THE MEANING OF THE REVELATION

THE MEANING OF THE REVELATION

BY

PHILIP CARRINGTON, M.A.

SOMETIME SCHOLAR OF SELWYN COLLEGE, CAMBRIDGE,
DEAN OF DIVINITY, UNIVERSITY OF BISHOPS COLLEGE,
LENNOXVILLE, QUEBEC.

*'Tis ye, 'tis your estrangèd faces,
That miss the many-splendoured thing!*

WIPF & STOCK · Eugene, Oregon

Wipf and Stock Publishers
199 W 8th Ave, Suite 3
Eugene, OR 97401

The Meaning of the Revelation
By Carrington, Philip
ISBN 13: 978-1-55635-673-5
Publication date 10/11/2007
Previously published by SPCK, 1931

THE KINGDOM OF GOD.

"In no Strange Land."

O world invisible, we view thee,
O world intangible, we touch thee,
O world unknowable, we know thee,
Inapprehensible, we clutch thee!

Does the fish soar to find the ocean,
The eagle plunge to find the air—
That we ask of the stars in motion
If they have rumour of thee there?

Not where the wheeling systems darken,
And our benumbed conceiving soars!—
The drift of pinions, would we hearken,
Beats at our own clay-shuttered doors.

The angels keep their ancient places;—
Turn but a stone, and start a wing!
'Tis ye, 'tis your estrangèd faces,
That miss the many-splendoured thing.

But (when so sad thou canst not sadder)
Cry;—and upon thy so sore loss
Shall shine the traffic of Jacob's ladder
Pitched betwixt heaven and Charing Cross.

Yea, in the night, my Soul, my daughter,
Cry,—clinging Heaven by the hems;
And lo, Christ walking on the water
Not of Gennesareth, but Thames!

FRANCIS THOMPSON.

(*By permission of Messrs. Burns Oates & Washbourne, Ltd.*)

PREFACE

THE object of this book is to provide a running commentary on the *Revelation*, elucidating its meaning. Other considerations are subordinated to this main quest. Illustrative matter from the Old Testament, from the apocalyptic writings, from the Rabbis, or from the speculations of Gnostic heresy, is only adduced where it is necessary for the explanation of the meaning. Many points of homiletic or doctrinal or historical value are passed over. The authorship of the book is not discussed. It is accepted as a great monument of mystic poetry from the last decade of the first century, and the only question really asked about it is *What it means*.

It is hoped that this question has been answered in a manner sufficiently free from technicalities to make it of use to the general reader who is not familiar with the conventions and formulæ of theological writers. Here and there a closely-reasoned passage has been necessarily inserted, where the author has not accepted the orthodox opinions of the modern critics; but these passages are not very frequent.

When the *Revelation* was originally written it was naturally accepted as an account of current events and of events " shortly to come to pass "; that is how it describes itself, and that is how it was naturally taken. The key to its meaning was soon lost, and its mystical symbolism was taken as literal description. As the centuries passed by, and its great symbolic scenes (now taken in a literal or material sense) did not become history, its scope was gradually lengthened. Some were taken figuratively, it is true, and applied to various historical events, such as the plunder of Rome by

Alaric, the Protestant Reformation, or the French Révolution; but others were still taken literally and looked for in the future. Hence arose the view that the *Revelation* is a forecast of the main events of history, a view which is still living in certain quarters. This view, the *Future-Historical* view, has collapsed so far as serious scholars are concerned; but nothing clear or definite has taken its place.

It is a distinct gain, however, that the whole system of historical " identifications " has gone; nobody now looks in the *Revelation* for the Pope or the Kaiser.

One group of interpreters holds that there are no historical references in the *Revelation* at all, hardly even to current events. The symbols represent abstract ideas or general principles which may be seen at work in any age; if there is any reference to current history it is only because figures in current history (like Nero) are good examples of the general principle in question. This may be called the *Spiritual* method of interpretation. It overlooks the fact that the *Revelation* was decidedly a message to its own age, that its tone is too fierce to be the product of a philosophical interest in the general laws of history, and that a Hebrew never thought of the spiritual except as an actual living force in present history. Nevertheless we have much to learn from this method, the chief exponent of which was F. D. Maurice.

Meanwhile those who still looked on the *Revelation* as an exposition of history, saw that its scope must be confined to the prophet's own life-time, and to events which were " shortly to come to pass." This may be called the *Present-Historical* school. Instead of the Pope and the Kaiser, the Roman and the Parthian were thought to be the theme of the prophecy; and so far as it went, this method was a great advance on what went before. So far as it reflects events of history, it is current events that it reflects; but it is far from being merely a highly-coloured review of historical events. The value of this method was exhausted when it had adduced all the illustrative historical material at its command; the *Revelation* was not yet explained.

The best commentaries of recent years have been those in which the *Spiritual* and the *Present-Historical* methods have been combined; the *Revelation* represents great principles working themselves out in actual history. These are the lines followed by Milligan, Swete, and Anderson Scott; and these are the lines of the present book. They seem to the present author to be the normal sane lines of interpretation to which scholarship is feeling its way.

The progress has, however, been held up by two other theories of the *Revelation*, both of which have contributed something, though both are in the main erroneous. One is the *Mythical* theory, and the other is the *Eschatological* theory.

Those who uphold the *Mythical* theory regard the *Revelation* as a mass of contradictory fragments by various authors. Some of the fragments are then explained as pieces of heathen mythology, Babylonian, or Persian, or Greek, or mixed. The theory contains this much truth; the *Revelation* can be divided into strata which seem to have been composed at different times and in different places; and there are some visions which do seem to be coloured by conceptions which are not drawn from orthodox Judaism or Christianity. But the theory is broken on the fact that the book is a literary unity stamped throughout by the mark of a great genius; and there are simpler ways of accounting for its different strata and its very occasional non-Jewish colouring.

The *Eschatological* theory is a more serious business. It too is often based on a theory of composite authorship, but it does not stand or fall by it. Its real basis is the comparative study of apocalypse. The great majority of Jewish apocalypses contemporary with St. John (or a little earlier) look forward to a catastrophic " end of the world " as we call it, and a visible coming of the Christ. This seems to fit the *Present-Historical* method; and critics of this type hold that St. John is interested only in the events of current history, and in the celestial intervention by which current history is shortly to be interrupted. A certain allowance is necessarily made for historical and " spiritual " interpretations; but, wherever possible, the symbols of St. John are taken as naked material fact.

The latest and most important commentary on *Revelation* is of this type; and Dr. Charles, its prodigiously learned author, has produced two magnificent volumes which will henceforth be the necessary handbook of any scholar. In two ways they mark a great advance on previous Eschatological interpretations; they insist that on the whole the book is a literary unity; and they also insist that its visions are in chronological or logical order. *Revelation* is restored to its position as an orderly literary composition produced by the imagination of one man; but Dr. Charles has unfortunately marred his work by a number of eccentric theories of omissions, interpolations, and transpositions, in which his most devoted disciples are hardly likely to follow him.

It is presumption perhaps to praise a scholar of the international eminence of Dr. Charles for the twenty-five years of labour which have gone into this monument of scholarship; for the work on the text, the grammar, and the style; for the wealth of illustration from all sources, and in particular from the contemporary Jewish apocalypses; but it is a pleasure to offer this humble tribute before disagreeing with him on points of literary judgment and poetical criticism.

The Jewish apocalypses which Dr. Charles has collected are admittedly mere religious journalism destitute of the higher gifts of imagination; the *Revelation of St. John* is admittedly one of the loftiest mystical poems the world has produced: and Dr. Charles is obviously making a mistake when he interprets the higher by the lower. Quite consistently throughout his Commentary he assumes that the symbols of St. John must be employed by him in the same sense as they are employed by the anonymous authors of *Enoch*, *Esdras*, and the rest; he brings down the meaning of the *Revelation* to their level of literalism, materialism, pessimism, and puerility. This will not do. The *Revelation* is capable of a high spiritual meaning throughout; and this can be no accident. A highly spiritual symbolic poem can, of course, always be interpreted literally and materially by literal and material men; it is inconceivable that a literal and materially-minded man could by accident create a poem which is capable of being interpreted spiritually; and in this matter we must trust the poets and saints and visionaries who have found that spiritual truth in the *Revelation*.

What St. John has borrowed from the apocalypses of his time is their literary form; but he has used that literary form to convey his own meaning. It is rather as if Mr. John Masefield, let us say, has been asked to prepare a film version of the Legend of King Arthur; it would be necessary for him to master the technique and conventions of the film, and to recast the legend so as to fit into it; but we may feel quite certain that he would not use the accepted ideals and sentiments of the average film play. His production might be a re-arrangement of Mallory; it might owe much to Tennyson; but it would be marked throughout by his own power and beauty of thought and style. In a somewhat similar way the *Revelation* is a re-arrangement of the visions of Ezekiel and other ancient Hebrew writers; it owes its main message to the preaching of our Lord; and it is everywhere marked by the distinctive and lofty genius of its author. Only in a few places do we find the characteristic symbols of Jewish apocalypse; and even there the meaning is not always the same.

The Jewish apocalypses were " eschatological "—that is to say, they looked forward to the very rapid approach of the " end of the world " as we call it, the sudden spectacular intervention of God in the affairs of the world, a smashing up or burning of the cosmos, and a universal and vindictive judgment. The first Christians also looked forward to the rapid approach of certain events of world-wide importance; the nature of these events was expressed in symbolic language of an eschatological character; but the language is symbolic, not literal. It is probable that many of the early believers took it literally; it is possible that St. Paul in his earliest period took it literally; but it is quite clear that our Lord and St. John did not take it literally. They agree with the Jewish apocalypses in prophesying events of world-wide importance " shortly to come to pass "; they also agree with them in using the figurative language of the ancient prophets; but while the Jewish apocalypses understood this language literally, our Lord and St. John used it to convey a spiritual meaning, or to describe the way in which the great principles of justice work themselves out in human history.

The first thing, then, which we find in common with the other apocalypses is the insistence that certain events of world-wide importance are coming immediately; these things are the same both in the Gospels and in the *Revelation*, and may be tabulated as follows :

Gospels.	*Revelation.*
1. Wars, Earthquakes, etc.	Wars, Earthquakes, etc.
2. Fall of Jerusalem.	Fall of " Babylon."
3. Coming of the Son of Man.	Coming of the Messiah (xix.) ; Son of Man (xiv.).
4. Kingdom of God.	Descent of Jerusalem.

The meaning of these events is discussed in the body of the book. The relative order of 3 and 4 cannot be determined either in the Gospels or the *Revelation*, and in any case they refer to what is practically one process. In the *Revelation*, a period of a " Thousand Years " is interposed before the final annihilation of evil and the great judgment.

The second thing we learn from the apocalypses is the nature of the literary form employed by St. John. Two points here are essential. The first is that an apocalypse surveys the whole field of history from the beginning to the end, so that the first half of our book (chapters iii. to ix. inclusive) deals with the past history of the race; the second is that the writer places himself mentally at a point in past history, and treats of current events as if he were foretelling them. It follows that we must not look for anything specifically Christian before chapter x., which narrates the call of the prophet, and also that we must not be surprised to find that the mental standpoint of the book is about the year 69 A.D. under the rule of Vespasian, though it was actually composed under Domitian about 95.

It is now possible to tabulate the principles which have guided the present author in the interpretation of the book; and it will be seen that they are the principles of accepted, moderate criticism, modified by study of the researches of the eschatological school.

1. The *Revelation* is spiritual. Its symbols stand for great invisible forces which are at work in human history.

2. It is occupied with the current history of its own times, not with the far future.

3. In so far as it looks into the future, it thinks of certain events of world-wide importance which are to come to pass immediately. As a matter of fact they had already begun to come to pass when the book was written.

4. After the manner of apocalypse, events which had already happened, or begun to happen, were treated as future; the author goes back in his mind to the decade 60–70, just before Jerusalem fell.

5. The visions of the *Revelation* were not all composed about the year 95, the date of the compilation and publication of the whole book; most of them were earlier. Some date from the decade 60–70. Some may be even earlier than that.

These principles are fairly generally accepted; but it is now time to warn the reader of others over which there is likely to be argument.

1. The central event of *Revelation* is the fall of " Babylon," and the view taken is that it refers to the fall of Jerusalem. This view was advocated by Dr. Milligan, one of the most eminent expositors of the book; but it has not met with general acceptance. It is to be feared that Dr. Milligan's view has only fallen to the ground because it has been overlooked. I note that Dr. Swete, Dr. Anderson Scott, and Dr. Charles fail to refer to it at all; and it does at least deserve respectful attention. I have urged a number of new arguments in its favour; and I think it impossible to make sense of the book without it.

2. St. John narrates his call to prophesy and his particular work in chapters x. and xi. In chapters xii. and xiii. he describes the origin, diffusion, and persecution of Christianity. (He had no choice about the relative order; he could not insert the account of his call into the middle of chapters xii. and xiii.)

Two things follow from this, which I do not think have been properly grasped. The *Revelation* is written in chronological and logical order (Dr. Milligan was wrong there, and Dr. Charles is right); and it follows that chapters x. and xi. are the earliest visions in the book, and that they are the work of the author of the whole book. It also follows that we must not expect that chapters iv. to ix. will deal with the Christian church or its problems; they are the survey of world-history previous to that date.

These principles clarify the interpretation of the book as much as the identification of " Babylon " with Jerusalem.

3. The presence of heathen Mythological elements in *Revelation* has not been established. Every element in the principal debated chapter (xii.) can be shown to rise naturally out of Hebrew thought; and yet there is a flavour about this chapter, and also about a few other passages, which is foreign. This flavour (we cannot call it much more) needs to be accounted for.

I am suggesting that the explanation is to be found in the fact that St. John is refuting certain " gnostic " speculations which he considered dangerous to the Christian church. Gnosticism is a blend of Hebrew, heathen, and Christian mythology; we only know of its developed form in the second century; but it is possible for us to form some idea of the preparation for it that went on in the first century. We know for certain that a type of Hebrew gnosticism did threaten the church even in apostolic times, and it is generally admitted that the *Gospel* and *Epistles of St. John* are antignostic in tone. It is a very reasonable hypothesis to suppose that Hebrew Gnosticism of this type has also left its mark on the *Revelation*.

Mythological theories which explained features of the *Revelation* by the influence of Babylonian or Persian religion were always a little in the air, partly because the exact parallels in those religions were seldom forthcoming, and partly because it was difficult to see how the influence was exercised; in the case of Gnosticism, the mode of contact is clear, and the parallels are very close.

This suggestion is the only one I have to offer for which I can claim originality; and even here it is more than likely that I have been anticipated. It will be seen, therefore, that this little study of the *Revelation* can only claim to follow out methods and principles which have been already established or suggested.

What, then, is its value? It is hoped that it may form a guide to those whose object in reading the *Revelation* is merely to enjoy and understand it. It attempts in a small way and in a small compass to explain the meaning of the book along sane and spiritual lines of scholarship; avoiding the age-long errors of conservative study, and the eccentricities of critics who affect the latest modes. It is natural that under such circumstances it must be indebted on every page to various authorities on this complex subject; an indebtedness which will be too apparent to need pointing out.

We run through the *Revelation*, translating and quoting where necessary, and explaining as simply as possible what each passage means. Here and there a digression cannot be avoided; here and there the reader will find a page or two of argument: but in the main the book is designed to run smoothly on, unfolding the meaning of the visions. Passages which are quoted from St. John are printed in a different type, and so occasionally are other quotations from the Bible. Words used by St. John in a symbolic sense, or abstract words characteristic of him, are given a capital letter. The different sections are given titles in order to make reference easy. The Bible and Prayer Book usage has been followed as regards capitals in pronouns referring to divine Persons, the publishers having departed from their usual practice in deference to the author's wish, since most of the book is a running commentary on the words of Scripture.

It is hoped that a simple treatise on the meaning of this book will help clergy and others who often have to deal with people who take it in a false and literal sense. I have from time to time referred to the errors of Adventism, and particularly of the Seventh-Day Adventist sect. It is not enough, however, merely to expose the false exegesis of sects of this type; the only defence of the book is to grasp its true meaning, and make more use of it in preaching and in the devotional life. No one who has once seen its real power and beauty can ever be led astray into the dreary mazes of literal and historical application.

The same is true of the eminent scholars who have failed to see the poetry and spirituality of these amazing visions. Without believing in Adventism themselves, they still miss the real meaning of the book. Often in reading a discussion of the Johannine problem, I have come across some such statement as this: "It is impossible to suppose that the author of the Fourth Gospel could have written so crude and materialistic and vindictive a book as the Apocalypse." When I read this, my blood boils; I feel that I do not care who wrote the Gospel or who wrote the Apocalypse; let those problems go; let us grant for the sake of argument that Timothy wrote the Gospel and Papias wrote the Apocalypse; let us give them to Cerinthus and Elchasai; but do not let us disgrace our birth and breeding by calling the Apocalypse crude or materialistic or vindictive.

Mr. G. K. Chesterton has said with some truth that in *The Ancient Mariner* Coleridge glorified the penny ballad, just as in *Treasure Island* Stevenson glorified the penny dreadful; they took these literary forms out of the gutter and consecrated them to the service of the highest art. But what should we think of the literary critic who deduced from this that *The Ancient Mariner* was no better than a penny ballad, and *Treasure Island* no better than a penny dreadful? St. John did the same thing; he took the penny apocalypse out of the gutter and used it as a vehicle for the expression of supreme beauty. Yet "critics" maintain that because he employed the literary form, his spiritual vision can be no wider than the vision of others who employed it.

You cannot argue with this kind of judgment. You cannot prove that the *Revelation* is one of the world's greatest poems. When the old lady said that Bach was an old gentleman who wrote five-finger exercises and had the audacity to call them fugues, there was nothing to be done. She was blind. She was not only unable to see the beauty of the music; there are thousands like that. She was unable to see the possibility of any beauty; she was unable to guess at the spiritual secret which enchanted those who could see the beauty. She could hear the noise and follow the mechanics; there her vision ended.

But in the case of the *Revelation* we are dealing with an artist greater than Stevenson or Coleridge or Bach. St. John has a better sense of the right word than Stevenson; he has a greater command of unearthly supernatural loveliness than Coleridge; he has a richer sense of melody and rhythm and composition than Bach. The painter selecting and arranging his colours; the sculptor massing his great shapes; the musician delicately picking out his chords; no artist in any medium has ever surpassed St. John in heart-searching and blood-curdling effects. It is the only masterpiece of pure art in the New Testament; it is immensely greater than *Job*, the only possible rival from the Old. Its fulness and richness and harmonic variety place it far above Greek tragedy; there never has been any author who could handle the vast themes used by St. John with such balance of technique, such epic power, and such lyric beauty.

Nor is this all. It is not only a question of weaving words, like Shelley; the imaginative structures of the *Revelation* are built up of great spiritual ideas. Behind the rush and melody of the words, behind the glorious display of images and symbols which are a triumph of art merely in themselves—behind all this literary and artistic achievement lies an architecture of ideas which leaves Shelley or Milton or Dante far behind. Behind the phenomena of nature and history and personality, St. John has seen great laws and principles and influences working themselves out; the colossal invisible energies which explain the crash of mighty empires and the triumph of despised truth. He has seen the limitless joy and energy of creation as it vibrates in unity and obedience; he has seen the glitter and the loathsomeness of sin as it rises out of the unknown abysses of the human mind; he has seen the utter purity and intense heat of truth and justice going out to battle with flaming eyes; he has seen the corruption and cynicism of a religion which prostitutes

b

itself to the cult of success; he has seen the flames in which sin destroys itself; he has even seen the pure and paradisal life of the blessed in their meekness and singleness of heart.

I saw. That, after all, is the key-note of the book. St. John has a superhuman capacity for vision; he sees conquest, and ambition, and lust, and patience, and endurance, and truth; he sees what it is that ruins men and empires, and what it is that saves them; he sees the power of Christ in his witnesses and martyrs and foretells their victory. These are the ideas that lie behind his symbols, and if we have a little vision we can see something of them too.

Why, then, it may be asked, does he not say clearly what he means instead of wrapping it up in a fantastic dance of symbols? One answer may be that he prefers that we should do some thinking ourselves, as our Lord did when he taught in parables; but there is a better answer than that. The things cannot be said more clearly than he says them; no simple explanation is quite so clear. The " plain " explanation is only a partial one, a mere stimulus to meditation; the symbol blazons the whole truth.

Take the Rider on the White Horse. Does he " mean " Selfishness, or Ambition, or Conquest, or what? The more we look at it the more we see that these abstract terms are only aspects of the solid spiritual truth blazoned by the symbol. The symbol is man himself in his foolish innocence, utterly confident, making a hero of himself, riding out conquering and to conquer. He does it on every conceivable occasion; he is quite sure of himself each time, and each time he makes a mess of it: the other three riders always come cantering along behind. The symbol is the actual thing, or at any rate as near to the actual thing as words can get; the abstract terms are feeble in comparison.

Theologians and philosophers have an immense trust in vocabulary; they multiply technical abstract terms in their anxiety to analyse and define. That is their work; and very necessary it is. But it explains why they have not done very well with the *Revelation*. To them a symbol is a figure (probably clad in a Grecian robe) which rather arbitrarily stands instead of an abstract notion; real symbolism, the symbolism of the poets, sweeps the abstractions on one side and grasps the reality by a kind of inspiration. At their best they stand nearer to the truth than the philosophers. Once you have seen that St. John is a poet, and that his symbolism is immediate and inspired, you can never be argued into taking him literally; you also have *seen*.

It will be said now that all this is only assertion; which is very true. It is very difficult to see how æsthetic judgments can be more. But this is where the specific thesis of this little book comes in. We can begin by pointing out that each vision is capable of two interpretations, a major and a minor. The major is poetical and spiritual; the minor is low and materialistic. We may take our choice. If we grant the dilemma, and accept the lower interpretation in every case, we find ourselves in a difficult position; we hold that the *Revelation* is the work of an unspiritual man with a narrow and material mind, and yet by accident he has achieved a poem which can be interpreted throughout as an artistic triumph of high spiritual beauty. Now it is clear that a great spiritual poem might easily be taken literally by literal men; but it would be a miracle if a crude materialistic and vindictive mass of prophecies could yield a highly spiritual meaning in every section. It is not in reason that the lower can by accident create the higher.

Nor is it reasonable to admit a spiritual meaning in some cases but not in others, though this is what is often done. I do not suppose any critic takes every vision literally. But if certain visions are interpreted spiritually, we are entitled to ask why the whole book is not treated in the same way, and on what principles passages are selected for different treatment. The sad fact is that on the whole such critics explain visions which they think refer to the past as allegorical, and visions which they think refer to the future as literal, a method which has little to commend it.

It is possible, I think, to demonstrate (if not precisely to prove) that certain visions are meant to be taken spiritually; in some cases they cannot be taken literally; and in others there are strong indications that a spiritual meaning is intended. The vision of the locusts is a case in point; it can only be taken in a material sense in defiance of the evidence. In all cases it is possible to point out the nature of the spiritual facts blazoned by the symbols.

The reader will see, therefore, that the title of this book, *The Meaning of the Revelation*, is an over-description. Such a title should be given to a study of the spiritual facts with which the *Revelation* deals. In point of fact it does no more than indicate what those facts are, and give sufficient argument and illustrative material to prove that the indication is reasonable. In doing so it only follows humbly in the footsteps of Maurice, Benson, Milligan, and Swete.

The decision of this point is very important for theological scholarship. It is admitted on all hands that the Gospel, the Epistles, and the *Revelation of St. John* were all written in Ephesus towards the end of the first century, and that in some way they are connected with a Jewish Christian called John, who has always been regarded as the Apostle. This identification is now questioned, and there is also little agreement on the relations of the writings to one another, or their exact connection with the illustrious John. It is commonly said that the Gospel and the *Revelation* are totally unlike in grammar, style, and outlook, and that while the Gospel is spiritual and gentle in tone, the *Revelation* is, as I have quoted above, harsh, crude, and materialistic. This statement is true of the grammar and style, but profoundly untrue of the spiritual value of the *Revelation*.

Before going any further with the discussion of the authorship of these books, it will be necessary to revise this low and even hostile view. I have therefore neglected the question of authorship, and concentrated on the meaning. I have referred to the author as John, and very occasionally I have spoken of him as if he were the Apostle. I have casually noted a number of cross-references to the fourth gospel; but they are only such as occurred to me naturally as I went along; I made no search for them. The identity of the author makes no difference whatever to the soundness of my interpretation.

A decision that the *Revelation* is to be understood in a spiritual fashion is bound to influence the whole Johannine problem. But there is also the question of the relations between the *Revelation* and other New Testament literature, St. Paul, *Hebrews*, and the first gospel; the dating of the different sets of visions, in which I agree fairly well with the results of Dr. Charles, may help to illuminate earlier periods of New Testament history, and give us some insight into the obscure problem of the church in Jerusalem.

PHILIP CARRINGTON,
January 1931.

University of Bishops College,
   Lennoxville, Quebec.

CONTENTS

BOOK I.—INTRODUCTORY MATERIAL

PAGE

PART I.—PRE-CHRISTIAN 31

History of Israel principally post-exilic—Daniel's outline of history—Characteristics of apocalyptic literature—Symbol and myth—The new view of the universe—Syncretism—Apocalyptic hopes.

PART II.—CHRISTIAN 50

The two ways—The kingdom of God—The prophecies of Jesus—The Christian prophets—The *Revelation*.

BOOK II.—ST. JOHN'S INTRODUCTION

PART I.—INTRODUCTORY VISION (Rev. i–iii) . . . 71

Title and greetings—The vision of the Risen Lord—Psychology of prophetic vision—The Seven Angels.

PART II.—THE LETTERS TO THE SEVEN CHURCHES . 91

Literary composition and inspiration—The future Coming of Christ—Condition of the churches—The Synagogue of Satan and Gnostic heresy—The Serpent.

BOOK III.—THIS AGE

PART I.—GOD, MAN, AND CREATION (Rev. iv–vii) . 109

The vision of God enthroned in his glory, worshipped by men and angels and all created things—The Book which symbolises the riddles of faith—The Lamb alone able to solve them—The first four Seals, an " outline of history " showing the progress of humanity through imperialism to the grave—The fifth shows the souls of the innocent dead crying to God for justice—The sixth shows how the prophetic dooms have fallen upon the guilty nations.

A Parenthesis—The avenging forces are restrained by God while the number of the martyrs is completed—They are assured of a blessed immortality.

The Seventh leads to a pause.

There is as yet nothing relative to the Christian church. The past is depicted.

BOOK IV.—THIS AGE

PART II.—THE SERPENT, SIN, AND THE THREAT OF DOOM (Rev. viii–xi) 151

The Seven prophetic Trumpets prelude the approach of judgment—The first four symbolise the fall from righteousness and the destruction worked by sin—The fifth shows by a plague of Locusts the power that sin has gained over man—The sixth shows by the demonic cavalry its destructive power. This is the inner history of humanity corresponding to the outward course of empire.

A Parenthesis—The strong Angel descending from heaven symbolises the Word of God inspiring the prophets—The call of John to prophecy—His theme the building of the spiritual temple and the witness against the earthly Jerusalem—The witness for God in Jerusalem—The martyrdom of the prophets and their " ascension "

Past judgments on the city.

The Seventh Trumpet leads to the annunciation of the final doom.
—The spiritual temple opened in heaven.

BOOK V.—THE GREAT INTERLUDE

PART I.—CHRIST (Rev. xii–xiv. 13) 201

The woman in heaven signifying the Spirit of God and the holy community—The birth of the Christ—Under the name of Michael he defeats the Serpent—Persecution of the woman and her seed, the church of Christ in Jerusalem.

PART II.—ANTICHRIST 226

The beast rising from the sea symbolises the Roman Empire and its god-emperor Nero—His divine pretensions and persecutions—The beast from the land signifies his allies—The mark and number of beast—The Lamb and his faithful followers face the beast.

BOOK VI.—THE AGE TO COME

PART I.—THE DOOM OF BABYLON (Rev. xiv. 14–xix. 10) . 247

The threefold message of Christian prophecy announces the worship of the true God, the doom of Babylon (Jerusalem) and of the Beast (Rome), the two persecutors: the Son of Man appears in judgment over Jerusalem, and war and bloodshed begin—The Seven Plagues are poured out on the Land, the first four symbolising the horrors of invasion and civil war—The fifth shows the death of Nero and the confusion in the Roman army—The sixth shows the massing of the Roman armies round the city—The seventh symbolises her end.

Jerusalem is now shown as the Harlot after the fashion of Ezekiel, and her sins and her punishment described—The lamentations show that her fall is irrevocable.

Her place is taken by the Bride, afterwards to appear as the New Jerusalem (the Christian Church).

BOOK VII.—THE AGE TO COME

PART II.—THE TRIUMPH OF CHRIST AND HIS CHURCH (Rev. xix. 11–xxi. 8) 301

The King-Messiah appears with his saints, symbolising the advance throughout the world of the gospel and the church—The whole god-emperor system to be overthrown and obliterated—The " millennial kingdom " shows that Christ and his saints will succeed to their place of domination in the world—This ascendancy not secure, Satan not destroyed—Further battles in the far future against further enemies, Gog, and Magog—Sin to be finally destroyed—The judgment of God—God dwelling with men—Creation renewed and restored.

BOOK VIII.—IN CONCLUSION

PART I.—ST. JOHN'S EPILOGUE (Rev. xxi. 9–xxii. 21) . 341

Relation of the earthly church and the ultimate perfected humanity —The New Jerusalem symbolises both—The new Eden or Paradise Regained—Final attestations and conclusion.

PART II.—RECEPTION AND INFLUENCE OF THE BOOK . 353

The church in Ephesus in the Johannine period—Gnostic heresy—Montanism and the Greek type of prophet—Chiliasm or the secularisation of apostolic prophecy—Hermas and the prophets of Rome—Subsequent history of *Revelation* in the church.

APPENDIX I.—THE LEVITICAL SYMBOLISM OF REVELATION 381

The poem offers a scheme for Christian worship in chapters iv. and v. —The older parts of the poem have a structure which is based on the sacrificial worship in the temple—Outline of the ceremonies of the daily burnt offering and comparison with the structure of *Revelation* vi.–xix.

APPENDIX II.—PRIMITIVE HEBREW GNOSTICISM 395

The mythology of Ophite Gnosticism shows elements similar to some of the symbolism of *Revelation*, especially chapters xii. and xiii., which are not based upon the temple ritual or upon *Ezekiel*. Attempt to recover elements in primitive Gnosticism which have Hebrew affinities—Comparison with *Revelation*.

ILLUSTRATIVE MATTER

Tables and Charts

Prophetic View of History	34
Time-Chart of N.T. Prophecy	59
Analysis of O.T. Sources (Ezekiel, etc.)	64
Prophecy of Jesus: Gospel Sources	196
Ophite (or Gnostic) Universe	238
Symbolism of the Divine Activities	278
Historical Background of Jerusalem Visions	298
Liturgical Structure of Revelation	378

Indexes

Passages from the Revelation	418
Other Biblical Passages	420
Supplementary Subject Index	422

THE MEANING OF THE
REVELATION

BOOK I
INTRODUCTORY MATERIAL

PART I. PRE-CHRISTIAN
  Old Testament Prophecy.
  The Apocalyptic Literature.
  The New Universe.

PART II. CHRISTIAN
  The Gospel of Jesus.
  The Kingdom of God.
  The Prophecies of Jesus.
  The New Testament Prophets.
  The Revelation of St. John.

LINES FROM THE EVERLASTING GOSPEL

Thunders and lightnings broke around,
And Jesus' voice in thunders sound :
" Thus I seize the spiritual prey.
Ye smiters with disease, make way.
I come your King and God to seize.
Is God a smiter with disease ? "

The God of this world raged in vain :
He bound old Satan in his chain,
And bursting forth, his furious ire
Became a chariot of fire.
Throughout the land he took his course,
And traced diseases to their source.
He cursed the Scribe and Pharisee,
Trampling down hypocrisy.
Where'er his chariot took its way,
There Gates of Hell let in the Day,
Broke down from every chain and bar ;
And Satan in his spiritual war
Dragged at his chariot-wheels ; loud howled
The God of this world : louder rolled
The chariot-wheels, and louder still
His voice was heard from Zion's Hill,
And in his hand the scourge shone bright ;
He scourged the merchant Canaanite
From out the Temple of his Mind,
And in his body tight does bind
Satan and all his hellish crew ;
And thus with wrath he did subdue
The serpent bulk of Nature's dross,
Till he had nailed it to the Cross.

WILLIAM BLAKE.

BOOK I

INTRODUCTORY MATERIAL

Part I. Pre-Christian

The World of Apocalypse.

THE *Revelation of St. John the Divine* and the Gospels of St. Matthew, St. Mark and St. Luke belong to a world which is otherwise unknown to most readers. It is quite a different world from the world of the Old Testament, with which they are moderately familiar; it is a world of which something can be seen in the Apocrypha, a collection of sacred books written in Greek, added to the Old Testament in Alexandria, and accepted by the whole Christian church for the first fifteen hundred years of its existence; it can be seen more clearly still in the apocalypses and other anonymous literature which never even got into the Apocrypha, books like *Enoch* and the *Twelve Patriarchs*, which were read by the first Christians and were then forgotten till the last manuscripts of them were examined and given to the world by the labours and energies of Dr. Charles and others; and finally it is the world of the three great religions, Christianity, modern Judaism, and Mohammedanism, and of other religions great in their day but now forgotten or decayed, like Gnosticism and Manicheism. The conceptions of heaven and hell, angels and devils, a future life, a last judgment, so natural and familiar to all these religions, are not to be found in the Old Testament; they arose after the Old Testament period, after the conquests of Alexander the Great, in a composite cosmopolitan civilisation, when Greek philosophy and poetry, Babylonian astrology and Persian dualism were combined in a glittering, unstable equilibrium to form the mental and imaginative background of a whole world. The Caliph Haroun al Raschid, the great Byzantine Empress Irene, the Pope in Rome, the first Western Emperor, Charlemagne, the Rabbis, and the Manichees all lived in this same world.

The world of the Old Testament is a smaller world; it is the world seen by a tribe of savages, a world taken for granted and not speculated upon. The great sea stretches away to the sunset, and the great plains and hills stretch away to the sunrise; the whole forms a flat disk, in the centre of which lies Israel upon her holy and familiar hills. Overhead, like the roof of a cave, is the firmament in which the heavenly bodies are set; and there is all your cosmos in a nutshell, and a very small nutshell too. There were vague impressions of a continuation of the sea underneath the land, "the great deep," and of more waters on top of the cave, "the waters above the firmament," a view shared by most of the Semites. The science of the Hebrews was, in short, the science of their day.

Politically Israel was at first only a small cluster of tribes surrounded by other tribes who were hostile, "the nations," "the gentiles," "the heathen," as they appear in the Bible, Ammonites, Moabites, Edomites, and so on, not very different in culture and speech from the Israelites themselves. Jehovah was at this stage their own tribal god, and Israel was his land; the progress of Israelite religion is seen in the steps by which they came to extend his power to the whole earth and sea and firmament which they affirmed he had created, to affirm, further, that he was not localised in any particular spot, and to deny that any image of him could be made; for he had no form or likeness; he was spirit and not flesh.

As their horizon enlarged, the great empires began to appear, and Israel, which had held out gallantly against the surrounding tribes, and even set up a little Palestinian empire under David and some of the later kings, suddenly found itself no more than a plaything for the great powers, a mouse between the paws of the cat—several cats. The whole history of it is telescoped in the first eight verses of the seventh chapter of Daniel, *I saw in my vision by night, and behold the four winds of the heaven strove upon the great sea, and four great beasts came up from the sea, diverse from one another* (*Dan.* vii. 2, 3).

By these four beasts (and we shall meet the symbolism again in *Revelation*) Daniel meant the four great world-empires, though in another vision (that of the Image) he makes it clear that they are only one world-empire appearing in successive forms. The four empires are the Babylonians, the Medes, the Persians, and the Greeks.

Daniel was essentially right in his view of history, at any rate from his own point of view, which was that of the Jewish nation; history from the point of view of the mouse is very different from history from the point of view of the cat.

In mere historic detail he is wrong. There never was a Median world-empire; Darius the Mede only exists in the imagination of Daniel. But there was an empire before Babylon which might well be included in order to make up the mystic number Four; that empire was the Assyrian. By including Assyria and omitting Media, we get a prophetic outline of history which has the advantage over Daniel of being accurate; not that Daniel would have cared about that.

The four empires are these. The first is Assyria, whose king Sennacherib destroyed Samaria, the northern capital, in 622 B.C. and added Israel to his empire; the second, *which was like a lion and had eagle's wings*, is Babylon, whose king Nebuchadrezzar completed the work of subjugation by destroying the southern (and less important) capital, Jerusalem, in 586, and carrying off the principal Jews as captives to his own country; the third, *like a leopard*, is Persia, whose king Cyrus captured Babylon in 538, and allowed the captive Jews to return. The fourth was *dreadful and terrible and strong exceedingly; and it had great iron teeth; it devoured and brake in pieces and stamped the residue with the feet of it; and it was diverse from the beasts that were before it; and it had ten horns.* This beast represents the triumph of the disciplined army and the heavy-armed soldier under Alexander the Great, who conquered Persia in 332.

THE PROPHETIC VIEW OF HISTORY
CREATION
The Fall of Man.
The Flood.

ARCHAIC PERIOD
Babylon and Egypt.   Abraham and Moses.
                            Legend.

THE KINGDOM OF DAVID
FIRST EMPIRE
Assyria.   The Prophet Isaiah.
Sennacherib, 701 B.C.   *First written prophets.*

SECOND EMPIRE
Babylon.   Jeremiah : Ezekiel.
Nebuchadrezzar, 586 B.C.   *Literary work begins.*

THIRD EMPIRE
Persia   2 Isaiah: Zechariah.
Cyrus, 538 B.C.   *Literary work concludes.*

FOURTH EMPIRE
Greece.   Daniel: (Apocrypha).
Alexander, 332 B.C.   *Canon of Old Testament closed.*

Break. ### THE KINGDOM OF THE MACCABEES
ROMAN EMPIRE
Cæsar.   (Apocalyptic): New Testament.

This chart shows the Outline of History according to the prophets. The four empires under which Old Testament religion developed are the four beasts of Daniel, though he also regards them as four forms of one empire. In St. John's *Revelation* this fourfold empire is seen again, and is finally identified with Rome. The dates are those of the siege of Jerusalem by Sennacherib, its destruction by Nebuchadrezzar, the capture of Babylon by Cyrus, and Alexander's victory at Issus. The word "Cæsar" stands for the "seven" Cæsars down to Domitian, under whom the *Revelation* was written. The date of the Revelation is about A.D. 96.

It is well worth noting here how the historical sense arose in Israel long before we find it anywhere else in the world. Israel was the spectator of the whole drama of man and civilisation; she had faced the archaic empires of the Euphrates and the Nile a whole millennium earlier, and still clung to her memories of those far-off times. She now watched the rise of Assyria and the new Babylon, of magnificent Persia and glorious Greece, and the pages of her prophets are commentaries in which all their greatness and all their weakness can be clearly read. And far back in the mind of the prophets rested the sure conviction that, despite their power, they could do no more than carry out the will of God. *Shall the axe boast itself against him who heweth therewith?* (*Is.* x. 15).

Now almost the whole of the Old Testament was written before the Greek period. Isaiah prophesied in the Assyrian period; Jeremiah and Ezekiel in the Babylonian; the Persian is marked by the re-writing of history, the editing of prophets, and, above all, the codifying of laws. The Old Testament appears to us to be pre-Persian; but in actual fact the Jewish religion as we know it, and the Jewish scriptures as we know them, were finally systematised in the Persian period. When the Greek period opened it was very difficult to get in anything new; it could only be done by representing it as the work of some earlier writer. The canon was closed; the scriptures were sacred; and the whole of this important process took place between Cyrus and Alexander.

At Alexander's death the gigantic world-empire was divided into four parts, which were ruled by four of his generals. Syria with Jerusalem was ruled by Seleucus, and Egypt fell to Ptolemy; each had a new city as its capital, Antioch and Alexandria. The two rulers appear in Daniel as the king of the north and the king of the south. In the year 169 Antiochus IV, the Syrian successor of Alexander, decided to reduce Judea to conformity with the Greek culture and the Greek religion, which the whole known world was then copying. The epic of the resistance made by the loyal Jews under the old priest Mattathias and his five sons is to be found in the *First Book of Maccabees,* preserved in the Apocrypha, and I am very sorry for anyone who has not read this magnificent record of a magnificent war. Partly by alliances with Sparta and Rome, but mainly by their own valour and diplomacy, the Jews won their independence, and the Maccabees became High Priests and kings in Jerusalem.

Among the books which can be traced to this epoch is *Daniel.* The great Nebuchadrezzar is a symbol of the mad Antiochus, with his arrogant claims to divinity; the burning fiery furnace and the den of lions are the persecutions and wars through which the faithful had to go. There is no pretence of history in it; its author cared so little for actual facts that, in his description of the fall of " Babylon," he makes Belshazzar, not Nabonidus, king of Babylon, and Darius, not Cyrus, the conqueror.

Daniel was written at the beginning of the war, before the Maccabees had come forward to lead the people. We have seen how he describes the whole past history of the human race as a succession of brute empires, whose motive was cruelty and greed, whose method was fraud and force; the present one, the Greek, is the fiercest and most terrible. His message is that, like all the others, this heathen empire will pass, that God will protect his saints, whatever they have to suffer, and that God's own empire will at length be set up on earth (*Dan.* vii. 9).

I beheld till the thrones were cast down and the Ancient of Days did sit, whose garment was white as snow, and the hair of his head like the pure wool ; his throne was like the fiery flame and his wheels as burning fire. A fiery stream issued and came forth from before him . . . the judgment was set and the books were opened. . . . I beheld even till the beast was slain and his body destroyed and given to the burning flame ; as concerning the rest of the beasts, they had their dominion taken away ; yet their lives were prolonged for a season and time.

I saw in the night visions, and behold, one like the Son of man came with the clouds of heaven, and came to the Ancient of Days, and they brought him near before him, and there was given him dominion and glory and kingdom, that all people, nations, and languages should serve him ; his dominion is an everlasting dominion, and his kingdom that which shall not be destroyed.

The Apocalyptic Literature.

Before attempting to explain this piece of symbolism, it is best to point out the contrast between this new Jewish literature of the Greek period, and the old literature which was codified and canonised during the Persian period.

The first point, which has been already noted, is that the work is anonymous. The old prophet had received his inspiration from God at first hand, and had himself at once given it to the people, not as his opinion, but as the word of Jehovah. It was not intended to be written down; writing it down was in the primitive period an afterthought. It was a live message for the moment.

By the time of Antiochus the prophets were already thought of as existing in a holy and remote past, their number was complete, the editing of their books practically finished. In the cultured cosmopolitan half-hellenised Jerusalem of 200 B.C. a prophet would have been unthinkable. Those who had prophetic messages to give wrote them in secret and circulated them under the names of the saints of long ago; some of these writings were incorporated into the canon, a chapter or two into *Isaiah* (chapters xxiv–xxvii) and several chapters into *Zechariah* (chapter ix to end). In the case of *Daniel*, a whole book received recognition. It is impossible for us now to say how far this was actual fraud, and how far mere literary convention; it is unlikely that the scholars of the time ever took them to be the work of the saints whose names they carried. It was at the same time that the psalms were being collected under the name of David, and the proverbs under the name of Solomon.

These books ought not, strictly speaking, to be called anonymous (without a name), but pseudonymous (with a false name). They have been collected in the two-volume *Apocrypha and Pseudepigrapha* of Dr. Charles, where they are translated with notes. Many of them are compilations of different works which were written at various times between

200 B.C. and A.D. 100. The most important of the early ones is the *Book of Enoch*, some parts of which were perhaps earlier than *Daniel;* another is the *Testament of the Twelve Patriarchs*. Both of these books were finished before the time of Christ, though there may be interpolations, especially in the latter. Two of the latest are *Baruch* and *Esdras*, which are about contemporary with St. John's *Revelation; Esdras* has found its way into the Apocrypha.

A second point which is very clear from the extract quoted from *Daniel* is the copious use of symbolism. The old prophets had used whatever symbols came handy to describe spiritual things; sometimes, no doubt, the symbols were seen in actual visions. In every case they are used to blazon spiritual things which cannot be literally described. Indeed, a primitive people is bound to use symbolic or figurative language, owing to its lack of abstract words. There are practically no abstract words in Hebrew, and metaphor is the only way of alluding to the abstract. Where we would say that God is both immanent and transcendent, the Hebrew said, *Who is like the Lord our God, who hath his dwelling so high, and yet humbleth himself to behold the things which are in heaven and earth?* (*Ps.* cxiii. 5). The power and the poetry of all primitive races lie in this deficiency of abstract words.

But the use of symbolism in the new literature of the Greek period is quite different. The symbols are not used to explain spiritual things; the symbols need explanation themselves. The writer is engaged in managing a whole system of symbolism which he has inherited from the past. It has become rigid, hard, and connected. It is no longer a poetic flash of language which illuminates a deep spiritual experience. The spiritual experience may, for aught we know, be entirely lacking. What is presented to us is a logical system of allegorical figures, which themselves have to be interpreted. The whole process has been reversed.

This systematisation may be accompanied by a still further stage of degeneration. The mass of metaphors has become a system of allegory; the system of allegory may become a myth. Now a myth is simply a story; a myth is always the work of a poet. The gods and goddesses, the angels and devils, with which a myth deals are characters in a drama or novel. The dead system of allegory springs to life again; but the life it has is the life it shares with Hamlet or Don Quixote or Pickwick; it is the living creation of the imagination of the poet. Now the authentic Old Testament is miraculously free from mere myths; the story of Enoch was known, and so was the story of the fall of the angels, but they were deliberately passed over in a verse or two. This mythology which failed to get into the Bible is found at full length in the pseudonymous book of *Enoch*.

There are two stages also in the history of mythology. There is the first stage of original creative effort which produces a story about imaginary persons in whose characters eternal principles work themselves out; in the second stage the eternal principles (the ideals) are forgotten, and the story is everything; the persons are real, and the events historical. A good example is the Adam and Eve story. Originally a pure product of the imagination depicting the process of sin and temptation, it was after a time taken literally, and looked on as an event in the chain of events.

It is quite clear that the passage in *Daniel* is capable of being interpreted mythologically; it might be an account of a future event as the prophet imagines it will occur; it might be a pictorial and objective description of an event as visible as the coronation of Queen Victoria. On the other hand, it might be allegorical; that is to say, every detail may have a " meaning," if only we can find out what it is, and once the " meaning " is discovered we shall not need the symbols any more. In the book of *Enoch* there is plenty of imagery of both kinds; but I do not think either way will do here. Both methods of interpretation are literal, material and degenerate. If we use them here, we shall have to apply them also to the earlier part of the vision where the four world-empires are described as various beasts; in this case it is admitted that the vision is symbolical and not literal, and we may imagine it will be symbolical throughout. With reference to the second or allegorical method, the case is not so simple; there are points at least in every parable or symbolic narrative which have to be given " meanings " or interpretation, but no sustained symbolic narrative of any artistic or spiritual merit has ever been able to keep up a system of " meanings " successfully; and indeed what would be the value of a narrative whose symbolism merely consisted in substituting one set of words for another throughout? It would hardly reach the level of a cryptogram.

We are forced back on the old simple idea of the early prophets, that spiritual processes can best be described symbolically. Sin is called a dragon, because sin is much more like a dragon than it is like a doctrinal definition. God is called a king, because God is much more like a king than he is like the first of the Thirty-nine Articles. The dragon and the king are helpful symbols as long as it is remembered that sin is not a dragon and God is not a king: that would be mythology. They are helpful symbols until we begin asking what the dragon's claws or the king's crown " mean "; for that is allegory.

Now in the narrative before us there are allegorical details. We are told, for instance, that the ten horns are ten kings, and the three ribs in the mouth of the bear, and the four wings on the back of the leopard doubtless have " meanings " too, which have long been lost. But on the whole it is a symbolic narrative asserting spiritual truths, the eternity, the majesty, the terror that is God, the sure overthrow of the brutal and lustful empires, the utter destruction of all evil from the universe, the judgment to come on all deeds and words (the symbolism of the book), the eventual establishment of a kingdom which may be compared to a man, not a brute, a kingdom of humanity which shall stand for ever. Even here there is a maximum and a minimum method of interpretation; the seer may be expecting a day of dramatic and supernatural overthrow, or he may be expecting the silent and invisible laws of God's justice to work themselves out in history as they always have done; the " Son of Man " may be a supernatural leader out of heaven, or he may stand for the reign of justice and mercy, as the four beasts stood for the reign of brute force. Or the seer may be content to write his faith in flaming symbols, and leave all that open.

The simplest and the wisest thing is to resolve all these symbols into the great spiritual concepts of the triumph of justice and mercy. Daniel himself begins doing this for us, so far as he interprets his vision; and the coming of the Son of Man seems to correspond to the expression, *The saints of the Most High shall take the kingdom and possess the kingdom for ever even for ever and ever* (vii. 18). The vision of a spiritually-minded man may easily be interpreted materialistically; but it would be a miracle if the vision of a materialistic man could so naturally and easily be interpreted spiritually. The lower cannot create the higher by accident.

Antiochus will go where all the idols and evils of men ultimately end; *and he shall speak great words against the Most High and shall wear out the saints of the Most High, and think to change times and laws, and they shall be given into his hand until a time and times and the dividing of times.*[1] *But the judgment shall sit, and they shall take away his dominion to consume and to destroy it unto the end; and the kingdom and dominion and the greatness of the kingdom under the whole heaven shall be given to the people of the saints of the Most High whose kingdom is an everlasting kingdom and all dominions shall serve and obey him* (vii. 25-27). Israel as a world-empire in the immediate future seems to be the be all and end all for Daniel, just as it was for the early prophets. *Hitherto is the end of the matter* (vii. 28).

The third point is the most important of the three, and will be further developed in the next section. In the earlier prophets down to Isaiah and Jeremiah God is close and familiar, and his working is seen in the world all the time; in the later prophets from Ezekiel to Daniel God seems remote, transcendent. We do not feel in Daniel that he is overruling all things in the world all the time, though I do not doubt that Daniel would have agreed to this. Isaiah felt that the destroying Assyrian was the axe in the hand of God; Jeremiah felt that Nebuchadrezzar was doing God's work of vengeance in destroying Jerusalem; Isaiah the

[1] The three and a half years during which Antiochus controlled the Temple.

second said that God had raised up Cyrus for the special task of taking Babylon and setting free the Jewish exiles. These Napoleons of the ancient world set themselves to follow the desires of their own hearts according to their own wills; God did not interfere with their free will, but in the end it was his will that they had done. In *Daniel* the feeling is not that of God overruling all the time, but of his interfering with doom at the end.

It went with the new feeling of God's overwhelming majesty, of the awful difference between God and man, of the sense of man's insignificance and sinfulness and defilement. The old familiarity went; the old joy in his intimacy and nearness was discouraged; men's thoughts were concentrated now on the great gulf that was fixed between. Hence the system of sacrifice and reconciliation was developed; hence the old ministry of prophecy and inspiration died. The earliest prophets had not doubted that their inspiration was God himself speaking in the silence; the latest prophets felt it could not be the Most High himself. It was an influence from him, a power, a manifestation, but not simply and literally the Very God: they called it his Word, his Wisdom, his Angel, his Spirit, his Glory, his Presence, activities or energies or manifestations of God rather than God absolute.

The New World.

The task of the Jews was to adapt their old monotheistic faith to a new world. It was the Hellenistic era in which national and religious barriers were disappearing and men were proud of being citizens of the whole world. All that could be given by Persian and Babylonian, Greek and Egyptian, Hindu and Roman, was pouring into the great melting-pot of civilisation; the Jew alone shut himself up behind high barriers of race and religion. But he was a soldier and a merchant; his colonies were spreading east and west, and he had to accommodate himself to the world as he found it. The little cave-world of the primitive Hebrews had vanished in the high universal dawn of science and philosophy.

It is impossible to say from what sources the Jews took the new elements—scientific, philosophic, mythological, and astrological—which made up their new universe; and this alone shows how all the religions and philosophies were blending into syncretisms of various kinds. But a study of the new literature, produced in great profusion subsequent to the book of *Daniel*, enables us to give a fairly clear notion of the new world in which they lived and thought. The old limited world had given way to a universe in which thought was free to explore in every direction; it was possible now to speculate on what lay above the firmament or below the great deep, or even of what lay beyond this life in the far future.

The new world may be illustrated graphically by means of the duality (perhaps dimly Persian in origin) which was one of its peculiar features. Draw a line horizontally across a piece of paper, and you have that division into upper and lower which conditioned their view of space. Earth, with its firmamental dome, was the lower part of existence; above it lay heaven, the dwelling of God. The earlier Hebrews had occasionally thought of God as seated in majesty above the blue dome; but this was only a symbol of theirs; he was no more localised there than anywhere else. Babylonian astronomy had now interposed seven such domes between earth and the outer infinite space; these seven spheres were strict scientific abstractions, like the ether or electrons of modern science; each sphere was the orbit of one of the seven wandering stars or planets which circled so curiously and irregularly round the earth. This idea was forced upon the Jews, for it was the best science of the day; it had been adopted by Aristotle. With it went the astrological idea that each star was a god whose influence might be for good or evil; the Jews could not, of course, accept the idea of a god, but it was possible to put an angel in charge of each of the planets.

Enoch passes through all these spheres, past angel after angel, past the treasuries of the snow and the gates of the winds, before he finally arrives at the Throne of the Great Glory. Enoch also traverses much of the earth and gives us vague and strange accounts of curious lands, mainly to the eastward. The Jew was not really interested in mere speculation as such; he had no mind for spatial imagination; and we must not expect this curious geography and astronomy to be consistent.

Quite inconsistent cosmogonies are cheerfully woven together in the new universe. The rooted dualism of the Jew's view of the universe made him think much more naturally of the contrast between heaven and earth than of the theory of seven spheres which he had imported into it. The good things of earth were pale replicas of the good things of heaven. In heaven there was an " Upper Jerusalem " corresponding to the Jerusalem on earth, an altar, a temple, the ark of the covenant, and so forth, as we find them in the *Revelation of St. John*. It was impossible for a Jew to look on the earth and its life separated from God by the seven spheres as evil; for it was his creation; but it was possible for him to look on it as an inferior copy of the good things in heaven.

A further and very natural step was to think of all future things as existing now in heaven. The Messiah, for instance, was to come at the end of the world to redeem God's people; but inasmuch as God had already thought of him and predestined him, he must now exist in heaven, along with the new Jerusalem, waiting to be revealed. So it is natural that Enoch should find the " Son of Man " already in heaven beside the Ancient of Days. The thought of the pre-existence of all good things is curiously like Plato's.

The system of angels was developed to a very great extent indeed. The celestial monarch was surrounded with thousands of them, even thousands of thousands. Their names, their numbers, their grades, are told us with much confidence. Some of them had fallen into sin by marrying the daughters of men, and Enoch is much concerned with their fate; according to one view, these fallen angels (the Watchers) became the gods of the heathen and led them astray. This view lasted long enough to colour the thought of Milton. According to others, they were bound in prison awaiting judgment; they were often placed in one of the lower heavens.

The earth was an inferior place, and was doomed to destruction; it was not fit for God's kingdom, though some asserted that the Messiah would defeat all the heathen and reign in Jerusalem for a long time before the earth was finally annihilated. This temporary kingdom of the Messiah before the end of the world is clearly reflected in the New Testament. The thought of the inferiority of earth and the impossibility of redeeming it from sin is the base and heathen element in all this new thought. It despairs of creation.

To return for a moment to our horizontal line which graphically represented the new space idea: it serves to remind us that the earth we live in is but a line between the heavens above and the deep below; but their thought did not penetrate into the deep below. The firmament is the real dividing line between the Upper and the Lower; and in the thought of some the very rulers of the spheres were not free from evil. *In whose sight the very heavens are not clean* (*Job* xv. 15).

The hell below the earth is a European idea. The hell of the Christian religion came to us through the second-century *Apocalypse of Peter*, which relies on Orphic ideas such as we find in Vergil, and may come into Orphism ultimately from the northern nations. Vergil is Dante's guide to hell. In Jewish books we occasionally find evil arising from the abyss, a thought allied to that of the primæval serpent at the bottom of the sea; but hell generally means no more than the grave, the actual pit dug in the earth into which the dead are put. Hell is no more than the abode of the dead. As for the punishment of the wicked, the commonest idea was that it would take place on earth within sight of the saints who are enjoying life in the new Jerusalem.

Let us now turn to the question of time. A vertical line drawn from top to bottom of the page will serve to indicate their notion of time; the present is but the moment which separates the past and the future.

No nation had such a rich sense of the past as the Jews. Their own continuous national existence and memory went back into the past further than any other nation; their scriptures were older; and this sense of their antiquity profoundly impressed the whole world. Beyond that, their thought took them back to God, the creator of all things.

The apocalypses and the rabbinic writings are deeply interested in origins, the origin of the world, of man, and of sin; the myths which they tell attempt to account for these mysteries. In exactly the same way they look forward into the future, and sketch the destinies of all things—of angels, of men, of Israel, of the world. Just as their new view of space broke the little cave-world in which they had so long lived, and thrust right up into infinity, so the new conception of time broke right out of the narrow limits of prophecy, which had never looked beyond this life for the individual, or this generation for the race; it was now a question of the destiny of the whole human race for all eternity. And the end of all things, like the beginning of all things, must be God.

The pseudonymous writers love to go back to the beginning, and to map out the whole course of the history of creation up to its consummation; the Jewish apocalypses are the first Outlines of History. The work can, of course, only be done with the help of the mythological and the symbolic. The very numbers are symbolic. Just as the upward axis thrust up into heaven was divided into seven heavens, so the onward course of time was divided symbolically into seven ages, the spectrum or octave of space and time. The old Hebrew system, with its unit of one generation for the life of a man and many generations for the life of a tribe, was insufficient, though it was taken up symbolically into the new system. A very good example is to be found in the first few verses of St. Matthew's gospel which groups the whole genealogical history of the Hebrews into seven ages of seven generations each, two ages from Abraham to David, two ages from David to the Babylonian exile, two ages from the Babylonian exile to Christ; the conclusion being that with Christ Israel was entering into its seventh age (or "week") which would prove its consummation.

It must be noted that the number seven stands for the whole course of a thing, its completion and perfection. The system of seven "weeks" with which the first gospel opens is similar to the seven "days" with which the story of creation opens, beginning from the chaos and the void and ending with the sabbath rest of God. St. Augustine takes this system to cover the whole course of time; we are still in the sixth day, for the creation of man is not yet complete; before us is the seventh age, the sabbath of God. It may well be that he is right.

But, as in the case of the space system, we do not expect to find one logical scheme even within the covers of one book. Far more common is the simple dualism of This Age, and the Age to Come. The world in which we live is merely the line which trembles between past and future; and the common conviction in all the apocalypses is that we are entering into the last age of the world. This view is the view properly called eschatological, and the word ought not to be applied to any Old Testament book, not even *Daniel*, which is not concerned with the end of the world but with the immediate destinies of Israel.

The eschatological outlook grew up between *Daniel* and the New Testament, and is intimately connected with the disillusion created by the Maccabean kingdom. Antiochus was defeated and the saints of the Most High did possess the kingdom; the sons of old Mattathias reigned in Jerusalem as Priests of the Most High God. They extended their empire over Galilee and Idumea. But there was no increase of justice and mercy and true religion, and men began to doubt whether this earth was a fit place for the establishment of God's kingdom at all. They looked forward to a new heaven and a new earth, with a new Jerusalem and a new temple descending from God. The promised Messiah, or king like David, was almost forgotten; the bringing in of the New Age was God's work, or the work of the heavenly pre-existent Son of Man, who will come on the clouds of heaven with thousands of his holy ones to execute justice and vengeance on the earth.

The new mythology rises at its best into very fine poetry; it sinks at its worst into a welter of dreary allegory. It is vitiated at its heart by the poison of pessimism; it has committed the deadly sin of despairing of the universe. It has rightly been excluded from the canon of scripture; though one of the best apocalypses, *Esdras*, is to be found in the Apocrypha. Its notions pass into the theology of the orthodox Rabbis, and their recorded sayings shed some light upon it. It is impossible to construct any consistent picture of what was expected in the near future, but we can indicate some of the features which are most frequently found in it.

The old prophecies were preserved in many cases by the device of a temporary intermediate messianic kingdom before the actual end. A military leader will arise who will chastise the heathen and establish the world-empire in Jerusalem. Sometimes he is provided with an antagonist worthy of his steel, a messiah of evil, the " antichrist " who will be destroyed by fire from his mouth. The ungodly will be thrown into the valley of Hinnom outside Jerusalem, where the saints can watch their torments. The kingdom will last for a long time, and be incredibly rich and prosperous; the earth will be miraculously fruitful, and all the good will be happy. The righteous dead, especially the martyrs who died in the Maccabean wars, will come out of their graves to share in all this bliss; but in the end it will pass away like smoke; the new heaven and the new earth will take its place.

It is time now to put out of our minds the horizontal line which divides the world above from the world below, and the vertical line which divides This Age from the Age to Come. It is clear that the world below is This Age, and the world above is the Age to Come. Those lines were a mere scaffolding on which we built our thought. The Jews had in their minds something very like the modern notion of a space-time continuum. The mysterious Hebrew word '*Ōlām* (Greek *Aion*) originally meant a long passage of time; the " everlasting hills " are the " *hārē 'Ōlām*," the hills of an age; the Jews had not grasped the philosophic notion of infinity. When they wished to express the idea of permanent or enduring, they said, " Into the Age and onward " (" *lʿōlām wʿād* "). The Coming Age was simply another enormous stretch of time, the last one in the course of creation. But the word '*Ōlām*, by a kind of transference, was also used of the world which so endured or so passed away, just as we can speak of the mediæval world or the classical world. The Age to Come was also the World to Come, and the World to Come was the World Above; strictly speaking, the gospels never talk of the end of the World, but of the end of the Age; nor of the World to Come, but of the Age to Come.

Such were the expectations and dreams, in some circles of Judaism at least, when Christ was born. They had been terribly intensified by the rise of a new world power, the empire of Rome. Pompey had come eastward and easily deposed the last degenerate successor of Alexander reigning in Antioch. He had come south and without the least difficulty made Judea a province of the Roman Empire; he had even gone into the Holy Place of the temple to see what manner of god the Jews worshipped, and had been amazed to find no god there. The brief ascendancy of Jerusalem was over; the saints of the Most High had lost the kingdom.

But the Jews did not acquiesce in this new order of things. They had seen too many great empires pass by and fall, to imagine that they would not outlast the new one from the west; had not Ezekiel pictured all the glorious ghosts meeting in the shades of sheol, tarnished and dingy? The conquest only served to re-animate their faith. The belief in the military Messiah, the king like David, revived; we find it clearly expressed in the *Psalms of Solomon* written shortly after Pompey's desecration of the temple. We find it still more clearly expressed in the desperate rebellions which broke out from time to time under messianic leaders. Jerusalem was still very powerful; it was very rich; the Jews were very numerous and made good fighters; they would yet fight to the death with Rome for the mastery of the world, and Romans would not sleep safely till the queen city was destroyed and the Jewish nationality utterly abolished.

Part II. Christian

The Gospel.

WHEN Jesus was born in Bethlehem of Judea, Judea was a province of the Roman Empire, and had long been part of a brilliant and cosmopolitan civilisation. The official scriptures were the primitive Hebrew scriptures; the system of sacrifice and priesthood was narrowly and exclusively Hebrew; the prayers of the synagogue did not go much beyond the same orthodox range; and the national hope was that Israel and its law should dominate the Roman world. But in the minds of men these things had long been woven into the new Hellenistic background, with its fierce symbolism borrowed from Babylonian and Persian sources. Non-biblical mythologies and allegories were commonly accepted; wild visions of the future were eagerly read; and new doctrines like the resurrection of the dead had become a permanent part of men's faith. All this *mêlée* of incongruous conceptions was to fuse into a harmonious picture and become the accepted background of a new world; and the work of selection and simplification was done by Jesus of Nazareth. It was Jesus who fixed the conception of the cosmos for the Rabbis and the Mohammedans as well as for his own followers.

In the first place, he rejected the merely mythological and the merely allegorical. He talked almost entirely in symbolic language, which he shared with the pseudonymous writings; but the symbols are never so arranged as to form a system. He was careful in all he said to speak so that no fool could possibly take his words literally; it is an unfortunate fact that the fools so often have. No system of heavens, no machinery of rewards and punishments, no programme of the judgment day, can be deduced from the gospels.

Secondly, he rejected material that would make his message exclusively Jewish. He took the broad universal things in the national religion with which to build the new temple for all the world to worship in. He betrayed no consciousness of doing this; but it is what he did. He built within the old Judaism the new church of all humanity; and when the old Judaism fell, that remained standing.

Thirdly, he subordinated it to the great spiritual and moral ideals which had inspired the prophets. These had been lost to sight in a profusion of speculation and imagery; mere supernaturalism had taken the place of a simple faith in the justice and mercy of God; and the secret of real religion is that the good is the only supernatural. If we return for a moment to our old graph of the upright line dividing past from future, and the horizontal line dividing heaven from earth, upon which we have managed to plot the whole system of heavens and hells, angels and devils, ages and eras, things past, things present, and things to come, we note that it is flat; it is in two dimensions only; it is no solid reality, but is, after all, only beautiful scenery. Jesus gave the whole thing perspective and solid reality by adding the third dimension, the dimension of spiritual destiny; there is not only Up and Down, Past and Future; there is Good and Evil, and that is the duality that matters. The world is much more than a space-time continuum; what gives the thrill and drama to human existence is that we are going either to salvation or to ruin. A third line must be drawn at right angles to the other two (it will have to go straight out into the air), and this line will represent the pathway of the soul.

The whole power of the gospel is derived from the doctrine it teaches that there are only two directions in which the soul can go as it passes through this world of space and time: it can go upward along the narrow and difficult path to salvation, or it can go downward along the broad and easy path to ruin. No third possibility is considered. There are five wise virgins and five fools; the house may be built upon rock or upon sand; there are beatitudes for the poor and woes for the rich, no moderate criticism or faint praise. The first name for the new religion was *The Way*; its first manual for novices was called *The Two Ways*, and began *There is a way of life and a way of death ;* its characteristic is this sense of direction and destiny, the direction being the destiny. Souls are either being saved or being lost.

The Kingdom of God.

It will now be easy to approach the main subject of the teaching of Jesus, the coming of the kingdom of God. (The word "heaven" in *Matthew* is merely a respectful way of saying God, and makes no difference to the sense.) The kingdom of God is, of course, the World Above; it is also, of course, the Age to Come; but it is above all things the reign of justice and mercy; there is no difference between these three.

To Jesus the terms Above and Below are purely symbolic. God is not far away from him above seven heavens; he is close at hand. This is the way in which he begins his preaching: *The kingdom of God is at hand* (*Mk.* i. 15) (has come close). The kingdom of God is an invisible world, not apparent to the senses, not involved in the space-time continuum; but very close to us.

Similarly, though it is called the Age to Come, that does not mean that it does not exist now. The Coming is to be *in power* and *in glory*; but even now it exists among men like a minute invisible germ of life, the leaven that is to leaven the whole lump, the seed which will develop into a tree whose branches will give shelter to all the birds of the air. Already the *poor*, and the humble, and the penitent belong to the kingdom; the scribe who praised him in the temple is not far from it; and in his wonderful works its glory is already to be seen.

The term *kingdom of God* is not taken from the eschatological vocabulary at all. This is a fact which many champions of "eschatological theories" of the gospel have passed very lightly over; but it is significant. It is taken from the synagogue prayers of the day, and the orthodox Rabbis explained it as meaning the rule or sovereignty of God; where God's law was obeyed, there was the kingdom of God. Jesus himself, in making it the principal petition in his pattern prayer, subjoins a paraphrase: *Thy kingdom come*, that is, *thy will be done on earth as it is in heaven.*

We must be careful here not to tie down the conception of the kingdom to a cold and narrow ethic, or a passive and resigned obedience. The kingdom was a power, an overwhelming power, now entering into the lives of men. The truth is that Jesus brought back what the pseudonymous writers and the orthodox Rabbis had so long forgotten—the faith that God was working in the world all the time, that his justice and his compassion overruled all things, from the rise and fall of mighty empires down to the untimely death of the fledgling bird. This invisible power, this inner history, was the kingdom of God; God himself, not remote and separate from men, but familiar with them and entering into communion with them; God himself, surrounded by his angels, God himself in the company of his saints, Moses and Elijah, Abraham, Isaac, and Jacob.

The kingdom of God is the invisible world of power and glory, parallel with the visible world of space and time, breaking in upon it and subduing it. It is in Jesus himself that this process begins; in and through him the kingdom of God is coming to men. To accept him is to accept God, and to reject him is to reject God. He is the divine Son of Man who symbolises God's kingdom; he is here now in poverty and lowliness and humility, but he is to come again in power and glory on the clouds of heaven—or the kingdom is to come, it does not matter which you say; it comes to the same thing. Those who accept him on earth already belong to the kingdom; he will acknowledge them when he comes *in glory*. Those who are ashamed of him will be denied.

The divine Son of Man, the champion of the kingdom of God, appears on earth to do a work which is hid in mystery from his followers. It begins with a battle with Satan. Jesus never mythologises Satan. Satan in the gospel is a splendid example of pure religious symbolism. Satan is a name for a spiritual fact, the strong, cunning, vicious opposition to all good which we find in the world. Jesus never speculates whether the evil in the world is a person or a force or a tendency; he never speculates on its origin; he just names it: Satan. Jesus is a spiritual realist; he finds in his heart and in the world a set of forces working for good, and another working for evil; one is the kingdom of God, and the other is Satan.

He found Satan first in his own inner life, and overcame him; he found Satan next in his opponents and denounced them; he found Satan thirdly in his own chief disciple and warned him. Peter had suggested that there was no need for him to go up to Jerusalem and die; Jesus replied by saying that the narrow way must lead to the cross for every one of them, and that unless they took up the cross they could be no disciples of his. The way of justice and mercy and love would also be the way of patience and suffering and sacrifice. Jesus went up to Jerusalem to meet force with endurance and to overcome death by dying, and as he went he told them how through this death they might find their way into the kingdom of God, and how it was to be a ransom for the sins of the world. On the cross he met the last of Satan's terrors, and overcame it; his disciples were convinced that he had vanquished not only sin, but death also, and carried through all the world the news of their meeting with him risen from the dead. These are the things which the men who knew Jesus best reported about him.

The Prophecies of Jesus.

The prophet is the man who sees more clearly than anyone else the justice of God at work in the world; he therefore sees more clearly than anyone else the working of evil; and it is his duty and inspiration to announce these things to the world. Jesus was a prophet, and much of his prophecy has come down to us. The prophet, being the man who can really see the forces at work in the world, will see further than most into the future; we also possess some prophecies of Jesus about the future. These prophecies form the basis of St. John's apocalypse. One we have already noted is his own future *coming in glory*; the other deals with the doom of Jerusalem, and the two are related. It is very doubtful indeed how far any prophecies of Jesus can be said to deal with the end of the world or with a last judgment. One principal group of prophecies is to be found in *Mark* xiii.; this was probably in existence as a separate document before St. Mark incorporated it into his gospel; it was probably written in Jerusalem, and claims to have the authority of the apostles Peter, Andrew, James, and John. Two versions of another are to be found, one in *St. Matthew*, and the other in *St. Luke*; they differ slightly in vocabulary and style, but must be drawn ultimately from one tradition, which scholars call Q. (*Matt.* xxiv. 25-28 = *Luke* xvii. 23-27, xii. 29: *Matt.* xxiii. 34-39 = *Luke* xi. 49-51).

The Q prophecies tell us how the Son of Man, after being rejected and killed, will come again in vengeance; the day of vengeance appears to be identified with the doom of Jerusalem. The same is probably intended by the reply of Jesus when the high priest asked him whether he was the Christ, the son of the blessed; he answered, *I am, and thou shalt see the Son of Man coming on the clouds of heaven* (*Mk.* xiv. 63), Plenty of other passages in the gospel make it clear that Jesus did prophesy the doom of the city that rejected him. Jerusalem had always rejected the prophets. There was a cult at the moment of building tombs for them, and decorating the tombs and making speeches at their festivals; but Jerusalem was breeding true to type; they were the sons of those that slew the prophets. Ritual and sacrifice were duly carried out, and this was to the good; but mercy and justice and the great things of the law were passed over. Money and power were the ideals of Jerusalem, just the same as in any heathen kingdom; cunning and cruelty and force were her methods. She was like one of those great beasts in *Daniel*, with the added sin of being false to her God; and her last chance had come. God's last messenger, no servant this time but his own Son, offered her the last chance, and she refused it; and as he returned from the temple, he told the disciples with tears that within one generation every stone of the temple would be cast down, and the ruin of Jerusalem complete.

He was asked by his disciples what the signs of the future doom would be, and the end of the age; and it is at this point that St. Mark inserts his Little Apocalypse (chapter xiii.). It is divided into three stages. In the first he speaks of a period of wars and famines, of false Christs and false prophets. Then comes a parenthesis, which may be lifted from some other context, in which he warns them of persecutions, but assures them of the inspiration of the Spirit. Then comes the second stage, which is a repetition of the horrors and abominations of Antiochus alluded to in *Daniel*; Jerusalem will be besieged and there will be horrible atrocities; there is also a further warning against false Messiahs and false prophets. The third stage is described only in symbols drawn from the older prophets; there is a studious lack of detail about it. The sun and moon will be darkened, a quotation from *Isaiah*, which refers in its original context to the fall of Babylon; the Son of Man will come on the clouds of heaven, which means in Daniel the setting up of the kingdom of the saints; and messengers shall gather into it the elect from the four winds of heaven—that is, from all over the earth.

I see no reason to suppose that this refers to the end of the world. The darkening of the sun and moon need only mean the capture of Jerusalem; the coming on the clouds need only mean the establishment of the new religion. I am aware that this is a minimum method of interpretation; but the words are capable of this meaning, and this is all that is required. If we want prophecies of the end of the world (in our sense of the term), we must look elsewhere for them; what we have here is the end of one age and the beginning of another. A whole stretch of history from Abraham to John the Baptist, the whole of significant history up to that date, was over; a new era would begin, the era of the Son of Man, or, as we call it, the Christian era.

In denouncing Jerusalem Jesus was turning his back on the apocalypses (which never dominate his thought) and going back to the real prophets. He differed from them, however, in making the doom of Jerusalem final; there was no remnant, no restoration. But a saying quoted at his trial does suggest his view of what lay beyond that doom. *Destroy this temple that is built with hands, and in three days I will build another not made with hands* (*Mk.* xiv. 58 plus *Jn.* ii. 19). The material was to give way to the spiritual, the human to the divine, the earthly to the heavenly; a better temple would take the place of the old, the kingdom of God would come in, the Son of Man would return in glory.

We are amazed at the powerful restraint of the prophecies of Jesus. They announce definitely the fall of Jerusalem within this generation; it took place in precisely forty years, which is the conventional length of a generation in the Bible. Before it he prophesied wars, disturbances, false Christs, and false prophets; after it, his own triumph in the establishment of the true universal spiritual religion. The how and the when are thrust on one side; the symbols merely blazon out the spiritual convictions. "You destroy me now; my day will come. Your city will be destroyed: my kingdom come in."

The Christian Prophets.

It is plain that the disciples did not know what to make of these prophecies. He had flung out the symbols, and left who would to interpret them. They were sure of his resurrection, and in the strength of that they could no longer doubt his prophecies. They sat down in Jerusalem to await his coming in glory; for most of them seem to have taken his promises literally. They do not appear to have continued his denunciations of Jerusalem and the established religion; for the authorities recognised them as orthodox. They were just one among many sects who had unusual views about the Messiah.

The prophetic witness was not, however, permitted to sleep. For one cause or another there was dissatisfaction with the twelve within a couple of years, and a group of Hellenists, seven of them, rose to some considerable power in the church. One of them, St. Philip, was a prophet and had daughters who prophesied; St. Stephen also was of the prophetic type. He continued the denunciations of Jerusalem, and was finally charged with saying that when the Messiah came he would "*destroy this place and change the customs*" (*Acts* vi. 14). His words were plainly based on the sayings of Jesus, though he went beyond them in definiteness. His death as the first martyr shows the close connection between prophecy and persecution; prophecy invites persecution as surely as persecution produces prophecy. The martyr and the prophet are closely connected. To him, as to Jesus, heaven and earth were close together; *Behold I see the heavens opened and the Son of Man standing at the right hand of God (Acts* vii. 56). The twelve did not share in this persecution, so that it looks as if they did not approve of St. Stephen's views.

A school of prophets soon arose, but its origin is lost in the obscurity which clouds the whole Palestinian Church. We first hear of prophets as going from Jerusalem to Antioch, and one of them, Agabus, foretold a famine, which was no doubt one of the signs of the end. Possibly the prophets too were driven from Jerusalem by persecution. As we are told that this famine came to pass in the days of Claudius, it is reasonable to assume that the prophecy of Agabus may be dated in the reign of Caligula, the previous emperor. Caligula attempted to force the Jews to put up his image in the temple at Jerusalem and worship it; the nation declared they would rather suffer martyrdom than consent. The Roman governor in Syria, Philo the distinguished Jewish philosopher of Alexandria, and Herod, who was living in Rome, not yet a king, joined in protesting; and then fortunately the emperor died. It is quite possible that this event brought into existence the Christian school of prophecy; they may have seen in Caligula the new Antiochus predicted by Jesus (*the abomination of desolation spoken of by Daniel the prophet, Mk.* xiii. 14), and this in turn may have led Agabus to prophesy famine. It is not impossible that some of the visions in St. John's apocalypse may date from this period.

It is quite certain, at any rate, that there were Christian prophets in Jerusalem, that they did make some sort of witness, and that Jerusalem visions of different periods are incorporated in the *Revelation of St. John.* St. Paul spoke of the church as founded on the apostles and prophets, and when he entered Europe he was accompanied by Silas, a Jerusalem prophet. His epistles to the Thessalonians are filled with a confident expectation of the end of the world, and there are mysterious references to a man of sin exalting

TIME-CHART OF NEW TESTAMENT PROPHECY

This Age Ends

Jesus prophesies that within a generation Jerusalem will fall and the Son of Man come: the Kingdom of God: the Temple not made with hands.

A.D.
- 29. Crucifixion.
- 30. ? St. Stephen martyred: prophetic type.
- 31.   Witnessed against Temple.
- 32. St. Philip's preaching: also prophetic.
- 33.   The Spirit: the desert.
- 34.   Christianity spreads to gentiles.
- 35.   St. Peter's vision.
- 36.
- 37. Caligula. A possible antichrist.
- 38. ? Jerusalem prophets: Agabus: " famine."
- 39. St. Paul's mystic friend.
- 40.
- 41. Caligula dies. ? Jerusalem prophets: Agabus: etc.
- 42. First Period of Christian Prophecy.
- 43. St. James martyred: call of St. John? (*Rev.* xi.).
- 44. Herod dies. A possible Antichrist.
- 45. ? First visions of St. John.
- 46. ? St. Paul visits the " pillar " apostles.
- 47.
- 48.
- 49. Jerusalem Council. Silas the Prophet
- 50.   accompanies St. Paul. Thessalonians.
- 51.
- 52. Expansion of Church westward.
- 53.
- 54.
- 55.
- 56.
- 57.
- 58.
- 59.
- 60.
- 61. St. Paul in Rome.
- 62. St. James the brother of Jesus martyred in Jerusalem.
- 63.
- 64. Persecution in Rome. Nero Antichrist. (*Rev.* xiii.)
- 65. Second Period of Christian Prophecy.
- 66. ? SS. Peter and Paul martyred in Rome.
- 67. Roman army in Palestine under Vespasian.
- 68. Suicide of Nero: civil war: Vespasian emperor.
- 69. St. John writes as from this Date.
- 70. Jerusalem destroyed by Titus.

The Age to come Begins

So ends the Generation of which Jesus spoke. Twenty-five years later (A.D. 95), during the persecution of Domitian, came the Third Period of Christian Prophecy, in which St. John wrote new visions and combined them with the old to form the book we now possess. But he still writes as if from the year 69, treating of subsequent events as if they were still in the future. He sees Domitian as Nero over again; he sees the coming of the Son of Man in the invisible presence of Christ conquering the world through his martyrs and witnesses; he sees the coming of the Kingdom of God in the extension of the Church.

himself over every alleged god or object of worship, so as to seat himself as God in the temple of God, making himself out to be God, and there is an equally mysterious restraining power or person. He also speaks of the Jews in Jerusalem as having killed the Lord Jesus and the prophets and " persecuted us," and mentions the sufferings of the churches of God that are in Judea. All this represents, not so much primitive gospel Christianity, as the wave of Palestinian prophetism under Caligula, and in particular the influence of Silas.

To return to the Agabus period, the Caligula episode was closely followed by the succession of Herod to the throne of all Judea. The facts about Herod are obscure, but we have positive evidence in *Acts* that he was regarded by St. Luke at least as a second Antiochus. His policy was fanatically pro-Jew and anti-Hellene, and he was afflicted in some way or other with the religious obsession which has caused so many kings to think of themselves as gods; he posed as some sort of a divine person (Angel or Messiah?), and in the height of some splendid ceremony was struck with the same loathsome disease as Antiochus. Both Josephus and St. Luke look on his death as a divine punishment for arrogance, and St. Luke narrates the story in terms borrowed from the story of Antiochus in 2 *Maccabees*.

This king put St. James to death, *and because he saw it pleased the Jews, he proceeded further to take Peter also* (*Acts* xii. 1). No reason is given by St. Luke, and we are therefore quite in the dark as to the motives of this murder; but there must have been accusations made, pretexts put forth, and reasons which led up to it. The apostles must have been against the exaltation of Jerusalem and the king's extreme Judaism. They must have denounced the divine king; they may have thought of him as the new Antiochus. It is significant too that persecution has now extended to the apostles for the first time.

It is certain, at any rate, that a school of Christian prophets in Jerusalem did keep up the old prophetic message of doom which Jesus himself had so clearly enunciated. We know this because the document preserved as *Mark* xiii.

was drawn up, and given to the world under the names of the four chief apostles; we know it because we find visions in the apocalypse in which Jerusalem is called quite clearly *Sodom and Egypt, where also the Lord was crucified* (*Rev.* xi. 8); we know it because of all the clear denunciations which were handed on and at length written down in the gospels. The antagonism was bound to become more and more bitter between the jingoistic zealots who were determined to fight the Romans for the empire of the world, and could not doubt that God would uphold his own city, and the Christian prophets who were sure that God had doomed it. The cleavage came when at last the Roman army appeared before Jerusalem, and the Christians, in obedience to their Lord's prophecy, fled from it to Pella.

By this time the Emperor Nero had begun the imperial policy of persecution by his burnings and tortures in Rome; there was no doubt at all now that he was the antichrist, and as such St. John described him. St. Peter and St. Paul had perished in Rome, and St. James the Lord's brother in Jerusalem; these were apparently the last times, and when in the year A.D. 70 Jerusalem actually fell Christians must have looked up to see the Son of Man coming on the clouds. Though much of the *Revelation of St. John* was already in existence, the book as we know it was not written. It was not till twenty years later that it was worked into a complete whole with the addition of much new matter, during the persecution by the Emperor Domitian between A.D. 92 and 96. It looks back on the tremendous events of the century and interprets them in the light of the words of Jesus; it calls itself the apocalypse of Jesus, not the apocalypse of John.

The Revelation of St. John.

I do not propose to worry much over the authorship of the book. It is enough to say that someone wrote it about the year A.D. 95 and meant it to mean something. He incorporated into it visions which belong to the Jerusalem of an earlier period, which may, of course, be the work of somebody else; I shall bring reasons to show why this is not likely, but in any case it does not much matter. Whoever wrote them, he incorporated them because they meant something to him, and that meaning fitted into his scheme. It is the meaning attached to the whole book by its final author that I intend to consider.

The book cannot be understood in detail without some study of the pseudonymous Jewish apocalypses of the period, because it shares some ideas with them, and has the same general conception of the universe. But the influence of these books is subsidiary. Dr. Charles, their great champion, can adduce only a very few quotations. All this has been much exaggerated.

Much more important is the prophecy of Jesus. It is, in fact, decisive. Dr. Charles has shown how the whole book runs parallel with the events of *St. Mark*, chapter xiii.; wars, famines, and disturbances, false Christs and false prophets, the destruction of a great city, the coming of the Son of Man on the clouds of heaven, the new Jerusalem . . . and yet Dr. Charles has not even considered the suggestion that the great city whose downfall is described and lamented over is Jerusalem. This suggestion was strongly urged by Dr. Milligan in a book which is a recognised authority on the subject, and yet neither Dr. Charles nor any other commentator [1] has taken it seriously. If the Babylon of St. John is not Jerusalem, what has happened to that central prediction of our Lord?

This suggestion is reinforced by other considerations. The second leading influence in the book is the prophecy of the Old Testament. There is plenty of evidence to show that the primitive Jerusalem church devoted a great deal of time to searching the prophets, and that they actually drew up tables of proof texts. Dr. Charles has shown that the author of the *Revelation* read his Old Testament in Hebrew, and made his own translation; the *Revelation* is a mass of quotations. The *Psalms* have contributed the largest number of quotations, and after that come the prophets such as Isaiah and Zechariah; but the formative influence from the Old

[1] But see note appended by Dr. Goudge to commentary on *Revelation* in Dr. Gore's *New Commentary* (S.P.C.K.).

Testament is *Ezekiel*. The plan of *Ezekiel* is the plan of the *Revelation*; the *Revelation* is a Christian *Ezekiel*. In a sense we may say that the best of all the Hebrew prophets is selected and clarified for us in the *Revelation*, and that every leading idea in Hebrew prophecy is to be found there illuminated and christianised. But in the case of *Ezekiel*, it is more than that.

Make a synopsis of *Ezekiel* and divide it into sections, and you will find those sections correspond to sections of the *Revelation*. The first part of each leads up to the doom of Jerusalem, and the last part of each dwells on the glory of the new Jerusalem. The spirit, the colour, and the imagery are the same; the repulsive figures of Oholah and Oholibah are the originals of Babylon the great harlot. Step by step they agree.

The object of the *Revelation of St. John* was in a secondary sort of way to collect a number of visions dating from various periods and arrange them; but this is a minor matter, a piece of literary labour. The primary object of *Revelation* is to take the course of prophecy down to Jesus and show how it had all been fulfilled. The two main sequences involved are the sequence of the prophecies of Jesus and the sequence of the prophecies of Ezekiel; these are woven together without breaking their order. Into the web there also go the other prophecies, in particular those of Isaiah and Zechariah; but the whole thing is skilfully mingled with more or less independent Christian prophecies made in Jerusalem before its fall, by lamentations over its fall, and by gorgeous visions which had been seen since.

Yet the book is, as Dr. Charles says, a unity; it marches forward with one purpose, and every movement in it is subordinate to that purpose. It bears the mark of one mind, and (except for minor passages?) is written in one style. It rises to the highest poetic vision which the human mind can attain; it has passages of sheer beauty and terror utterly beyond any other writer. It is the world's supreme masterpiece of imaginative art.

We shall not therefore do it the injustice and insult of giving it a lower meaning when it cries out for a higher.

64   THE MEANING OF THE REVELATION

ANALYSIS OF THE REVELATION SHOWING THE SOURCES OF ITS SYMBOLISM

Revelation.	Gospel.	Ezekiel.	General.
1. *Preliminary*, i.–iii.			
Patmos Vision.		(Ez. viii.)	(Dan. x.)
2. *Throne of God*, iv.–v.		Ez. i.–ii. The Throne.	*Is.* vi.
The Book.		Ez. ii. The Book.	
The Lamb.	*John* i. 29.		(cf. Enoch.)
3. *The Seven Seals*, vi.–viii. 5.			
Four Destroyers.	*Mark* xiii. 3–8.	Ez. v. (vi.–vii.) Four Judgments.	Zec. i.
Souls under Altar.	*Matt.* xxiii. 34	also Ez. xiv.	
Prophetic Dooms.	*Mark* xiii. 24.		(Is., Joel, etc.)
Sealing of Elect.		Ez. ix. Sealing of Faithful.	
New Creation (anticipated).		Ez. xi. 19. New Covenant (anticipated).	(Jer. xxxi. 33.)
Fire from Altar.		Ez. x. Coals from Altar.	
4. *The Seven Trumpets*, viii. 6, xi.			*Joshua* vi.
Fall of Star.			*Is.* xiv. 12 (cf. Enoch).
Locusts and Demon Horses.			*Joel* i.–ii.
Angel of Revelation.		Ez. viii. Angel of Revelation.	*Dan.* x.; viii. 16; ix. 21; xii. 7.
Call of Prophet.		Ez. ii. Call of Prophet.	
Against Temple.		Ez. ii.–iii., etc. Against Temple.	
Two Witnesses.			*Zec.* iv.
(Dead in Streets.)		Ez. xi. Dead in Streets.	
Ark in Heaven.		Ez. xi. Glory leaves Temple.	
5. *The Great Interlude*, xii.–xiii.			
Birth of Messiah.			*Is.* vii. 10; ix. 6.
Woman in Heaven.			(Is. vii.; Canticles Gen. Wisdom.)
Michael			*Dan.* vii. 7; x. 13 and 21; xii. 1.
The Beasts.			*Dan.* vii. 1–8.
The Battle to come.			*Dan.* vii. 15–28.
6. *The Coming of the Doom*, xiv.–xviii.			
The Son of Man.	*Mark* xiii. 26.		*Dan.* vii. 13.
The Harvest of the Land.	*Matt.* xiii. 39.		
The Vine of the Land.		Ez. xv., etc. The Vine of Israel.	
The Wine-press.			*Is.* lxiii. (*Joel* iii.). *Exodus.*
The Seven Plagues.			
Great Hail.		Ez. xiii. 11. Great Hail.	
The Harlot.		Ez. xvi., xxiii. The Harlot.	
The Great City.		Ez. xxii. The Bloody City.	
		Ez. xxiv. Jerusalem Destroyed.	
Lament over "Babylon."		Ez. xxvi.–xxvii. Lament over Tyre.	(Is. xiii. xiv., etc.)
7. *Future Judgments, etc.*, xix.–xxi. 8.			
Wedding of Messiah.			(Ps. xlv.; Cant.)
The King-Messiah.		Ez. xxxiv., xxxvii. David.	*Is.* ix. 6, etc.
Wars of Messiah.			*Is.* ix. 6, etc.
Invitation to Birds.		Ez. xxxix. 17. Birds of Heaven.	
First Resurrection.		(Ez. xxxvii. ? Resurrection, Restoration.)	
Gog and Magog.		Ez. xxxviii.–xxxix. Gog and Magog.	(Jer. i.)
The Judgment.			*Dan.* vii. 9.
New Creation.	*Mark* xiv. 58.	Ez. xxxvi. 27–8. New Covenant.	*Lev.* xxvi. 11 (Jer. xxxi. 33).
8. *The Holy City*, xxi. 9–22.		Ez. xl.–xlviii. The Holy City.	(Is.; Tobit.)

SOURCES OF THE SYMBOLISM OF THE REVELATION

The Analysis printed opposite is a synopsis of facts which must be thoroughly grasped if the *Revelation* is to be understood. It traces the Old Testament origin of each of St. John's visions, but does not show the extent to which he is influenced by the Old Testament, since it does not deal with mere quotations and allusions. In each case the subject-matter and symbolism of the whole vision are borrowed from the Old Testament passage printed opposite to it; St. John has taken the Old Testament passage and re-written it.

The main parallel column shows the material taken from *Ezekiel*. Smaller columns show the influence of the gospel prophecies, and of other Old Testament literature. The whole synopsis traces every vision to its main literary source. Where an Old Testament passage has exercised a strong influence without contributing the main symbolism of the vision, I have sometimes put a reference in parentheses.

The result shows that the material is drawn in an overwhelmingly large proportion from *Ezekiel*. More than this, it is easy to see that the order of *Ezekiel* is fairly faithfully followed. The only serious dislocation is that the call of the prophet to witness against Jerusalem and the temple is later in *Revelation* than in *Ezekiel*; chapters viii., ii. and iii. are thus out of place in the *Ezekiel* column. The plan of the *Revelation*, which devotes the first chapters to a survey of past history, necessitated this arrangement; but it is worth asking whether in the original Palestinian form of the visions, the section which described the call of the prophet did not come first. The present first chapters of *Revelation* (iv. and v.) show signs of a later date.

The *Revelation* is a Christian re-writing of *Ezekiel*. Its fundamental structure is the same. Its interpretation depends upon *Ezekiel*. The first half of both books leads up to the destruction of the earthly Jerusalem; in the second they describe a new and holy Jerusalem. There is one significant difference. Ezekiel's lament over Tyre is transformed into a lament over Jerusalem, the reason being that St. John wishes to transfer to Jerusalem the note of *irrevocable* doom found in the lament over Tyre. Here lies the real difference in the messages of the two books. Jerusalem, like Tyre, is to go for ever.

It is now worth noting that there is a whole section which is not based upon *Ezekiel* at all; it is chapters xii. to xiv., the Great Interlude, as I have named it. Its independence of *Ezekiel* still further justifies the title. If it were totally omitted, the *Revelation* would flow continuously on, and it would be more than ever obvious that the great city whose destruction it portrays is Jerusalem.

Other symbolic material from the Old Testament is worked into the scheme in a subordinate way, the Plagues of Egypt, the Seven Trumpets of Jericho, the Messianism and Fallen Star of *Isaiah*, the Horses and Olive Trees of *Zechariah*, the Locusts and Dooms of *Joel*, and the Eschatology of *Daniel*. We need not go to the contemporary apocalyptic writers for any principal piece of symbolism except perhaps the Souls under the Altar; their influence may perhaps be discerned in the imagery of the Fallen Star and the Lamb as Messiah, though this symbol owes much more to current Christian thought.

The influence of the Gospel prophecies is harder to show in tabular form, though I have added some references. St. John in re-arranging the Old Testament prophecies is avowedly interpreting them in the sense of the prophecies of Jesus. The complete ruin of Jerusalem and its supersession by a heavenly or spiritual religion is not drawn from the prophets, but from the Gospel. The *Revelation* might be summed up in the words, " *Destroy this temple which is built with hands, and in three days I will build another not made with hands* " (*Mark* xiv. 58; *John* ii. 19). There was probably more temple symbolism in the earlier drafts of the *Revelation* than there is now.

I have noted in the Gospel column a few actual parallels : Jerusalem as persecutor, the souls of the innocent dead crying for vengeance, the prophetic dooms as a sign of the end, the coming of the Son of Man, the Harvest symbolism, the destruction of Jerusalem, and the coming of the kingdom of God and of his Christ; this is the outline of Gospel prophecy and also the outline of the Revelation. The Harvest symbolism seems characteristic of the Gospels only; the other Gospel symbols are drawn from the Old Testament. It will be seen, therefore, that in giving a new meaning to the Hebrew prophets, St. John was continuing a process begun by our Lord.

Parallels with the fourth gospel, like Lamb of God and Word of God, are often noted in the course of the book.

E

We shall not betray our own lack of humour and imagination by supposing that its author thought that all his weird creatures had a material existence somewhere, and that Christ had a sword protruding uncomfortably out of his mouth. We shall not look for references to the time in which we live, and suppose that the Beast is the Kaiser and the Scarlet Woman the papacy. We shall see what spiritual realities are blazoned by these creatures of the imagination, and the only historical references will be to the writer's own time.

The literal-minded man will have nothing of this treatment of the *Revelation*, or indeed of the faith in general. The literal-minded believer, in his solid material way, wants his brimstone hell, and everything else according to catalogue; he thinks the book really means that, and that heaven really has those animals, just four of them and no more; he is the Fundamentalist. The literal-minded sceptic also thinks the book means exactly that, and that it is absurd; he is the mental and moral double of the Fundamentalist, only inside out. Both of them think that when we talk about spiritual meanings we are trying to find a low and cunning way out of what the book actually says; but if we want to grasp all its beauty and all its power, we must pay no deference to them. We must march on.

Our treatment of the *Revelation* will be guided therefore by three main principles.

In the first place, we shall assume that it deals with spiritual realities, which are very different from abstract ideas. It rests on the faith that in history great invisible powers are at work, and it attempts to describe those powers in symbolic terms, much as the political cartoonist does, or the poet in such a verse as

> *Slowly comes a hungry people, as a lion drawing nigher*
> *Glares at one who nods and winks behind a slowly dying fire.*

Just as Tennyson is here concerned with the rise of the proletariat, so St. John is concerned with the advent of the kingdom of God, by which is meant, not some outward spectacular event in the sky, or even some outward ecclesiastical progress on earth, but the certain conquest of cruelty and greed and brute force by the powers of justice and mercy and love.

In the second place, we must illustrate our studies from the pseudonymous apocalypses of the time, because St. John has cast his work in the same literary form, and arranged his system of symbols against a similar background of space and time. The publication of Dr. Charles' splendid commentary has made this task an easy one; but we must be careful not to be led away by his enthusiasm for the pseudonyma. St. John does not, except in a very few cases, derive his ideas from the previous apocalypses. We are likely to be wrong if we suppose that the symbols in *St. John* must have the same meaning they have in *Enoch* or *Esdras*; the contrary is the case. He does not even draw from them his conception of the universe; they both use the same conception, which is quite another thing; and how differently they use it!

The space conception of the world Above and the world Below is purely symbolic in *St. John*, as it is in the gospel; the picture of the seven heavens is utterly abolished, and the world of heaven interpenetrates the world of earth. Future time is not pictured spatially; it is not a map along which mankind is inevitably progressing; it is dynamic, it is rolling in upon us; the Age to Come is God and all his invisible powers. It is the triumph of the kingdom of God and his righteousness, which is only visible to the prophetic eye, and to the prophetic eye has already begun. The determining and formative influences in the thought of St. John are Jesus and the older prophets.

In the third place, we shall test Dr. Milligan's theory that the great city whose destruction is the central event of the book is Jerusalem; we shall bring forward what I believe to be conclusive reasons for accepting this theory. The fall of Jerusalem was the central event in the century which John reviews in his vision, and it marks the end of the ancient world; a whole continuous age of history, beginning with Hamurabi and Pharaoh and ending with Cyrus and Alexander and Cæsar, is wound up; the world enters on a new age, the age of Christ, before whom all the older gods and idols are destined to fall. John, looking up, sees the victorious Christ and his martyrs riding in to possess the world, and the new Jerusalem descending out of heaven from God.

BOOK II
ST. JOHN'S INTRODUCTION

PART I. INTRODUCTORY VISION
Title and Greetings.
The Vision in Patmos.
The Seven Angels.
Vision and Composition.

PART II. THE LETTERS TO THE SEVEN CHURCHES
Their Future Destiny.
Their Present Condition.
The Synagogue of Satan.
Primitive Hebrew Gnosticism.

INSPIRATION

Saint Francis, he was merry;
His heart was like a bird
That sang and throbbed with music till the leaves and grasses stirred.
His heart was like a well of fire,
A roaring sun of love,
A fountain of compassion
That drowned the world in love;
And out of cold and misery,
And out of hate and shame,
And out of pain and poverty,
He rose like a golden flower,
He rose like a golden flame,
To the peaks of holy ecstasy, the heights of mystic power,
The sunshine of eternal God, the saints' unfailing dower.

Up from the leafy forest in the blue September air
His spirit soared like a skylark, singing, singing, singing;
He heard the Holy, Holy, that never ceases ringing
In the heaven beyond the heavens where he rose on wings of prayer:
Holy the Lord of angels, Holy, Holy, Holy:
And the bells of a million churches were mingled into the cry;
Full is the heaven of Glory: and full is earth and sky.

And the seraph wings unfurled
Till they overbore the skies,
And the emerald rainbow shone,
And the dim blue throne was shown,
And HE that sat thereon
Was a glory of blinding rays;
And gazing into the blaze
Of light invisible,
Light intolerable,
Unendurable,
He saw what is seen by none,
The Love that moves the sun
In heaven, and all the stars:
God's sorrow and God's pain,
The Lamb as it had been slain
And the broken heart of God.

    STANZAS FROM THE CHANSON OF ASSISI.

BOOK II

ST. JOHN'S INTRODUCTION

PART I. INTRODUCTORY VISION

ARGUMENT

ST. JOHN sends greetings to the Seven Churches of Asia, and narrates his Vision of the Risen and Present Christ in Patmos, which is his authority to prophesy to them. He then writes messages to each of the Seven Churches, encouraging them in their trials, promising rewards for constancy and judgments for unfaithfulness, and warning them against the Synagogue of Satan.

The tone of the Introduction is that the Christ is not far off in a distant heaven, but present now, and triumphing in his Church and in his Martyrs.

Title.

St. John gives the title of his book as *the Apocalypse of Jesus Messiah;* it is not therefore the Revelation of St. John the Divine. Revelations were not given by writers now living on earth, but by holy men of old, Enoch, Ezra, or Baruch. Daniel is a case in point. The prophets had received inspiration from heaven and given a living message to living men. The authors of apocalypses were not so bold; they concealed their identity and put their messages into the mouths of ancient worthies whose names would carry more weight. The *Revelation* differs in being attributed to one who had lived and died not long before; it differs also in disclosing the name of its author. The revelation by the supernatural person is combined with the inspiration of a prophet now living, known and named: it is therefore double in character and can be regarded as

1. The Revelation of Jesus Messiah,
2. The Prophecies of John his servant.

The Revelation did not originate with the Messiah. God gave the Revelation to the Messiah, and the Messiah was *to show it to his servants*, a useful text for those who hold that the *Revelation* contains the work of other prophets; on the other hand, the words might imply that the message was originally given to the Old Testament Prophets, or more likely that Christ while on earth gave it to his disciples.

In harmony with the utterances of our Lord and his apostles, we are told that the content of the *Revelation* is *bound to happen shortly*. This statement, so frequently repeated, cuts out altogether the idea of an outline or survey of many centuries of future history. What is revealed is shortly to come to pass.

The Revelation was made known through one particular servant whose name was John; but he did not act directly. There is another link in the chain; *he signified it to John through his Angel.* The word *signify* is an interesting and uncommon word; it suggests that through St. John the meaning of Christian prophecy was first made plain. The Revelation had already been given (*to show it to his servants*); its meaning was supernaturally revealed to St. John. An Angel-Guide or Angel-Companion or Angel-Interpreter is almost universal in Jewish apocalypses. Often he is Uriel, and practically always one of the Seven (Four) principal Angels. The question is very complicated, because almost at once we lose sight of the Angel, and St. John receives a revelation from Jesus himself; on the other hand, the Angel-Guide does appear later in the book. Two considerations may help to explain this.

1. In St. John's earlier visions, which come at a later stage in the *Revelation*, the Angels played a more important part than they do at present. The reference appears to be to the Angel in chapter x through whom he received his call to prophesy. This Angel is the Angel of Prophecy, a kind of personification of Prophecy or Revelation. At a later stage St. John's visions appear to have come more directly, and the Angel was allowed to recede into the background.

2. The Angel may represent Jesus himself. In *Exodus* and elsewhere the *Angel of the Lord* (*i.e.* Angel of Jehovah) is a representative of Jehovah, the activity or energy or manifestation of Jehovah in history. He appears in the burning bush and says, "*I am the God of Abraham.*" In a similar way this Angel, *his Angel*, may be a personification of the energy or activity of Jesus, a projection of him into the mind of the prophet.

The difficulty arises from the attempt to personify a process, and particularly a spiritual process like prophecy. Prophecy is an activity of God; it is also an activity of the prophet; it is that manifestation which occurs where the two minds meet. Hence the lack of logical system in John's orders of Angels; hence his difficult phrases like *the Spirit of Prophecy*, or *the Spirits of the Prophets*. The same difficulty occurs when we come to other Angels and other processes. There are powers and influences at work among men, some of which come from God. St. Paul does not fully personify them; he calls them "*powers and authorities.*" St. John calls them Angels; at times he thinks of them as distinct from God, and at times as his identical activities.

We now have three links in the chain:

1. God who gave the Revelation to the Messiah,
2. The Messiah who gave it to his Servants,
3. The Angel, or prophetic power by which it was *signified* to John.

Lastly we have the prophet himself, *who Witnessed the Word of God and the Witness of Jesus Messiah, the things which he saw.* This appears to refer to the contents of the book, which he hereby claims as his own actual visions, though it could mean that he saw the trial and crucifixion of Jesus; this, however, would be contrary to what the same words mean in other parts of the book.

There follows a benediction upon the officer whose duty it would be to read the book in the assembly of the church, upon *those who hear*, and *those who observe* its contents.

For the time is at hand.

Greetings to the Seven Churches.

Grace to you and Peace. All the Epistles start with such greetings; but those we find here are peculiar, because St. John makes no claim upon his readers by calling himself apostle or prophet; he is simply *John*. It is not likely, therefore, that there were two Johns in Ephesus at this time, but one only, whose name and authority were known and accepted.

The *Seven Churches* are the churches of the actual seven towns. Most of the fantastic schemes which twist the *Revelation* into a forecast of modern history begin by making each of the churches an age in the history of the church universal; for without this indefensible proceeding it would be difficult to get down to modern times at all. All these schemes are contrary to the plain warning of the prophet, *what must quickly come to pass: the time is at hand.* This argument alone is enough to refute every kind of Adventism.

Grace to you and Peace is the familiar salutation which he has perhaps borrowed from St. Paul, and which St. Paul had adapted from the ordinary letter formula of the day; but St. Paul would have said *from God the Father and our Lord Jesus Christ.* St. John expands this in symbolic language borrowed from Isaiah and expressed in his own amazing and ungrammatical Greek, *from the Being and the Was and the Coming.* Dr. Charles has shown that St. John does not wantonly or carelessly break the rules of the Greek language, and in his monumental commentary has tabulated the strange rules of grammar which he obeyed. Was it perhaps the Greek spoken in some Palestinian circle to which St. John belonged? This book is not concerned with linguistic problems, but we must once and for all note that the book is written in this barbarous style, and also that it does just here in a very magnificent manner blazon the word Eternity.

The Seven Spirits before the Throne must be dealt with later. They are all that is left of the Seven Great Angels of *Enoch* and contemporary apocalypse; here we cannot doubt that they are identical with God and represent the Holy Spirit.

(For this reason Dr. Charles regards them as the unintelligent gloss of some later editor or scribe.)

Jesus is described first as *the Martyr, the Faithful* Witness to God who gave his life for the truth, then as the *Firstborn* (or more probably *Sovereign*) *of the Dead*, then as the *Ruler of the Kings of the Earth*. All that Jesus said and hoped in Palestine is here seen as done; he has given his life a ransom for many, he has risen on the third day, he sits with God in glory; and so the prophet, carried away by his ecstatic faith, breaks into lyric in praise of his Redeemer.

> *To him who loves us,*
> *And loosed us from our sins by his Blood,*
> *And made us a Kingdom, Priests to God and his Father,*
> *To him be Glory and Power into the Ages.   Amen.*

It is the first of those lyrical cries which are so often heard in this book, like the song of a Greek chorus, interpreting the symbolic action of the drama. The terrible and glorious symbols of apocalypse are not very suitable for the delineation of sorrow and love; St. John has not mentioned the cross or redemption in his picture of the exalted Jesus, but the lyric shows how the redemption is his real inspiration, and fills with tenderness and love the hard outline provided by the symbols. It is an amazing fact, however, that the word "cross" is not found in the *Revelation*, and proves very forcibly St. John's determination not to go beyond the symbols already used in prophecy and apocalypse. Hence the extraordinary effect of the one occurrence of the word crucified (xi. 8).

The *Kingdom of Priests*, as we may perhaps translate it, is the *Royal Priesthood, the Holy Nation* of St. Peter's Epistle, the *Peculiar People* singled out for God's special possession, the new Israel taking the place of the old.

It is startling to see how much in St. John's vision is already accomplished. Not only has Jesus risen from the dead as prince of life; he is now *Ruler of the Kings of the World*, and Christians are already a *Kingdom*. One thing waits—outward and visible expression of these truths; but that is what is coming so quickly. As Daniel says, *Behold he cometh with the Clouds*; or to quote Second Zechariah, *Every eye shall see him, and those that pierced him ; and all the tribes of the land shall wail.* (See Note on Second Zechariah in Book vi, page 268.)

Yes : Amen, adds St. John.

St. John began to write a greeting, but lost himself in contemplation of the exalted Jesus. He now adds a line which has little connection with the context, as it appears to come from God himself; Dr. Charles takes it to be another gloss. I think we ought to translate it *I am the A and the Z says the Lord God, who Is and who Was and who is Coming, the Ruler of the World.*

Almighty is a poor translation of *Pantokrator*, which means " having all the power " or " ruling over everything." It represents the title which occurs so commonly in Jewish prayers, *melek ha'olam*, King of the Age (or world), and this, in turn, represents the much older *Yahweh S'baoth* or Jehovah of Hosts. Jehovah of Hosts originally meant Jehovah, Lord of the armies of Israel. In time the title *Adonai* (Lord) was substituted for the personal name, Jehovah, which was thought too sacred to pronounce; and the *Hosts* were taken to mean the stars or angels. The title, *Lord of Hosts*, thus came to mean supreme ruler of all the forces of heaven. The Greek equivalent *Kurios Pantokrator*, meaning the Lord who rules over all things, extended its meaning to earth and hell as well as to heaven. The title *Alpha and Omega* (A and Z) extends it throughout and beyond the whole process of time and of creation, so that, as in Aristotle's philosophy, God is both the Origin of all things (*Arche*), and the Consummation to which all things are moving (*Telos*) ; *who Is and who Was and who is Coming.*

The Vision in Patmos.

So far we have had no visions recorded. We have had no more than a title-page and a greeting; but the style is full of symbols drawn from the later visions and ultimately from prophets like Second Isaiah, Second Zechariah, and Daniel.

Now comes the record of a Vision, one of the latest of

all visions, because it is given as the authority for his letters to the Asian churches. Every prophet has a "Call" or initial vision, in which he is commanded and authorised to prophesy; the Call of St. John is described in chapter x. The Vision here described is his authority to prophesy in Asia, opening a new and final period; it forms an introduction to his letters to the seven churches, and also in a sense to the whole collection of earlier prophecies which is appended to them and arranged so as to form a unified composition.

Little is told us of the circumstances of the Vision, though much may be imagined. St. John describes himself merely as a fellow-Christian in persecution, *your Brother, and Companion in the Persecution, and in the Kingdom, and in the patient Endurance in Jesus*: in the *Kingdom* or Royal Power, because in *the Persecution*, and therefore also in that *Patience* or *Endurance* which is the key-note of the whole book. Persecution is its background; patience is its gospel.

He is *in the island called Patmos through the Word of God and the Witness of Jesus*. The word *Witness, Marturia*, has almost already become the technical term for martyrdom; and the traditional view is that John was suffering exile for the faith; but the words might equally well imply that he was there in loneliness and meditation as a result of a spiritual call. They are the same words that we find in verse 2, where he describes himself as *John who Witnessed the Word of God and the Witness of Jesus Messiah*, where, however, he adds the words *which he saw*.

He passed into a state of ecstasy; *he was in the Spirit* (or *in spirit*) *on the Lord's day*. References to the Holy Spirit are rare in this book; and this rarity is one of the few points that definitely mark it off from the fourth gospel and link it with the other three. There has already been much about the Almighty Ruler of the world and much about Jesus the Messiah; next to nothing about the Spirit in whose power the whole book was written.

The traditional view of *the Lord's Day* is that it means Sunday, already kept as a weekly festival of the Resurrection; but it could mean the Day of the Lord—that is, the

Day of Judgment—though this on the whole is not likely.

The Vision begins with a Voice that breaks in upon his trance *from behind;* it is a *loud Voice like a Trumpet blast*, and its function is to draw his attention to the Vision proper. It commands him to *write that Vision in a Book and send it to the Seven Churches*. The Trumpet Voice recalls at once the Angel with the Trumpet who was expected in Jewish mythology to sound the reveille for the Judgment Day. It is quite uncertain whether it is meant to be the voice of Jesus or of the Angel of Revelation; very likely St. John had no clear idea on the subject.

Vision of the Risen Lord.

Nothing is more important than to make the most of every occasion on which St. John describes his own words, actions, or feelings during a vision; in this case when he saw the glorious being who had spoken to him *he fell at his feet as if dead*. This terror is an authentic part of prophetic communion with God. Moses covered his face with his hands, Isaiah said *Woe is me, for I am a sinful man;* Jeremiah said, *Ah, Lord God, I am but a child;* Ezekiel and Daniel both fell in a swoon; and we shall see that in other ways St. John's experience was like theirs.

But little more is said of the prophet. It is one of the strangest parts of this strange book that he so completely effaces himself.

As he lay there the being *laid his hand upon me and said, Do not be afraid; I am the First and the Last and the Living One; I too became dead, and behold I am living into the Ages of Ages, and I hold the Keys of Death and of Hades*.

Then he knew who this being was; it was the risen and glorified Jesus, now possessed of power over life and death, and clothed with the majesty of the eternal God; for the words he used were those used by Isaiah to describe Jehovah.

The description of the risen Jesus is based on visions of Ezekiel and Daniel in which they beheld a figure who is nothing short of a manifestation of Jehovah, his Word or his Angel.

In *Ezekiel* viii. we read that *the Hand of the Lord God fell there upon me, and I beheld, and lo a Likeness as the appearance of Fire : from the appearance of his loins even downward, fire ; and from his loins even upward, as the appearance of brightness, as the colour of amber.* This is the likeness as the appearance of Adam (man) that he had seen in his initial vision of the Throne of God, except that there the symbolism is more confused and the amber and fire are mixed. This is the image of man that is conceived of in Genesis i. as existing in the nature of God; it is also the power of God which came to the prophets.

This figure is further elaborated in the Gabriel (man of God) of *Daniel* viii. 16; x. and xii. 7, who is *Clothed in Fine Linen, whose Loins were girded with fine gold of Uphaz : his Body also was like Beryl* (= *the Amber of* Ezekiel) *and his Eyes as Lamps of Fire, and his Arms and Feet like in colour to polished Brass . . . and when I heard the voice of his words then was I in a deep sleep on my face, and my face toward the ground, and behold an Hand touched me.*

This figure is probably also to be identified with the Son of Man (x. 16). It is not conceived mythically, but is a personification of something which the last great prophetic thinker of the old Israel really thought to exist in God, something similar in nature to man, something that enters into communion with him in his soul, the revealing Word which came to the prophet.

In this passage St. John has identified this figure with Christ, and the point is important because it carries with it something more; the Strong Angel of chapter x who appears to St. John in his first call is the same figure differently described and conceived; this becomes apparent on comparing *Daniel* xii. 7 with *Rev.* x. 5.

Dan. xii. 7. *He held up his Right Hand . . . and his Left Hand unto Heaven, and sware by him that liveth for ever and ever that it shall be for a Time, Times and Half a Time. . . .*

Rev. x. 5 . . . *lifted up his Hand to Heaven, and sware by him that liveth for ever and ever . . . that there should be time no longer.*

The Strong Angel of chapter x., then, who brings St.

John his first call to prophesy is to be identified in some way with the Christ; but he is conceived primarily as the Word of God, that human something in the divine nature which all through history has revealed the will of God to man; he is the whole course of prophetic activity, God's aggressive truth, coming at last to St. John: the Gabriel of Daniel, Man of God and Son of Man.

Here in the second call to prophesy he is that Word of God, once incarnate, now risen, glorious, and triumphant. The Word of God is the Angel of the divine will: St. John's vision is an Angel of that Word. The risen Christ, the Angel of the divine will, speaks to his servant John; there is real communion between the Lord of the invisible world and the disciple still in the flesh; but the spiritual experience clothed itself in visible and audible form, and the clothing that it took was woven of symbols with which the mind of the prophet was already stored; and the words he heard were drawn from books with which he was familiar.

The spiritual fact which St. John sees is the Lord risen and reigning in his church; despite persecution and suffering, or rather because of persecution and suffering, he knows that the kingdom of Christ is victoriously advancing in the world, and Christ himself gaining power over the lives of men. Because the church is *in persecution* it is therefore *in Royal Power;* it is suffering for the *Word of God and the Witness of Jesus,* and he can see Jesus powerful and prevailing in the midst of his martyrs. That is the whole message of the *Revelation,* Christ is here; and when we come to the point of crisis and culmination of the whole book, it is only to see the heavens opened and this figure ride out on the White Horse of conquest, armed only with the sharp point of his all-powerful Word.

In the Patmos Vision this tremendous Presence clothes itself in the familiar symbols of prophecy and apocalypse. *Seven golden Lamps* flare against the void of eternity; among them stands *One Like a Son of Man,* whose priestly robe is gathered at the breast with a golden girdle and hangs in massive folds to his feet; *his Head and his Hair White as Wool like Snow; his Eyes like a Flame of Fire; his Feet like Brass glowing in the Furnace ; his Voice like the Voice of Many Waters ; in his Right Hand Seven Stars ; out of his Mouth a sharp double-edged Sword issuing ; and his Face like the Sun shining in his power.*

Now the important and original parts of this Vision are explained by the Voice itself. The Seven Lamps are the Seven Churches, and the Seven Stars are the 'Angels' of the Churches. The Priest-Messiah is in the midst of his church; yet the church is held firm in his right hand. *God is in the midst of her : therefore shall she not be moved.* The weakness in all Adventist thought is the assumption that God and his Messiah are a long way off; it is the familiar heresy of the " orthodox," a one-sided enthusiasm for the " transcendent." In the Jewish apocalypses the seer has to journey through heaven after heaven until he finds the Throne of the Great Glory; St. John clears that error away at the very outset. The Messiah is not far off in the infinite; with all his transcendent glory he reigns here on earth among his martyrs. It is true to say with Browning that God's in his heaven; but the kingdom of heaven is within reach of earth, as Jesus in his apocalyptic was constantly telling us.

We cannot take too much trouble to get this clear in our minds. St. John wrote his *Revelation* to show that the victorious Messiah is with us now *in affliction, in royal power, in much patience.* Any future coming can be no more than the " unveiling " of this fact. Apocalypse means Unveiling, Revealing.

A further proof that this is the central meaning of the Vision is found in the fact that this alone is explained. The imagery woven about the person of the Messiah is taken for granted; the reader is not expected to mistake anything so easy. The Seven Lamps and the Seven Stars need to be explained; they are the new and original part of the Vision.

The Details of the Vision.

To people who expected their Messiah to " come " from a distant heaven, St. John gave the message that he was now present among them in his glory. But this certainty had itself come to him as a revelation in a vision; and it is our duty to reconstruct, so far as we can from the fragmentary evidence and the known (or partly known) principles of psychology, how this came about.

The stages of this particular Vision are:

1. The trance: *I was in the spirit.*
2. The voice: arousing him and arresting his attention.
3. The vision.
4. The terror: *I fell as if dead.*
5. The voice of encouragement.
6. The command to tell what had been seen.

Point by point this is parallel with the " conversion " of St. Paul, which has been so often studied from the psychological point of view, though St. Paul is at pains to make it clear that his *heavenly vision* is to be classified with the resurrection appearances of the Lord. Both, however, may be described as the sudden presentation of a new truth in the form of a vision or an " audition."

Now psychologists point out that this is liable to occur when the truth in question has for some time been consciously or unconsciously repressed, and in this case may indicate that St. John himself had for a long time adhered vehemently to the view which he now combats—the view, namely, that the Messiah was to " come " from a distant heaven; and I feel sure that a psycho-analyst would agree that the hearing of the Trumpet Voice *from behind* might well indicate that for some time previously the prophet had turned his back on the truth which the Vision expressed. Now, if St. John is the apostle of that name, there is every reason to believe that his views of heaven and of the " coming " may have been of this material nature, and if so he had no doubt conscientiously repressed the opposite conviction, that the Messiah in his glory was invisibly present. The Vision is the moment in which these " repressed " thoughts surge up and overwhelm the older system of thought; but they do not destroy the old; the Messiah is still *in Heaven, at the Right Hand of God,* but he is also present in his church. He is still "transcendent" and clothed with all the glory of transcendence; but he is also "immanent."

In the strength of this knowledge he is prepared to rearrange his old prophecies and to prophesy anew *what is about to happen hereafter*.

I have pointed out that the symbols from which a vision is woven must already exist in the mind. The revelation, coming from God, is pure spirit; it clothes itself in form from such materials as it can find, and this is the origin of all those symbols which here blazon the "glory" or transcendent state of the Messiah.

The Hairs White as Wool symbolise in Daniel the eternity of the *Ancient of Days* : *like Snow* suggests the transfiguration, itself a kind of apocalypse; the *Eyes like Flame* and the *Voice like Many Waters* derive from the visions in which Ezekiel and Daniel saw the Angel of Revelation who is the Angel of Jehovah himself; even the phrase *Son of Man* goes back to visions of God or of his kingdom seen by those prophets; the *Sharp Sword* is found in Second Isaiah's vision of the servant of Jehovah; the *Sun shining in his power* comes from the song of Deborah, and symbolises the victorious career of the armies of Israel; the *Long Robe* is found in the visions of Ezekiel and Daniel.

It is not to be supposed that St. John deliberately pieced these texts together; he was not aware perhaps in every case where the words came from. No pedantic accumulation of quotations could produce the fine imaginative unity of this Vision. For an image which is a unity is created before us; and this creation is much more powerful than any of the prophecies from which the separate quotations are made.

On the other hand, it is not a realistic picture; it could not be painted. It is no more than a group of symbols massed together to produce a certain effect. There is no possibility that the prophet believed that there existed in time and space such a physical object as he describes; the various elements of the Vision could not be combined to form such an object, and if this were attempted the result would be ludicrous, whereas the Vision itself is magnificent. The Sword, for instance, which issues from the Mouth, is a powerful symbol of the all-conquering gospel, *the Word of God;* as a physical substitute for a tongue it is merely ridiculous.

It follows from this that we have not got a plastic or paintable vision such as we see in dreams: we have a spiritual reality which has attracted to itself a number of symbols, mainly visual, which do in combination blazon the significance of that reality. The word " blazon " is an excellent one to employ. It is a technical term from heraldry; and heraldry, where it is not pedantical or over-systematic, has much of the spirit of religious symbolism.

The spiritual reality entering the prophet's mind is the unity underlying the Vision; otherwise it would have none. The process requires a biological metaphor to illustrate it; biologists tell us that in the first stage of conception the male sperm unites with the female and produces a kind of directing centre which organises and develops the new body out of such material as exists. Rather in the same way the spiritual truth enters the mind of the prophet, and organises itself a body out of such material as is at hand; after finding union with the mind, it collects and arranges the symbols in such a way that all are harmonious with the inward and spiritual unity. Nothing but symbols are presented to us; yet the symbols convey the unity.

To the prophet it is only the spiritual truth that matters; it is this that he conceives with labour and brings to birth in a material or symbolic form.

The principles are so important that they are worth tabulating.

1. John did not believe that there was a material object existing in space, corresponding to his description.
2. He did not have a dream-vision of such an object.
3. He did not invent such an object by piecing together various symbols, each of which had a " meaning."

The last point is very important, because so many people " interpret " the *Revelation* in this way, as if each detail of each vision had a definable meaning which could be explained in so many words. These commentators are rationalisers, deficient in the mystical sense. Symbolism is a way of suggesting the truth about those great spiritual realities which elude exact definition or complete systematisation; that is why it is so much employed in worship. If they could have been expressed as a rationalised logical system, the prophet would have so expressed them; but his symbols, because they are not tied to a system of " meanings," express the truth better.

Very often it is quite easy to attach definite " meanings " to elements in the vision; and almost always there are one or two significant points to which we must attach " meanings "; they are usually made quite clear. In all cases it is very tempting. We read of the *Feet* like *Brass glowing in a Furnace*, and we recollect that the image in *Daniel* which represented the imperialism of this world had Feet of Clay. But there are, no doubt, other meanings possible. The symbol is much richer in meaning than any meaning we can draw from it. The same is true of the parables and symbolic teaching of Jesus. The same is true of the sacraments and symbolic acts of the church, or even of society. Many logical systems can be made up to explain the " meaning " of shaking hands or making the sign of the cross; but because of their simplicity and universality these actions mean more than words can explain.

These successive steps, therefore, in the development of a vision are to be noted:

1. The spiritual truth enters the mind.
2. It finds contact with the mind of the prophet.
3. It attracts to itself harmonious symbols already existing in the mind.
4. This occurs by free association, not by conscious effort.
5. It " organises " them into an imaginative unity.
6. The whole picture is then presented to the mind.
7. These steps may be taken unconsciously.

The production of visions is not a mechanical or rationalising process, like piecing together the parts of a Ford car; it is more like a biological process, such as conception. On the other hand, we should note that such mechanical visions are found in Jewish apocalypse; we may note the Eagle of *Esdras* xi.; and here and there we find an element of conscious construction in *Revelation* itself.

The Seven Angels.

An example of the futility of rationalising the imagery of the *Revelation* is to be found in the attempts to explain the Angels of the Seven Churches. By the end of chapter i the number Seven has occurred four times:

1. The Seven Spirits before the Throne,
2. The Seven Churches,
3. The Seven golden Lamps,
4. The Seven Stars;

and we are told that *the Seven Stars are the Angels of the Seven Churches, and the Seven Lamps are the Seven Churches.*

Now it is clearly quite futile on any rationalised or materialist system to imagine St. John sitting down to write a letter from the Messiah to the Seven Stars in his Right Hand; yet that is precisely what he is told to do. It is plain that we must search for the spiritual reality symbolised by Seven.

Any hardened reader of apocalypses expects to find Seven spirits or Angels by the Throne of God; they are the Seven Angels of the Presence, Michael, Gabriel, Raphael, etc., to whom the church afterwards gave the name of Archangels. In the New Testament there is only One Archangel, as in Philo.

These Seven appear to derive originally from the seven planets, Sun, Moon, Mars, Mercury, Venus, Jupiter, Saturn, the erratic and eccentric movements of which perplexed the astronomers of ancient times. The Babylonians regarded them as heavenly beings with a powerful influence over human lives, seven baneful gods, in fact, under whose motions the lives of nations and of men were swayed. The thought was taken over into Jewish apocalyptic, where they became the Seven Angels nearest the Throne of Glory, or sometimes the Seven Eyes or Spirits of God searching out all the world. We can hardly help connecting them with the seven-branched "Candlestick" or lampstand which stood before God in the Holy Place of the Jewish Temple; and this, in turn, is connected with the Seven Lamps of our Vision. Angels, stars, lamps, and eyes all turn out to be identical.

But here we are perplexed at first by the unsystematised nature of Hebrew thought. An Angel might be regarded as

1. The activity of God himself, identical with him,
2. An independent agency, either a vague influence as in St. Paul, or a named person as in *Enoch*.

But just as the Angel of the Lord was a projection of God, having some kind of identity with him, so nations or persons, or even natural objects, might have their Angel. The Angel of a person was a phantasmal representation of himself, a "Doppel-gänger," as the Germans call it, or an "astral body," to use the theosophist jargon; or else he might be an independent spirit guiding or controlling the person, a "Guardian Angel." Michael, for instance, is described in *Enoch* as the Guardian Angel of Israel; in *Daniel* he appears to be no more than a personification of Israel. It is hard to say whether Michael means Israel, or the spirit animating Israel, or the angel sent by God to rule the destinies of Israel—the Captain of Jehovah's Army, mentioned in *Joshua*. It was an age like ours, when men felt the whole world was dominated by powers and influences which were beyond their control. A Jew could not doubt that ultimately they were under the control of God; but to some they were his own activities, to others they were independent and incalculable forces.

When the Jew said that the world was subject to Angels, he meant that it was under the sway of these incalculable, perhaps capricious forces; they therefore appear in the Jewish apocalypses as independent beings. But in *Revelation* these independent Angels, with names and personalities and spheres of influence, are fairly consistently ruled out; God is in control of his own universe.

The Seven Angels or Seven Spirits are close to God and his Messiah; they are the Angels of the Presence; they are forces which may be regarded as activities of God. On the other hand, they represent or rule over the churches; what Michael was to Israel, the Seven Spirits are to the Christian church, Guardian and Inspiration.

The net effect is clear, and the claim made is colossal in its calm. Jewish apocalypse had depicted the Great Glory seated on his Throne above the Seventh Heaven, and the Seven Angels adoring his Presence; the chief of these, Michael, was the patron and champion of Israel. The Christian apocalypse brings down the Great Glory into the church itself, and places beside him the crucified Messiah, Jesus. Christians are not content with having one of the great Angels for their champion; the whole Seven become Angels of Christendom, representing God to the church and the church to God. The whole Glory of God, his Presence, his Majesty, and his Worship, are enshrined in the Christian church; and all his Powers and Influences and Activities flow into the church, so that they become Powers and Activities of the church. Heaven has broken in on earth and is moulding a kingdom there; the Seven Angels of the Presence of God and the Seven Angels of the church are identical; the transcendent has become immanent.

The Holy Spirit.

It is a trouble to the orthodox that St. John does not use the accepted terminology of Father, Son, and Spirit. In the Vision and the greetings prefixed to it a high place is given to the Messiah, but God is not described as Father, nor Messiah as Son; the Trinity is made up by a reference to *the Seven Spirits before the Throne*, which seems an unsatisfactory way of describing the Holy Ghost. Dr. Charles finds this Trinity so grotesque that he rejects this reference as the work of an interpolator.

In the particular letters to the different churches the

deficiency is made good. The words Father and Son are used there quite in the spirit of the fourth gospel. *I will give him to sit with me on my Throne . . . as my Father hath given me to sit with him on his Throne*, and still more definitely, *thus saith the Son of God*. The Spirit is also named in the phrase *What the Spirit saith to the Churches*. What is possible in the letters is excluded from the definitely apocalyptic part, where St. John is limited to the traditional imagery.

Let us now consider the view of Dr. Swete, based on all the Latin commentators, that the Seven Spirits are the Holy Ghost, and that the number Seven is introduced because the churches he works in are Seven.

The Seven Spirits are first of all introduced in close connection with the Father; they are *before the Throne of God*. In chapter iv. they appear again for the last time, unless we are to include the Seven Thunders of chapter x.; they are *Seven Lamps of Fire burning before the Throne, which are the Seven Spirits of God*. The words *Spirits of God* give us food for thought. Later on the Messiah is introduced as a *Lamb standing as it had been Slain, having Seven Horns and Seven Eyes which are the Seven Spirits of God sent out into all the Earth*. The Seven Spirits are therefore just as much Spirits of the Son as Spirits of the Father.

The Seven Spirits are organically one with Father and Son; they are forces which go forth from Father and Son, and have an identity with Father and Son; and we have noted that this is the traditional and natural Jewish idea of an Angel. In the Old Testament we find several names for the creative and inspiring energies of God. The world is said to be created and renewed by his Word and by his Spirit; revelations are given to men by his Word, his Spirit, or his Angel. The title "Word" is, of course, appropriated in Christian thought to the Son only; but both Son and Spirit might conceivably be called an Angel; for the term is very vague.

If we think of Angels as separate independent beings, possibly with wings, as Dr. Charles appears to do, then it is grotesque enough to call the Holy Ghost Seven Angels; but if the view I have given above is accepted, there is no difficulty. The term "Word" is reserved for the Messiah; the Holy Ghost appears as the Seven Angels proceeding from the Father and the Son. The Holy Spirit is the life, the power, the wisdom, the energy of God; as such he dwells in the church and energises it; looked at from this point of view, he can fairly be called the Spirit (or Angel) of the church, the true activities of the church being the activities of the Spirit that energises it. The Spirit of God is identical with the Spirit of the Church.

There are three good reasons why St. John should give us Seven Spirits rather than One. First he is working with the accepted symbols of Jewish apocalypse, and weaving them into his scheme. The Seven Angels or energies of God are part of the apocalyptic system; they are the language he is talking. If they are identical with God, how much more are they identical with one another, forming a unity?

A second point is that they do blazon the *diversities of operation* spoken of by St. Paul. Isaiah speaks in a notable passage of the six great gifts of the Spirit, and these are mentioned in an ancient confirmation prayer; but orthodox thought has not shrunk from the thought of the Spirit itself as Sevenfold: *Tu septiformis*, says the old hymn. The number Seven would therefore symbolise the multiplicity, the richness and complexity of the energies of God. It is not that the One develops into the Many; the One is Many in himself.

Thirdly, it blazons the "particularity" of the Spirit, if I may coin a word to express a characteristic mark of St. John's thought. Ephesus does not have its share of the Spirit; it has the whole Spirit. It is a corollary of the richness and complexity of the infinite God; he is poured out in all fullness on each church, and though each church is inspired by him to a particular life and a particular character of its own, yet it has the whole Spirit. The "Sevenness" of the Spirit is a symbol, therefore, rather than a number. It collects all the energies and activities of the eternal into one perfection, and yet allows for that "particularity," which is, of course, the essential character of creation in time and space. And if it is a mark of God in his dealings with creation, it must also be a mark of God as he is in himself. These are the manifold activities which the prophets and wise men had perceived of old, and called his Spirit, his Word, or his Angel. Ephesus has the whole Spirit of Gold; Sardis has the whole Spirit of God; but it is one Spirit that energises all in all.

On the other hand, there is a real distinction. The term Spirit is used for the conception of the energy as it goes forth from God; the term Angel is used for the same energy as it works in the church, and at times as a personification of the church. The system is not completely logical; it does not quite cohere; that is its value.

It is worth while remarking that no complex system of symbols ever does quite cohere. No long parable, no sustained allegory, no involved myth, no complex analogy or system of symbolism ever quite holds together as a consistent unity. It is the underlying truth, the inward and spiritual reality, the thing symbolised, that gives unity to a number of different symbols. It is always possible, of course, to express your spiritual truth in terms of the philosophy or science of the day; it is even a duty: but had St. John done this, I shudder to think how much more obscure his work would now be. The symbol has this great advantage: it cannot change its meaning; it remains the same for ever. A crown is always a crown, and a lamp, a lamp. Trouble only arises when we meet some such symbol as an Angel which was a fluctuating and uncertain term blazoning a complex spiritual process, an energy, an influence, or an agency that can be detected at work in the world.

PART II. THE LETTERS TO THE SEVEN CHURCHES

The Writing of the Book.

The Seven Churches of Asia have been shown by Sir William Ramsay to be the churches in the actual cities answering to those names, and he has worked out the symbolism of these letters in a way which is always interesting and on the whole convincing, though here and there too ingenious in detail. He shows how the seven cities lay along a loop of road in the order named in the *Revelation*, and how each would form a convenient postal centre from which to distribute the letter to the country of the interior. In every case the symbolism of the letter is delicately adjusted to the circumstances or history of the city, in accordance with St. John's remarkable sensitiveness to new symbolic values. For the details of the letters the reader is referred to Sir William Ramsay's book.

The point which interests us here is that the Seven Spirits of the Presence have been assigned to churches of Asia to the exclusion of Antioch, Rome, Jerusalem and Alexandria. To a certain extent it is merely that the vision of the prophet is focussed upon the Asian churches, just as in earlier visions it was focussed upon Palestine; the remainder lie in the penumbra. But it is obvious too that the Asian churches must be regarded in some sense as central and representative of all Christendom. This concentration of his attention does rest on historical fact. For a time the primacy of Christendom rested over Ephesus. The glory of Jerusalem was gone; Rome had not yet risen to her place of ecumenical prestige; Alexandria was in obscurity; Antioch, the only possible rival, had long been outstripped by the Pauline church of Ephesus, where, under the apostolic name of John, a whole body of sacred books was being written, ultimately to be accepted as canonical by the universal church. Ephesus, therefore, was leading and guiding Christendom; it actually was central, representative, and primatial. And if, as seems possible, persecution was there more intense than anywhere else in the Empire, there, according to St. John, must be the Presence of God and the royal Power of his Messiah.

The Presence of God resides in the whole church; but the prophet narrows his vision to Ephesus, the centre and heart of the church; and it was a simple and obvious matter to assign the Seven Angels to the Seven Churches and to regard each Angel as the soul and character of his church.

Even in *Enoch*, where the Angels are well-developed personalities with individual names, we find men writing divine messages to them. Enoch writes a message from the Fallen Angels, and reads it to God; he writes God's reply, and reads it to the Angels. St. John's letters are written to the churches themselves. It is the church that has suffered, or been lukewarm, or hated heresy; the Angel is the spirit of the church.

The task of writing is one invested with great dignity in the apocalypses. In the days of the prophets the message of God was always a spoken one; but after the time of Ezekiel the speaker gave way to the writer. The ancient books of the Law and the Prophets now received a sacred character, and the Jewish apocalypses were palmed off as ancient books. Writing itself was still perhaps something of a craft and a mystery; and the act of writing had a sacred character. It was no doubt felt that the author of an apocalypse must write it with his own hand. Enoch is called the Scribe.

The business of writing takes us a stage beyond vision. The work is now mainly intellectual, and must generally have followed vision, though in *Revelation* it sometimes appears to be simultaneous; but we cannot believe that it was the mere mechanical work of a clerk or stenographer; still less the unconscious act of a medium, though perhaps it may have been in some stages of Jewish apocalyptic.

Revelations can come through a medium in the following ways:

1. *Clairvoyance.* Something " spiritual " is seen in a dream, or in a crystal, or in the mind, and the medium describes it.
2. *Clairaudience.* A " spirit " voice is heard, and the medium repeats its words. More often the " spirit " speaks through the medium while the medium is unconscious.
3. *Automatic writing.* The hand of the medium writes under the control of the " spirit," the medium being unconscious, or at least unconscious of the hand's

activity. This is called "verbal inspiration" when applied to the scriptures.

Before any of these phenomena occur it is necessary for the conscious mind to go to some extent into abeyance; the clairvoyant, for instance, hypnotises herself by staring at a crystal. Many odd religions have been founded by hysterics or neurasthenics of this type, and many sacred books have been written by them. Montanus in the second century, who made the mistake of treating the *Revelation* as a prophecy of physical and material events, was of this type; when under the control of the "spirit" he was quite sure that God was speaking through him: "I am not an Angel or a Messenger; I am God the Almighty." The same is the claim of the false prophet down all the ages. "It is God who has spoken," said Ellen Gould White, the founder of Seventh Day Adventism, "not an erring mortal." An excellent example of clairvoyance is to be found in Joseph Smith, the founder of Mormonism, who "saw" the golden plates on which was written the Book of Mormon. All of these left an extensive literature.

This type of "inspiration" is very like the "gift of tongues" described in St. Paul's epistles; but it is sharply distinguished from the prophecies and apocalypses of New Testament authors. The man who speaks with tongues is like the medium; he is more or less unconscious of what he says, and sometimes cannot understand it. The prophet uses his understanding; he is represented as clearly conscious of what he sees and says; and, unlike the dreamer, his whole intellectual and critical self is active. As St. Paul says, *the spirits of the prophets are subject to the prophets.*

Then too we have seen that the whole psychological process of vision is normal and natural. Exactly the same process is found in all imaginative writing, though the processes may be more conscious, and the result less sudden or symbolic. Coleridge's conception of *Kubla Khan* is the pattern of most poetic creation. As a matter of fact, it is the way most of us do our thinking, though we flatter ourselves that we reach our conclusion by what Sherlock Holmes calls "irrefragable processes of logical reasoning."

But when it came to writing down what he had seen, the prophet's work was almost entirely intellectual; he had to remember; and as he exerted his memory, he had to concentrate on the truth itself as much as on the symbols; and even as he re-thought the living truth, it must have been modified in his mind. He had to select: the most difficult part of composition. He had to arrange; and a literary study of the *Revelation* shows that he was a master of his art. He had to choose words and phrases. Sometimes, no doubt, vision and writing went on almost simultaneously; at other times his work was purely literary or editorial. Some portions of *Revelation* are not visions at all; they are straight-out composition. Here and there a vision has been made more comprehensible by an added touch or hint; here and there it has been perhaps elaborated and enriched. Sometimes it is hard work to weave together visions from different periods in which the symbolism is used rather differently. All these tasks, however, are successfully achieved, and the book as it stands is a masterpiece of imaginative art.

What is to Come.

Write what thou hast seen, and what is, and what is to be. So far we have dealt mainly with what is; the present is the main pre-occupation of every prophet. But if you know the present, you also know something of the future, because it is all one process. God himself is described as *who Was and who Is and who is Coming;* the prophet is to write in his book *what thou hast seen, and what is, and what is to be.* The process of temporal history reflects the eternal nature of God.

In no less than six of the letters to the churches there is a reference to the future, and in each case it is to the coming of the Messiah. These quotations are of great importance. The most interesting problem of New Testament criticism is the question of the "Parousia" (or "coming of the Messiah") expected both by Jews and Christians. If we may trust the extant apocalypses, many Jews must have looked for a destruction of the visible universe and the appearance of a visible Messiah; the Christians used this kind of language, but it is doubtful how far they intended it in a literal sense. The words they employ appear to mean the destruction of the visible world and the appearance in the sky of a visible Messiah; but they may equally well mean the end of one age in the political and religious history of the world, and the beginning of another in which God and his Messiah are invisibly present, and through the church rule the world.

It is the standing puzzle of gospel criticism that words of Jesus can be found to support either theory. St. Paul in his earliest epistles seems to favour the literal view, and so does the unknown author of the *Second Epistle of Peter*; it is a genuine surprise to find that the *Revelation* favours the spiritual view.

Consider the evidence.

In four cases the " coming " of the Messiah is conditional; *repent . . . if not . . .*; Ephesus, Pergamum, Thyatira, and Sardis are all told that if there is no repentance the Messiah will " come " to them in judgment. Now if these four " comings " are each dependent on the conduct of the different churches, they must all be at different dates; they cannot refer to one colossal outward " coming " on the clouds of heaven, visible to all. They are spiritual. In one case he says, *I will make war on them with the Sword out of my Mouth*—that is to say, the Word; the " coming " is not to be taken in a literal or visible sense.

In one case a visitation is actually represented as going on, *Lo, I am casting her into a bed*; but perhaps an imminent future is intended.

In the case of Laodicea there is a promise of a " coming " in blessing; it is plainly spiritual, and contains an uncontestable reference to the Eucharist, *Behold I stand at the Door and knock; if anyone hear my Voice and open the Door, I will come in to him, and sup with him, and he with me.*

It is plain that the prophet saw the hand of God in many calamities with which the churches were threatened; the Messiah would " come," and *remove their Lamp*—that is to say, the church would be punished and the mystic presence within it disappear.

He also saw the hand of God and the " coming " of the Messiah in an *Hour of Trial which was to come on the whole world;* but we have seen that in the minor cases where the Messiah says *I am coming,* he refers to an invisible spiritual visitation, and this leads us to suppose that the same is the meaning when the " coming " is on a larger scale.

In point of fact, the literal visible " coming " in the sky is not a thought natural to John, because he has accepted the belief that the Messiah is already present in glory in the church; this being so, there is no coming from a distant heaven, but only an unveiling of what already exists. The " coming " is a useful symbolic word for what we call (equally symbolically) a visitation.

Two ideas, therefore, have been rejected by John, both derived from a too material and too transcendent idea of God.

1. The idea that God and his Messiah and his Angels are a long way off in a distant Heaven.
2. That the Messiah's coming is a visible arrival in the sky accompanied by the destruction of the world.

These ideas he may once have held, and traces of them may possibly be discernible in earlier visions; but they have been abandoned in favour of the new view of the immanence in the church of the transcendent Messiah. They are not the leading ideas of the *Revelation.*

The new view of the Presence in the church is emphasised by the audacious identification of the Angels of the churches with the Angels of the Presence; it is the inspiration of the whole book, and is clearly stated at the end of it:

> *Behold the Dwelling of God is with men,*
> *And he will dwell with them ;*
> *And they shall be his people,*
> *And he, Immanuel, shall be their God.*

The Seven Churches.

I do not propose to study here the individual characteristics of the churches of Asia; it has been done often enough. It is forty years after their evangelisation by St. Paul; and much has happened in that time. Forty years is a long time in the history of a church. It allows for organisation and solidification and tradition; the original pioneering days are forgotten. St. Paul can only have been remembered by a few old men, who probably told pointless anecdotes about him; but we know from other sources that he had become a glorious, unassailable tradition. His letters had already been collected and published; this collection was called "the apostle," and what was admired in it was not so much his intense faith or burning charity as his divine wisdom. The word "wisdom" is bandied about by the writers of the sub-Pauline age when they refer to St. Paul; and it probably covers the fact that they did not understand much of his message . . . *as also our beloved brother Paul, according to the wisdom granted unto him, wrote unto you; as indeed in all his letters, talking about these things; in which there are some things hard to be understood, which the ignorant and unstable twist, as they do the rest of the scriptures, to their own destruction* (2 Peter iii. 15).

His great church of Ephesus remained faithful and orthodox; it hung on to the tradition; it hated heresy. But despite all this, St. John felt that it had deserted its first love, a rare word by which he means that divine mystic union with God which had also meant everything to St. Paul. Smyrna was in persecution and poverty; but this persecution and poverty meant spiritual victory and riches. Pergamum had passed through the persecution and remained faithful; a martyr, Antipas, had been killed there. Thyatira was full of good works. Sardis was spiritually dead. Philadelphia was a weak church, but had been splendidly faithful. Laodicea was rich and worldly and lukewarm. It was all just what one would expect.

It has always been recognised that if we are to understand the *Revelation* we must grasp the fact that its thought is conditioned by persecution and martyrdom. Mystical love and good works are highly prized; but its real keynote is faith and courage and "*witness*," and that tough, prolonged endurance which the Authorised Version translates "*patience*."

On the other hand, it has not been so widely realised that St. John feared much more another enemy of the churches, something much more insidious and dangerous—the enemy of heresy. He does not really think that persecution can do anything against the church of God; but he does warn his readers with desperate earnestness against the Synagogue of Satan; and just as the thought of persecution runs right through the book, and colours it in almost every section, so the thought of heresy is the explanation of certain odd and enigmatic passages which will not yield to any other treatment.

The Synagogue of Satan.

The strong and faithful church of Ephesus has tested and rejected certain men who *claim to be apostles and are not ;* it hates the works of the Nicolaitans. The martyr church of Smyrna suffers *blasphemy* (perhaps merely slander) from men *who say they are Jews and are not, but they are the " Synagogue of Satan ";* it is possible they are the source of the persecutions. At Pergamum is the *Throne of Satan ;* and this church, which has been so stedfast in persecution, contains in it men *who hold the teaching of Balaam, who instructed Balak to cast a stumblingblock before the sons of Israel, to eat things offered to idols, and to commit fornication.* There are also some *who hold the teaching of the Nicolaitans.* Thyatira, which has a very good character otherwise, gives encouragement to *the woman Jezebel, who calls herself a prophetess, and teaches and leads astray my servants, to commit fornication and to eat things offered to idols ;* there is a reference to those who claim to know *the deep things of Satan,* and a promise that they shall discover that *it is I that search the reines and the heart* (that is not someone else). Sardis has a few who have not *defiled their garments,* a clear synonym for fornication and idolatry. In Philadelphia there is a *Synagogue of Satan of those who say they are Jews and are not,* but a speedy victory over them is promised. Laodicea alone has no reference to the heretics, unless we see it implied in the counsel to buy *white garments, that thou mayest clothe thyself, and the shame of thy nakedness not be revealed.*

The first point to note is that one sect appears to be

described throughout, except perhaps for the Nicolaitans, of whom no description is given; they may, therefore, be left on one side.

The characteristics of the sect appear to be inconsistent; they amount to this:

1. They claim to be Jews,
2. They join freely in pagan religious rites,
3. They belong to Satan,
4. They have prophets.

In the reference to the Thyatiran heretics there appear to be twisted quotations from St. Paul, who speaks of the Spirit as *searching the deep things of God* (1 *Cor.* ii. 10); so we may add,

5. They appear to claim the authority of St. Paul.

Now St. Paul, when he dealt with the question of meats offered to idols, did admit that an idol was nothing, and that meat offered to idols was the same as any other meat; but he *advised* his converts not to touch it, for the sake of weaker brethren who had not so clear a faith. He could therefore be quoted on their side. On the other hand, he strongly condemned the fornication that accompanied the heathen religion of the time. St. John goes on to quote the decree of the Jerusalem council which laid upon them *no heavier burden* than to abstain from things offered to idols, from fornication, from things strangled, and from blood; a decree to which St. Paul had given his consent.

The heretical party, then, advocated full participation in heathen rites (thus avoiding persecution), and, we deduce, claimed the authority of St. Paul for their views. It is clear that such a policy would mean ultimate relapse into heathenism.

The odd thing is that it is Jews who take this stand, or men who claim to be Jews, and make much of their apostles and prophets. The forerunners of these men, however, appear in *Corinthians*, and they are still more clearly defined in *Ephesians* and *Colossians*; and *Colossians*, it must be remembered, has many affinities with *Revelation*. Dr. Hort always claimed that these were Jewish heresies, and although they have Gnostic and pagan characteristics, he is certainly right.

The church was not the only circle in which a blend of Jewish and heathen ideas had been effected. Archæological and literary evidence shows that all over Asia Minor, as well as in Alexandria, the process was at work. The Pauline church was the Jewish cradle of what was to be catholic Christianity; in some other Jewish cradle lay the infant that was subsequently to develop into Gnosticism.

The Beneficent Serpent.

The key lies in the word Satan. It has been customary to treat it merely as a piece of abuse. Its use four times suggests that it has a subtler point than that; St. John is a great writer who uses every word with accuracy and tact, and there is no reason to suppose that this word was employed at random.

Later in the book (chapter xii.) we find that by Satan he means *the Primal Serpent who deceived the whole world*—that is to say, the Serpent who tempted Eve; and there really were Jews or pseudo-Jews who did worship this Serpent. We know a little of them through St. Irenæus and St. Hippolytus (much later writers), who inform us that they were the first Gnostics. They are called Ophites or Cainites.

A rough date for St. Irenæus is A.D. 175, and a rough date for St. Hippolytus is 225. St. Irenæus actually came from Ephesus, and is one of our leading authorities on the Johannine tradition; but the Gnosticism he knew was the developed philosophic and "catholic" Gnosticism of Valentinus, which bore about as much relation to original Gnosticism as the present Christian Science Organisation in Boston does to Dr. Quimby. Valentinus was a man of great intellectual gifts who took the old Gnosticism, and combined it with Christian and Persian and astrological and Egyptian and Platonic elements into a complicated and coherent system which appealed to the cultured religiosity of the second century. This was the Gnosticism that St. Irenæus had to fight; and therefore he concentrates on it.

Luckily he gives us a little information about the older, simpler Gnosticism.

Valentinus may be dated from A.D. 120 to 140; so that the first Gnostics (the Ophites or Cainites) were earlier, let us say A.D. 100 to 120. He claimed that he had a secret tradition handed down from the apostles and not known to the generality of Christians; he and his sect were the "gnostics," the men who knew, the spiritual; ordinary Christians were merely the righteous. There is no reason to doubt that there did reach him a Jewish Christian tradition of a kind, sponsored by apostles of a kind, and that he took it seriously. It is quite possible that in the *Revelation* John is referring to the forerunners, or even the authors of this tradition . . . the Ophites or the pioneers before them.

The Ophites (from "ophis" a serpent) were so called because they believed that the Serpent who tempted Eve was the great benefactor of mankind, persuading her to eat of the Tree of the Knowledge of Good and Evil, which Jehovah the jealous god was keeping from them. The Serpent was the Mind or Spirit of the high God who was unknown to Jehovah. It was not at all unnatural that ordinary Christians should call this sect the Synagogue of Satan; and the first originators of these opinions must have been Jews, who, like St. John, could read the Old Testament in the Hebrew tongue; for their views are based on a minute study of the first chapters of *Genesis*.

They had observed the fact that the first two chapters contain two different accounts of creation. In this, they anticipated modern scholarship; but their deductions were different. They held that chapter i. narrated the heavenly creation by the high God, and that chapter ii. narrated a second creation by an inferior God; there was, therefore, first a heavenly man created, and then an earthly, a view attacked by St. Paul in *Corinthians*. The creation that we know is, therefore, badly done, and its author, if not evil, is a bungler. It is the lower God who forbids man to touch the Tree of Knowledge; it is the high God who sends the Serpent to tell Eve that it is a fruit to be desired, to make her wise.

The law of Mount Sinai was given by the lower God, and the "spiritual," who have a knowledge of the high God, take no account of it. They are "antinomian," free from any law, perfect. Their heroes are the rebels, Cain, Korah, and so on.

I have no doubt that these were the pseudo-Jews, with pseudo-apostles and pseudo-prophets who taught St. John's Christians to join in the heathen religious rites. They took in a certain element of heathen worship; they took in a certain element of Christian faith; and they used the name of St. Paul, the great enemy of legalism, to conjure with. This explains the emphasis laid by St. John on the blessedness of the *righteous* and of those who *keep the commandments of Jesus*. This is not a relic of some supposed primitive Palestinian Christianity; it is directed against men who thought themselves so perfect that they were freed from every moral law.

It has been universally recognised that the fourth gospel is directed against some primitive form of gnosticism, the nature of which is made clearer by the author in his epistles; the Gnostic views there combated are known as Docetism. The Docetists held that Christ was a spiritual being sent from the high God in the upper heaven to save us from the lower god and his inferior creation; but they could not believe that he took a body. The body is the source of all the evil in us, an inferior thing, tainted with the evil that marks all creation. Christ therefore had no body; he only *appeared* to have a body. Hence the name Docetist—from *dokei*, it appears. In consequence he never suffered, though he may have *appeared* to suffer. He was a glorious phantom from the upper world.

The fourth gospel insists that the body of Christ was real, that he suffered, that he died, that he was tired, that he wept; and that it is written by an eye-witness who saw, and witnessed, and handled. It repeats and emphasises these points. It also insists that Christ was divine, the Word, the only-begotten; for Gnostics looked upon him as some sort of angelic emanation from the supreme being, divine yet inferior to the divine. The *Revelation* also emphasises these points; it has the same stress on his divinity, and the same stress on the actuality of his sufferings and death and resurrection; it speaks of the blood that was shed for us.

If we examine those titles of Christ which are employed in the letters to the seven churches, we shall see that they assert his share in creation (not permitting it to an inferior God) his identical deity (the First and the Last), his sovereignty over the heavens (which are therefore not evil), and his actual death and resurrection. The *Revelation* makes sure both of the humanity and divinity of Christ. It will allow him no intermediate position, in which he is neither one nor the other, but only a glorious splash of spirit out of heaven; but it principally aims at denying the older and more fundamental Jewish Gnosticism to which the Synagogue of Satan had wedded their Docetism. It asserts God, creating his whole universe and ruling over it all; it asserts evil as the rebellious will of man riding out to conquer for himself, as a star meant to be bright and shining, fallen from its sphere, as the primal serpent rising from the abyss, but not as an element of evil introduced into creation itself by a bungling creator, and thus inherent in our bodies.

It is in the twelfth chapter, which tells of the Woman, the Serpent, and the Man-Child, that the Ophites are most obviously attacked; and the subject will be taken up again there.

No one can say how old the idea of the bad creator and the good serpent may be. Very odd combinations of Jewish fantasies and Greek myth had long taken place. When St. Paul first came to Ephesus, he found there a group of magicians practising under the name of the Sons of Sceva, who, says St. Luke, was a Jewish high priest. But St. Luke can hardly be right here; it would be like finding seven sons of a President of the United States practising spiritualism in Paris. " Sons of " obviously means " the guild of," as in the case of " sons of Korah "; Sceva was their patron saint. Now the only easy explanation of the word Sceva is the Latin adjective, *scæva*, left-handed. If this conjecture is sound, they were the Guild of the Left-handed one, a very likely name for a group of magicians; for Satan was often called Sammael, the left-handed, by the Jewish Rabbis; and Michael and Sammael were the two great adversaries in the war of good and evil. St. Irenæus tells us that in the Gnostic system Sammael was one name for the Serpent. The " Sons of Sceva " is equivalent to the " Synagogue of Satan," or of the Serpent.

The Guild of Sceva adopted the name of Jesus, and even the name of Paul, to conjure with; and though they failed on one occasion, it is not recorded that they gave up using the name, or that they joined the church. A number of magicians (presumably Jews) did burn their books and join the church, thus providing a little hot-bed for strange notions later on.

No wonder that when St. Paul left Ephesus he warned the elders that there would be heretical teachers who would do much harm to the church, and that some even of themselves might develop along those lines, tempted by the pride of having a personal following of disciples. The next stage can dimly be seen in the Ephesian and Colossian letters; the next in the Pastorals; and the next in *Revelation* and the fourth gospel.

NOTE 1.—The Serpent was compared by the Gnostics to the intestines coiling in the hidden parts of the body: this may explain St. John's assertion (in the name of Christ) *that it is I that search the reines and the heart.*

2.—The Serpent in some systems took the place of the Spirit moving on the abyss (*Gen.* 1); hence perhaps *the deep things of Satan.* The abyss or deep below was called the left-hand (sinistral) as well as the lower (inferior) parts; the abyss above (heaven) was the right-handed or dextral.

3.—The word " Dragon " (Greek *Dracōn*) means no more than a snake. The reader must beware of confusing it with the mediæval "fabulous monster" which had wings and claws.

BOOK III
THIS AGE

PART I. GOD, MAN, AND CREATION
The Throne in Heaven.
The Sealed Book.
The Lamb of God.

THE SEVEN SEALS :
1–4. *The Four Riders.*
5. *The Souls under the Altar.*
6. *The Prophetic Dooms.*
(*Parenthesis : The Sealing of the Elect*)
7. *The Silence in Heaven.*

THE BEATIFIC VISION

*In that profound abyss of light most high
I saw three moving spheres of equal might
But various colours ; one from one reflected
Like rainbow out of rainbow ; and the third
Of fiery nature, like a breath inspired
The other two.*

   *O words are weak to blazon
The image in my mind ; and this compared
With what I saw, is such that if I said
" Little," the very word were insufficient.
O Light Eternal, in thyself alone
Thou dost abide ; thou dost thyself behold,
And by thyself alone art comprehended ;
And in beholding makest love and laughter.*

*Now as mine eyes followed the inner ring
That circled in thee like reflected light,
I saw within it, painted of its colour,
The likeness of the image of a man
So that my gaze was fixed upon it wholly.*

*As when a master of the mathematics
Pores on the circle, but with all his thought
Can find no ratio to measure it :
So when I saw this vision strange, I fain
Would see how image and circumference
Were joined and fitted ; but for such a flight
I had no wings, had not a flash of glory
Struck through my mind that had the will to know.
Then all my tower of imagery fell ;
And yet my will went onward like a wheel
That moved in even motion, drawn by love,
The love that moves the sun and other stars.*

        IMITATED FROM DANTE.

 *The glories of our blood and state
  Are shadows, not substantial things ;
There is no armour against fate ;
  Death lays his icy hand on kings :
    Sceptre and Crown
    Must tumble down,
And in the dust be equal made
With the poor crooked scythe and spade.*
       J. SHIRLEY.

BOOK III
THIS AGE

Part I. God, Man, and Creation
Argument

St. John first sees God as primal Light and invisible source of countless energies and activities. His Glory is reflected in the worship of his creation, but the Book with the Seven Seals symbolises the mystery of the apparent triumph of evil in human history.

The divine Son of God is alone capable of solving this mystery.

The first Four Seals symbolise the domination of the world by Conquest and War and Famine and Plague. The Fifth shows the souls of the innocent dead crying for justice, and the Sixth shows the dooms spoken by the prophets on the imperialisms of the past; these dooms, however, are not final or sufficient. The process continues.

A parenthesis follows the Sixth Seal. The avenging forces of God are held back while the number of the Martyrs is completed. They are " Sealed " and assured of a blessed immortality which anticipates the conclusion of the whole book.

The Seventh Seal is then broken.

The Vision of Heaven.

It has already been pointed out that the Jewish apocalypses are materialistic. Heaven and hell are localities in space, and Enoch the seer has to pass through heaven after heaven, each more glorious and terrifying than the last, before he arrives, dazzled and fainting, before the Throne of the Great Glory. There is another type in which an Angel descends out of the heavens and dictates to the seer his summary of future history. The one appears to be based on *Ezekiel*, the other on *Daniel*; and both conceptions are found in the *Revelation*. We begin with a Vision of Heaven; but later on our standpoint appears to be Palestine, and Angels descend out of heaven; the Palestinian Visions are obviously the earlier.

Dr. Charles has pointed out that St. John has abandoned the whole machinery of Seven Heavens; almost always he uses the word in the singular, which is contrary to the prevailing practice.

It is also worth noting how easily he gets there. *After this I saw, and behold a Door opened in Heaven, and the first Voice which I heard like a Trumpet talking with me, saying, Come up here, and I will show you what must happen.* The transition from earth to heaven is particularly easy.

> *The gates of heaven are lightly locked,*
> *We do not guard our gain,*
> *The heaviest hind may easily*
> *Come silently and suddenly*
> *Upon me in a lane.*
>
> *The meanest man in grey fields gone*
> *Behind the set of sun,*
> *Heareth between star and other star,*
> *Through the door of darkness fallen ajar*
> *The council, eldest of things that are,*
> *The talk of the Three in One.*

The simple spiritual nature of this transition is made perfectly clear by two considerations. A verse or two earlier occurs the beautiful saying, *Behold I stand at the Door and knock;* this is the converse of it, *Knock and it shall be opened unto you.* A verse later he says, *After this immediately I was in the Spirit;* it is never definitely stated that he passed through the Door, because going into the Spirit is merely another way of saying that he entered the Gate of Heaven.

The Vision of the Throne.

The Throne as a symbol of the sovereignty of God goes back through all the apocalypses and prophets to the vision of Isaiah; it is older than that, for it occurs in the visions of Moses and of Micaiah ben Imlah.

Upon the Throne one Sitting . . . like in appearance to Jasper and Sardius Stone. The word " Sitting " suggests to the Hebrew mind both ruling and judging; to us it has something of the notion of presiding; he is the bishop of the presbytery of heaven.

The Precious Stones suggest Light—Light, cool and hard and indestructible, concentrated into its most costly form; light and eternity. Looking into the Throne, he sees nothing in the first place but the dazzling rays of the primal source of light; nothing but unsearchable rays, white like the diamond, blood-red like the ruby, green-haloed like the emerald : prismatic, varying—kaleidoscopic if you like: Light shining from its primal source, undifferentiated in origin, yet differentiating into iridescent colours.

Note once more the " particularity " of St. John. God is Light, as he said in his epistle; but it is Light full of particular and different manifestations. The simplicity of God is rich in its complexity. It has colour, even colours.

Out of the Throne proceed Lightnings and Voices and Thunders, and before the Throne Seven Lamps of Fire which are the Seven Spirits of God. These are the powers and energies and activities of God as they issue forth from him in their infinite multiplicity, and yet, remaining in him, continue to be himself.

The Oneness of the Hebrew God is not a still and solitary thing; it is not inactive and detached like the absolute being of the philosopher. It is pure energy, creative spirit, raging and devouring fire, as Moses called it.

The philosopher is anxious that the Oneness should remain One and undisturbed, not acting here and there; he shudders even to think of creation. The prophet is anxious that God should inspire him and speak with him, here and on this spot. Here, he can say, and at such a time the Word of God came to me; and there he revealed his Glory. Here, he says, and there; yet not denying that God was infinitely present in all places and to all people; nevertheless here he is, and giving the whole of himself to me.

The completion of this theology was the work of the Rabbis of St. John's own age. God in himself, and God in his activities and manifestations; yet one God. The Word coming to the prophet; the Angel coming to Moses; the Glory descending on the landscape or the temple ritual; the Breath or Wind or Spirit; the Life; the Indwelling and the Tabernacling. All these are Names of God and energies of God, and are identical with God. God in himself is free from time and free from space. Those of us who are under time and space must be here or there; God, in dealing with time and space, must himself become here and there. The integrity of the One God must be divided or multiplied out into a Many if he is to reveal himself to us and work with us; and yet the Many must be the One. And if he must become Many in order to work with his creation, then he must be Many in himself; his Oneness must be a Oneness that is Many, and his whole nature must be a complex of infinite forces; and that is what Oneness must mean: Many and yet One; changing yet for ever the same.

This thought is characteristic of Jewish religion of St. John's time, and may be christened Dynamic Monotheism; not an unrelated absolute God like that of German philosophy, but an infinitely related God, first self-related, and then related with his creation by Word, by Angel, by Spirit, by Wisdom, by Glory, and by many other activities which are all identical with himself.

This doctrine is the basis of the Christian Trinity and also the starting-point for the gnostic systems which we shall also have to consider. Jewish thought did not make these energies into persons, it did not grant them independent existence; they were no more than processes of God.

The Twenty-four Elders.

It is significant that the first thing he sees is the Throne; there is no ascent by degrees to the Christian vision of God. The next thing he sees, as his eyes grow accustomed to the divine Light, is a vision of *Four and Twenty Thrones around the Throne* and upon them *Four and Twenty Elders sitting clothed in White Robes and on their Heads Crowns of Gold.* Before going any further, St. John introduces humanity; not angelic creatures as in the conventional visions of his time, but men, redeemed, purified, and reigning, sharing in the All-sovereignty of

God. The nature of God is reflected in them; they are his images, his viceroys, lords of creation; they wear robes of redemption and kingly crowns. They are *a Kingdom, Priests to God*.

The word Elder is a magnificent word. It suggests men of kingly character and function sitting in senate and ruling justly. It is modelled upon the organisation of the Christian church, the senate of Smyrna or Ephesus sitting in council round their bishop. Such councils of Elders ruled in the power and presence of the Almighty; and what they bound on earth was bound in heaven. The whole congregation was priestly; but these represented and summed up the congregation. They were *Kings and Priests to God*: and nearest God's Throne in heaven we are shown such a senate, just and holy. The church on earth mirrored the church in heaven; nay, it is the church in heaven.

The number Twelve is the number of the Tribes of Israel, the people chosen by God and invested with his grace and sovereignty; it stands therefore for the full number of his saints, the whole army of his people. It is also the number of the Twelve apostles, the rulers of the new Israel. It has been suggested that it is doubled here to include both covenants; but the simplest of all suggestions is that the number was chosen because there were twenty-four " courses " of priests who served the temple in Jerusalem. It is better not to identify them with any definite twenty-four people; they represent the worship of mankind offered through its spiritual leaders, the highest and noblest of the race.

The imagery of this chapter represents the whole of creation as it reflects the glory of God and offers him praise and honour; it is based on the ritual of the temple, as the following table will show:

The Revelation.	*The Temple.*
The Throne.	The Mercy-Seat.
The Invisible Glory.	No Image.
The Seven Lamps.	The Seven-Branch Lamp.
The Four Living Things.	The Cherubim.
The Glassy Sea.	The Brazen Sea.
The Twenty-four Elders.	The Twenty-four Courses of Priests.

The parallel with the Temple and its ceremonial is worked out more fully in Appendix I.

H

The Sea of Glass.

The Elders are grouped round the Throne in a circle: they do not appear to have been derived from any known apocalyptic imagery, and they are probably a conception of St. John's Asian period. The other parts of the Vision are all traditional.

The Sea of Glass like Crystal is derived from the "waters above the firmament," which are often represented in apocalypses as a Sea. As water descends from heaven, it was natural that the seers should find there a sea of water, or even frost, snow, hail, or dew. But the spiritual meaning of the symbol goes deeper than that.

In traditional myth among the Jews and elsewhere there is a story of a battle between God and Chaos; Chaos, the primæval enemy, is often represented as the Sea or a Sea-Monster or a Dragon which personifies the Sea. This myth has been eliminated from the Old Testament as a living thing, but in apocalyptic and liturgical writings it remains as symbolism. *Art thou not it that pierced Rahab?* (*Is.* li. 9) we read in a late apocalyptic chapter of *Isaiah*. *Thou smotest the heads of Leviathan in pieces* (*Ps.* lxxiv. 14) says a psalm: and in many another psalm the same myth provides the basis of the imagery. In the creation psalm xciii., for instance, we read:

> *The Floods are risen, O Lord,*
> *The Floods have lift up their Voice,*
> *The Floods lift up their waves.*
> *The Waves of the Sea are mighty,*
> *And rage horribly,*
> *But yet the Lord who dwelleth on high is mightier.*

In the prophets the symbolism is often transferred to the enemy civilisations of Egypt and Babylon which were built upon great rivers; Egypt is called Rahab. It thus comes to refer to the unruly wills and affections of sinful men. In the Vision of St. John the wild monster is spread calm and peaceful and tame before the Throne of the Almighty. It corresponds to the Brazen Sea which stood in the Temple; but the origin of this was quite utilitarian, though by now it had become the subject of mystical interpretation.

The Four Living Things.

And in the midst of the Throne and around the Throne Four Living Things full of Eyes before and behind. These beings, unfortunately translated beasts in our Authorised Version, correspond to the two Cherubim in the Temple of Solomon whose wings overshadowed the Mercy-Seat and the Ark of the Covenant. They had already been doubled in the Vision of Ezekiel which St. John follows pretty closely here; but it is a mark of the " particularity " of St. John that one has the Head of a Lion, the second of an Ox, the third of a Man, the fourth of an Eagle. In *Ezekiel* they are all alike, each having four different heads.

In Ezekiel's case we should note that they remind us of the great winged stone figures so common in Babylonian architecture. It has also been suggested that they correspond to the four principal constellations of the zodiac which mark out the four quarters of the sky, or, as we should say, points of the compass. These constellations are Bull, Lion, Scorpion, and Water-carrier; and a great deal of manipulation is necessary to make them fit the Four "Beasts" of our text. Like most of the astrological identifications, it seems very far-fetched; but we shall have reason later on to remember the four points of the compass.

The original form and meaning of the Cherubim in Hebrew art are lost in obscurity; some say that they were the old nature gods of Palestine now represented as subservient to Jehovah. These living things, and the number Four generally, symbolise all the powers and forces of nature, including man and his empires. The Eyes, so suggestive of the peacock, unquestionably recall Stars; and the Vision is linked to that of Isaiah by the Six Wings of each creature and the Isaianic song which they perpetually sing, *Holy, Holy, Holy, Lord God Almighty, who Was and who Is and who is to Come.*

They are not only the Cherubim of Ezekiel, but also the Seraphim of Isaiah, and their song represents the worship of all creation. They are forces or agencies which are not to be identified with God, but work according to his will. This entirely differentiates them from the Seven.

The impressive thing is that St. John has eliminated all the technical terms of apocalypse, Cherubim, Seraphim, Watchers, and even at this point Angels. We only have Spirits, " Pneumata," the higher activities, which are energies of God, identical with him; and Living Forces, " Zoa," which are the lower activities and inhere in creation, though they act according to his will. It is not fair, when St. John has pointedly omitted the apocalyptic mythology, to bring it back and say that is what he means. The term " Zoa " is a translation of " Hayyim " or " Hayyoth," an accepted Rabbinic name also found in the synagogue prayers.

Liturgy and Symbol. (See Appendix I.)

The connection between prophetic symbol and the ceremonial of worship is a subject which has never received fair attention, mainly because of the curious modern idea that the prophet and the priest are naturally antagonistic. This is no more true of St. John than it is of Isaiah, Ezekiel, or Zechariah; it may be partly true of Jeremiah. Prophets do denounce priests when they are corrupt; but the prophet and the priest are natural allies, and the whole progress of Hebrew religion was due to that alliance. The natural enemy of the prophet was the false prophet.

The prophet was continually deriving his inspiration from the ceremonial of temple worship; and worship, in its turn, was continually being enriched by prophetic interpretations of its ceremonial. The *Revelation* lives and moves and has its being in the atmosphere of such ceremonial, and it is best understood by one who is accustomed to it. Both in liturgy and prophecy the function of the symbol is the same: it is not there because it has one definite and rational meaning; it has a hundred meanings. It may mean different things to different ages or to different men; but it never changes. Lights and colours and vestments and song and processions are used by all religions for this reason; they can be misunderstood, but not so badly misunderstood as sermons and philosophies.

Now the *Revelation* is filled with the spirit of worship. It has a definite liturgical movement which can be traced to its culmination in the great burnt sacrifice of Babylon.

But though this background is mainly Jewish, the opening movement is more akin to the great Thanksgiving of the Christian Eucharist. It lifts up the soul to heaven; it joins with angels and archangels; and the hymn it utters is the Sanctus.

It is uttered first by the Four Living Things that represent all the orders of creation. It is uttered first by them because their worship and order are perfect; it never varies: but it is taken up by the representatives of humanity, the Four-and-Twenty Elders, who rise from their Thrones, and worship the Eternal, *casting their Crowns before the Throne and saying, Worthy art Thou, O Lord our God, to take Glory and Honour and Power, because thou hast created all things, and through thy Will they came into existence and were Created.*

Man, the rational creature, made in the image of God, and reigning with him on his throne, is distinguished from the Living Beings; he can give a reason for his worship. He can offer a rational and fully conscious homage to the God who has created all things. The worship of creation—a familiar thought in Jewish psalmody—lies only in its beautiful and faultless obedience to the order which God has given it; the worship of man must spring from gratitude and wonder and awe.

The Vision of the Sealed Book.

God has been represented to us as the fountain of light and ruler of the universe, the eternal creator whose praise is in the order and beauty of his creation; the worship of nature and of man goes up to him in an unbroken harmony. But in actual fact the harmony is broken. The order of nature goes on in uninterrupted perfection; but man has escaped from this orbit; he is lawless, and his crimes make continual discord.

It is characteristic of St. John to state first the grand truth of the perpetual harmony, and, having stated it, to make in a second stage of the vision the necessary qualification. It is perhaps a necessary characteristic of symbolic thinking. He sees first the great principle of the universal harmony; having seen the harmony, he becomes aware of the discord. *I saw in the Right Hand of him who sat on the Throne, a Book written on the back and front and Sealed with Seven Seals.*

St. John is not afraid to bring his doubts into the presence of the divine Light. In fact the divine Light is itself the cause of those doubts; it is not until you have seen the vision of heavenly Justice that you can doubt the just government of the world. The question cannot arise. The vision of a righteous and Almighty God is a magnificent and illuminating revelation; but such a vision does carry in its right hand a whole volume of difficulties—difficulties that no prophet or philosopher *in heaven or earth or under the earth* had ever solved or even looked in the face—*to open the Book or to look upon it.*

St. John had felt the difficulties deeply. They were a challenge to his faith; it was *a strong Angel proclaiming with a loud Voice* that asked *Who is worthy to Open the Book and Loose the Seals?* It was perhaps at a later date, when he came to write it down, that he felt that these doubts were themselves divine, the Voice of a Strong Angel, and that it was a noble and inspired impulse that made him face unwelcome truth. It came perhaps after the martyrdom of his brother James; for the thought of martyrdom underlies the whole book. At any rate it was not done without agony. Despite his insight into the nature of God and the governance of the world, he was one of those sensitive souls that feel deeply its sorrows and inequalities. *I wept long because no one was found worthy to open the Book or look at it.* He went through a long period of doubt and tears and distress, torn between his faith in God and the perplexity over the evil and injustice permitted in the world.

He found comfort at last through the words of the prophets. *One of the Elders says to me, " Weep no more ; the Lion of the Tribe of Judah, the Root of David, has conquered !—to open the Book and its Seven Seals."*

If we wish to identify these Elders as ancient worthies of Israel, this may perhaps be Isaiah, who wrote of the Root of Jesse to which the gentiles should seek, an identification which supports the view that the Twenty-four represent the prophets and apostles. To make a precise identification would probably be a mistake; but in any case the comfort came through the witness of Isaiah, or rather through the Messiah foretold by him, in whom all the enigmas of history would be solved; and it is important to remember that he is the great Messianic prophet, and that the Messiah is introduced in the terms of his prophecies.

The Lamb of God.

Once more he gazes into the Great Glory that blazes in the midst of the Living Forces of nature and the Thrones of the spiritual leaders of Humanity, and now he sees further into the heart of it. At first he saw merely the Light and the worship; then he had looked deeper, and seen the Sealed Book in the Right Hand; now he looks deeper still, and sees *the Lamb as it had been Slain,* a word which implies Slain in Sacrifice. At last he sees the Heart of God, and finds that it is broken in sorrow; it is the Bleeding Heart; it is the Crucifix. Forth from the heart of God, *ex Parentis Corde natus,* comes the Lamb, and takes the Book, and opens the Seals. In one symbolic vision he sees the going forth of the heavenly Word; the divine Son, the essence of the Father, Light out of Light and Very God out of Very God, endowed in his own right with the perfect powers and energies, *the Seven Horns* of power, and *the Seven Eyes* of insight, comes forth to solve the tragic mysteries of human life.

I pointed out that the word Slain implies Slain for Sacrifice; and this word begins the great sacrificial movement of the whole poem. It is the first action in the sacrifice, but not the sacrifice itself; it is offering, not killing, which makes the sacrifice: the blood poured out, or the smoke going up.

The mysterious word " standing " must, I think, have the same meaning; for, taken literally, the phrase *Standing as it had been Slain,* is difficult. I suggest that the word is a rough Greek translation of the Hebrew Tamid, which means " standing " or " continual," and refers to the daily burnt-offering in the Temple. It is the regular technical term, and forms the title of the section of the Mishnah which deals with that sacrifice. The Lamb of the Tamid is an intelligible expression, which might well have been turned into the *Arnion Hestekos* of the Greek. The Greek word *Hestekos* does not mean " continual," but only " standing " in the literal sense ; but it might be a rough equivalent like *Christos* (smeared), which stands for Messiah. *Arnion Hestekos* might thus be " baboo " Greek for Lamb of the Sacrifice.

The word *Arnion* has also aroused discussion. Our Lord is called Lamb of God in the fourth gospel (i. 29), just as he is here called Lamb of the Tamid; but the two words are different, *Arnion* here and *Amnos* in the gospel. It is possible that while *Amnos* is the more common and natural word for Lamb, *Arnion Hestekos* might be a technical term of the Jewish Temple; for there must have been Greek equivalents for Hebrew terms in use among the priests themselves, and the Greek of *Revelation* may represent an illiterate Greek used in Jerusalem. Josephus, himself a priest, uses the word *Arēn*, of which *Arnion* is a diminutive; but *Arēn* is not a New Testament word except for St. Luke (*Luke* x. 3).

In its position here it serves a double purpose :

1. The culmination of the act of Christian worship which fills chapters iv. and v.

2. It is the first act in the Hebrew liturgical worship which runs through the poem from chapter vi. to chapter xix.

In the *First Epistle of St. Peter* there is a reference to Christ as a *Lamb ordained before the Foundation of the World* ; and it is difficult to believe that it is not a definite reference to this Vision of St. John, which must be much older than Patmos.

There is a kind of theology which affects to believe that God learnt something by becoming man, and that after the cross and passion he was different from what he had been before; his experience had given him something new. Such a theology holds that the eternal God lived in perfect bliss, and knew nothing of suffering or sorrow; but it is a doctrine that can scarcely commend itself to any clear thinker, critical or orthodox. If the cross reveals God, it must reveal him either as he is or as he is not. If it reveals him as he is not, it is a lie; it fails to reveal him at all. If it reveals him as he is, then the cross blazons the very secret of God's essential being; his emblem is the broken heart; he suffers.

The doctrine of the suffering God, or at any rate of the sorrow of God, is daring and difficult; but it is the only way of reconciling the doctrine of his just government with the actual fact of the crime and misery of the human race. It does not explain that contradiction; it does not attempt such a task; it introduces a third mystery which reconciles the other two. God is love, and love suffers more than we do; all his infinite being is in agony over the sins and follies of man. He suffers more than any prophet or philosopher. It is his eternal nature.

More. He comes forth, and suffers in and for his creation, thus making the reconciliation or atonement actual. This is the everlasting gospel of the Christian church; the world suffers because of sin, but not so much as God does.

This view is quite different from the Patripassionist error, which held that God the Father suffered the actual bodily pains of the cross. This is impossible because God is pure spirit. The church, therefore, denies this; but it does not deny that God suffers.

It is frequently represented that the *Revelation* lacks the supreme Christian ideas of grace and love and mercy; it is said to be hard and legal and inspired with the spirit of vengeance. The truth is that the apocalyptic symbols do not lend themselves very readily to the theology of grace; they incline more to majesty and terror. Yet St. John has so transformed them that the meaning ought to be clear to anyone on purely rational grounds. He does not adopt the new symbol of the cross, as St. Paul does, because he is working with the old Jewish symbolism. The Lamb is well understood there to mean the Messiah; but, strange to say, it means the fighting Messiah. In *Enoch* the Lamb who grows Horns is Judas Maccabaeus and his army. The Lamb is a constant symbol of the Messiah; but not the *Lamb as it had been Slain*. That is a new thought.

The Worship of the Lamb.

It has been pointed out before how the symbolic visions are supplemented and enriched by songs like those of a Greek chorus. It is a device which enables the prophet to supply those elements of love and devotion which the hard shining symbols cannot quite convey; they have the effect of emotional revival hymns introduced into a correct and beautiful liturgical worship. They leave no doubt in the simplest mind of the intention of the whole.

The divine honours of the Lamb had also been partly anticipated in Jewish apocalypse. It has already been remarked that Ezekiel discerns on the Throne of the Great Glory one having *the Appearance of the Similitude of a Son of Man* (i. 26). By this he meant to suggest that there is a likeness in nature between God and Man; but Daniel appears to have taken it to imply a second person sharing the divine sovereignty, and he introduces this divine Son of Man as the companion of the Three Children in the furnace of persecution, and as the final triumph of God's sovereignty *on the Clouds of Heaven.* The last word has yet to be said on what Daniel intends by this figure; but there is no doubt that in *Enoch* it means a divine Messiah, ready to come from heaven. In our *Revelation* it is the crucified Jesus, the eternal Word of God.

The adoration of God now becomes the adoration of God and of the Lamb. We have seen how the first chorus of worship, addressed to the Creator, represents the first " movement " in the Eucharistic prayer of the church, and culminates in the Sanctus; the Vision of the Lamb corresponds to the second movement in that symphony, and culminates in the orchestral worship to which every created thing contributes.

Man, as is right, leads this adoration. The Twenty-four Elders now appear definitely as Priests with the music of Lyres and the Golden Censers, whose Smoke represents the prayers of the faithful; they sing a *New Song,* a song never heard before the sacrifice of the Lamb on Calvary, and praise *the Lamb who was slain and has Redeemed to God in his own Blood out of every tribe and tongue and people and nation, and made them a Kingdom, Priests to our God, and they are reigning on the Earth.*

The New Song is a regular type of Psalm, quite common in the Temple Psalter, and always of a triumphant character, celebrating the triumphs of Jehovah.

> *O sing unto Jehovah a New Song:*
> *For he hath done marvellous things.*
> *With his own Right Hand and with the Arm of his Holiness.*
> *Hath he gotten himself the Victory.*

But all this imagery of conquest is transferred to the victory of the cross; *thou hast bought for God at the price of thy Blood.*

Man, the Redeemed, leads this new worship; but the strain is taken up by the Living Forces and by the millions of Angels round the Throne, now mentioned for the first time to be brought into the chorus of praise. *Worthy is the Lamb that was Slain to take power and riches and wisdom and strength and honour and glory and blessing.* And in the grand doxology which concludes it, every created thing in heaven and earth and under the earth and on the sea sings a part. *To him that sitteth on the Throne and to the Lamb, blessing and honour and glory and power unto Ages of Ages.*

And the Four Living Things said *Amen;* and the Elders fell and worshipped.

The First Four Seals.

So far, then, the Vision blazons the story of creation in four stages which may be represented thus:

1. Harmony.
2. Discord.
3. Resolution of the Discord.
4. Restoration of the Harmony.

But it is now necessary for St. John to hark back. He sees his Vision in stages; but he loves to show each stage reaching its full and perfect climax. In this case the Sealed Book has been left behind, and faith has swept on to the vision of the restoration of the harmonies of creation. He now has to go back to the opening of the Seven Seals by the Lamb.

The number Seven most naturally divides into a four and a three; in the case of the Seals, and also of the Trumpets, this division is very marked. The first four seals make a group; the last three are of quite a different character. This division is made fundamental by the connection of the first Four Seals with the Four Living Things.

The Book, as has been seen, symbolises the discordant note in creation, the apparent injustices that give pain to the prophet. It is interesting to remark that in ancient times no difficulties were felt about nature. Despite its " cruelty " and " immorality," nature was felt to be a harmony; and so it is : it obeys its own laws of life and force, moving unerringly in its perfect circle of order and beauty. The difficulty felt by the Hebrew mind was that man does not obey *his* laws, the laws of reason and goodness. Why does evil triumph? Why do the poor suffer? Why have godless imperialisms dominated the earth? In particular, why has Israel been trodden under by the great heathen powers? These are the problems which arise as the Seven Seals are opened; but they do no more than arise. They are stated, not answered.

The Rider on the White Horse, summoned by the first Living Thing, represents the spirit of ambition and conquest, not specifically the Roman or the Parthian, as some commentators have supposed, but the " lust of gain in the spirit of Cain " wherever it may be found. History has recorded the domination of man by this spirit through century after century. *He goes out conquering and to conquer* with his *Crown* and his *Bow*. The name blazoned on his forehead is Cyrus or Alexander, Cæsar or Napoleon, but the spirit is always recognisably the same. The marvel is not merely that men suffer these ambitious adventurers to ride over them; they adore them and deify them. So much so that some commentators have been carried away with the enthusiasm themselves, and held the Rider on the White Horse to be Christ. It is, of course, the lust for power, the arrogant pride of the self-made man as opposed to the God-made man.

What follows is simple. When the Second Seal is opened, the Second Living Thing summons a *Red Horse*, whose Rider carries a *Great Sword* and represents war, slaughter, and massacre.

The third is the *Black Horse*, whose Rider carries a *Balance*, and brings famine.

The fourth is the *Pale Horse*, literally a *Green Horse*, whose Rider is *Death* or possibly *Pestilence*, and with him comes the *Grave—Hades*. Green in Homer is the colour of fear (*chlorons deos* = " blue funk "); it is also the colour of corpses; and these two riders complete the procession.

One magnificent point in this succession of symbols is the change from splendour to horror. The first rider, with his White Horse and Golden Crown, is a splendid figure; you would like to be that figure. The second is less attractive; the third is evil; the fourth is horrible. Such is the progress of man; for the lust of conquest and domination is the spirit that ruins not only great nations and empires, but also businesses and homes and all beautiful simple human things. God, as it appears, does nothing to check it; the ungodly triumphs, and the result is hell.

Apocalyptic History.

It has already been pointed out that in *Ezekiel* the Four Living Things are the forces of creation, the laws which govern all things within the four points of the compass. In *Zechariah* they are the Four Winds, or Four Horses of various colours which represent the forces of God which work in human history. St. John has kept both conceptions and cunningly woven them together. There is a hint of this in *Daniel*, where Four Winds (or spirits) strive together on the face of the waters before the Four Beasts arise to dominate the earth.

Neither in *Ezekiel* nor in *St. John* do the Four spirits of life signify the energies of God himself; they are not identical with him. They are forces at work in the world; but they are distinct from God. Nor is there any suggestion that they are moral forces; the following interpretation of this symbolism is put forward tentatively.

The Four Horses have Riders, and, unlike the horses of *Zechariah*, are independent of God, and work contrary to his will; they represent the lawless spirit of man dominating creation and ruining it; they represent in particular the godless heathen empires. The number Four had been used thus before; but it had been differently worked out. In *Daniel* there is one world-empire appearing in successive forms, the Babylonian, the Mede, the Persian, the Greek; this can be seen quite clearly, in the vision of the statue. Ezekiel, on the other hand, uses the key number Four to represent the different ways in which Jehovah brings punishment upon the Jews; they are the *Four sore judgments, the sword, the famine, the noisome beasts, and the pestilence* (xiv. 21). St. John has combined these views. The Four Riders represent both the self-willed, domineering, conquering spirit of imperialistic man, and also the judgment which God brings upon his people Israel.

This double meaning is found in the ancient prophets, and is also very characteristic of St. John. In the *First Isaiah* Sennacherib is the fierce bloodthirsty, self-willed tyrant conscious of nothing but his own will which he is fulfilling; yet he is a mere tool in the hand of God; though he does not know it, there is a destiny above him, and he is being used for the service of the righteous God. His free will is not infringed; but the omnipotence of God is using him all the time for higher purposes. *Ho, Assyrian, the rod of mine anger* (*Is.* x. 5). Similarly, in the *Second Isaiah* the much greater conqueror, Cyrus, is said to be raised up and endued with power by God to serve purposes of which he knows nothing: *I girded thee though thou hast not known me* (*Is.* xlv. 5). The same figure represents both the vain, self-willed ambition of man and also the avenging power of God.

Throughout the whole *Revelation* we must be prepared to find this double character in the symbols employed. The Seven Spirits represent both the Spirit of God working in the churches, and also the human communities in which it works. The Strong Angel of chapter x. represents both the Word of God inspiring and strengthening the prophets, and also the activities of the prophets themselves.

In this particular case, however, the overruling power is clearly indicated for us. The Four Riders represent man going out conquering for himself, forgetful of God, and uninspired by the Seven Spirits; but as each Rider comes forth it is one of the Four Living Things which says Come. Nothing within the Four corners of creation can escape from law of some kind; we may emancipate ourselves from communion with the spirit of truth and goodness which was meant to be our guide; we only fall more completely under the control of the lower laws, the laws of creation which apply to the animals as well as ourselves, and work in their way too the will of God. They belong to creation; they are not identical with God; but though they may work slowly, they work exceeding sure. Man makes force his ideal; he falls under the laws of force, and progresses through War and Famine to Pestilence and the Grave. He has come under laws from which he was meant to be free; and he has found ruin and death and hell.

There is another point to mark about St. John's use of symbols. It is the underlying spirit of a movement in history which he grasps and displays. The identification is nothing; sometimes, as here, there is no identification. His system is much deeper and much more philosophical than that of Ezekiel or Daniel.

It is the nature of the process which he has here depicted. A process is a difficult thing to handle either in symbolic or apocalyptic terms; we tend to fix it and give it a static abstract existence; but it is in its essence something which is going on. It changes, it develops, and yet it has an inherent character which explains all those developments. Daniel merely gives us four successive examples of the world-empire which are antiquated at once by the appearance of Rome, a fifth; Ezekiel merely gives us four different ways in which judgments may fall upon the chosen nation; it is only St. John who asks what *is* this process that lies behind the vast phenomena of history?

St. John begins with man and ends with Death. His first Rider is simply man in that simple self-sufficiency of his, supposing himself "lord of creation," imagining that he is here to acquire, to enjoy, to "get on"; that is the initial mistake, for he is really here to learn, to serve, and perhaps to suffer. He is the "natural man," the contrary of Jesus; he is the man who has fallen in all three temptations. He thinks of his rights rather than of his duties. He may have all the four cardinal virtues; but as he sits in his arm-chair and makes plans for his business, or his home, or his future, he is blissfully ignorant that he is in the world to serve higher purposes than his own.

Out of this grows that lust of empire and conquest that has so often ruined human civilisation; out of that lust of power and possession grows war; out of war, in logical sequence, come famine and pestilence. We saw it all happen sixteen years ago, and in the history of the human race it recurs and recurs and recurs.

We are conscious in history of what we call movements. Not only does one nation rise to power and another sink, but within the nation one class rises to power and another sinks. The art of history consists in grasping the character of these "movements."

St. John always thinks first of the "movement" or process, and depicts its character; he may then exhibit it as for a moment taking bodily form in some nation or group; it may even for a moment be incarnate in an individual. Later on—for instance, in chapter xiii.—the "Beast" is this very world-conquering process taking bodily form in the Roman Empire; for a moment it appears as an individual, Nero; but later on it is Domitian. As the Beast represents worldly royalty, so "Babylon" represents worldly priestliness; but it is in each case the underlying essential character of the process which he is depicting.

In the Four Riders there is no definite identification intended; they represent simply the recurring rise and destruction of great worldly systems; they also represent, in consequence, the recurring nemesis or fate (the judgment of God, he would call it) that comes upon them under the laws of history.

We have thus a sort of Outline of History.

Such is the meaning of the Four Riders, and later on,

when St. John mentions the Four Winds, or the Four Horns of the Altar or the Four destroying Angels, these are the thoughts he wishes to come into our minds.

An interesting parallel to this use of the figure Four is found in the writings of the late Gnostic author, Justinus, whose works, though they are mixed with a very curious Greek-Syrian mythology, yet reflect also a stage of early Gnosticism of the same period as St. John, or not much later. He says that the Fourfold river of Eden which watered the whole earth symbolises Four bands of destroying angels which in turn dominate the material world, bringing upon it famine, disease, and other evils. This connection of a Fourfold destroying influence with a river is also found in *St. John*; for in ix. 13 a voice comes from the Four Horns of the Altar, saying, "Loose the Four Angels who are bound at the Great River Euphrates." (See p. 165.)

Now the Throne and the Altar are connected, so that the Four Living Things and the Four Horns of the Altar would naturally be the same; but it is curious that the Four destroying agencies which first appeared as Riders on Horses should now appear as Four Angels bound at the Great River Euphrates. But this Great River is the first of the Four rivers that watered Eden, and might itself be regarded therefore as a fourfold river. A river is a very natural description for a destructive agency, when one considers its likeness to a serpent and its power in flood.

Earlier and Later Strata.

I pointed out on p. 109 that there are two strata distinguishable in *Revelation*, an earlier Palestinian stratum in which angels descend from heaven to earth, and a later Ephesian stratum in which the seer himself is in heaven. It is at this point that we become conscious that we have gradually passed from the later stratum to the earlier. I am distinguishing the earlier series of visions by the letter J because they were composed in Jerusalem; I am calling the later visions P because of their connection with Patmos. P provides the introduction and conclusion of the book, and also the anticipatory vision of the Great Multitude in chapter vii.; J provides the main outline (chapters vi. to xx.).

1. P is more free and universal in tone. It has the Throne, the Twenty-Four Elders, and the Four Living Things.

2. J is Jewish and does not look much beyond the bounds of Palestine; it has an Altar, Four Horns, and a multitude of Angels often conceived as priests. It is concerned throughout with the fate of Jerusalem. Its local character is obscured by the A.V. translation of " dwellers upon the earth " for " inhabitants of the land."

The structure of J is based on that of *Ezekiel* (see p. 64) and on the ceremonial of the temple (see p. 378). These features are not shared by the P material, or by chapters xii. and xiii. (see p. 228).

The Altar.

Quite suddenly there rises before us an Altar, a piece of symbolism founded upon solid earth. We must imagine it like the great four-cornered altar at Jerusalem, which covered the sacred rock which the Mohammedans still reverence on Mount Moriah; it is a huge structure of stones which have not been hewn by any metal tool; at its four corners rise the Four " Horns " which are so common in East Mediterranean religious art.

It is difficult to connect it with the previous visions, because these Four Horns now take the place of the Four Living Things. Angels are now very prominent in the action of the poem, and move about doing the work of priests. It is all in the open air; and we do not hear for a long time of any holy building or Naos: and when we do, it is a Naos in heaven.

The Altar represents earth, and in particular the land of Israel, on which has been poured out so often the blood of prophets and saints; in conformity with the double signification of symbols, St. John makes it represent now the innocent dead whose blood was poured out, now the guilty nation that shed the blood.

The martyrs are the genuinely priestly; the nation is the falsely priestly.

The Innocent Dead.

The first Four Seals outline the domination of the world by self-will and brute force, and exhibit history as a record of battles and conquests and plague and desolation. It is suggested that these calamities occur as a result of natural law once the spirit of Cain is introduced into the history of man. We shall see that the story of Cain is actually in the author's mind.

But there is a further question. What of the innocent sufferers? Why does God allow massacre and famine and plague? It is like a change in the structure of a musical composition when the Fifth Seal introduces this question. *The Souls of those who were killed for the Word of God and the Witness which they bore are seen under the Altar crying with a loud voice, How long, O Master, Holy and True, dost thou delay to judge and avenge our Blood on the inhabitants of the Land?*

I translate it Land rather than Earth, because, as we shall see, the earlier (or J) visions have Palestine in view rather than the whole world.

These words have in them the very dawn of the world's history, and the cry of Abel's blood going up to Jehovah for vengeance. The whole system of blood-revenge which is symbolised in that story provides also the symbolism for this. The Earth (or Land) which had previously been favourable to Cain was defiled by the blood which he shed upon it, and cursed "from him." The innocent blood calling to God for vengeance was taken up in many writings of this period as a symbol of the blood of the innocent dead in general, shed by the oppressors of mankind. The system of blood-revenge demanded that a "Redeemer," the next of kin, should avenge the dead by shedding the blood of the murderer; and it must be remembered that this was not revenge in our sense of the word, but the strictest justice that a primitive culture could manage. The cry for "vengeance" which we find throughout *Revelation* is a cry for justice; how long will God permit the oppressor to crush the innocent?

It is important also that this is the first clear echo of the words of Jesus; for he says that there shall *come upon you all the Righteous Blood which is being shed upon the Land from the Blood of Righteous Abel to the Blood of Zacharias son of Barachias, whom ye murdered between the Naos and the Altar : verily, I say unto you all these shall come upon this generation.* (*Matt.* xxiii. 35.) Not only is the symbolism of blood-revenge the same; but it points out what later study will confirm; it is the land of Israel, and in particular the Temple at Jerusalem which is to suffer. And we must remember that there is a hint of the same idea in the Four Seals; for the Four Judgments in *Ezekiel*, to which they correspond, were all to come upon Jerusalem.

The martyrs of which St. John is speaking here are not Christian martyrs, but the innocent dead in general. It is not said that they were killed for the Witness of Jesus, but for the *Witness which they bore*, an awkward phrase which purposely avoids making them Christian.

The *Revelation* is written in an orderly fashion, and as the birth of Christ is not narrated until chapter xii., we should not expect to find Christian martyrs yet unless they are mentioned by way of parenthesis of anticipation. I have already pointed out how the Apocalypses go back to the origins and review history from the beginning.

The Blood Sacrifice.

Dr. Charles has collected a great deal of evidence to show that in this period the death of the martyr was commonly regarded as a sacrifice. It began in the Maccabean period, where those who fell fighting against the Greeks were thought of as giving their lives as a sacrifice for the nation, and fully assured of a joyful resurrection. Behind that is the Suffering Servant of *Isaiah* liii.

There was by now a natural connection in thought between the Altar and Martyrdom; and this led in its turn to the Christian custom of building an altar over the body of a martyr, or enclosing the body or relics of a martyr under the altar. The whole cult of the martyrs is linked with the *Revelation*.

With regard to the symbolism of *Revelation*, we must bear

in mind that in Hebrew theology it was not the death that was the sacrifice, but the presentation on the altar, the whole blood splashed upon it, and part or the whole of the animal burnt upon it. It is naturally only the pouring of the blood which finds its way into the symbolism at this point. The martyr or prophet who died for his religion was a sacrifice, because his blood was poured out on the Land; the Land must therefore be thought of as an altar, and he himself priest as well as sacrifice.

Looked at from the opposite point of view, the persecutor is the priest who has poured out the righteous Blood on the Altar of the Land; this, then, is the Blood offering which priestly Jerusalem has offered to the Lord.

The thought already occurs in *Ezekiel*; the passage is too long to quote or explain in detail; a couple of verses must suffice. *Woe to the Bloody City . . . for her Blood is in the midst of her; she set it upon the bare Rock; she poured it not upon the Land (Earth) to cover it with dust. That it might cause fury to come up to take Vengeance, I have set her Blood upon a bare Rock that it should not be covered* (*Ez.* xxiv. 6-8).

The twin ideas of Blood-offering and Blood-revenge must be kept in mind if we are to understand *Revelation*.

The White Robe.

The answer assures us that the blood of the innocent dead is a sacrifice of which God does take notice. *They are given each one a White Robe and told to rest for a little till the number of their fellow-servants and brethren is fulfilled, who are going to be killed as they were.*

This conception also is common in the apocalypses. God will not interfere with vengeance until the number of the martyrs is complete; the fellow-servants and brethren can be nothing else but the Christian martyrs. Heaven and earth are thus both waiting upon them as they go out to their agony. This is the very picture in 1 *Corinthians*, where St. Paul compares the apostles to gladiators marching into the arena before a vast audience of spectators both in heaven and in earth. The death of the righteous is not unobserved by God; it has value; it fulfils a predestined purpose.

We are told elsewhere in *Revelation* that the White Linen is the Righteousness of the Saints; but Dr. Charles regards this as an interpolation by a later hand, and proposes another explanation. He shows that in " apocalyptic circles " the Robe was a regular symbol for the resurrection body; in the *Assumption of Moses*, for instance, these robes are stored in the seventh heaven. We cannot accept anything so materialistic as this; and it still remains to be proved that St. John belongs to the " circles " in question. No literary dependence of St. John on any surviving apocalypse can be shown, and the best explanation of the few ideas he shares with them is that they were very widely accepted in Judaism generally.

On the other hand, we need not accept that idea in its crudity; in any case we are involved in contradiction if we do, for it is difficult to say how the Christian martyrs later on in the book can be said to wash their Robes in the Blood of the Lamb.

The Robes are something which they clearly have already, and yet they are something which can be said to be given them; if we accept the spiritual view of the resurrection body as propounded in St. Paul, we can combine Dr. Charles' view with the view that they are the " Righteousnesses " of the Saints. As priests they offered themselves, their souls and bodies, their thoughts and words and acts; in death they laid all this down to receive it glorified and spiritualised, to *be clothed upon that mortality might be swallowed up in life* (2 *Cor.* v. 4). The Robe is thus the glorified, spiritualised human nature or character fitted for the heavenly life; it is their Righteousness also, their true self. (This view should be compared with the conception of the heavenly Robe in the Egyptian Gnostic *Pistis Sophia* and the Syrian Gnostic *Hymn of the Soul;* see also p. 143.)

The study of Jewish apocalyptic is undeniably helpful; but it was thoroughly materialistic, and if it had imagination it was usually imagination of the very lowest order. If we drag down the level of our apocalypse to that dreary commonplace we shall not do it justice. The original pre-Shakespearian *Hamlet* does not survive; but scholars assure us that it was a very poor production, full of murders and ranting and melodrama. Shakespeare's *Hamlet* is built up on just such a basis of murders and ranting and melodrama; it is all there; but how much else as well? Much of the machinery of contemporary apocalypse is to be found in *Revelation*; but if we are content to take it in a low and literal way, how much we shall miss! We shall, in fact, be omitting the Prince of Denmark from the play.

These same considerations must guide us in the next section, which tells of the stars falling and the heavens in dissolution.

The Prophetic Dooms.

The Sixth Seal opens, and with it comes the annunciation of those prophetic signs with which the day of God's vengeance was always proclaimed: *there was a great Earthquake, and the Sun became black like Sackcloth, and the whole of the Moon became like Blood, the Stars of the Heaven were falling on the Earth . . . the Heaven departed like a Scroll rolling up, and every Mountain and Island were moved out of their places.*

We must deal at once with these symbols of doom. Either they are to be taken literally or not. If they are to be taken literally, there is no room for any more apocalypse, or any more history; the physical structure of the universe is at an end. If they are not literal, what do they signify?

The problem has to be solved for the whole book. Either it is the work of an inspired poet dealing with invisible ideals and forces and principles, and expressing them in an imaginative system of starry symbols; or else it is the work of a narrow-minded, materialistic, adventist fanatic, who believed that there were really stables in heaven for four horses, no more and no less. I cannot disguise from the reader the fact that I believe he was a poet; on the other hand, some modern critics seem to think he was an adventist of the grossest type. Dr. Charles really seems to believe that St. John thought that when Jesus of Nazareth appeared again in triumph he would come with a short Roman sword protruding uncomfortably out of his mouth. Yet Dr. Charles took the Four Horsemen as symbols; why does he not treat the whole book in a consistent manner? And on what principles does he choose some things to be taken literally and others symbolically?

A second point is that these Signs in the Sun and Moon, as St. Luke calls them, are borrowed from the Old Testament prophets. In those prophets they refer to political disasters; Isaiah uses them, for instance, to symbolise the fall of the great Babylonian Empire. They have no precise "interpretation," though you may, if you like, say that the heavenly bodies stood for the gods and rulers of Babylon. But that is not necessary. Babylon's power vanished in a moment; her Sun went down at mid-day. That is all.

Thirdly, the prophets in general constantly speak of the destruction of the universe when they really mean the political structure of the world-empire. Haggai says, *I will shake the heavens and the earth . . . and the desirable things of all nations shall come, and the glory of the latter house shall be greater than the glory of the former house* (ii. 7). It is plain that, though the heaven and earth are shaken, the Temple will still be standing, and all the nations still in existence; what Haggai hoped for was political upheaval in the Persian Empire which would leave Jerusalem free to develop and dominate.

Fourthly, the prophets in general use a great deal of hyperbole and picturesque exaggeration in the manner of Oriental poetry. *As the days of a tree shall be the days of my people* (Is. lxv. 22). *Yet destroyed I the Amorite whose height was like the height of the cedars* (Amos ii. 9) : statements which mean respectively "very old" and "very tall." It goes right back to quite primitive poetry: *The mountains skipped like rams. . . . The earth trembled and shook* (Ps. cxiv.). Poets, even Western poets, will always continue to use it. It includes the use of huge figures; a reign of forty years means a good long reign, and a kingdom of a thousand years means a good long kingdom. The poetry of Jesus has it to a superlative degree; camels are swallowed or passed through needles' eyes; mountains are thrown into the depths of the sea; a man gets a tree-trunk stuck in his eye.

People without sufficient imagination to understand this and to enjoy it ought to steer clear of the Apocalypse. Just as a witness has to understand "the nature of an oath," so the commentator ought to understand the nature of a poem, or even of a joke. Many who are deficient in a sense of poetry and a sense of humour have tried their hands on the Apocalypse, and made a mess of it. Astonishing to relate, Sir Gilbert Murray is among the culprits. It is no excuse that even in the period itself unspiritual men took these poetic visions in a literal sense, and that all round St. John unspiritual men were writing unspiritual apocalypses. Just as the fourth gospel is the spiritual gospel, so the *Revelation* is the spiritual apocalypse.

The Signs in the Sun and Moon.

There are therefore two ways of approaching this passage:

1. *Hyperbolically.* It may refer to such natural phenomena as earthquakes, eclipses, and falling stars, and these may be regarded as warnings to sinners, and signs of judgment approaching. This would be quite in harmony with some of the more primitive Hebrew prophets.
2. *Symbolically.* It may refer to vast political upheavals, the decline and downfall of empires and religions, gods and kings.

The second is much to be preferred, though the first may not be excluded. Though the world-empire re-constitutes itself, and goes on, each successive phase of it, the Assyrian, the Babylonian, and so on, does meet its downfall; kings and kaisers and dukes do fall from their thrones; and for a moment the monarchs, the militarists, and the millionaires are terrified. *They hid themselves in the caves and the rocks and the mountains, and say to the mountains and the rocks, Fall upon us and hide us from the Presence of Him who sitteth upon the Throne and from the Wrath of the Lamb, for the Great Day of his Wrath has come, and who is able to Stand?*

The terminology of these verses is so thoroughly Jewish in tone that for the moment St. John's horizon does not appear to be much wider than Palestine. The question is complicated by the ambiguity of the word *Ge*, translated either "earth" or "land." The phrase *kings of the earth*, which is used here, can equally well be translated *rulers of the land*, and it is only the rulers of Israel who would fear the Great Glory on his Throne, and the Lamb who symbolises the Warrior Messiah in Maccabean apocalypse, a Warrior Messiah of Zechariah's type, who will execute vengeance on the "wicked shepherds," *defend the poor and fatherless, and see that such as are in need and necessity have right* (*Ps.* lxxxii. 3). This confirms us in the supposition that we have reached an earlier stratum of vision seen in Palestine, which owes much to the gospels, and has a similar background to the Maccabean apocalypses like those of *Daniel*, *Enoch*, and *Second Zechariah*.

The Great Day of the Lord has not come. That ought surely to appear in the Seventh Seal, though we shall see that, as a matter of fact, it does not. The prophets and apocalyptists are disappointed; there is an inexplicable silence in heaven.

The Outline of History.

To recapitulate. The Seven Seals give us an outline of history as the prophets see it; it is the earliest philosophy of world-history, and bears an odd resemblance to the Spenglerian theory. A world-empire of a brutal and godless kind has dominated mankind; it repeats itself in a series of cycles, but each cycle follows the same logical form, under the influence of irresistible law, a law from which mankind was intended to be free.

The Seven Seals outline the progress of the cycle.

1. *The First Four.* The rise and triumph of brutal militaristic imperialism.
2. *The Fifth.* The souls of the innocent victims look to God as their champion, their blood calls to him to execute vengeance.
3. *The Sixth.* Vengeance does fall on the godless empire, and, to anticipate,

4. *The Seventh.* God holds his hand. The final establishment of a just empire does not come.

It is clear that so far we are dealing with the past.

The Restraint of Judgment.

The Seventh Seal ought now to be opened, and, according to apocalyptic hope, we ought to have the Great Day, and the establishment of Justice; as a matter of fact, we get

1. Delay. The Sealing of the Righteous who are still in the world.
2. Further Delay. Silence in heaven. The prophetic hopes are not fulfilled.

This doctrine of a restraint of judgment is also to be found in St. Paul; God suffers the reign of sin in the world for a long time, because he desireth not the death of a sinner, but rather that he should turn from his wickedness and live. The purpose of God is to save to the uttermost, and vengeance must wait.

The Destroying Forces.

Once more we are introduced to the Four beings who symbolise the forces at work in the world, but in these earlier visions they appear as *Four Angels standing at the Four Corners of the Earth restraining the Four Winds that the Wind may not blow upon the Earth nor upon the Sea nor upon any Tree.* If we take our cue from Zechariah, and substitute Horse for Wind, we see that we are still dealing with those Four Riders, which symbolise the unruly wills and affections of sinful men, but yet, without knowing it, become the instruments of God's judgment on earth. Nebuchadrezzar, for instance, thinks he is fulfilling his own heart's desire; but the prophet sees that all he actually achieves is the execution of God's vengeance upon Jerusalem. And indeed, as we look back through the centuries, that is almost all he has achieved which is of any importance to us to-day.

The power of the Four Riders is to hurt the Earth and the Sea—that is, to execute material judgments upon mankind. The physical framework of the universe signifies political and social organisation. Meanwhile they are restrained. *Another Angel arises from the East with the Seal of the Living God,* and calls for a truce until *we Seal the Servants of our God upon their Foreheads.*

The Sealing of the Elect.

The symbolism of the Seal is taken from *Ezekiel*, where the faithful Israelites are sealed on the forehead to protect them from death when God punishes Jerusalem. Though St. John has a judgment on Jerusalem in his mind, he does not mean that the elect are sealed to protect them from death; if anything, they are to be martyrs. They are those who declare themselves on the side of God, and they are sealed as his in the resurrection, and as members of the new Jerusalem which will take the place of the old.

In the original Hebrew of *Ezekiel* the sign was the Hebrew letter *Tau*, which in some scripts had the form of a cross; this coincidence must have helped to originate the very early Christian custom of the sign of the cross. Ezekiel himself probably drew it from the sign made by Jehovah on Cain's forehead to protect him from the consequences of the blood feud. Its general implication is exemption from God's judgment.

One Hundred and Forty-four Thousand.

The use of the numbers is, of course, entirely symbolic. The Sealed are drawn from all the tribes of Israel, Twelve Thousand from each. In the Old Testament a Thousand is a rough name for a subdivision of the tribe, consisting theoretically of a group of families; it is a " clan." A good parallel is the division of an English shire into " hundreds." " Come in your Thousands " means " Come in your clans."

Here we have the Twelve Tribes, the total number of the Elect People, the Redeemed. But not only is the Number of the Elect People perfect; each Tribe is perfect, containing Twelve clans or Thousands. The Day of Judgment is being held back so that the perfect number may be made up, and the roll of God's elect completed. This may be the Book of Life mentioned later on.

The number of the tribes is peculiar, because Joseph is not divided into two, Ephraim and Manasseh, according to the usual rule. Joseph is mentioned; but Manasseh, which is half of the tribe of Joseph, is also mentioned. This would make thirteen; so one tribe has to be omitted, and this tribe is Dan. Two explanations have been given of this. One is that Dan represents the traitor; and there is evidence that Antichrist was expected from this tribe. The other is that the intrusive tribe, Manasseh, has accidentally taken its place, the original Dan being miswritten Man by error, and Man being taken as an abbreviation of Manasseh. (But see p. 269.)

This roll of the elect represented originally, I think, the elect from among the actual Israel; they are Jews. We have had no reference so far to Jesus, or to Christianity, or to the persecution of Christians; we are still in the pre-Christian stage of the world's history.

But it would be misleading here to make no reference at all to gentile Christian martyrs, as it might give the impression that only Jews were to be saved: so he adds a section which looks on into the future and sees the " whole ransomed church of Christ " when it is " saved to sin no more." Such anticipations are naturally found from time to time in the Apocalypse; indeed, it would have been impossible to write it without them. Their lyrical style and universal symbolism show that they were written at a later date, and belong to the stratum we have called P. The intrusion of this passage here is responsible for an inconsistency. Here the Hundred and Forty-four Thousand are Jews and the great Multitude are gentiles: in xiv. 1 the Hundred and Forty-four Thousand include both.

The Great Multitude.

The vision is of *an immense Multitude*, countless, beyond calculation, *whom no man could number*. These are not Israelites; they are *of every nation and tribe and people and language ;* they too *stand before the Throne and before the Lamb.* They are *clothed in White Robes ;* they have *Palms in their Hands,* and they add a new kind of chorus to the great liturgy of creation,

SALVATION *to our God*. The thought of the prophet has taken wings and soared on to the very end of the process with which he is dealing; he sees the full number of the Redeemed, gentile as well as Jew, as they shall be presented spotless before the Throne of God.

The first point I want to make is that there is a very striking echo here of *St. John's Gospel*. S*alvation to our God* is an echo of the Hosanna of Palm Sunday. Hosanna means " Save now," and critics have often pointed out how ungrammatical and illogical is the expression " Save now to the son of David." *Salvation to our God*, while not actually ungrammatical, is nearly as awkward, and clearly represents Hosanna. An interesting confirmation is found in the fact that the word translated Palm (*Phoinix*) is only found twice in the New Testament, here in the *Revelation,* and in the Palm Sunday story in *St. John's Gospel.* One echoes the other. The Gospel shows the Lord of the Martyrs going to his triumph; the Apocalypse shows those who have followed and triumphed with him. The use of the Palm as a symbol of martyrdom is derived from these passages in the Johannine literature.

The second point is that the Palm and the Hosanna were connected in the Jewish ritual of the Feast of Tabernacles; and on this Festival the present passage is modelled. As a historic commemoration it was connected with the victorious passage of the Red Sea, and the huts or booths built at Succoth where the Israelites rejoiced in their freedom; in this passage the martyrs have passed the Red Sea of death and are enjoying salvation and victory. The Feast of Tabernacles (Succoth) was the last festival of the year, and far the most merry and popular; it marked the final ingathering of the harvest, and the harvest symbolism in New Testament literature is connected with the gathering of the elect into the kingdom. The pouring of water was a great feature of the ritual of Succoth; and in verse 17 we have a reference to the fountains of the Water of Life (the similar reference in *John* vii. 37 is admitted to be a reference to Succoth). The festival received its name from the huts or booths made of branches in which the people " tabernacled " during the feast; and in verse 15 it is said that God would *tabernacle* upon them. *Psalm* cxviii (with the Hosanna verse) was sung by a procession of priests waving palm-branches round the altar; and here it is sung *before the Throne and before the Lamb.*

It can hardly be doubted, therefore, that the final joy of the martyrs is pictured as a heavenly festival of Tabernacles, in which God himself makes his Tabernacle among them and they act the part of priests. It seems worth while, therefore, to give the explanation of the White Robe suggested by John Lightfoot in the seventeenth century; this master of Hebrew lore pointed out that when the priests reached the canonical age they came up to the Temple to have their claims tested. If their genealogies were found correct, they then underwent a physical examination; if they were found to be without blemish, they were accepted as priests and given a White Robe. If St. John has this in his mind, then the White Robe given to the martyrs is the recognition of their claim to priesthood; and this explanation is a very good one, because their White Robe then corresponds to the White Robe of their master the High Priest (see comments on xix. 12), and great force is added to the expression *made white in the Blood of the Lamb* which corresponds to the *dipped in Blood* of his own garments.

It will thus be seen that all that is most characteristic in this vision is based upon the ceremonial of the Hebrew Temple; yet it is linked with the very latest and most un-Jewish strata of the poem by the Throne, by the Elders, by the Four Living Things, and by its simple lyrical tone. It also anticipates the conclusion of the poem; it reads, in fact, like an alternative draft for that conclusion: for it uses that transparent imagery in which the meaning shines through with a clarity like plain white light.

These are they that have come through great tribulation
   And washed their Robes,
And Whitened them in the Blood of the Lamb.
They shall hunger no more . . .
The sun shall not smite them . . .
The Lamb . . . *shall lead them by the Wells of the Water of life,*
And God shall wipe away every tear from their eyes.

NOTE. ORIGINAL POSITION OF THIS PASSAGE

1. This passage is unquestionably in its wrong place; many reasons may be given for this. (*a*) The Hundred and Forty-four Thousand, though Judaistically conceived, are meant to include all the elect, gentile as well as Jew; they reappear in xiv. 1 without any reference to the vision of the Great Multitude. When xiv. 1 was written, this interpolation did not stand here. (*b*) The style belongs to a later period; the Throne, Elders, and Living Things link it with the last visions. (*c*) It is obviously anticipatory or " proleptic," as Dr. Charles calls it. The martyrs are now specifically Christian martyrs who have washed their Robes . . . in the Blood of the Lamb. (*d*) They have passed through "the Great Tribulation"; the use of the definite article implies that this is some well-known universal crisis, which so far has not occurred. (*e*) The Feast of Succoth was the last festival of the whole year; this passage, which is based upon it, is a grand finale to a history which has included a colossal persecution.

2. In character it is perplexing because it is double. On the surface it belongs to the later universalist period of the P visions; as I have pointed out, the Throne, the Elders, the Living Things, and the style generally make sure of this.

Underneath, however, we have detected a reliance upon the ceremonial of the Jewish Temple; we have: (*a*) copious use for so short a passage of the ceremonial of Succoth; (*b*) an actual use of the word Naos or Temple (*i.e.* the building which enshrined the Holy Place and Holy of Holies).

The last point is important; for while in other respects this reads like another draft for the conclusion of the book, we have here a contradiction. At this point (vii. 15) *They serve him day and night in his Naos*, and at the end (xxi. 22) *I saw no Naos in it; for the Lord God ALMIGHTY is the Naos of it*, and further (xxi. 25) *There is no night* there. Here, then, lies the difference between this draft conclusion and the actual conclusion in xxi. and xxii. This preserves the notion of a Temple; that does not.

3. The natural deduction is that a passage originally intended as the climax of the book was not used for that purpose, but worked over, and placed here. Originally it conceived the bliss of the redeemed under the symbolism of the Feast of Tabernacles as celebrated in the Temple; the passage was worked over in the later period, and what was specifically Jewish removed. It now bears the marks of the later period, and is linked to the Patmos visions and the symbolism of the universal worship of mankind.

4. The Revelation can be easily divided into two strata, an earlier (J) series of visions seen in Jerusalem, and a later (P) series of visions seen in Patmos. The present conclusion belongs to the later (P) series, and depicts a universal worship for all mankind, not tied to a local Temple or a hereditary priesthood; Jewish liturgical symbolism is strictly excluded. The J series, on the other hand, forms the body of the poem, but now has neither beginning nor end; its symbolism is based throughout on the ceremonial of the Temple (see Appendix I) and the structure of the prophet Ezekiel. In these visions a Naos or Temple is of great importance, as I shall show in the next chapter; it is announced in xi. 1; it appears in heaven in xi. 19; it is filled with the divine Glory in xv. 8; out of it comes the Voice of God (xvi. 1), and the Angels with the Last Plagues (xv. 6); but when the earthly

THIS AGE 145

Temple is destroyed with the fall of Babylon, we hear no more of the heavenly one either.

It is not unlikely, as I shall suggest in the next Book, that the J document ended with the descent of the heavenly Naos on Mount Sion; in xiv. 1 we have the Lamb and the Hundred and Forty-four Thousand assembled on Mount Sion as priests, but they are left there; nothing happens to them. And iii. 12 and vii. 12 both seem to anticipate the establishment of a Naos as the consummation of the poem.

5. Even as it stands *Revelation* has a double conclusion: (*a*) xxi. 1 to 8 begins, *And I saw a new heaven and a new earth . . . and the Holy City, New Jerusalem I saw coming down out of heaven;* in verse 8 it comes to a natural conclusion. (*b*) The new conclusion begins with xxi. 9, *And there came one of the Seven Angels . . . saying, Hither: I will show thee the Wife of the Lamb . . . and he showed me the City, the Holy Jerusalem, coming down out of heaven;* this vision comes to an end in xxii. 5. This second and longer conclusion belongs to the later (P) visions, and excludes liturgical symbolism; but in the first (and shorter) conclusion the liturgical symbolism can just be detected, exactly as it can in the passage we have been considering.

Behold the Tabernacle of God is with men :
And he shall Tabernacle with them.
And they shall be his People :
And he . . . shall be their God.

This is quoted from *Leviticus,* so that the divine order is regarded as a consummation of priestly hopes; it is linked to a reference, not to the Naos, it is true, but to the Tabernacle, which is a Naos not tied down to a locality.

6. My suggestion is, therefore, that the passage we have been considering is part of the conclusion of the original J document which ended with the establishment of a heavenly Naos, and symbolised the joyful consummation of the ages as a heavenly Feast of Tabernacles. What was symbolised was, of course, the substitution of a human universal worship (*a Temple not made with hands*) for a local and national one; but the old Levitical ceremonial of the Temple was used to symbolise it. Later, in the Patmos period, the new conclusion, with the Holy City as its main feature, took the place of the old ending with the Temple as its main feature. Traces of the old ending remain, however, in vii. 9 to 17 and xxi. 1 to 8, and possibly in xiv. 1 to 5.

Note.—It is very odd indeed that Ezekiel uses the same passage out of *Leviticus* in xxxvi. 27 in the description of the New Jerusalem which is the climax of his book; he also anticipates that climax by quoting it earlier in xi. 14.

Subjective and uncertain as such reconstructions are, I here subjoin a suggestion as to how such an ending might have run.

The Noble Army of Martyrs. (Conceived as Priests.)

And I Saw and behold the Lamb upon the Mount Sion, and with him the Hundred and Forty and Four Thousand, with his Name and the Name of his Father written upon their Foreheads. And I heard a Voice out of Heaven as the Voice of Many Waters and as the Voice of Great Thunder; and the Voice which I heard was like that of Harpers harping upon their Harps; and they sing a New Song; and nobody can learn the Song except the Hundred and Forty and Four Thousand, who have been redeemed from the earth.

K

These are they which were not defiled with women; for they are Virgin.
These are they which follow the Lamb wherever he goeth.
These are they which have been Redeemed from among men: for they are a Sacrifice to God and to the Lamb; and in their mouth was found nothing False; for they are without Blemish. (xiv. 1 to 5, omitting 3*b*.)

Descent of the Tabernacle (or Temple).

And the Tabernacle of Witness (or the Naos of the Tabernacle of Witness, cf. xv. 5) *I saw descending out of heaven from God,*

Or

And the Naos of God which is in Heaven I saw descending out of Heaven from God. (Based on xxi. 2.)

Here would have followed a description of the Naos, some of which would have been incorporated in the present description of the Holy City. It would have included a measurement of the Naos by the prophet (not the angel) (cf. *Rev.* xi. 1 and xxi. 16 and *Ezek.* 40, etc.). It would probably have included also the foursquare shape (*Rev.* xxi. 16 = *Ezek.* xlviii. 16) and the twelve gates according to the tribes of Israel (*Rev.* xxi. 12 = *Ezek.* xlviii. 30, etc.). We learn from *Rev.* iii. 12 that it would have included pillars.

> *And I heard a Great Voice out of the (Naos?) saying*
> *Behold the Tabernacle of God is with men,*
> *And he shall Tabernacle with them;*
> *And they shall be his People,*
> *And he (Emmanuel) shall be their God;*
> *And he shall wipe away every tear from their eyes;*
> *And death shall be no more.*
> *And mourning and weeping and pain shall be no more;*
> *For the first things have passed away.*

And he who sat upon the Throne (i.e. the Throne of the Judgment, xx. 11) *said, " Behold I am making everything new "; and he says, " Write: these are faithful and true words."*

And he said to me, " IT IS DONE. I am the Alpha and the Omega, the Beginning and the End. I will give to him who thirsteth of the Well of the Water of Life freely. He who overcometh shall inherit all things, and I shall be God to him, and he shall be a son to me.

But for the cowards and the faithless and the defiled and the murderers and the harlots and the magicians and the idolaters and all who are False: their portion shall be in the Lake that burns with Fire and Sulphur, which is the second Death " (xxi. 3 to 8).

Here perhaps would have come the descriptions of the Water of Life and the Tree of Life which are based on *Ezekiel* xlvii. (See also *Zech.* xiv. 8.) They are found at present in *Rev.* xxii. 1 to 2.

The Victorious Thanksgivings. (Feast of Tabernacles.)

After this I saw and behold a Great Multitude whom no man could number of every nation and tribes and peoples and tongues, standing before the . . . Lamb. clothed in White Robes and Palms in their hands, and they cry with a loud voice, " Hosanna to our God who sitteth upon the Throne and to the Lamb." (vii, 9 to 10.)

And one of the (Angels?) answered and said to me, " These who are clothed in White Robes, who are they? And whence came they?"

And I said, " Sir, thou knowest."
And he said unto me, " These are they who have come through the Great Tribulation, and have washed their Robes, and made them White in the Blood of the Lamb. Therefore are they before the Throne of God and worship him day and night in his Naos; and he who sitteth upon the Throne shall Tabernacle upon them.

> *They shall hunger no more and thirst no more;*
> *Nor shall the sun smite them nor any burning.*
> *For the Lamb that is amidst the Throne shall Shepherd them*
> *And guide them by the Wells of the Water of Life,*
> *And God shall wipe away every tear from their eyes."*

(vii. 13 to 17.)

Note.—I have ventured to restore the original Hosanna in verse 10 instead of the Greek paraphrase *Soteria* or Salvation. An original Alleluia has been similarly paraphrased in xix. 5.

I do not claim that this is a " restoration " of the text of the original J document. It is only an attempt to show how that document would have ended if vii. 9 to 17 does represent its original ending. Some such ending the document demands, and in xiv. 1 to 5, xxi. 1 to 8, and vii. 9 to 17, we find material that may once have belonged to it. In any case, they have been worked over to remove any strong Jewish colouring, and to fit them for the positions they now occupy.

BOOK IV
THIS AGE

PART II. THE SERPENT, SIN, AND THE THREAT OF DOOM

The Seven Trumpets.
   1-4. *The first Four : the Fall.*
   5-7. *The Three Woes :*
       5. *The Locusts from the Abyss.*
       6. *The Demonic Cavalry.*
(Parenthesis : *The Call of the Prophet to witness in Jerusalem.*)
        The Angel of Revelation.
        The Little Book.
        The Two Witnesses.)
       7. *Song of Triumph and Victory.*
        The approaching Doom.
The action of the Poem is broken off and the Great Interlude concerning the Saviour from Heaven and the Adversary from the Abyss follows.

THE DAY OF THE LORD

The Day of the Lord is at hand, at hand :
  Its storms roll up the sky :
The nations sleep starving on heaps of gold ;
  All dreamers toss and sigh ;
The night is darkest before the morn ;
When the pain is sorest the child is born,
  And the Day of the Lord is at hand.

Gather you, gather you, angels of God—
  Freedom and Mercy and Truth ;
Come ! for the Earth is grown coward and old,
  Come down and renew us her youth.
Wisdom, Self-Sacrifice, Daring, and Love,
Haste to the battle-field, stoop from above,
  To the Day of the Lord at hand.

Gather you, gather you, hounds of hell—
  Famine, and Plague, and War ;
Idleness, Bigotry, Cant, and Misrule,
  Gather and fall in the snare !
Hireling and Mammonite, Bigot and Knave
Crawl to the battlefield, sneak to your grave,
  In the Day of the Lord at hand.

Who would sit down and sigh for a lost age of gold,
  While the Lord of all ages is here ?
True hearts will leap up at the trumpet of God,
  And those who can suffer, can dare.
Each old age of gold was an iron age too,
And the meekest of saints may find stern work to do
  In the Day of the Lord at hand.

CHARLES KINGSLEY.

BOOK IV
THIS AGE

PART II. THE SERPENT, SIN, AND THE THREAT OF DOOM

ARGUMENT

AFTER a pause the prayers of the saints are answered. The Seven Trumpets begin to sound.

The first Four Trumpets show the principle of evil as the Fall of something originally high and heavenly; this Fall opens up the Abyss which is the source of everything contrary to God. The Fifth shows that out of the Abyss there rises in the heart a cloud of dominating, fascinating, and yet destroying passions. The Sixth shows the enormous and universal destroying power of sin, so that it brings with it its own ruin.

A parenthesis now shows the intervention of God through his aggressive Word, in prophecy, in the Gospel, and in the call of St. John himself to be a prophet. He proceeds at once to his task, which is to prophesy against Jerusalem, where God's witness has always been strongest, and always consistently persecuted.

It has now become clear that the Judgment is to be directed not so much against heathen persecuting empires, as against the corrupt religion of the true God, Jerusalem which is still unrepentant in spite of warnings in the past.

The Seventh Trumpet sounds, and the Glory of God's presence leaves the temple.

The Seven Trumpets.

After the opening of the Seventh Seal there is Silence in heaven for half an hour, and this is followed by the offering of Incense and the sounding of the Seven Trumpets.

The Trumpet is first found in the Old Testament story of the descent of God upon Mount Sinai and the giving of the Law. This is what theologians call a theophany, or visible manifestation of the glory of God; there were fire and thunder and lightning and smoke and the continual pealing of the Trumpet.

In war the Trumpet was used to sound an alarm. The watchman on the wall or tower blew the trumpet when he saw the enemy; and the prophet was set for a watchman over Israel.

At the long blast of the Trumpet the walls of Jericho fell flat; and the Seven Trumpets of the *Revelation* are also a prelude to the fall of a great city. Seven priests with Seven Trumpets encircled Jericho seven times before that long blast.

It was part of the popular expectation of the Jews that on the Judgment Day the great Reveille for the dead would be sounded by the Angel Michael, and in one case at least he is said to give a sevenfold blast. This use of the Trumpet is not, however, to be found in the apocalyptic of Jesus as handed down in either Q or *Mark*, though the church early adopted it; for it is to be found in 1 *Thessalonians*, and "Matthew" has added it to Mark's Little Apocalypse (chapter xiii.).

The force of the symbolism in *Revelation* seems to depend mostly on the Old Testament precedents. The Seven Trumpets represent the prophetic warnings all down the ages; they lead up to the fall of the great city, Babylon.

The Temple Worship.

As already pointed out, our earlier system of visions, which we have called J, is fitted into a liturgical framework which is based upon the ceremonial of the Jewish Temple. I have worked this out more fully in Appendix I, so I may content myself here with pointing out that the liturgical action now begins. So far we have been presented with the Altar with its Four Horns which corresponds to the great square stone Altar of the Jerusalem Temple built in the open air in front of the Naos or holy house. We have had no Naos; that is to appear when the Seven Trumpets have been sounded.

(Chapters iv. and v., which describe the universal worship of the Lamb, are based on the furniture of the Naos as it existed in the time of Solomon; chapter vii. contains an anticipatory vision of the *triumphant* worship of the martyrs "in the Naos"; but both these belong to the later stratum P.)

The sounding of Trumpets was an important feature of the Temple service. At daybreak the Trumpet sounded three times, and as it sounded the Lamb of the burnt offering was killed and its Blood splashed on the Altar, while the great gates of the temple were opened. We have already had the Lamb as it had been slain for sacrifice; and we have already had the Altar with the Blood of the Innocent Dead at the foot of it. We have now a series of Seven Trumpets (chapters viii. to xi.), and the opening of the Naos (xi. 19); but at present the Angels who hold them are only preparing to sound.

Meanwhile the Incense is offered. This came at a later stage in the daily ceremonial, though on the Day of Atonement it was more nearly at this point. It was followed by a period of Silence, prostration, and intercessory prayer; but St. John has placed the Silence earlier.

The Incense offering signified the presenting of the prayers of the faithful before God; yet even before this presentation the answer is ready; the Seven Angels are preparing to sound. The prayer is a prayer for vengeance on the blood which has been spilt upon the land; the Seven Trumpets represent the long course of prophetic warnings given by God all through the history of Israel down to and including St. John himself. At the conclusion of the Seven Trumpets the time comes for final judgment, and the Naos of the new Covenant is opened to all mankind.

Let us now follow the text.

The Incense.

Another Angel came and took up his stand by the Altar with a Golden Censer. He is the Angel of Prayer. Just as the

Seven are given Trumpets, so *he is given much Incense* and the great Cloud of it going up from his hand represents the prayers of the saints. At last those prayers reach the Throne of God; at last they are to be answered. I have pointed out before that the great difficulty in fixing the meaning of an Angel lies in the fact that he represents a process. The process of prayer is communion between God and man; the Angel symbolises that process; he may therefore be viewed either as an activity of God, or as an activity of man, or as both. Through him the prayers of the faithful go up to the Throne; through him comes the answer.

The answer is presented in a dramatic manner. The censer itself, its smoking incense and its glowing coals, is thrown into the earth, and there follow Thunders and Voices and Lightnings and Earthquake, symbols of the power and presence of God. This symbolism is borrowed from the same section of *Ezekiel* as describes the sealing of the elect, and shows how in the Apocalypse the two visions are continuous and belong to one stratum (J).

The Altar, we must remember, symbolises the martyrs or innocent dead, so that it is in response to their intercession that God intervenes. The prayers of the faithful, especially of the faithful dead, do hasten the judgment; as our Lord said, *How much more shall he not avenge his own elect which cry to him day and night?* (*Luke* xviii. 7).

This parallelism with the prophecies of Jesus and the dependence on the symbolism of Ezekiel show that the doom of Jerusalem is still in St. John's mind.

The First Four Trumpets.

The first Four Trumpets, like the first Four Seals, compose a unit. Dr. Charles thinks the last three Trumpets may have been originally a little apocalypse of their own called the Three Woes, and these four devised to fill out the number Seven and link the Three Woes with what goes before. Under cover of the Seven Trumpets a further set of visions is worked in, so that we are still a long way from the culmination of the J series of visions.

Each of the Four Trumpets brings disaster upon a different element:

    1. The earth.
    2. The sea.
    3. The rivers.
    4. The sky.

The style is very conventional and monotonous; but there is one point to be noted: the judgment in each case covers only one-third of the element, and of the living creatures that inhabit it. The meaning is obvious. Judgments in the past have been only partial. They have not met the whole case, or anything like it.

It had better be repeated that the physical structure of the universe symbolises the political and social structure of mankind, and that there is no reason to suppose that the seer's vision goes beyond Palestine.

On further studying these partial judgments which have taken place in the past, we are struck with an odd and original point in a series which is otherwise so conventional. The judgments are linked one with another by a series of "falls." After the First Trumpet a third of the earth is burned up with hail and fire and blood which fall from heaven; the symbolism suggests both Sodom and Egypt. After the Second the sea is turned into blood by a great Burning Mountain which falls from the land, which had in its turn been set on fire from heaven. But after the Third *there fell out of heaven a great Star, burning like a torch: and the name of the Star is called Wormwood, and a third of the Waters became Wormwood.*

We have, therefore, a series of three "falls" which we might not have inquired into closely but for the luminous and picturesque language of the Third. It seems to be a new form of the myth of the Fallen Angels, which we shall deal with shortly; and if so, that proves we are dealing with moral and spiritual catastrophes, one leading to another. If the fall of the Star signifies the Fall of the Angels (and in *Enoch* it does) or the introduction of sin into human life, then the whole imagery of the Four Trumpets will apply to political and social catastrophe arising out of sin. In this case they will correspond much more closely to the first Four Seals which symbolise the progress of human society to ruin and destruction. There, however, it is the outward progress that is traced in conquest and war and death; here it is the inward and psychological development, the fall from righteousness which occasions all that.

Except for the darkening of the sun and moon which is a familiar figure in prophecy, and signifies that complete eclipse of nations to which the first three stages lead, the symbolism seems to be drawn from the plagues of Egypt, narrated in *Exodus*. The symbolism of the Star Wormwood may be drawn from the episode at a place called Mara (Bitter), where the only water was too bitter to drink; at the command of Moses palm trees were thrown into the water and it was sweetened. Here we have the reverse; the sweet and healing waters of earth are made bitter by admixture with Wormwood. The Fallen Star is a kind of Anti-Moses; just as the law of righteousness entered into the world through Moses, so sin entered into the world through the Star. Sin embittered the sweet waters; justice restored them. *There*, says *Exodus, he gave judgments and ordinances*. The passage in *Exodus* itself seems to have been worked over by its priestly author so as to give it a symbolic meaning.

If this is correct, the Burning Mountain of the Second Seal may be the evil counterpart of Sinai, the burning mountain of God. Sin is opposition to law: Anomia (1 *Jn*. iii. 4).

The gap in the middle of the Seven Trumpets is even more marked than in the case of the Seals. The last three Trumpets were originally a vision by themselves called the Three Woes; even as it is, they are introduced in a very remarkable manner: *And I saw, and I heard One Eagle flying in Midheaven, saying with a loud voice,* WOE, WOE, WOE *to the inhabitants of the land because of the rest of the voices of the Trumpets of the Three Angels which are going to sound.*

The structure is as follows:

1. *The first Four Trumpets*, which show the trail of ruin in the world, due to sin. Perhaps they were originally a separate prophecy like the first Four Seals; and their Four Angels may have corresponded to the Four Living Things.
2. *The Three Woes*, which is linked to the above by the myth of the Fallen Star.
    (a) The Fifth Trumpet (= First Woe). The Swarm of Locusts.
    (b) The Sixth Trumpet (= Second Woe). The Demon Horsemen.
    (c) The Seventh Trumpet (= Third Woe). God's Kingdom is announced.

This is the structure of the book at this point; but just as in the case of the Seven Seals, there is an interpolation between the Sixth and Seventh; it is a longer one this time, and describes St. John's own call to prophesy, and his witness against Jerusalem. The background throughout is Palestinian, and I am therefore venturing to translate *Ge* as Land, not as Earth; this substitution makes all the difference in the world to the sense of the passage.

The Eagle.

It is difficult to give any particular interpretation to the Eagle, unless it represents Prophecy; it certainly suggests that bird's-eye view of world-history which we have seen to be characteristic of the prophets. Later Christian thought has found in it an excellent symbol for St. John himself, with his lofty flights of vision and his steady gaze into the depths of the infinite.

Heaven is not the circle of God and of the blessed, but simply the sky; the Eagle is seen high up in the air under the firmament, where it can see all things, and announce its message to the whole land. The symbolism is based on true observation; the eagle hovers, a mere dot in the empyrean; yet nothing escapes its all-seeing eye; *Where the carcase is, there the eagles are gathered together (Matt.* xxiv. 28 = *Luke* xvii. 37).

If the Eagle signifies prophecy, the Midheaven signifies the highest and most spiritual part of mankind.

The Fallen Angels.

The *First Woe* (or Fifth Trumpet Blast) is the introduction of sin into the world.

There are two Hebrew myths which attempt to give some account of the origin of evil, one tracing it to the disobedience of Man (Adam), the other to the disobedience of the Angels (the Watchers). The first myth is very familiar to us; it depicts Man as the servant of God, but lord of the world, free to pick and choose in it as he likes within certain limits. He is tempted—or, to be more accurate, Woman is tempted by the Serpent—to do what is known to be wrong. They both fall, and are driven out of Eden, which signifies the blessed state of happiness for which they were created.

Sin, therefore, entered into the world by Man's deliberate choice; he was tempted and disobeyed. Adam is merely a Hebrew word meaning Man; the woman is merely called Ishshah (the woman): the name Eve is given her later; the Serpent signifies the psychological fact of temptation.

It will be seen, therefore, that this myth sheds little light on the origin of evil. It is more in the nature of a study of the psychology of sin and temptation, asserting Man's responsibility for the sins he commits; but the human mind is bound to go on and ask the question, Whence came temptation? or, to put it symbolically, How came the Serpent into God's Eden? The myth of the Fallen Angels attempts an explanation.

This myth is almost unknown to-day; but in New Testament times it was as familiar as the story of Adam. It is the principal subject of the very popular *Book of Enoch*, and explains the introduction of evil into the world by the influence of evil spirits. These spirits were originally good angels; but they fell in love with women, left heaven, intermarried with the daughters of men, and taught mankind idolatry, superstition, and every moral evil. They are often identified with the heathen gods, a tradition which lasted till the time of Milton. The *Book of Enoch* contains several versions of this story with variations in names and places; its last literary expression is in *Paradise Lost*, which held a pseudo-canonical position in Protestant England, much as *Enoch* did in the gospel period.

The Old Testament knew the myth, but deliberately passed it over; it could not omit it altogether, but it is reduced in *Genesis* to a colourless summary. It has no advantages over the Adam myth; it tends to shift the responsibility for sin from Man the actual sinner; and it is no easier to say why God should have created angels who were capable of sinning than men.

The Fallen Star.

St. John's version of the Fall is singularly pure and unspeculative; we have already read it under the first Four Trumpets: it is the Fall of the Star.

Enoch applies the word Star to the Watchers, or Fallen Angels, just as Shakespeare does in the case of the peers who were involved in the Mary Queen of Scots conspiracy:

> *Certain stars shot madly from their spheres*
> *To hear the sea-maid's music.*

So, too, our international democracy of to-day bestows the same title on the fairest and noblest creatures which are permitted to dazzle its million eyes; it speaks in adoration of "film-stars."

In *St. John* there is only one Star, and there is no mythology. Whether the Star is an Angel or a man is not clear; according to apocalyptic conventions it might be either. The point is purposely left vague. Something made to be clear and high and shining and near to God fell from its lofty position. That is all.

No one can deny St. John an exuberant and powerful imagination. Nothing, therefore, is more remarkable than his austere restraint in this matter of the origin of evil. A Star fell; that is all he has to say. Some glorious being, endowed with noble ideals and the supreme gift of free will, used that free will amiss; it fell, and with its fall there came a trail of ruin for all mankind . . . a Third of it suffered, to use the symbolic figure.

Something is owed, no doubt, to the single line from *Isaiah, How art thou fallen from heaven, O Lucifer, Star of the Morning;* but this seems originally to have referred to the fall of Babylon.

The Key of the Abyss.

We now pass to the First Woe. *And the Fifth Angel sounded, and I saw the Star which had fallen upon the Earth, and there was given it the Key of the Pit of the Abyss.*

The Abyss is different from Hades, though often we find the two conceptions confused. Hades (hell) means the grave, the actual pit dug in the earth, and hence never means more than death or the abode of death. For instance,

*On this Rock I will build my Church,
And the gates of Death (Hades) shall not prevail against it*
(Mt. xvi. 18).

The Abyss is the bottomless void of infinite space, over which the earth was thought of as a floating disk like a flat lid. It is the ancient chaos and darkness with which, according to many mythologies, the Creator had to contend. It is conceived of as watery and shapeless, full of dragons and serpents, always restlessly moving, continually in rebellion against God. Contemporary Jewish thought was full of speculation upon it; it was the home of evil spirits, and in the miracle of the Gadarene demoniac the demons pray not to be sent there. Odd mythological sects like the Ophites brooded upon it, and built a whole mythology of fairy tales out of it; and these odd sects were ultimately to give birth to the Gnostic heresies.

In *St. John* the Abyss only ever means one thing: it means the depths of sin and wickedness, the home and origin of all evil.

To the Fallen Star was given the *Key of the Pit of the Abyss.* The Pit is simply a hole dug in the earth, a shaft sunk down until it communicates with that bottomless chaos of nameless horrors which coil and seethe below the solid earth. The Star opens this Pit, *and there came up out of the Pit Smoke like the Smoke of a great furnace, darkening the sun and the air. And out of the smoke came Locusts upon the earth, and authority was given them as the Scorpions of the earth have power.*

The first fall, therefore, lets loose upon the earth the whole horror of sin and all the destruction it brings with it.

The Demon Locusts.

The swarm of locusts is suggested by the prophecies of Joel, which dominate the thought of this chapter. In *Joel* we find:

1. A swarm of locusts *has* devastated the land: it is a judgment of Jehovah.
2. A swarm of soldiers, innumerable like the locusts, *will* devastate the land.

Similarly in *St. John* we find two stages, which are a little harder to distinguish:

1. A swarm of locusts which represents sin in all its destructive force,
2. An army of locust-soldiers which represents the consequences of sin.

The distinction is difficult, because, of course, sin itself is its own destructive consequences.

Unfortunately a majority of commentators, in defiance of common sense or any other restraining mental force, such as imagination or humour, take these avenging forces to be the armies of Parthia raiding the Roman Empire. A hundred reasons forbid it. We have not yet got to the future; we are still in a stage before the call of the prophet. It is out of place, absurd, and inadequate.

Others seem to think that St. John is dully and scientifically describing monsters which he thinks have a physical existence somewhere, and that one day he expected to wake up and see them cantering down from the North-East. The plain, straightforward meaning of the words forbids these appalling theories.

L

The Scorpion-Locusts were never intended by John to come under the department of entomology; they are invisible things; they do not belong to the insect, but to the spirit world. *They had no power to hurt the grass or any green thing or any tree :* they are not actual physical locusts. *But only men ; and only such men as have not the Seal of God on their foreheads.* And even these they cannot kill, *but to torture them Five Months ; and their torture was like the torture of a Scorpion when he stings a man.*

The Locusts have no power over nature, but only over man; they do not even possess power over all men, but only over those who abandon themselves to sin. They are spiritual, therefore, and they confine their attentions to sinners; they can be nothing else but the next stage in the progress of sin, sin as a power in the human heart, sin welling up out of the abyss of the " subconscious " and spreading over the soul, sin with its torture and degradation.

The spiritual nature of the Locusts is still more convincingly proved by their appearance, which is compared to

> *Horses apparelled for war*
> *on their heads Crowns of Gold*
> *their faces like the faces of Men*
> *Hair like the Hair of Women,*
> *Teeth like Lion's Teeth.*

Eloquent theological entomologists have endeavoured to prove that the locust of Palestine is exactly like that, and I am not entirely incredulous; I think it possible that at the back of his mind the prophet still had the actual locust in view; but the force of the passage is symbolic. Many of these are exactly the forms in which temptation expresses itself; the War Horse and the Golden Crown recall the Four Riders and symbolise the lust of conquest; the Faces of Men and the Hair of Women would suggest the fascination of sex; the Lion's Teeth preserve the demonic character of the whole picture.

When sin enters the imagination in the initial form of temptation, it naturally has to be tempting; it must present itself in attractive form, the golden gleam of ambition, or what counts in the world for love; but the Sting of it comes after; it is in its tail. *They have Tails like Scorpions, and Stings ; and in their Tails is their power to hurt men Five Months. And they have over them as King, the Angel of the Abyss ; his name in Hebrew Abaddon, and in Greek Apollyon,* or in English Destruction.

The Angel of the Abyss.

The difficulties of fitting together a symbolic system are very great. We need some figure to symbolise evil in itself, and we want it to arise like the Locusts out of the Abyss; but we cannot do that because we have so recently seen it fall from heaven, and open the Pit of the Abyss. So it is introduced cunningly and silently without a word as to his origin, and thus two inconsistent symbols are unobtrusively welded together; he appears two chapters later as *the Beast which arises out of the Abyss.*

The word Abaddon is simply a Hebrew word meaning Destruction; but in the Wisdom literature it appears to go along with Death, and to signify Hell, either the grave or, as here, the Abyss, or possibly a conception which is intermediate between the two. It is as clear as daylight, therefore, that we are already introduced to the Devil and his Angels, of whom we shall hear more later, and that the Locusts represent the forces of evil: sin and temptation in every form in which they attract and afflict mankind; and in the name of their chief is summed up their whole work and nature, the Ruin and Destruction of mankind.

Doctrine of Sin.

How clear becomes the parallel with the first series of Seven, which outlines the outward progress of history and the domination of the innocent poor by the ruthless strong. Here we have the inward history, origin, and motive of that outward progress. An inward spiritual thing explains everything: Sin.

It is the familiar myth which is enshrined in stories so simple as Bluebeard and Cinderella. Adam and Eve touch the forbidden tree, and all Eden is lost. Pandora opens the forbidden box, and all evils fly out. The curses and afflictions of mankind are all consequences of that original act of treachery which first let disobedience into creation. Such are the forces let loose in every human soul, when it yields to sin and lets the imagination dwell on the fair images it presents. In each soul the history of the race is repeated.

The doctrine is characteristic of Christianity as a whole; but surely an echo of this actual symbolism is found in St. James' Epistle, a Palestinian document. Chapter iv., which deals with temptation, begins, *Whence are wars, and whence are fightings among you? Is not this their origin, from sensual delights which make war in your members?* The word for "making war" (strateuomenon) suggests a whole army in array. In i. 13 we read: *Let no one who is being tempted say, I am tempted of God. . . . Every man is tempted by his own lust, being dragged away and enticed; then lust conceives, and brings sin to birth, and sin, when it is fully developed, generates death.* The whole process is summed up by St. Paul in a single epigram, *The wages of sin is death.*

Some ingenuity has been expended by scholars, who, realising that the background of these visions is Palestinian, have sought to localise the Pit of the Abyss. The question is unnecessary. We all have a key to the Abyss, and no commentator need look far to find the door. It would be fashionable, I suppose, to call it the sub-conscious mind; but by any name it smells as bad, and is the same reality to-day, as in the days when St. John prophesied. It is that bottomless sea in all our souls, from the great deep of which do arise monstrous and amazing suggestions of evil; from which arose every crime, and before it was committed looked good in the eyes of some human being. *For from within, out of the heart of men, do all evil arguments proceed, adulteries, thefts, murders, harlotries, covetings, evil living, guile, lasciviousness, envy, insults, arrogance, folly . . . all these originate from within,* says our Lord Jesus (Mk. vii. 21).

The Devastation of Sin.
 The First Woe is gone; behold there come still two Woes after this. And the Sixth Angel sounded; and I heard a voice out of the

Four Horns of the Golden Altar which is before God, saying ... Loose the Four Angels who are bound by the Great River Euphrates.

The River Euphrates has led astray many commentators who are anxious, as has been stated above, to turn these Four Angels into Parthian kings; Parthian kings are to some writers on the Apocalypse what King Charles' head was to Mr. Dick.

We have had these Four Angels before; they are the agents of vengeance and destruction, and they are connected with the Four Living Things of the P. visions. Here we find them connected with the Four Horns of the Altar, which correspond to the Four Living Things. The stages are:

1. *P. visions* (Throne)
    Four Living Things   control   Four Horses.
2. *Intermediate stage*
    Four Angels   control   Four Winds.
3. *Here: J visions* (Altar)
    Four Horns   control   Four Angels.

The symbols in the first column represent the natural laws or forces in the world which control the destroying agencies in the second column; the intermediate stage probably represents an easy transition from one set of visions to the other, as in the case of the Beast arising out of the Abyss.

In the intermediate stage we saw that the destroying agencies were being restrained while the servants of God were being Sealed and their number completed; we have seen since that the Seal protects them from the Locusts which signify temptation. In the Intermediate stage the Four Angels stood at the *Four Corners of the Earth*, restraining the Four Winds; why do we now find the Four Angels, which now signify destroying not restraining forces, bound by the Great River Euphrates?

The River Euphrates was the scene of Israel's captivity six hundred years before. From the River Euphrates had come Sennacherib and Nebuchadrezzar, destroyers of Samaria and Jerusalem; by now the Euphrates has become a mere symbol for the quarter from which judgment is to come on Jerusalem. Dr. Charles has shown how well-known apocalyptic symbols, when introduced by St. John for the first time, always have the definite article; he also notes that geographical names do not. Now the Great River Euphrates *has* the definite article, and so Dr. Charles puts it down as the one strange exception to the latter rule; it does not seem to occur to him that it is an example of the first rule. It is a well-known symbol introduced for the first time.

The words themselves are taken from *Genesis*, and until we can track down St. John's use of the *Genesis* symbolism, we shall not quite understand this passage, nor, for that matter, one or two others. It has something in common, as we shall see later, with the notions of the Jewish Serpent-worshipping sect, from which sprang the Ophites and other Gnostic Christians, including Justinus, from whom I have quoted. Now Euphrates is the first and largest of the four branches of the river that watered Eden, and we have seen that Justinus regarded these four as bands of destroying angels. Also, in the original Hebrew, the Tree of Life is actually the Tree of Lives (plural), 'Etz Hayyim, and might mean, Tree of the Living Things; somewhere here, I think, lies the solution. From the Tree of the Living Things flows the Fourfold Destroying River.

The Demonic Cavalry.

All is predestined. The hostile army is ready to go over the top at the exact *hour, day, month, and year*. In his vision St. John heard the army of vengeance numbering, and it comes to the incalculable number of Daniel, *myriads of myriads, ten thousand times ten thousand*, and that twice over (200,000,000) it means nothing but countless, complete, colossal, overwhelming numbers.

The picture of the demonic cavalry is one of the most vivid and gruesome things in the Apocalypse. Their breastplates are fiery-red, smoke-blue, and sulphur-yellow; the heads of their horses are like lions and breathe out of their mouth fire and smoke and fumes of sulphur. They not only kill with their heads, but, like the Locusts of the first Woe, with their Tails; their Tails were not like Scorpion

Stings, however, but like live Snakes with heads and power to hurt.

It is an absurdity to pretend that this ghastly creation of the imagination represents any human empire; it is the empire of hell. The first Woe symbolised the growth of sin in the heart; here we have it sweeping the whole world. First we had its insidious attack upon the soul, and the sting that it brings with it; now we have it gathering body to itself, incarnating itself, raging through the earth like a destructive fire. Under those even laws of God, Man brings in sin, and sin brings in its own destructive vengeance upon Man. John is not afraid of the Parthian or the Roman; he is afraid that the whole of Man's civilisation may crash, because he has allowed himself to be ridden by his sins. Now he knows why the great empires, after rising to such heights, crashed to ruin. The only real conqueror is Apollyon, and his invisible army of destroyers; and he is chasing Man to ruin and the Bottomless Pit. Thus he explains the judgments of the past. He that takes the sword perishes by the sword; sin itself has ridden and ruled and ruined the sinner. And yet he maintains his faith in the just government of the world; looking up, he sees the operation of those great four-square laws which condition the history of Man; *they were prepared for that hour and day and month and year to kill the Third part of mankind.*

But mankind is not only sinful; it is blind and foolish. It continues to play with the destructive thing. *And the rest of mankind who were not killed by the plagues did not repent of the works of their hands, not to worship Daimons and the Idols of gold and silver and bronze and stone and wood . . . neither did they repent of their murders or their witchcraft or their adulteries or their thefts.* Man never learns.

So ends St. John's recasting of the vision of Joel, and a powerful thing he has made of it. Joel's vision, like the visions of Ezekiel, which St. John has used as a framework before, was directed against Jerusalem; but St. John, though he has had Jerusalem in mind all along, has not been thinking exclusively of her. His thought is that judgments have fallen in old times upon the nations that forgot

God; judgments have fallen on Jerusalem because she forsook Jehovah and worshipped the idols of silver and gold; and he sees just how and why those judgments fall as they do. Sin is itself the executioner; and though it appears to be lawless, it is controlled by those inscrutable four-square laws, so that in rebelling against God it is overruled to serve his purpose, and bring vengeance upon itself.

He must now go on to develop the main thesis of his book—that such a judgment is about to fall upon Jerusalem. And so we step from the past into the present, meaning by the present the near past, the events of St. John's own lifetime.

The Angel of Revelation.

After the Sixth Seal there was a digression before we came to the last of the series; after the Sixth Trumpet (or Second Woe) we find an even longer digression. It is necessary because St. John must give reasons why he should be in a position to add to the revelations of the past, to indicate the time for the fulfilment of all prophecies and the destruction of Jerusalem; he must narrate his call to prophesy. We have now reached the very earliest of all his visions; but we find it in its logical place.

At the moment of deepest depression and gloom comes the radiant vision of a *Strong Angel descending out of Heaven, arrayed in a Cloud, and the Rainbow about his Head, and his Face like the Sun, and his Legs like Pillars of Fire.* The Cloud is always a symbol of the presence of God; the Rainbow was round the Throne; it was the Face of the divine Christ that shone like the Sun, and the Pillars of Fire blazoned the Presence of Jehovah with his people in the wilderness. Why the critics who want the Woman of chapter xii. to be a Sun Goddess do not make this figure a Sun God I do not know.

The chapter is based on *Ezekiel* again. Ezekiel's call came through such a figure, which represented the " Word of God " which came to the older prophets; the same figure is found in a more developed form in *Daniel*. In both cases it represents divine inspiration. Here it covers a whole process of revelation which can be divided into four stages:

1. The Hebrew Prophets.
2. The Incarnation of the Son of God.
3. The Preaching of the Gospel throughout the World.
4. The Inspiration of the Christian Prophets by the Holy Spirit.

St. John does not distinguish between Christ's own work and witness on earth, and the same work and witness carried on by the saints in his Name, and under the direction of the Holy Ghost. It is all one process, beginning in Galilee and spreading through the whole world: in short the Gospel of Christ.

The Angel has a message to the whole world. *He put his right foot on the Sea, and his left foot on the Land, and cried out with a loud voice like a lion roaring.* This amazingly vivid verse recalls the line out of our Lord's own Apocalypse, *But first must the Gospel be proclaimed to all the gentiles* (*Mk.* xiii. 10). The Gospel, foreshadowed in the prophets and first proclaimed in Galilee, now reverberates through the world; and behind it *the Seven Thunders utter their Voices*, the Holy Spirit, confirming the Gospel as it goes triumphantly on.

Utterances Unutterable.
And when the Seven Thunders spoke, I was about to write, but I heard a Voice out of Heaven saying, Seal up what the Seven Thunders spoke, and do not write it.

The parallels to this in the other New Testament passages are too numerous to mention. In the epistles we constantly hear of the Gospel and Spirit as a pair, the Spirit confirming the Gospel, so that the faith comes *not in word only, but in power and in the Holy Ghost and in much fulfilment* (1 *Thess.* i. 5). Then there is the written Gospel which announces at the beginning that Jesus is to baptise in Holy Spirit, and says nothing more about it. The Gospel material is a fit and proper subject for writing, but the

Spirit is not. The Spirit confirms, and no doubt explains the Gospel, but cannot itself be explained or expressed; it tends to express itself in "tongues" and non-rational forms. Jesus is Logos, Word, matter for speech; the Spirit is mystery: it is not Word.

There is an interesting parallel adduced by St. Paul under the heading of Visions and Apocalypses. He says, *I knew a man in Christ fourteen years ago, whether in the body I do not know, and whether out of the body I do not know (God knows) who was caught up to the Third Heaven. And I know that Such-a-one, whether in the body or out of the body, I do not know (God knows) was caught up into the Paradise, and heard unspeakable words which it is not permitted to utter. About Such-a-one I will boast; but about myself I will not boast, except in my weakness* (2 Cor. xii. 2 ff.).

Despite the tradition among scholars, this visionary cannot be St. Paul himself; and it is unlikely that it is St. John, because in the Apocalypse the Angel comes down to earth as in *Ezekiel* and *Daniel;* St. Paul's seer also accepts the apocalyptic system of seven heavens, which St. John does not use. Yet there is the important parallel of the Unutterable Utterances (Arreta Remata).

Date of the Vision.

If the fourteen years is accurate, St. Paul's visionary had his mystical experience about A.D. 41; but we cannot be sure, because the figures are round numbers (two sevens), and fourteen is a figure which seems to come readily to his mind. It may be two years more or less. In any case it is very important, because it lands us in the period just before the martyrdom of St. James the brother of St. John (A.D. 44) during the reign of Herod, and just succeeding the attempt of Caligula to have his image worshipped in the temple. The gospel had begun to reach the gentiles; Cornelius had been baptised at Cæsarea, and there were Christian communities at Damascus and Antioch. Prophets had come down from Jerusalem to Antioch, and St. Paul and St. Barnabas were making their collection to take to Jerusalem. It was perhaps 46 when they paid their visit.

Acts and St. Paul coincide, therefore, in giving this as the first period of Christian prophecy. Prophecy sent out St. Paul and St. Barnabas on their missionary journey in 48, and on his second journey St. Paul took with him Silas, who was a Jerusalem prophet; the influence of Jerusalem prophecy, through Silas, colours the Thessalonian epistles very strongly. We detect much that is characteristic of St. John—the " restraining force," for instance.

Caligula's pretensions had caused a ferment among the Jews; but there were pretensions of Herod too. It is hard to make out what they were, but both Josephus and St. Luke regard his death as a judgment. As a Jew and a strong patron of the national religion, he could not pretend to be a god-king; but he did claim to be messiah or angel or some other figure in the Jewish mythology. His pretext for putting St. James to death is not given, but there must have been one. You cannot put a man to death merely to please your constituency; you must assign reasons, and the most obvious reasons are the old ones alleged against our Lord and St. Stephen: prophesying against the temple. If this guess is true, St. John's call to prophesy may have had some definite connection with the martyrdom of his brother; he felt it his business to carry on the tradition.

Whether or not St. James was a prophet, whether or not he was the visionary friend of St. Paul; we have enough evidence between *Acts* and St. Paul to prove to us that the year or two before his death were years of prophetic ferment, and of persecution by Jewish authorities. This earliest Vision of *Revelation* well fits that period, when a great change was taking place in the minds of the original disciples; when the gospel was getting itself proclaimed to the gentiles almost as if it were a living thing; when St. Paul and St. Barnabas were given the right hand of fellowship, and even St. Peter began to travel abroad.

The Call of St. John took place under these circumstances:

1. The Gospel was spreading rapidly among the gentiles,
2. Persecution had broken out at Jerusalem, and his brother James had been beheaded.

Both thoughts were bound to create great upheavals in the minds of the Hebrew Christians; both are impressed on the *Revelation*, throughout its course.

A further point which has some interest here is the nickname *Sons of Thunder* given to the two brothers in St. Mark. The apostolic nicknames found in the Gospels were not necessarily bestowed in the gospel period; they may have been given later. One of them certainly was; this is the name Zealot which was not in use till some time after the crucifixion, and was given to the second Simon. *Sons of Thunder* may be no more contemporary with Jesus than *the father of Alexander and Rufus*, which is plainly an identification for the benefit of St. Mark's readers.

The original Aramaic form of this nickname, " Boanerges," is given by St. Mark, in a form so corrupt that it seems impossible to restore it; Boanerges seems to mean nothing, though various conjectures have been made. But *Sons of Thunder* is a recognised Greek equivalent, dating from a sufficiently early period. It may be that as in the case of St. Barnabas a punning re-interpretation of the name was made later on; and even if it is a misunderstanding of the original Aramaic (or Hebrew) original which gave rise to the form Boanerges, it is so early a misunderstanding as to be of great importance. It is peculiarly applicable to the prophet at whose call the *Seven Thunders* uttered their voice.

In conclusion there is a strange passage in the fourth gospel where our Lord is speaking with some Greeks in the temple, and a peal of thunder is taken by the by-standers as a voice from heaven. The passage is symbolic in tone and has four connections in thought with this:

1. The extension of the gospel to the Gentiles.
2. A last chance given to the Temple.
3. Thunder, regarded as an incomprehensible message from heaven.
4. The approaching Martyrdom of Our Lord.

The coincidences are far too complete to be accidental. I cannot help feeling myself that the simplest and easiest thing is to identify the John of Ephesus, who (at the very lowest critical estimate) inspired the Johannine writings, with St. John the son of Zebedee; but nothing in my book depends upon it. I am merely investigating its meaning as it stands.

What is demanded is that these earliest Visions were seen by a Hebrew Christian prophet in Jerusalem at an early date.

The Angel of Revelation. (See also p. 79.)

I have already pointed out the identity of this Angel with the Angel of Revelation who appeared to Ezekiel and Daniel; and a careful study shows that the account of St. John's call is based in detail on that of Ezekiel. The importance of this will appear later.

In both prophets the figure, though blazoned as an "independent" Angel, is divine, an energy of God, God himself in action, his divine Word inspiring the prophets from age to age.

St. John has followed Ezekiel in giving first the picture of the high God on his Throne, and later on his own call. Ezekiel saw in the Throne *the likeness of the appearance of a Man*, and I have already pointed out how Daniel turned this symbol into the much more separate and independent *Son of Man*. He probably also identifies the Son of Man with the Angel of Revelation; his name for the Angel of Revelation is Gabriel, and Gabriel means Man of God.

This figure is sharply distinguished in *Revelation* by its colossal size and its divine attributes; it corresponds to the Word-of-God, Man-of-God, or Son-of-Man group to be found in the heretical Hebrew speculations of the period. In them it is the sum of the male functions and attributes of God differentiated first into a single figure, and later into a chain of them; it is the primal Adam, according to whose image the earthy Adam was formed; it is the Second Man, son of the First Man, who is God. Over against him is the primal Eve, the sum of all the female attributes of God—Wisdom, Spirit, Life, and so forth; St. John has a figure corresponding to this in the colossal Woman standing on the Moon in chapter xii.

But St. John's figures are not used in the same sense as the mythological fancies of the forerunners of Gnostic heresy; he is writing to refute them. He returns to the Hebrew prophets, and starts from the great conceptions he finds there; he uses them to symbolise great processes and movements which are actually discernible in history.

This figure represents the whole process of God's Revelation. It is the Word of God which came to the prophets of old; it is the message which they gave the world with such remarkable continuity and purity; it is the gospel of Galilee in which it all culminated; it is the propagation of that gospel by Christian evangelists, and its enrichment and explanation by Christian prophets. It is the whole gradual evolutionary process now seen as complete. It is the Logos: the aggressive working of the divine.

The Angel . . . raised his Right Hand into Heaven and swore by the eternal creator *that there shall be no more time.* The three and a half " Times " of Daniel (xii. 7) are over.

It is the mark of the Christian primitive gospel wherever we find it. An end has been reached; a beginning lies before us. *The time is fulfilled; the Kingdom of God is at hand; repent and believe the Gospel,* is the message of our Lord in *St. Mark.* This is the same message with further elaboration: *In the days of the Blast of the Seventh Angel, whenever he sounds, the Mystery of God is fulfilled, according as he gave the Gospel to his servants the Prophets.* All they foresaw, all they foretold, all they groaned for, is on the point of coming true.

One function of all the Apocalypses was to explain or re-state the teachings of the prophets, especially those which had never been fulfilled. Daniel, for instance, gives a new interpretation to *Jeremiah*. Jeremiah had promised that seventy years after the exile Jerusalem would be restored, and a king like David would flourish there and subdue all his enemies. The restoration took place, and some of the Jews returned from Babylon; but there was no flourishing Messianic kingdom. Daniel explains this by counting the seventy years as seventy *Weeks of Years,* or four hundred and ninety in all.

This was only one of many similar re-interpretations; but as time went on, even the re-interpretations failed. The people waited, but there was no flourishing Messianic kingdom; they grew as sick of re-interpretations as of prophecies.

Now, says St. John, the Seventh Angel is about to sound; time is up; the last age of the world is to open, and every prophecy, however mysterious, will be fulfilled. This is the standpoint from which he dates all his Visions and prophecies; and that is why, even when he arranged and re-wrote them in the time of Domitian, he still proclaimed them as from this date, when he saw the doom of Jerusalem and the end of the old dispensation so clearly impending.

The Call of St. John.

He is bidden by the Voice from Heaven—that is, by the inspiration of the unseen God—to take the Book from the hand of the Angel, and the Angel tells him to eat it. It is *honey-sweet in the mouth*, but *bitter in the stomach*. Though the metaphor is a violent one its meaning is quite clear; prophetic vision is sweet, but the labour and agony of the prophet's work are bitter; and the content of the message itself is doom and woe.

In *Ezekiel* it is filled with *lamentations and mourning and woe* (ii. 10). *And they say unto me, You must prophecy again upon peoples and nations and languages and many kings*—a comprehensive command, but one which does describe the contents of our book.

The word *again* may mean that St. John has prophesied before; but it is probable the word ought not to be pressed. It is more likely that it represents some Hebrew particle (e.g. *gam*) which is more of an " also " or " even." The suggestion in it is, You are to re-open prophecy; you are to carry on the great process; the tradition is in your hands.

The prophesying against peoples and kings is based on the call of Jeremiah (though repeated in the case of Ezekiel); it refers to opposition and prejudice on the part of their own countrymen, the Jews.

The book in *Ezekiel* is inscribed within and without with woes and dooms which are to fall upon Jerusalem. The inference is that the same may be the case here, and the book may therefore refer specifically to the contents of the next chapter, though its general reference is to St. John's prophetic work as a whole.

The Measuring of Jerusalem.

St. John now goes on to the specific work to which he is called—the continuation of the witness of all the prophets against Jerusalem. This is his special commission; this is the work for which he receives authority in his call. That is why this Vision must belong to the Jerusalem period, and must be the work of the author of the whole book; he claims this Vision as his own. This, too, is why he needs a fresh call to prophesy to the Seven Churches of Asia; his original call was to witness in Jerusalem like most of the prophets before him.

He is given a Reed, an object commonly used for measuring buildings. It is stiff *as a Rod ;* it is an exact standard that will measure justly. He is to *Measure the Temple of God and the Altar and the Worshippers in it.*

We must now give some account of the Temple which is the scene of these earliest prophecies of St. John just as it is the scene of much of the preaching of Jesus and of the apostles.

There were three principal mountains on which Jerusalem stood:

1. The highest, Mount Zion, where the Upper City or City of David stood.
2. The next, Acra, "sustains the Lower City." The height of this hill was reduced by the Maccabeans, thus making it lower than the third hill on which the Temple stood. They also filled up the dividing valley.
3. The third, Moriah, on which the Temple stood.

Such is the statement of Josephus, and without entering into the controversies on the subject, we may safely assert:

1. The principal division of the city is the " Valley of the Cheesemongers " of Josephus, which divides the higher mountain (Zion) on the west from the other two on the east.

2. Josephus is wrong in supposing that this high western mountain was the Zion of David: it was uninhabited in his time. David's city on Mount Zion was identical with the Temple site.

No doubt, however, it was called the City of David in his day, as the palace of the Herods stood there.

3. The present " Haram," in which stands the " Mosque of Omar " or Dome of the Rock, marks the place where all the successive Jewish temples stood. Its walls (with some extensions) are the walls of Herod's Temple; the " Rock " is the original altar, probably much older than the time of David.

The whole of Jerusalem in the period of these visions was defended by a system of walls, some of which had been recently built to enclose the new suburb of Bezetha (New City), which was built on yet another hill north of Mount Moriah.

Imagine the city as a triangle, with its base to the north and its apex to the south. That apex is almost impregnable, for it is formed of the two deep ravines which made attack almost impossible; the Valley of Hinnom (Gehenna) on the west, the Valley of the Kidron on the east. Along these two sides of the triangle one wall was sufficient; the base of the triangle which faced the north was the dangerous quarter, and here there had been built a series of three parallel walls. It was natural therefore that in apocalyptic symbolism the north should be the quarter that symbolised danger.

Within the walls of the city, the Valley of the Cheesemongers, a shallower depression, separated the Upper City or Market Place, with Herod's Palace and fortifications upon it, from the eastern group of rather lower hills, on the southernmost of which was the Temple. The Temple itself was so solidly built as to form a fortress which might well defy attack; in fact it was in the Temple itself that the Zealots entrenched themselves against the Roman armies; and as God himself was believed to dwell there, they had no doubt of their security.

Let us now in imagination enter the Temple.

The top of the hill has been levelled until it forms a plateau rather under a quarter of a mile square. It is surrounded by massive walls, on the inside of which are cloisters upheld by rows of Corinthian columns; we enter by the "Royal Cloister," which runs the length of the south wall, and find ourselves in a spacious square called the Mountain of the House, though in modern books it is called the Court of the Gentiles. Here the palace of Solomon once stood; here Jesus cast out those who bought and sold animals for sacrifice, or transacted other business. In front of us, and towards the north of this court, rises a rectangular block of buildings in which stands the temple proper.

In the New Testament there are two words which are both unfortunately translated Temple. The word Hieron means the whole sacred enclosure in which the buildings stood; the word Naos means the holy house, the Sanctuary or Shrine in the midst of the buildings, where God was believed to dwell. As we advance, we pass from one enclosure to another, each more holy than the last.

We cross the quadrangle, turning to the right as we do so, so as to approach the sacred buildings from the east, which is the front. The Temple is built east and west like a modern church, only the sanctuary is at the west end, not the east. The front gate, therefore, faces the east. It is the greatest of the nine gateways, each with its massive two-storied tower over it. We pass through it and find ourselves in an open courtyard with a mosaic floor, and surrounded by a cloister; before us towers a magnificent gateway or arch.

This first court in which we now find ourselves is the Court of the Women, so called not because it was principally used by women, but because they could go no further. The gate by which we have entered it is probably that called the Beautiful Gate of the Temple (*Acts* iii. 12) and is made of Corinthian brass plated with gold and silver. This is where Jesus preached; and along the cloisters are the trumpet-shaped boxes (Corban) into which he saw the widow casting her two mites, which together make a farthing. It is the regular place for religious services, preaching, etc., and commands a splendid view of the Naos itself.

Exactly opposite us as we enter we see the gate of the innermost court of all. It has no doors; it is a great arch or doorway rising seventy cubits, says Josephus—that is, about fifty feet. It is covered with plates of gold, and through it appears the Naos or dwelling of God. "It had no doors," Josephus said, "for it symbolised the invisible and omnipresent character of the heavens" (*i.e.* of God). Perhaps St. John had this gate in mind when he wrote of the door opened in heaven in *Rev.* iv. 1. Over it was a golden eagle.

We ascend to this gate by fifteen steps, and pass through into the central enclosure, the Court of the Priests, in the centre of which was the Naos itself. A narrow strip was marked off round this court for the lay Israelites (male), a set number of whom must be present at every sacrifice. In front of the Naos in the open air was the great altar of unhewn stone built over the sacred Rock; it was square in shape, measuring fifty cubits (about thirty-four feet) each way, and at its corners were four horns. On the right of the altar were rings in the stone floor for tethering animals, and marble tables on which they were skinned and cut up. The place would present to us the appearance of a vast butcher's shop and abattoir combined. We must imagine the priests armed with knives and their white robes splashed with blood; joints of meat lying on the marble tables or hanging up, and on the huge altar the smoke of burning flesh perpetually rising before the holy house, and him who dwelt therein. Blood poured out and smoke ascending are the two principal thoughts of sacrifice; the killing of the animal is not the sacrifice.

The whole group of buildings which we have been considering is the Hieron or sacred enclosure; all round it there runs a low wall or balustrade on which at intervals are stones carved with an inscription which warns gentiles that if they enter it the Roman authorities will not be responsible for their lives. One such stone has been discovered. *Acts* xxi. gives us a vivid picture of what did happen when it was thought that St. Paul had brought a Greek into the sacred precincts.

The Naos or actual Sanctuary is the building which stands behind the Altar. What we see of it is a Porch or Cloister probably with pillars like those of an Egyptian temple, and over it a tower. It is of white marble plated with gold. Josephus says, "It was covered on all sides with heavy plates of gold, so that under the first rays of sunrise it reflected back a radiance like fire, and made those who forced themselves to look at it turn away their eyes as if from the beams of the sun; and to strangers who arrived from afar it shone like a mountain covered with snow, for wherever it was not covered with gold it was purest white."

The entrance of the Naos was covered by a veil, of which Josephus says, "It was a Babylonian curtain cunningly made of blue and fine linen and scarlet and purple, marvellously wrought, and the mingling of the material not without mystical significance, but as it were an image of the whole creation." He then explains how these signify the four elements earth, air, fire, and water, and the whole array of the heavens except the zodiac.

Over the door itself, which was also plated with gold, was carved a golden vine, "from which hung bunches of grapes the size of a man."

Through this door only the priests were allowed to pass. It led into the Holy Place, the central feature of which was the Golden Altar, where Incense was offered twice a day at the regular morning and evening Burnt Sacrifices. On the left was the Golden "Candlestick" or lamp-stand with seven branches, and on the right the Golden Table with the twelve cakes of "shewbread" laid there, symbolising the twelve tribes of Israel.

Beyond this lay the Holy of Holies or Most Holy Place, where God himself dwelt. It was hidden by a double veil, and there was nothing in it whatever except a stone on which the High Priest placed his censer when he entered there once a year on the Day of Atonement.

Let us now take the commission of St. John and consider it against this background. *And there was given me a Reed like a rod, saying, Arise and measure the Naos of God and the Altar and those who worship in it; and the Court which is outside the Naos, reject, and measure it not, because it has been given to the Gentiles; and they shall trample the Holy City Forty and Two Months.*

Let us get the actual symbolism clear before we study it. The Naos is the Sanctuary of God; the word Altar probably includes the whole space round it where the priests did their work in the presence of the faithful laity. That is the scope of the commission.

The Naos in Revelation.

This passage is one of the most complex in the whole of our study, and it is questionable whether a completely satisfactory explanation of it has been found.

In the first place we may ask whether St. John is speaking of the actual temple, or whether he is using the word Naos symbolically. In favour of a literal interpretation is the fact that this chapter quite certainly presupposes a Jerusalem background; and as we go on, we shall see that the main message of St. John has to do with the destruction of the Temple.

Then, too, it has been pointed out that the words fit a definite historical situation, that namely of the great siege by Titus, when the Temple was held by the nationalist party of the Zealots, while the Romans had gained possession of the outer court. It is suggested that we have here a fragment of Zealot prophecy in which an assurance is given that the faithful who hold the Naos and the Altar will be preserved, though the outer court is given to the gentiles, and the Holy City will be trampled down.

At first sight this seems very plausible; but the difficulty lies in explaining how it came to be included in *Revelation*. This difficulty is all the greater when we realise that it follows the vision of the Angel with the Book, and therefore is deliberately given to us as an authentic message of St. John himself, and the commission delivered to him at his call. We shall therefore be reluctant to accept this theory.

It is backed up by the fact that in this passage the stylistic argument against the Johannine authorship reaches a high degree of probability; during these few verses we find grammatical idioms which are hardly employed at all elsewhere. How much this really proves it is difficult to say. If this is really an early prophecy (as seems to be admitted) and if it was published in Hebrew, there is nothing to prevent us from supposing that it might have been translated into Greek by another hand, and this Greek translation in its turn worked into the complete *Revelation* when St. John set to work to produce it.

Again, the general reader will not find it very natural to accept the idea that measuring implies preservation. The precedent for this use of the symbolism is found only in 1 *Enoch* lxi., which is in any case a very obscure passage; cords are used for the " measures of the righteous," and in some way reveal secrets to them which will save them from destruction in the " day of the Elect One." There does not seem to be much real likeness, and Dr. Charles' citation of 2 *Sam.* viii. 2 is very remote indeed. We shall discuss the symbolism of measuring later; enough to say that all the elements of this vision—Angel, Measuring Rod, Temple and all—are to be found in *Ezekiel* xl.

So much for taking the Naos literally. The other possibility is that it may be a symbol for something, and in view of the general principles of *Revelation* this is *a priori* more likely. If so it can only represent the body of true believers who form the spiritual temple in which God dwells. As the period is that of the early church in Jerusalem, it will mean the primitive apostolic church, while the *Outer Court* will be the non-christian Jews who are " given " into the power of the gentiles. Dr. Charles, who holds that these verses were originally a Zealot prophecy about the actual Temple, insists that our present author, by incorporating them here, intends them to be understood of the spiritual temple; and it is their present meaning with which I am primarily concerned.

Secondly we must note that in each of the other fifteen occurrences of the word Naos in the *Revelation* it means a heavenly or spiritual temple. This is really its first occurrence so far as the main text of the poem is concerned; for iii. 12 is in the letters to the seven churches, and vii. 15 in an anticipatory vision of the triumph of the martyrs, both of which are later additions. So far as the plan of the poem is concerned, the concept is here introduced for the first time, after which it becomes constant.

Dr. Charles says that the phrase " the Naos of God " means in the diction of St. John " one of two things: (1) The spiritual temple (iii. 12) of which the faithful are pillars; (2) The temple in heaven (vii. 12)," etc.; but these concepts are, of course, the same. The faithful only make up the spiritual temple because God dwells in them; the temple " in heaven " is that same spiritual temple composed of all who worship him in spirit and in truth.

Thirdly we may note that no follower of Jesus could possibly stand in that Jerusalem Temple and look about it without reminding himself of those words that not one stone should be left standing upon another, and that when this Naos made with hands should be destroyed, he himself would build another not made with hands. To the first disciples of Jesus the earthly Temple was doomed; above and beyond it they saw Jesus the architect of a new Naos not made with hands.

We know that these sayings of his were treasured in the Jerusalem community because they were preserved not only in the tradition we call Q, but also in a Palestinian document preserved in *Mark* (chapter xiii.). St. Stephen was martyred because he developed them; and it is unthinkable that the prophets could have neglected them.

Fourthly we can trace some development of them in the writings of St. Paul. This same use of the phrase Naos of God is found in 1 *Cor.* iii. 16 and 2 *Cor.* vi. 16. What is more, it is symbolically conceived, and connected ultimately with Jerusalem; for in *Galatians* ii. 9 we learn that as early as the period A.D. 46 to 50 the three great leaders of the Jerusalem church (Peter, James, and John) were styled the Pillars, and this must be connected with the statement of *Rev.* iii. 12: *I will make him a Pillar in the Naos of my God.* The Naos imagery had been developed as early, then, as that.

Now I have pointed out that in the *Revelation* at least two strata of visions can very easily be detected: a later stratum in which the divine worship surrounds a Throne, and an earlier stratum in which it surrounds an Altar. This earlier stratum, as I show in Appendix I, depends for its symbolism upon the ceremonial of the Jerusalem Temple; but there is a heavenly Naos or dwelling of God in which the actions take place. As one studies this earlier material it becomes evident that its culmination was to be the establishment with men of the heavenly Naos after the earthly one (Babylon) had been destroyed; *Rev.* iii. 12, which I quoted in the last paragraph, looks forward to such a piece of Temple symbolism as the climax of the book, and an elaboration of it which will at least include Pillars.

This symbolism has gone, or very nearly gone; for its place is taken by a heavenly City in which the apostles of the Lamb are not Pillars, but Foundations. Yet the older conclusion has left a trace. The old conclusion is to be found in xxi. 1 to 8, introduced by the words: *And I saw the Holy City, New Jerusalem, descending out of Heaven from God;* but there is at this point no description of a City, but only a Great Voice which says: *Behold the Tabernacle of God is with men, and he shall Tabernacle with them, and they shall be his people, and he (God with them) shall be their God.* In these words we have first a reference to the Tabernacle which is a form of the Naos not tied to any locality; secondly we have a quotation from *Leviticus*, showing how in this New Jerusalem all the priestly and sacrificial hopes are to be consummated.

The Naos, then, means the community of men in whom God dwells, and in the original form of the *Revelation* it was much more prominent than it is now; but when St. John made his final draft of his great poem, he scrapped this conclusion with magnificent ruthlessness, and substituted for the spiritual Temple a City in which there was no Temple, and from which every trace of sacrificial, or Jewish-liturgical symbolism was expunged.

Some such change can also be traced in St. Paul, for in his later epistles the apostles are foundations, not pillars of the church, just as they are in St. John's New Jerusalem.

The Symbolism of Measuring.

Let us now ask ourselves, What is the most natural and rational explanation of the symbolism of measuring? We have rejected the idea of preservation, and the thought that probably comes at once into the mind is that of judgment: *with whatsoever measure ye measure, it shall be measured unto you* (*Matt.* vii. 1).

This explanation is probably wrong. The Measuring Rod was employed in building, and the picture of a man with such a rod suggests the idea of the erection of a building.

This suggestion is much strengthened by the fact that St. John is here reproducing the vision of *Ezekiel* xl., in which the prophet is planning out the newer and nobler temple which is to take the place of the old; the same imagery is used in a similar way in *Zechariah* ii. We must remember that throughout his book St. John is reproducing Ezekiel, and that in this particular chapter he is strongly influenced by Zechariah. These points make it much more difficult to assign these verses to a Zealot prophet. Their dependence upon Ezekiel and Zechariah claims them for St. John, and makes them suitable for this context.

By taking the most natural explanations, first of the Naos, and then of the Measuring, we are brought to a very simple and satisfactory explanation of the whole passage: it has to do with the building up of the spiritual temple of the true believers—that is to say, of the primitive Jerusalem church. We shall see later how this inner circle within the old Israel is regarded by St. John as the true Israel recognised by God.

The Outer Court, which is given over to the gentiles,

symbolises the other Jews who rejected Christ and are not being built into his spiritual temple.

So far so good; but what of the statement that *they (the gentiles) shall tread down the Holy City Forty and Two Months?* I must confess that I should very much like to approach this in the spirit and power of Dr. Charles and cut it out as an interpolation; I do, in point of fact, regard it as a comment added at a later date by St. John himself. Its phraseology does not fit the context, and its excision makes the sense flow on more smoothly.

In the first place, whatever may be said of an original alleged Zealot prophecy, our author could never use the phrase *Holy City* of the actual Jerusalem; in his use it means the community of true believers, and is therefore a synonym for the Naos of God. The plain meaning of the verse is that the Christian church shall be persecuted for a limited period only; the trouble is that such a statement is not required here, and that in a system of symbolism where the Naos and Altar mean the church, and the Outer Court means the anti-christian Jews, it is very confusing to bring in the symbolism of the City.

The meaning is clear, however, even though the symbolism does not harmonise: it is probably a comment which was added at a late stage in the compilation of the poem in order to link this vision of the Naos with the new finale of the Holy City. Let us summarise our results.

1. The Naos and Altar mean the same as the Holy City.
2. Their meaning is the inner circle of believers within Israel.
3. The Outer Courts symbolise the non-Christian Jews.
4. The inner circle of believers in Christ is to be built up into a spiritual temple which will take the place of the old when it is destroyed.
5. The anti-Christian Jews are rejected.

These results harmonise with the use of the same symbolism as it is found in *Ezekiel* and *Zechariah*, and there are also traces of it in St. Paul; it is a development of the main prophetic message of Jesus which St. John is professing to reproduce.

The Forty-two Months.

This period of time meets us again and again, and always with the same spiritual meaning. It is the period of time during which the enemies of God flourish; the time of persecution by godless heathen powers; or merely persecution in general. Its original meaning in this passage is persecution by Jewish authorities in Jerusalem.

The period of three and a half years is taken from the history of the Maccabean wars; it was for this length of time that Antiochus occupied the Temple and carried on the rites of Dionysus there; this profanation is called in *Daniel* the abomination of desolation, and is alluded to by Jesus in *Mark* xiii. By a curious coincidence, the war in which the Romans captured and destroyed the Temple also lasted three and a half months.

The number is found in *Revelation* in several forms:

Forty-two months.
One thousand, two hundred and sixty days.
Three and a half years.
Three and a half days.
A time, times, and half a time.

The number 1260 is peculiar; but Daniel appears to have used a year of 360 days, which explains this strange figure.

The number is symbolic only of persecution, and has no numerical value whatever; it does not even allude to any given stretch of time. It has one meaning only and that meaning is persecution.

By a curious accident, the period is half of Seven, halfway through a Week, which symbolises the perfection and fullness of time. Persecution has a period set to it. It is checked in mid career. It can never fulfil itself. The persecution of the Holy City will not last indefinitely.

The Two Witnesses.

We now come to the Two Witnesses who are to prophesy for 1260 days clothed in sackcloth.

Let us note first how simply the passage runs on if the reference to the Holy City is regarded as a later comment.

And the Court which is outside the Naos reject and do not measure it because it is given to the gentiles . . . and I will give to my Two Witnesses that they may prophecy One Thousand Two Hundred and Sixty Days. The Hebraic use of the word "give" links together the two passages; and, further, if the Outer Court represents the earthly Jerusalem, then the statement about the Two Witnesses follows naturally, as they are to do their work in the earthly Jerusalem.

Such comments inserted at a later date are frequent both in the *Revelation* and in the fourth gospel.

The Two Witnesses are *the Two Oil-trees (Olives) and the Two "Candlesticks" (i.e.* Lampstands) *which stand before the Lord of the earth.* The words are taken from *Zechariah* iv. and are interesting because in the time of St. John there was only one "Candlestick" in the Holy Place. On the other hand, we read in Josephus that a certain Joshua the son of Thebuthi, a priest, "handed over from the wall of the Naos two lampstands similar to those which were set in the Naos." This passage suggests to me that the two Lampstands in question stood on the wall which separated the Naos and Altar from the Court of the Women; there may therefore have been a basis in the Temple itself for this symbolism. On the Feast of Tabernacles four such lamps were lighted in this Court.

This is the second Vision which shows direct dependence on *Zechariah*; in *Zechariah*, the two *Sons of Oil*, which means no more than sources of illumination, are Joshua the High Priest, and Zerubbabel who is hailed as King. But in *St. John* neither Priest nor King will do, though we do draw this much from *Zechariah*: they are the spiritual leaders of the nation, standing always in God's presence and giving light to his people. They blazon the very function of Jerusalem itself, the candle of the Lord, a Witness to him throughout the whole earth.

Unfortunately the facts of history show that neither King nor Priest has fulfilled this idea. The rulers have failed; the rebels have been on God's side. One Witness appears to be an Elijah; *he has authority to shut heaven that it rain not.* The other is a Moses; *he has authority over the*

Waters to turn them to blood, and to smite the earth with every plague. In another way also they resemble Moses and Elijah; these are the two Old Testament worthies (besides Enoch) who escaped natural death; Elijah was taken up to heaven in a chariot of fire, and the death of Moses was regarded as a similar assumption. Hence they appear beside Christ in the Vision of Transfiguration.

The Two Witnesses of St. John were both taken up into heaven after their martyrdom; and for this reason they are not Moses and Elijah in person, for Moses and Elijah were not martyred. We are forced to regard them as the Law and the Prophets, of which Moses and Elijah were patron saints. Like the other principal characters of our poem, they represent great processes which do appear most clearly in definite epochs and are best summed up in definite persons. The Witnesses represent that process of Witness to the truth and justice of God which was the special function of the Jew; it worked most clearly and definitely through the Law and the Prophets; and Moses and Elijah were noble examples of it.

Though Moses and Elijah were not martyrs, though they were never in Jerusalem, yet the Two Witnesses are represented as martyred there. Martyrdom is the necessary condition of Witness; indeed, the two words are the same in Greek; and it is in Jerusalem, the holy city, designed as a witness to all the world, that the prophets have had most to suffer. We are reminded of our Lord's words: *It cannot be that a Prophet perish outside Jerusalem.*

The Death of the Prophets.

The Beast which rises out of the Abyss will make war with them and will conquer them and kill them ; and their body is in the streets of the Great City which is called in the spiritual manner Sodom and Egypt, where also their Lord was crucified.

The Dragon from the Abyss we have seen to be the power of evil; the Beast from the Sea, when we come to it, we shall find to mean evil organised in political form and ready to persecute. The Beast from the Abyss, which we find here, is an intermediate form. In the streets of

Jerusalem is found the same spirit of godless, self-seeking imperialism as in Rome or Greece; the priests and kings, instead of witnessing the truth, have schemed and fought to make Israel a world-empire just like any other. The prophets have always been rebels. They have uttered their voice; but they have always been persecuted. Behind it all we detect the words of Jesus: *Jerusalem, Jerusalem, which killest the prophets, and stonest them that are sent unto thee* (*Matt.* xxiv. 37).

Here, then, is the real battlefield of the war with evil. Here the prophets witnessed and were persecuted; here their Lord was crucified. This is Sodom; this is Egypt. Take note of it as you read; for here is the key to the whole book. The spirit of evil has always prevailed here; and spiritual men recognise it as the real enemy. Jerusalem, not Rome, is the real enemy of the prophet.

The truth, however, cannot be killed, and the witness of true men does not die with their death. It goes on. It revives. After the period of persecution new life enters into it; *a Spirit of Life from God entered into them and they stood on their feet* . . . (there is a touch of Ezekiel's Valley of Dry Bones here) . . . *and they heard a loud Voice out of heaven saying, Come up here! and they ascended into Heaven in the Cloud, and their enemies saw them.*

Though, no doubt, it is the Witness itself that the poet thinks of as reviving and ascending, yet his faith in the resurrection of the just is so strong that he is thinking also of the prophets themselves. Truth, smitten to the ground, revives again; the servant of truth passes through death to triumph. The Cloud means the power of God which upholds him.

In this thought St. John was not alone, as the Apocalypses testify; compare two of their titles, the *Assumption of Moses*, and the *Ascension of Isaiah*. There was more even than ascension and assumption in the popular religion; there was canonisation. We know from our Lord's words that there were decorations on the tombs of the prophets, and speeches were delivered there. The Maccabean martyrs were commemorated at the great mid-winter festival. The dead were not forgotten in the synagogue prayers. All this was filled with life and certitude for St. John by his faith in the resurrection of Christ, while his sense of it had been quickened by the recent martyrdoms of St. Stephen and St. James. To him (the Galilean), Jerusalem meant death and martyrdom and resurrection and ascension.

The City of the Martyrs.

We now reach the end of the first half of the book, the part which deals with things past, beginning from the creation of the world, and ending just when the doom of Jerusalem appears to be in sight.

The series of Seven Seals outlines the visible process of human civilisation in the triumph of a succession of brutal world-empires; the innocent victims cry to God, but though vengeance does fall on their persecutors, there is no complete and satisfying answer.

The series of Seven Trumpets outlines the inward and invisible causes, the Fall into sin, the ascendancy of evil in the human heart, and its ruinous results.

In each series there is a parenthesis after the Sixth point. In the case of the Seven Seals it deals with the restraint of God's judgment, but assures his elect that they are sealed as his, and destined for eternal bliss and refreshment. In the case of the Seven Seals it is longer and more complicated; it deals with prophecy, and St. John must first narrate his own authority to continue that divine activity. He can then contemplate the long battle carried on by these inspired men, who have thus won their immortality, and, unlike those who are merely expectant beneath the altar, are powers in heaven itself, triumphant and glorified.

The main point has to be firmly grasped if the book as a whole is to be understood. The whole stress has shifted. In the Seals the world-empires persecute and little Israel suffers; we think of the Twelve Tribes sealed and promised their reward; the gentiles are not forgotten, but Israel is the sufferer. In the Trumpets we are shown the real enemy, which is Sin; and the sufferers are those champions of God, the prophets, who boldly attack it. The place of conflict is Jerusalem, and it is there that the Witnesses of God meet the powers of evil, and ride through death to glory.

Jerusalem, the city of the martyrs, is also the city of the persecutors. There are two Jerusalems: the inner spiritual Jerusalem, the Jerusalem of the Witnesses; and the outer official Jerusalem, which is spiritually called Sodom and Egypt, where also their Lord was crucified. In this outward official Jerusalem, which is merely a world-civilisation, the powers of evil are concentrated in persecution, the Witnesses of God are concentrated in suffering.

Jerusalem, like the heathen world-empire, had had its warnings. They are symbolised in the *Great Earthquake*, in which *a Tenth of the City fell, and there died in the Earthquake Seven thousand Names of Men*. The remainder feared, but there was no repentance. *They gave glory to the God of Heaven;* but this formula does not imply repentance; it is used of Achan in *Joshua*. It is similar to the notion of Kismet; it admits that the Earthquake is God's doing; but it implies no difference in conduct.

Jerusalem admitted it had killed the prophets; it honoured them after their death; but it went on killing them.

We return to the Seventh Trumpet, which it must be remembered is the Third Woe.

The Second Woe has passed: Behold, the Third Woe comes quickly.

And the Seventh Angel sounded.

The Seventh Trumpet.

With *the Seventh Trumpet, Great Voices out of Heaven* announce the end of one Age, and the beginning of another; *the Kingdom of the World has become the Kingdom of our Lord and his Messiah, and he shall Reign for ever and ever;* and with this we are recalled to the original Vision, for the Twenty-Four Elders *fall on their faces and worship God* in a chorus of thanksgiving.

We thank Thee . . . because thou hast taken thy Great Power and become King: yea, though the Nations raged.

And thy Wrath came—that is, the great Day of wrath—*and the time of the Dead to be given Judgment, and to give the*

Reward to thy Servants the Prophets . . . and to destroy those who destroyed the Land.

The Day, then, implies that the Dead will receive the Judgment for which they have prayed, and the deaths of the Prophets and saints will be revenged. The principal *Kingdom of the World* in St. John's mind is Jerusalem, and it is vengeance on Jerusalem of which he principally thinks; and in answer to this hymn of worship the veil of heaven is withdrawn, and it is seen that, as in Ezekiel, the Glory of God has already forsaken the doomed city.

And the Temple of God in Heaven was opened, and in it was seen the Ark of the Covenant in its Shrine. . . . The Temple on earth has lost what status it had. It never did contain the Ark, which was lost when Solomon's Temple was destroyed by Nebuchadrezzar. It was a confident hope of some apocalyptic writers that in the Great day it would be restored; but St. John holds out no hope of any such restoration. God's covenanted presence is no longer in the City of David; it is a universal covenant now " in Heaven," visible to all mankind, and available for all. The earthly, local, temple is to be destroyed.

The long episode of the Angel of Revelation (chapter x.) and the Witness against Jerusalem (chapter xi.) has perhaps obscured the memory of that system of Seven Trumpets with which we began (chapter viii.). It will be remembered that this system was originally Three Trumpets only, which are also called Three Woes; it is the last which now sounds, and at its voice the Naos in heaven opens. This symbolism is borrowed from the Temple ritual; as the dawn rose, three trumpet sounds were heard and the gates of the Temple opened with a noise that reverberated through the city. In *St. John* it is the heavenly Naos which opens, and Thunders and Voices which are heard. The new Naos which he is to " Measure " appears; God's presence is there.

This corresponds also to the stage which has been reached in the reproduction of *Ezekiel*. In chapter ix. the Glory or visible covenanted presence passes from the cherubim within the Naos to the threshold; in chapter x. the Glory returns to the Cherubim and, riding upon them, passes out of the east gate; in chapter xi. the Glory leaves the city and comes to rest on the Mount of Olives across the river Kidron. Jerusalem is abandoned; *the land is full of blood and the city of perverseness* (ix. 9). As in the *Revelation* the dead bodies lie about the city. *Thus saith the Lord . . . Ye have multiplied your slain in this city, and ye have filled the streets thereof with the slain. . . . I will bring a sword upon you, saith the Lord God, and I will . . . deliver you into the hands of strangers, and will execute judgments upon you. Ye shall fall by the sword* (xi. 6 ff.).

If we turn to the *Jewish War* of Josephus, we shall see how terribly true the indictments of St. John were. The assassination and bloodshed increased as the doom of the city drew nearer; and Josephus, who composed his history rather in the spirit of the prophets, himself sees the hand of God in it, just as St. John did. He consoles himself with the thought that behind that great catastrophe lay the purpose of God, or, as he sometimes called it, Fate.

When the High Priest Ananus was killed by the Edomites, and " all the outer part of the sacred enclosure was swimming in blood, and the dawn revealed eight thousand five hundred dead bodies," he suggests that God permitted this because, " I suppose, God had condemned the city to destruction because it was polluted, and was determining to cleanse his holy places with fire." A little later he says that " there was an ancient oracle of men to the effect that the city would not be taken nor the holy places burned down by right of war, until civil strife should arise, and their own hands first defile the holy enclosure of God." When the siege had almost reached its end he addresses the defenders of the temple and says, " You are contending in robberies and murders, and devising strange new ways of evil. The sacred enclosure has become a receptacle for all men, and the divine place has been defiled by Jewish hands . . . so that I believe that God has abandoned his holy places, and stands with those against whom you are now making war."

His words have a prophetic lilt and parallelism, so that

it might almost be worth investigating whether some Hebrew or Aramaic metrical original may not lie behind them.

Conclusion of Part I of Revelation.

The action of the poem is now suspended. Chapters xii. and xiii. form a Great Interlude in which are played out the great facts of our redemption, and the story of the persecution of the Christian church both in Jerusalem and in Rome. Chapter xii., like chapter xi., which we have just studied, thinks of Jerusalem only; it is probably to be dated before the great Neronian persecution of A.D. 64; chapter xiii. deals with that persecution, and must be later.

In chapter xiv. the main action of the poem is taken up, and we find ourselves in the period of the Jewish war which began under Vespasian in 66 and was concluded by the destruction of Jerusalem in 70.

Chapter xi., which we have just finished, is the hardest chapter in the book, the least lyrical, and the most compressed. It is, however, of supreme importance. The very fact that it is enigmatical and resists solution shows that it would not have been included had not great weight been attached to it. It does not do (as many critics think sufficient), it does not do to give some sort of interpretation to these passages, and then pass on and forget them, as if they contributed nothing to the book. They are linked to the rest of the book by their dependence upon *Ezekiel* and upon the Temple symbolism; they are part of a unified and orderly composition; they definitely identify the Great City of which we are to hear more.

They are marked as passages of central importance by the symbolism of chapter x. This is the only chapter in which a passage based on *Ezekiel* is seriously misplaced. This is done for a purpose. Under the symbolism of the Angel and the Book it symbolises not only the whole course of prophecy, culminating in the Christian revelation, but also specifically the call of St. John himself to be a prophet. What follows in chapter xi. is therefore claimed as his own vision, as his first vision, as his primary witness; that witness is to prophesy against the earthly Jerusalem and the earthly Temple, and to announce the heavenly Jerusalem and the heavenly temple. The latter half of the book exactly corresponds to this programme. The earthly Jerusalem, under the figure of Babylon, is doomed and destroyed; the heavenly Jerusalem takes its place.

The narration of the call of St. John in chapter x. also fixes the chronology of the poem. What is previous to that call is past history, the whole extent of it from the creation. It is no good looking there for prophecies of contemporary or future events. It is not Christian; it is pre-Christian.

Why, then, does St. John place his call in chapter x. before the birth of the Saviour in chapter xii.? The answer is that the prophecies he makes in chapter xi. cannot be divorced from his authority to make them, which is received in chapter x.; chapters x. and xi. make a unit. The Angel of Revelation in chapter x. is the Prophetic Word coming to all the prophets, and now in these times to St. John; it must therefore come before the birth of the Saviour in xii. The coming of the Prophetic Word must be succeeded by the message which it brought to St. John. There is no other way of arranging it.

St. John has outlined the history of the world and the course of prophecy down to the middle of the first century A.D., when he is writing; he has so far introduced nothing Christian; he wants to show that the course of prophecy is continuous down to and including himself. He receives the Word as Ezekiel or Zechariah received it. He witnessed against Jerusalem as they did, and found Jerusalem hostile as they did; he distinguished between an earthly Jerusalem which shall be judged, and a spiritual or heavenly Jerusalem that shall be built up. Even in chapter xi., though we are contemplating in it the streets of Jerusalem after the time of Christ, nothing Christian is allowed to enter. Having brought his poem down to the end of the old age, the old order that is passing away, having indicated that there is even now a heavenly Naos or spiritual temple with open gates which is destined to be built up, he pauses and goes back a few years to the birth of the Saviour, which is to inaugurate the new age. Having described that birth and victory, he treats of the persecution of his followers in Jerusalem and Rome, and for the first time in the book (except for the anticipatory vision of chapter vii.) we are thinking of the sufferings of Christian martyrs. The Great Interlude over, he resumes the action of the poem where he suspended it, and shows us the Seven Last Plagues and the complete ruin which is to fall upon the earthly Jerusalem.

Such a treatment is unavoidable in the nature of his subject as he conceives it. " This Age "—the first age in the world's history—is marked by God's covenant with the Jews and culminates in his rejection of them which was announced by Jesus in A.D. 30 and effected by the Emperor Titus in A.D. 70. Part I, therefore, must continue up to A.D. 70 or within sight of it; Part II gives the events of A.D. 70 and the course of the Age to Come. But this Age to Come must in a sense begin with its announcement by Jesus in A.D. 30. You are left with an overlapping period from 30 to 70, and far the best way was to treat it as an Interlude.

THE PROPHECY OF JESUS. (Illustrative Chart.)

THIS AGE, which is passing away. (Rev. iv. to xi.)
   A.D. 29   The Son of Man rejected by Jerusalem.
                The Crucifixion.
THIS GENERATION. (Rev. xii. to xiv. 14.)
                The " seed grows."
                Wars, earthquakes, etc.
                False Christ: False prophets.
   A.D. 70   The Son of Man rejects Jerusalem. (Rev. xiv. 15 to end.)
                The Fall of Jerusalem.
THE AGE TO COME.
                The Coming of the Son of Man.
                The Kingdom of God in Power.

THE PROPHECY OF JESUS. This chart shows the division of time into This Age and That which is to Come, which was used by our Lord. The years 29 to 70 are the forty years during which his words were to be fulfilled: " This Generation shall not pass away till all these things be accomplished." The forty years is an overlapping, rather than an intermediate period, as the Age to Come and the Kingdom of God are thought of as breaking in on This Age even before the Crucifixion.

The two dates 29 and 70 are also the focal dates of the Revelation. Chapters iv. to ix. represent "This Age." Chapters x. to xi. tell of the call and special work of St. John, and chapters xii. and xiii. deal with the birth, diffusion, and origin of Christianity and the growth of emperor-worship and persecution. These chapters correspond to the intermediate period of This Generation. Chapters xiv. to xxi. deal with the Age to Come, the Fall of Jerusalem (Babylon), the victorious Coming of Christ, and the descent of the New Jerusalem.

The Montanist heresy preserves and perverts this arrangement in its system of three ages: the Age of the Father, the Age of the Son, and the Age of the Spirit.

The following table compares the three systems:

Gospels.	Revelation.	Montanus.
This Age:	*Part I* (iv. to xi.):	Age of the Father.
Prophets killed, etc.		
Innocent blood.	Souls under altar.	
	Earthquakes, etc.	
	Prophets killed.	
This Generation:	Interlude (xii. to xiv. 14):	Age of the Son.
Crucifixion.	Birth, etc. of Christ.	
Earthquakes, etc.		
Spread of Gospel.	(cf. Three Messages).	
False Christs.	The Beast.	
False Prophets.	The Second Beast.	
Persecution.	Persecution.	
	Three Messages.	
The Age to Come:	*Part II* (xiv. 15 to end):	
	Earthquakes, etc.	
Abomination desolation,	Gathering for Armageddon.	
The Son of Man.	The Son of Man.	
The Harvest.	The Harvest.	
Fall of Jerusalem.	Fall of Jerusalem (Babylon).	
Coming of Christ in power.	Coming of Christ in victory.	Age of the Spirit.
Coming of the kingdom in power.	Descent of the New Jerusalem.	Descent of the New Jerusalem.
		Coming of the Paraclete.

It has not been possible to attempt an arrangement of the events under the Age to Come in the Gospel column in a supposed chronological order. I have simply placed the Gospel prophecies opposite the events to which they correspond in Revelation. This table shows which sections of the Revelation are based on Gospel prophecies, and also makes it clear that the plan of the whole book is dictated by the Gospel outlook on current and future events. This plan, drawn from the Gospels, is skilfully woven into the plan of *Ezekiel*, which it so closely resembles.

BOOK V
THE GREAT INTERLUDE

PART I. CHRIST
The Woman in Heaven.
The Birth of the Man Child.
The Defeat of the Serpent.
The Persecution of the Woman and her Seed.

PART II. ANTI-CHRIST
The Beast from the Sea.
The Beast from the Land.
The Mark of the Beast.
The Lamb on Mount Sion.

I. THE LADY OF HEAVEN.

Thou art the Ancient Beauty,
  The Wisdom long-desired,
O Breath, O Radiance of God,
  O Grace of the inspired.
To thee the pale philosopher,
  The poet breathing spring,
Lift up enraptured hearts, O Bride,
  O Daughter of the King.

I see thee stand above the years,
  Within, beyond our range ;
With timeless life and spaceless light
  Thy shining vestures change.
Yet when the club's assembled,
  And human candles flare,
O lady of the deeps and heights,
  Thy Grace and Power are there.

Thy voice is laughter of the spheres,
  Thine eyes are lamps on high ;
O Star of all the aimless seas,
  O Queen of all the sky ;
The bliss of every noble heart,
  The fire by all adored,
O Wisdom ordering all things,
  The Spirit of the Lord.

Once in the darkest hour of earth,
  When shade on shadow fell,
We saw thee in the cave that's built
  Above the vaults of hell ;
Once in the light of Mary's face
  We saw thy beauties shine,
And left our gold and frankincense
  To burn before thy shrine.

Thou dost console the wounded,
  Thou shinest on the pure ;
Under the shadow of thy wings
  The saints have dwelt secure.
Mother of all the strong and brave,
  Dear love when all men sing,
We lift our hearts to thee, O Bride
  And Mother of the King.

      POEMS CELESTIAL: I. THE LADY OF HEAVEN.

BOOK V
THE GREAT INTERLUDE

Part I. Christ

Argument

THE action of the poem is suspended while the birth of the Saviour and the origin of Christianity are described. In this section alone St. John deserts the symbolism of Ezekiel.

The Saviour is born of the Heavenly Woman, who symbolises the community of elect souls in Israel, and overcomes evil by his Blood. He is given the name of Michael. His followers, under the symbolism of the Woman, are persecuted in Jerusalem, but are upheld and protected by God.

Persecution breaks out elsewhere. The Beast from the Sea means the Roman Empire, summed up in Nero, who is the Messiah of evil; the Beast from the Land means whatever forces are allied with him in spreading the cult of the Emperor. An immense battle is to take place between the followers of the Saviour and the system of the god-emperor.

Chapters xii. and xiii. are marked as an Interlude in more ways than one; some of the marks may be noted at once:

1. St. John goes back in time from the standpoint of his own call to prophesy in Jerusalem the birth of the Saviour.

2. Chapter xii. does not begin *And I saw*; it begins *And there was seen*. It is not a private revelation, but something open to all, the events of history which formed the preaching of the Christian church.

3. The difference in literary tone is felt at once by all critics.

4. In these two chapters alone St. John forgets *Ezekiel*; apart from this, *Ezekiel* is the groundwork of the book. Here there is much more reminiscence of *Daniel*.

5. These chapters are so modelled as to confute the propaganda of the Jewish sect which is called Ophite.

6. It forms a parenthesis in the action of the book; the action dropped in chapter xi. is taken up in chapter xiv.

On the other hand, the Interlude is linked to the remainder of the book in a number of ways.

1. The heavenly Woman, who represents the Spirit and the Church, is a counterpart of the Strong Angel of chapter x., who represents the Word and the course of Prophecy.

2. The heavenly Woman persecuted by the Red Dragon is planned to contrast with the Harlot of chapters xvii., xviii., who is seated upon the Scarlet Beast.

3. The Mark of the Beast is the antithesis of the Sealing of the Elect in chapter viii., just as the Beast is the antithesis of the Lamb.

4. Subsequent chapters refer to the symbolism of the Great Interlude.

It should also be noted that chapter xiii. was written later than chapter xii., so that the presentation of the two as an Interlude is part of the last editing of the book. Chapter xii. (the Woman in heaven) deals with persecution in Jerusalem, and is of much the same date and outlook as x. and xi., which also deal with Jerusalem. Chapter xiii. describes the Neronian persecution, and therefore must be later than A.D. 64. On the other hand, it has been suggested that while its present form belongs to that date, it may originally have been written in the time of Caligula, A.D. 37 to 41. In that case there is a very early *groundwork* (A.D. 40 onward) for the whole of the section x. to xiii., though there is much later work in xiii. How much further this very early series of visions may extend, there is no means of deciding; but they will at least include the Great Harlot and the Scarlet Beast of chapter xvii.

If it is conceded that St. Paul has been influenced by early prophecies of St. John, something may be done by careful comparative study of his Epistles.

The Woman in Heaven.

The vision of the Woman clothed with the Sun is a vision whose interpretation seems remarkably simple to the ordinary unlearned Christian; but among the learned it has roused great controversies. Catholics, of course, are sure that she represents the Virgin Mary, and Protestants are equally sure that she cannot. To-day many of our most learned and ingenious scholars are united in their attempt to sweep away any Christian interpretation at all. In their eyes it is a piece of heathen mythology which has found its way into a book which is only a mixed scrap-book of Jewish and Christian apocalyptic fragments.

With chapter xii. all commentators feel themselves in a new atmosphere. It has even been suggested that had the whole of Revelation after chapter xi. been lost, we should never have suspected that we had lost anything. I do not think this is true; but it is perfectly true that if we went straight on from chapter xi. to chapter xiv., verse 14, we should never have suspected any loss. The Trumpet of the Seventh Angel would have been succeeded by the Coming of one like a Son of Man on a White Cloud, the reaping of the Harvest of the Land, and the Seven Bowls which represent the Seven Last Plagues. It looks very much as if this was the original plan of the prophet, and represents the outline of the early Jerusalem apocalypse (J).

The Great Interlude, as we may call it, begins with a symbol of a strange kind. There is no parallel to be found in Jewish apocalypse, and a school of modern critics agrees in tracing it to heathen sources. There, however, their agreement ends; when it comes to deciding which heathen source, they take different sides. Persian, Greek, Babylonian, and Egyptian, have all been tried, but so far its origin has not been found. A survey of the evidence is given in Dr. Charles' Commentary, and it is sufficient to show that so far no case for heathen origin has been made out.

Superficially, of course, the elements of the story are to be discerned in all mythologies. It is the myth of the woman who bore a divine son, a hero who became the leader of his people, and killed a dragon or other monster. The two points are so common as scarcely to need illustration. Many heroes of Latin or Greek myth are the result of intercourse between a divine father and a human mother; many of them kill a dragon or sea-monster. Even the Red Indians and the South Sea Islanders have these stories. It is all the more startling that no clear parallel to this vision has been found; for in this case there is a divine mother and no father at all.

The theory that the woman is a sun-goddess is not only not proven; if that were all, the theory might still hold the field. The whole Vision, in all its perplexing detail, can quite easily be illustrated from other sources, all of them Jewish.

The Sign in the Sky.

This Vision differs from all the others in its introduction. It does not say, *And I saw*, as the others do; it says, *There was seen a Great Sign in the Sky*. It is not narrated as a private vision peculiar to the prophet; it is narrated as a piece of history open to everyone. The words *I saw* do not reappear till the next chapter.

I have translated it a Sign in the Sky rather than a Sign in Heaven in order to emphasise the fact that it does not here mean the dwelling-place of God and his angels. The standpoint throughout all this group of visions is earth with its seas and lands and deserts and rivers; the Heaven therefore means the space beneath our firmament, the highest part of this world, not the throne of God.

But, needless to say, the word here is not used in its geographical sense. It is symbolic. It symbolises the highest part of creation, or the highest part of our nature, just as the Abyss signifies the lowest. Just as Sin and its swarm of temptations arise out of the Abyss, so the Deliverer must come from Heaven. Up to this point we have been considering the worst that man has achieved—his wars and murders, and the ruin he has worked in his own nature; but there is another side to human history, a bright, idealistic side; there are activities which are inspired from heaven.

The actual words are drawn not from any heathen myth, but direct from the prophet *Isaiah, Moreover the Lord spake again unto Ahaz saying, Ask thee a Sign of the Lord thy God; ask it either in the Depth or in the Height above;* (vii. 10) or, to translate it into Johannine language, either in the Abyss or in Heaven. In *Isaiah* the language appears to be purely a rhetorical flourish; but it is obviously the origin of St. John's Sign in Heaven.

This is made perfectly clear by what follows in *Isaiah*. The king refuses to ask for the Sign, and Isaiah replies, *The Lord himself shall give you a Sign: behold a Virgin shall conceive and bear a Son, and shall call his name Immanuel*. The words of St. John are simply a quotation from the earlier prophet; *There appeared a great Sign in the Sky, a Woman* . . .

with child, and she cried in her pain and was in torment to be delivered. More than this, St. John has given us a much closer translation of the Hebrew than our Authorised Version, which is influenced by the Septuagint; the Greek translation does, indeed, say, *A Virgin shall conceive,* but the original Hebrew only says, *A Woman is with Child,* and St. John has given it us exactly. And, what is more, the words *Crying in her pain and was in torment* come from *Isaiah* also (xxxvi. 17).

St. John is therefore announcing the birth of the male child, the warrior king, foretold by the *First Isaiah*.

The Mother of the Messiah.

Before discussing the symbol of the Woman in itself, it is necessary to explode the curious fallacy that the Christian doctrine of the Virgin Birth is similar in kind to the stories of divine births in heathen mythology. It is loosely asserted that such mythology is full of virgin births.

The statement would never have been made if we were in the habit of using plain, straightforward language. The ladies in question were none of them virgins in any sense of the word; they have only been called so to make the myths sound respectable. Diana was not a virgin; far from it. Neither were the human maidens who gave birth to divine sons; for they had first been visited by male gods, who seduced them. The mother of Romulus was actually a Vestal Virgin who was persuaded by the God Mars to break her vows. To use a delightful phrase from the *Cambridge Ancient History,* the virgin goddesses were " dominant but unwedded."

The stories are therefore the very opposite of the story of the Virgin Birth of Christ, which says that a woman conceived a son in the power of the Holy Spirit, without a human male parent. This doctrine is not explicitly stated by St. John; all we know is that it was accepted teaching in the church before St. Luke and St. " Matthew " wrote their gospels—that is, before the *Revelation* received its final form. In *St. John* we are merely given the fact of the *Woman with child.* How she came to be so is left unexplained;

but the visit of a male god is an unthinkable impossibility. There is a strong resemblance here to the way in which the fourth gospel treats the same doctrine. It was, of course, known to the author who had read *St. Luke*; it is not asserted or denied; like so many cardinal events which are adequately dealt with in the synoptists, it is not narrated. But the divine origin of Christ is made absolute and unmistakable, and great reverence is given to his mother.

The use of this text from *Isaiah* both in *Matthew* and in *Revelation* is very interesting, and points to the fact that Jerusalem Christians must long have applied this prophecy to our Lord. St. John does not appear to use it as a proof that he was to be born of a virgin; but then can we be sure that St. "Matthew" does? Was it not originally used merely to link our Lord with the Messiah promised by Isaiah? And would not the significance of the word Virgin in the Greek version only begin to be felt as Christians lost their touch with the Hebrew?

This line of argument does not in any way affect the story itself, which rests on the evidence of St. Luke and St. "Matthew"; it only affects the modern theory, which suggests that the story sprang up as an explanation of the prophecy. The more we look into it, the less it seems likely that the prophecy would have suggested the story. The story has an independent origin, and it is difficult to resist the idea that St. John was thinking of it when he wrote this vision.

The Heavenly Bride.

The Woman is *Clothed with the Sun, and the Moon under her Feet, and on her Head a Crown of Twelve Stars.* Here we really have imagery that sounds heathen; and very close parallels to it have been quoted, particularly from Greek and Persian mythology. It is not impossible that St. John has borrowed the insignia of heathen goddesses to symbolise the dignity of his queen of heaven; but this does not justify Dr. Charles in calling her a sun-goddess, pure and simple, and still less her child a sun-god. There is no suggestion of either. Isaiah is entirely responsible for what is said about the child.

As a matter of fact, there is enough in the Old Testament to explain even this imagery, without recourse to heathen myth. The Bride sung of in *The Song of Songs* had already been interpreted by the Rabbis as the Ideal Israel, the mystic Bride of Jehovah, and we must not dismiss without examination the theory that this may really have been the idea of its final author. No one who has read that book will forget the magnificent line in which she is described as *fair as the Moon, clear as the Sun, and terrible as an army with banners* (vi. 10).

It is impossible to understand the *Revelation* at all without fixing clearly in the mind this conception of the Bride of God which is fundamental to so many of the prophets. It applies first to the early Israel of the wanderings in the desert, a period often thought of as the " honeymoon " of Israel and Jehovah; and, secondly, it applies to the ideal Israel, the souls in Israel who remain faithful to their God. The actual Israel is too often the faithless wife, the harlot who has gone a-whoring after strange gods. In *Ephesians*, just as in *Revelation*, the Christian church is the bride of Christ; for the thought of the true Israel as the bride of the Messiah was as simple and natural as the thought of the actual Israel or the actual Jerusalem as a harlot.

Here, however, the Heavenly Woman is thought of as the Mother of the Messiah, though later on the same figure will appear as his Bride; one of the masterly points of the *Revelation* is the way in which the transference from one thought to the other is effected without any of the incongruity which we find in heathen mythology.

This imagery appears to have been blended with the imagery of Joseph's dream, in which the Sun, the Moon, and the Eleven Stars bow down to him. The Sun and Moon symbolise Israel and Rachel; the eleven Stars, his brothers, the sons of Israel.

These symbols also associate the Woman with the true Israel, the glorious Bride of Jehovah; the figure Twelve alone is sufficient to do this, as in the *Revelation* it always means the full number of the elect souls. She is not the official Israel represented by the priests and scribes, or the official Jerusalem which we have been told is mystically called Sodom or Egypt, just as Isaiah called her Sodom and Gomorrha. She is the true people of God, the faithful remnant, the persecuted prophetic minority; at a later stage, without any controversy, she represents the Christian church.

We note again how St. John blazons in one magnificent symbol some general element at work in human history, which finds its classic expression at one particular epoch, in some particular nation or person. God has always had his Witnesses, for instance; but those Witnesses are best summed up for us in Elijah and Moses, the Law and the Prophets. Those witnesses have always been persecuted, even killed by the ruling powers; but neither they nor their Witness could really be killed: they have supernatural life; they live and are victorious.

It is so with this Vision.

God's people have failed him and are rejected; but there has always been an inner circle, a faithful remnant of visionaries and idealists, who remain true to him. They cry; they groan; they are bringing something to birth—something better than the crude imperialisms and commercialisms of the world. From this inner Israel the Messiah is born. We can sum the whole thing up in these stages:

1. Quite generally, the part of humanity that is nearest and truest to God; the "faithful few."
2. His Bride, the true Israel, the "inner circle."
3. The Mother of the Messiah; and here we must inevitably think of the actual Mother, Mary, in whose person, for these purposes, the true Israel is summed up.
4. The Primitive Christian Church, the inner circle within the false Israel, which is true to the Messiah.

The Dragon.

The Great Red Dragon is the persecuting power that watches the Woman and is ready to devour her Child. The Horns are borrowed from the vision of Daniel, and associate it at once with the great world-empire, and in particular with

Rome. We shall return to that later. The point to grasp here is that it is first of all essentially a general conception, the evil powers of history incarnate in some huge organisation and opposed to all that is good.

(We may note that if we are right in our rough division of the *Revelation* into two parts, we can distinguish now a further mark of difference: in one set of visions we find a Red Beast associated later on with a Harlot, and in the other a Dragon, a Beast, and a Second Beast, also called the False Prophet. Literary tests are largely subjective; but this and other evidence do give us some help in dating the parts of the book.)

Now though the evil forces of history are already conceived as incarnate in the Roman Empire, this chapter is really concerned with the force of evil in general, which earlier received the name of Abaddon or Apollyon, but is here described as the *Great Dragon, the Primal Serpent called the Devil or Satan.* The Great Dragon means the ancient enemy of God, sometimes symbolised by the Sea, and incarnate of old in Babylon and Egypt; the Primal Serpent is the serpent that tempted Eve; the word Devil or Satan means adversary or accuser or slanderer, and though the word appears to be drawn from Job (*who accused our brethren day and night*), it is a clear reference to the terminology of our Lord; it was he who finally fixed the name Satan as a comprehensive designation for the forces of evil.

As has already been shown in the case of the Two Witnesses, the forces of evil are always ready, even in the holy city itself, to attack, accuse, oppose, hamper, persecute, and crush all that is good or noble or true—whatever the Woman brings to birth: prophets, wise men, poets, philosophers, the Messiah himself with his followers, they all have the "world" against them. And in order to connect this Vision quite without any possible doubt with what has gone before, we are told that *his Tail drags a Third part of the Stars, and cast them to the ground.* He is that principle of evil which is responsible for the partial ruin of humanity; his power is in his Tail! He is Abaddon and his army.

o

The New Eve.

We must now add a third element to the Hebrew sources from which St. John draws his symbolism of the Woman in Heaven. On the one hand we have a Sign in Heaven, the Woman; on the other a Sign from the Abyss, the Serpent. Here we have repeated the drama of *Paradise Lost*, a contest between a Woman and a Serpent.

Bishop Gore has stated that there are only two elements in primitive catholic Christian thought which do not seem to be drawn from the circle of New Testament ideas: one is the thought of the bread and wine of the eucharist as in themselves an offering; the other is the thought of Mary as the second Eve. Well, here is the origin of the thought of Mary as the second Eve.

The first Eve was tempted and fell, and her son Cain was the first murderer; since then the spirit of Cain has dominated the kingdoms of man. The second Eve was saved from the hostility of the Serpent, and her son was to cast the Serpent down from his usurped authority " in Heaven." St. John is recording the fulfilment of the promise made to Eve by Jehovah of a Child that should crush the Serpent's head; the " enmity " placed between the Serpent and the " seed " of Eve is echoed in verse 7, *there was war in heaven* and in verse 17, *and the dragon went off to make war with the rest of her seed.*

It is obvious that we are now hard on the tracks of the Ophites or Cainites again. It will be remembered that they took the side of the Serpent and of Cain, and denied that the creator was the high God. That is why St. John has heaped up texts out of the Old Testament to identify the Serpent as the author of evil, and insists that he arises out of the Abyss. He does not name the evil one in every possible way, and dilate upon his origin and nature merely because of some personal pre-occupation with him; he does it because there are people who honour him as the origin of wisdom and goodness.

It will be remembered that these heretics are not the early Gnostics and Ophites dimly known to us through

St. Irenæus and St. Hippolytus, but only their more primitive Hebrew forerunners; but by comparative study of what we know we can get a fairly clear idea of some of their main tenets. Not only is the system of the first Gnostics (A.D. 100 to 120) based upon them; but there are primitive elements left in the systems of Marcion, and Marcus, and Justinus, later Gnostics; and there are strong traces in the Roman Christian writer Hermas, who only just succeeded in being orthodox. By isolating the Hebrew elements preserved in these curious and fantastic teachers, we can get some idea of the probable teachings of the Jewish Synagogue of Satan.

It is, however, impossible to make a logical system of it. It is chaotic, irrational, and unsystematic; that is why the Gnostics of the second century spent so much time spinning logical systems, which only became more and more absurd. It is possible too that they themselves are influenced by *Revelation*.

The Ophite Heaven.

God was called Aion (the Age) or Bythos (the Abyss), two words chosen originally to represent indefinite time and indefinite space. With the word Aion we have dealt; it was afterwards applied to all those intermediate divine beings which issued from God in a continuous chain. St. John does not use the word Bythos; and his word Abyssos is applied only to the deep below. He is making it clear that God and the Serpent are opposed.

God, then, is the Aion and the Bythos, or possibly the Aion in the Bythos. He is the Unnameable Father, not, of course, of creation, but of the heavenly Aions. Through Marcus we learn of an original female existence, Sige, the Silence, which he seems to claim became incarnate in himself; not very successfully, however. Sige is the womb of the all. Or it may be that the consort of Bythos was Ennoia, which means intellectual activity.

Symbolic as these names are, they point clearly to one dreadful weakness of Gnostic thought. They banned and detested all sexual intercourse as the work of Ialdabaoth, the creator; but when they meditated on the uncreated abysses and æons, they could only express their thoughts on the subject in sexual terminology. They thought of spirit only as a rarefied matter; they were materialists through and through; and this will be found to be true of their modern representatives, the theosophists and spiritualists.

Another and more simple name for God is Anthropos, or Man, and this seems to represent something more primitive and more Hebrew than the cosmology we have been considering.

Now as God did not create the world, we have to find out first what he did produce, and secondly how the world came into being.

We have seen how, in order to produce anything, God must first make himself male and female; for, after all, what happens on earth, bad as it is, is some sort of copy of what happens in heaven. It follows, too, that what is produced is itself male and female, so that from Anthropos, the First Man, proceeds the Second Man or Son of Man and a female counterpart, the Spirit. We are sure we are on Hebrew ground here, as the Hebrew word for Spirit (Ruah) is feminine.

Pushing the whole system of thought back to its orthodox Jewish origins, we can see that we have a degeneration of that noble Rabbinic thought of God as a complex of manifold energies and activities, Word, Wisdom, Light, Spirit, Angel, Presence, Glory, and so on. The power and helpfulness of the dynamic type of monotheism are only preserved by remembering that there is but one God, and these energies are identical with him. The weakness of Gnosticism lay first in separating them from God and giving them independent existence, then in arranging them in pairs, masculine and feminine, and thirdly in allowing each pair to produce a fresh pair a trifle less divine.

The logical system of this type is, however, the product of gentile speculation. The original Jewish pioneers of Gnosticism seem to have done no more than arrange on one side the activities whose Hebrew names were masculine, and on the other side the feminine ones; Word and Son of

Man on one side, and Life and Spirit on the other. Nor can we say when this was done; it is most likely that it was later than, or parallel to, the development of Christian thought. We find a reference to it in *Colossians* and the Pastorals.

It is probable that one stage of development further was reached while this heresy was still in its Hebrew stage. The original pair, Man and Spirit, which proceeded from God, became four. This Four (or tetrad) is pretty constant in Gnostic systems, and forms the group immediately below the Unnameable God. They are

> WORD: LIFE (Logos and Zoe).
> MAN: CHURCH (Anthropos and Ecclesia).

This should be contrasted with the Four Zoa or living forces in the *Revelation*, which are forces of creation distinct from God.

But these Four have grown out of the simple pair, Man (or Son of Man) and Spirit with which we began.

It may be thought that I have described this system in unnecessary detail; but the fact is that it illuminates from Jewish sources a portion of the *Revelation* which has quite wrongly been thought to be pagan. The Woman in Heaven corresponds to the Spirit-Life-Church æon; and the male æon (Word-Man-Son of Man) corresponds to the "Strong Angel" of chapter x. Both are figures of colossal proportions; both are heavenly in origin; and the figures in *Revelation* symbolise exactly the same as the abstract names of the Gnostic æons.

The gigantic angel with the book does symbolise the Word of God proclaimed through the prophets and incarnate in Galilee in the Son of Man; the woman who fills the heavens does signify first spiritual life, and then the church. St. John has boldly stolen the principal figures of his Gnostic opponents, and used them in his own characteristic way to blazon great spiritual processes at work in the world; and the fact that they form a pair shows that the Vision of the Woman is not a scrap from another source, but that it fits into a system. If our author is the Son of Zebedee, he had met this symbolism at least as early as A.D. 35, about which year he came in contact with Simon Magus of Samaria, who claimed to be the male æon, and Helen, his companion, to be the female æon. At least one Gnostic author understood St. John in this manner; the *Book of Elchasai* is unfortunately only known to us on third-century evidence, but it was supposed to be written about 101 A.D., and it claims to have been brought from heaven by a male angel ninety-six miles high and a female angel of the same size, who are said to be Christ and the Holy Spirit. This is very clearly a mixture of primitive Hebrew Gnosticism with a literal interpretation of the *Revelation*, in which one of St. John's gigantic figures gives him a book.

It becomes very clear that St. John needed no pagan model for his Heavenly Woman; she is Isaiah's virgin, Solomon's bride, and a second Eve, or universal mother, and among the Gnostic æons a very similar figure is to be found, even though as time goes on she develops into a chain of figures. It is also true that every Gnostic system known to us in any detail may have felt the influence of *Revelation;* but the general conception of the primal Adam and the primal Eve dwelling in God is older. The identification with Eve is made clear by the title of Mother of all Living given to the female æon, and in any case Zoe (or life) is simply a translation into Greek of the name Eve. Zoe Aionios can be translated " eternal life " if you like; it can equally well be translated the " Eve of the Aion," or the " heavenly Eve." Anthropos meant Adam; Zoe meant Eve. But these are, of course, the divine æons after whose pattern the earthly Adam and Eve were blunderingly made.

The Feminine Spirit.

We must now add a fourth element to the Hebrew sources from which St. John drew his inspiration for the figure of the heavenly Bride. She is the Holy Spirit: for Spirit and Bride are one. *The Spirit and the Bride say Come* (xxii. 17).

It takes some daring to suggest this; but for three centuries a whole branch of the catholic church called the Holy Spirit She; this was regular in the Syriac church, because in Syriac, as in Hebrew, the word Spirit (Ruah) is feminine. In the gospel used by the Jewish Christians the Spirit is also feminine, and is thought of as the mother of Christ. In the visions of the Roman prophet Hermas, a year or two later than St. John, the divine woman who appears to him is either the Church or the Spirit.

On the principle of double significance which we have seen running all through the *Revelation*, we must expect this identification. The woman in heaven is certainly the holy community or church; she is also the divine Spirit which animates the holy community, the Spirit of God working in the church, the Life of believers.

The Word of God which came to the prophets had already been personified by Ezekiel and Daniel as a male figure, called in the latter Gabriel or Man of God; yet he is divine, an activity of God himself, the creative intellectual power given to the prophets throughout history. He is the Word of God coming to the inspired leaders; from the opposite point of view, he is the activity of the leaders themselves. He represents both sides of the one process. This is the Strong Angel of chapter x. who came to St. John.

Here we have the counterpart, the Spirit (feminine) of the Lord, also so common in *Ezekiel*, though not personified. Such a personification is found, however, in the figure of Wisdom in the book of *Proverbs* and it is still further developed in the *Wisdom of Solomon* (vi. 22).

> *She is a Breath of the Power of God,*
>   *And a clear outflowing of the Glory of the Almighty.*
> *And from generation to generation passing into holy souls*
>   *She maketh them friends of God and prophets.*
> *She is fairer than the sun*
>   *And above all the constellations of the stars.*
> *Being compared with light*
>   *She is found to be before it.*

It will be seen that there is little difference between this conception of Wisdom and the conception of the Spirit; Wisdom in this passage is Spirit intellectually conceived.

The figure of the heavenly Woman in this chapter is therefore the counterpart of the figure of the heavenly Man or Strong Angel in chapter x. He represents prophetic activity, the masculine, aggressive power of God, the divine inspiration of all the leaders of the race in their battle against evil. She, on the other hand, represents the community or circle without which the prophet is an impossibility; the mother and nurse of the prophet. In particular, as we have seen, she is the community of Israel; she is shortly to become the Christian church; in either case she is only to be called the holy community because the holy community is moved and vivified by the Holy Spirit. It is that process which she personifies, from one side wholly human, from the other wholly divine.

This contrast between the male and the female runs through the book until it is consummated in the Wedding of the Messiah, and she appears as a Bride adorned for her Husband.

We shall have to note again the consummate art by which St. John avoids the genealogical confusions and immoralities which are inherent in this kind of imagery, the moment it is turned into heathen mythology or Gnostic allegory. The Strong Angel of chapter x. is the Word of God which spake by the prophets, and is in a sense that which spoke in Jesus. On the other hand, that which is born of the divine Woman in chapter xii. is Christ; in any mythological or Gnostic system you would have an immoral myth. St. John simply breaks off and starts afresh. Again, the divine Woman who is the mother of Christ appears again in chapter xix. as his Bride; there is no incongruity, for there has been a long break, and a fresh start under other names; and even then she is never described as a Bride, but only after a long interval as a City.

The fatal point in all mythology or allegorising is when the symbols assume an existence of their own apart from what they symbolise. In *Revelation* this is never allowed to happen. With all his imagination, St. John is a realist. He has in his mind the actual process or movement which he is describing; the Strong Angel is the masculine power which forces the prophet to speak and the people to hear; it is a fact. The divine Woman is the grace and beauty and refreshment which he finds in the holy community; the rest and loveliness which we do find in the church because the Spirit is in it. Hermas understood that.

The Preacher and the Congregation! he drawing his inspiration from her (if I may so allude to a congregation), she drawing the word from him. What matter whether we call the community the mother or the bride of the prophet? It is only mother or bride because the spirit is in it; and woe to the prophet who looks elsewhere for his inspiration; he will not find it.

I could wish at times that we had left the Holy Spirit feminine, and realised that Mother Church is only Mother Church if she is Mother Holy Spirit too.

The Ophite Cosmos.

From God came the primal Adam or Word of the Gnostics, from him also the primal Eve or Life (Spirit). From this pair came the Christ, and with him should have come his consort and sister, Sophia or Wisdom; but Wisdom is the errant æon who fell from the circle of divine beings which alone is true reality, and passed into the void or nothingness outside it. A splash of incorruptible light boiled over into chaos; and from her union with the dark waters proceeded the seven angels, the chief of whom, Ialdabaoth (child of chaos?), made this world. The rest of the story is too long to tell. (See Appendix II.) It is enough to say that through the intervention of Sophia, the earthly Adam and Eve had something of the image of the heavenly Adam and Eve; that the higher powers sent Mind or Spirit in the form of the Serpent to enlighten them, and that Ialdabaoth in anger threw both them and the Serpent out of his Paradise; and that in the end Christ came to redeem his bride Sophia and the race of Adam.

In some systems there is a higher heavenly Wisdom who did not fall, and a lower earthly Wisdom who is her daughter. The errant Wisdom is called Prunike, which seems to mean a harlot, and is curiously reminiscent of St. John's earthly

Jerusalem. Valentinus, grouping her with the seven creator angels, calls her the Ogdoad (or group of Eight), "mother and Ogdoad, and Wisdom and Earth, and Jerusalem, and Holy Spirit, and in masculine fashion, Lord." She is an earthly replica of her heavenly mother, the primal Eve, who is also thought of as the Heavenly Wisdom.

The Birth of the Child.

It is now time to return to the *Revelation* and follow the fortunes of the Male Child born of the Heavenly Woman: he is, of course, the Warrior-Messiah, *a Son, a Male, who is to Shepherd all the Nations with a Staff of Iron.* The language is taken from *Psalm* ii., and contemplates the inclusion of the gentiles among the redeemed.

Then follows a verse which is very hard to interpret: *And her Child was snatched up to God and to his Throne.* It may sum up in one line the whole earthly course of our Lord—crucifixion, resurrection, and ascension—or it may simply mean that the Messiah was all his life protected by the power and presence of God; or it may rank him with Enoch, Moses, and Elijah in that he was assumed to God. In the Ophite account of the birth of the æon Christ, it is stated that when the light that was to become Sophia boiled over into the void, the Christ æon was *snatched up into the incorruptible æon along with his mother who is also called the true Church.* See Appendix II.

In St. John's account the Woman takes refuge in the Desert.

Michael.

We now, unfortunately, have to spend some time in showing the truth of a fact which ought never to have been doubted—namely, that the heavenly warrior Michael, who defeats the Dragon, is himself the Messiah, the Man-Child. Dr. Charles asks why it is "Michael and not Christ" who defeats the Dragon; and in the strange confusion produced by this question-begging question, he finds his strongest evidence that the chapter is composite. The obvious identification of Michael with Christ is not even considered. It can, however, be demonstrated.

We will begin with the most obvious argument. It makes sense of the chapter. Of course if you want the book to be a Chinese puzzle, this will not weigh with you; but if you think that the author (or even the final editor) of the book intended this chapter to have a meaning, then you will think it reasonable to consider an interpretation of it which removes confusion. A Woman who is pictured as the Bride of the Lord bears a Son; she is the new Eve, and therefore her son is to crush the Serpent; she is the Virgin of Isaiah, and therefore he is a warrior-king. There follows a war with the Serpent, in which an opponent casts him out of heaven; the Serpent then *went off to make war with the rest of the seed of the woman*. Clearly, then, the person he had first fought with was also the seed of the woman. Why drag in anyone else?

The battle royal is followed by a choric song out of heaven, and, as we have seen, the function of these choric songs is to make clear the main action which is depicted in symbols. It says, *Now is come Salvation and Power and the Kingdom of our God and the Authority of his Messiah*, and then (going on to think of the followers of Christ rather than Christ himself), *They conquered him through the Blood of the Lamb and the Word of his Witness*. Now this admittedly means that it is the Christ whose power has come, and that it is through his blood that victory has been obtained. It tells us who conquered Satan and how; it was Jesus on the cross.

Dr. Charles says that this chorus is an interpolation by the author of the whole volume, who added it here to the Michael Apocalypse which he had copied from another source. If this is so, it shows that he identified Michael with the Messiah, and we are given strong support for our theory; for the objection to it can only be based on the notion that it is *impossible* for the Messiah to have received this title.

We need not linger on the fact that no Christian could conceive that anyone but Christ could have conquered evil; certainly the author of the *Revelation* could not.

By agreeing that Michael is the Messiah, the whole passage becomes simple and harmonious. The Mother gives birth to the hero; the Hero conquers the Dragon. If Michael is not the Messiah, you are reduced to a condition of absolute confusion. A heathen hero-myth has been tacked on to a Jewish myth about Michael and Satan in such a way as to produce a meaningless confusion; the author of the *Revelation* is so delighted with this piece of nonsense that he has translated it out of Hebrew into Greek and given it the central place in his great poem; he has added a chorus which introduces fresh misunderstandings, and then continued the myth in a way which shows that he had no comprehension of the original. The whole has been woven into a literary unity, and there is no sign of any other literary style than that of St. John. So much for a learned piecemeal criticism that despises imagination and common sense.

Angels and Archangels.

The objection to the identification is that Michael is the chief of the seven archangels, and that Christians could not call their Messiah an angel. These objections are based on a study of the apocalypses, reinforced by the Christian conceptions of a later age. A wider survey of earlier literature destroys them. We cannot submit to the thesis that the thought and phraseology of one of the world's greatest poets and theologians were entirely dictated by a group of second-rate books which there is little evidence that he had ever read. We have already seen that his whole thought and style are based upon the classic Hebrew prophets.

The name Michael first appears in *Daniel*, which we know did exercise a great influence upon him. In *Daniel* Michael stands alone, and is not one of a group of Seven or Four; this view is the only view to be found in the Bible, and is clearly earlier than that reflected in *Enoch*. In *Daniel* he is called *the Prince of your People;* he may be a divine leader (captain of the Lord's host) or a guardian spirit, or, more probably, Israel itself personified. In any case he stands alone. He is unique. That is the point. Michael, and nobody else, is fighting for God on earth. He may mean Israel fighting, just as the Son of Man means Israel victorious. Our Lord took the title Son of Man and transferred it to himself to mean the Messiah triumphant; it is equally legitimate to give him the title of Michael as the Messiah militant; and it is fair to say that even though most commentators take these figures in *Daniel* to mean Israel, they might be taken as persons even there.

Outside the pseudonymous apocalypses also we find the name Michael applied to an independent figure without any reference to a group of Seven or Four. We often find him contrasted with Sammael (Satan), just as we do here, leading the forces of good against the forces of evil. In the Ophite system, some form of which St. John is engaged in refuting, we find that the beneficent Serpent "has two names, Michael and Sammael," and the Seven angels of creation are Ialdabaoth, Iao, Sabaoth, Adoneus, Eloeus, Oreus, and Astapheus, which seem to be corruptions of titles of Jehovah. There is no trace at all in *St. John* of the system which makes Michael the chief of the Seven.

Catholic Christianity has adopted the system of the apocalypses, largely through the influence of Dionysius the Areopagite, a pseudonymous writer of the fifth century whose theology is barely orthodox. In the apocalyptic writers, only the first three names are fixed, Michael, Gabriel, and Raphael; Michael and Gabriel come from *Daniel*, and Raphael is found in *Tobit*. The fourth in the catholic series is Uriel, who is found in *Baruch*; but some parts of *Enoch* call him Phanuel, Gabriel, Raphael, and Uriel can easily be resolved into activities or energies of God; they are respectively God revealing himself to the prophets, God in his healing power, and God guiding the apocalyptic authors. But the *Revelation* has no room for this system; the Seven Spirits have become activities of God again, and are resolved into the Holy Spirit (compare Sophia and the Ogdoad), thus leaving no room either for the Ophite or for apocalyptic system.

It will be said that in the *Epistle of Jude* Michael is actually called an archangel, an important point, as *Jude* is also Palestinian, apocalpytic, and anti-Ophite. But mysterious as *Jude* is, it is clear that even here Michael stands alone. He is quoting from *The Assumption of Moses*, an apocalyptic writing which is only partly preserved; but we have enough to know that it contains no system of seven angels, and that Michael and Satan are simply leaders of opposing armies.

In addition, I have never yet seen any evidence that in pre-christian times the word archangel was ever applied to these seven angels, or to a superior "order" of angels. The first use of it in this sense which has come to my notice is in *Pistis Sophia*, an Egyptian Gnostic production, not earlier than A.D. 150; this work provides us with the vague phrase angels and archangels. It is used by modern writers in alluding to the seven (four) great angels of the apocalyptic writings; but it is not used in the writings themselves, so far as I know.

Further, the word archangel ought not to mean member of a superior class or group of angels. It ought to mean the chief of the angels, their captain or leader, just as the chief butler, chief baker, and chief jailer in the story of Joseph appear in the LXX as "arch-wine-pourer," "arch-bread-maker," and "arch-prison-guardian." Now this notion of head or chief of the angels is just the conception of Michael we find in the *Assumption of Moses* and other Jewish authorities.

The word archangel, then, by all the rules, ought to mean captain of the angels, an idea to be compared with the " Captain of the Lord's Host " of *Joshua* v. 15, which applies to an angel who is clearly a manifestation of Jehovah; it may even be compared with " Lord of hosts," and it may perhaps have meant that manifestation of God in which he appears as leader of the armies of Israel or of the heavens.

In the singular it is used by Philo; and this is the only use of it I have traced which is not later than the New Testament. In Philo it is applied to the divine Word which emanates from God: he is Archangel as he is Arch-priest. The title Word is applied by Christians to Christ, and it appears, therefore, that the word archangel would naturally apply to him also.

We may certainly disabuse ourselves of the idea that it applied to a group of seven. Gabriel is mentioned in *St. Luke*, but he is called an angel; he probably means the self-revealing activity of God, as he does in *Daniel*.

The word archangel only occurs twice in the New Testament, and then in the singular. In *Jude* 9 it is used in the Jewish sense, and refers to Michael, leader of the chivalry of heaven; in 1 *Thess.* iv. 16 it probably refers to Christ. St. Paul is here quoting a piece of Palestinian prophecy which he regards as throwing authoritative light on the original gospel; he probably owes it to his companion Silas, the Jerusalem prophet who aided him in composing the epistle.

> *The Lord will descend from Heaven*
> *With a Shout,*
> *With the Voice of an Archangel,*
> *And with the Trumpet of God.*

Now it seems fairly clear that we have one sound here, not three; the Shout is the Voice, and the Voice is the Trumpet. The passage is an obvious translation from Hebrew or Aramaic; for it the original Greek has *In a Shout, In a Voice* . . . *In a Trumpet ;* and the lack of definite articles with Voice and Trumpet is also a sign of a Semitic original. Now if the phrase Voice of an Archangel is Hebrew or Aramaic it would be better to translate it merely Archangelic Voice, and to interpret it as his own voice. And if this interpretation is as correct as it is simple and natural, then the word archangel applies to Christ. We have seen that we ought to think of one archangel only; on that point there is little room for doubt; and the easiest interpretation of it is to apply it to Christ.

The passage in *Thessalonians* proves, at any rate, that it was used in the primitive church at Jerusalem; and in Hebrew what can it be but Rosh Malakim? and what can Rosh Malakim be but Head of Angels? It is probably a Hebrew title of honour applied by Jews to Michael, and transferred by Philo and the Christians to the Word of God. Its natural meaning is that angel or power of God which leads the forces of God in their warfare against evil.

In the gospels our Lord represents himself as coming the second time with the holy angels, quite clearly as their leader. He comes, that is, as archangel; he represents himself as leading and commanding angels. What was to prevent the early Christian prophets from developing this element in his teaching?

This is a long digression; and apparently a useless one, as *Revelation* does not call Michael an archangel; but it has been vitally necessary in order to show that the accepted mythology which stands between us and the true interpretation of this passage is utterly unknown to the New Testament writers, or to any writers of their date. We read of Michael and his angels, exactly as we read of the Son of Man and the angels who accompany him.

Michael and Son of Man are related concepts drawn from the book of *Daniel;* and the Serpent who was defeated by him has characteristics which also link him with that book.

He is not even called an angel; though it would not matter if he were. But as a matter of fact he is not; and this fact vitiates the argument that Michael cannot be Christ, because St. John would not present Christ as an angel.

Why not?

An angel is not a visible creature with wings and a human shape; he is an invisible power proceeding from the Almighty. The use of the phrase angel of the Lord in the writings of St. Luke shows that the Palestinian church had revived the old belief in a manifestation or energy of God, and thoroughly understood it. The only reason why it did not pass into orthodox theology is that the other meaning—that of an independent subordinate spirit—gradually gained the victory.

But in Hermas, a Roman writer almost contemporary with St. John, Christ is identified with an angel; he is actually identified with Michael the leader of six who are called the first-created. In St. Justin Martyr (A.D. 130 to 156) Christ is frequently called an angel; it is one of his regular titles. Liturgical fragments (*e.g.* the Canon of Hippolytus, which is so closely related to the thought of St. Justin) call him the Angel of Great Counsel, even in the third century. This phrase is based on the Greek translation of *Isaiah* ix. 6; but it would scarcely have persisted so long in the face of a higher theology if it had not obtained a strong position in Christian thought. The use of it in Hermas and St. Justin must go back to something earlier; perhaps to a misunderstanding of this very passage, perhaps to something independent. But if it is a misunderstanding of this passage, then both of them identified Michael with Christ.

To conclude and to summarise; in *Daniel* Michael is the militant leader of Israel against the forces of persecution; in *Revelation* he is the militant leader of Christianity and all the forces of God against persecution and all the forces of evil.

The Persecutions in Jerusalem.

A decisive victory has been won by " Michael," and Satan is cast down from his high and dominating position. He is defeated; but the battle still has to be continued *on earth ;* he is, however, no longer in that position of power in which he *deceived the whole earth.*

It is characteristic of St. John that he does not distinguish the sufferings of the Messiah from the sufferings of his followers; just as in the symbolism of the Strong Angel he does not distinguish the Word spoken by the prophets from the Word proclaimed in Galilee and carried by apostles through the world. There is one war and one victory; and though a decisive victory has been won, the followers of the Messiah have to repeat it in their own lives. *They conquered him through the Blood of the Lamb, and loved not their lives unto death.*

There is no doubt in the minds of commentators that the Woman now represents the primitive church and its persecution in Jerusalem; for Rome, the Beast from the Sea, has not yet appeared in sight. But the details of the Vision are the most obscure in the book. Twice we are told that *the Woman fled into the Desert where she has a place prepared by God* for the prophetic period of three and a half years, which we know to represent the duration of persecution. I do not think, however, that the Desert represents the flight of the Christians to Pella before the siege of Jerusalem by the Romans; it is not the tone of the Vision, which in any case appears to date before that event.

I fancy that it has two references: one to the wanderings of Israel in the Sinai Peninsula, the other to the meditations of our Lord and the prophets in the desert.

When Israel escaped from Egypt the Desert was the refuge in which she could be in safety; here the mystic Bride was in spiritual union with her Lord. He protected her; *I bare you on Eagle's Wings* says Exodus xix. 4. Similarly the infant Church, though not literally in the desert, was brought safe through her Red Sea of suffering, and remained all the time protected by the presence with her of her Lord. *There was given her the Two Wings of the Great Eagle ;* Jehovah himself.

Her escape was not a literal escape into a literal desert, but into a vivid sense of communion with the Almighty; I dimly see in it a suggestion of loneliness, hardship, and want, but the continual presence of God. Had the Desert become not only a retreat for prophetic meditation, but also a symbol of union with God? In the case of our Lord and St. Philip the Deacon it is clearly literal; but later on, when St. John is taken into the Desert to see the Vision of the Great Harlot, it is surely a symbol equivalent to the words *in the Spirit.* The tradition is carried on by Hermas.

And the Serpent cast out of his mouth Water like a River to carry the Woman away ; and the Earth helped the Woman and opened her mouth and swallowed up the River.

This is the most mysterious verse in the whole book, and even when we have realised that its phraseology is consciously anti-Ophite, we are not much nearer to understanding it. Its main meaning is, of course, easy. The flood of Water represents the old enemy, chaos and void in the first place, and persecuting civilisation in the second. The dry land (like the desert) represents friendly influences. Persecution is aimed at the Church, but she is not overwhelmed.

There is a direct quotation from the Old Testament here which has been missed; it refers to Cain, the patron saint of the Ophites. *The Earth opened her mouth* and drank up the blood of Abel and was hostile to Cain; she is the enemy of the Serpent and the friend of the Woman. Is St. John insisting on the goodness of creation?

There is also a contrast intended with Prunike the Harlot, the Lower or Left-handed Wisdom, the æon who fell out of

P

the circle of divine beings into the void. Now the void is, strictly speaking, nothing at all; it is non-existent; but, as in the first chapter of Genesis, it is symbolised as water. This watery chaos was hostile and hateful to her, and yet she had to take a body from it; she attempted to escape from the waters, and reascend to her mother, the divine Eve, but could not, owing to the weight of the body. She leapt into the sky and became the heavens, *which still have a sort of watery body.* (See Appendix II.)

It is clear that St. John's Vision bears some kind of relation to this myth; but we are unable to say exactly just what relation, because we do not know what views of the Ophites St. John is answering; no doubt they had had something to say about the Christian church, which they must have regarded as a false church. In the Ophite system the woman is friendly with the Serpent, and enters into some sort of relation with the waters. In St. John the Serpent and the waters symbolise evil, just as they do in the prophets; the woman and the dry land (creation?) are good, and she is preserved by God from both the powers of evil. (See Appendix I.)

And the Dragon went off to make war on the rest of her seed who keep the Commandments of God and have the Witness of Jesus: and he stood on the Sand of the Sea.

We turn now to the persecution of gentile Christians, and at once find the Visions much simpler to understand.

The Great Interlude: Part II. Antichrist

The Beast from the Sea.
And I saw.

We now return to the Vision formula to which we have been accustomed, and as we look back on the whole picture of the Mother, the Dragon, and the Man Child, we cannot deny that it makes an impression upon us different from the rest of the book, even though it is marked throughout by the original style and unmistakable imagination of the author. And it is certainly curious that it is not marked definitely as his own vision by the words *I saw*.

It shares with the episode of the Two Witnesses a condensed involved manner in which poetry is sacrificed to a system of symbolism which is now hard for us to unravel: there is not a great deal of the free, bold and attractive style which the author appears to have learned later. The retention of this obscure Judaic material in the central position of the whole book at least makes sure of two things: it did convey a meaning to those who first read it, and that meaning was vital and essential to the whole composition. No method could be more unsound than that adopted by so many scholars in dealing with these passages: to regret their obscurity, discuss their origin, heave a sigh, and pass on to interpret the whole book without reference to them. You cannot make sense of a book by ignoring what the author considers essential. You may not like the discourses of the Father of Heaven in Milton's *Paradise Lost*, you may consider them obscure, and dry, and negligible; but if you want to understand the book, they are the most important passages in it.

St. John has finished his account of the birth of the Messiah, his contest with Satan in Jerusalem, and the persecution of his followers; by taking the Dragon to the Sands of the Sea, he leads us to contemplate the persecution of gentile Christians by heathen rulers, and this, of course, must be of a later date. For we are brought face to face with Antichrist; and Antichrist is for the moment the Emperor Nero.

When he wrote his earlier Visions, it is probable that gentile Christians did not come within the scope of our author; he knew they were there, of course, but they were a mere fringe on the borders of Jewish Christianity. Jerusalem had been the arena of conflict, and, in consequence, the focus of prophetic vision. Persecution abroad now brought into the limelight *the rest of the seed of the woman*.

The Emperor did not persecute before A.D. 64, so that the visions in their present form must be later than this; but it is possible that they are worked up from older visions in which some other personage (Caligula? Herod?) was identified with Antichrist. We appear, therefore, to have three strata of visions which can be distinguished and approximately dated. We may distinguish them by the familiar symbols J, E, and P. (See p. 131.)

> J means the earliest group of visions seen in *Jerusalem*, Jewish in form, pre-occupied with the persecution of the Jewish Church, and marked by the symbolism of the Red Dragon, the Woman, and an Altar in heaven. The prophetic standpoint in these visions is earth. Angels descend.
>
> E means the next group, which identify the *Emperor* Nero with Antichrist. They are marked by the "trinity of evil"—Dragon, Beast, and Second Beast—and their standpoint is also earth. They are less condensed and difficult.
>
> P means the latest group, connected with the last stage of all in *Patmos*. The style is freer, more lyrical, more simple, more universal; there are touches of gentile symbolism. There is a Throne, not an Altar in heaven; and the prophetic standpoint is heaven, not earth.

The Anti-Ophite propaganda is to be found in J and E even more strongly than in P, which shows that the sect did not originate in Ephesus, but, as we should have expected, in Palestine.

The Beast from the Sea.

In the *Book of Daniel* there is a vision in which the Four Winds break out upon the Sea, and Four Beasts arise in succession, each representing the world-power in a new form. The last and most horrible has ten horns, and represents the Greece of Alexander the Great; the ten horns are the ten successive kings of the Syrian division of his empire, who represented for the Jews the main line of succession.

In the *Revelation* one Beast arises out of the Sea; but he combines in himself the horrors of the whole Four described by Daniel. *He has Ten Horns and Seven Heads.* The Seven

Heads appear to be characteristic of the chaos monster, and the Ophite serpent, and, unlike the Ten Horns, do not come from *Daniel*. It is rather important to remember that St. John found these numbers fixed for him already.

It will be remembered that the Red Dragon in Jerusalem who persecuted the Woman had Seven Heads and Ten Horns; here too Antichrist had appeared; for a moment the Red Dragon appeared as the Beast. There can be no doubt that in *St. John* the number Ten has a connection with persecution, so that a monster with ten horns might in itself suggest a persecuting power, whether in Jerusalem or in Rome. The Beast is the Dragon, incarnate as a persecuting power.

There is no doubt, however, that in this Vision he now represents the imperial power of Rome; and the insignia of Roman power are not inappropriate even to the Red Dragon, who was hostile to the Man Child, for it was through the Roman imperial power that the Jewish persecuting authorities put Jesus to death. It was Rome (inspired by the Jews) that crucified Jesus; it was Rome that organised the great persecution of his martyrs; but it was the *Dragon* who *gave it its Power and its Throne and its great Authority*, titles which are quasi-messianic and quasi-divine. The Beast begins to appear as a blasphemous parody of the Lamb, a Messiah of Satan; he receives power from the Dragon, as the Lamb received power from God. Here is the Antichrist, or opposition Christ, foretold by our Lord.

Nero.

As in *Daniel*, the Ten Horns are meant to be identified with ten kings; but it is difficult to calculate who they are, and the consideration of this passage must be postponed. The Ten Horns have *Ten Crowns, and on its Heads a Name of Blasphemy, and one of the Heads was as if Slain unto Death, and its Mortal Wound was healed*. The Name of Blasphemy may be the name " Augustus " or " Worshipful " assumed by the Emperors; in any case it refers to their pretensions to deity. The vein of parody is also very clear; the Beast is a horrible counterpart of the *Lamb as it had been slain . . . who was dead and is alive.*

The Heads, like the Horns, represent kings (as we are told later); and the Head that received a mortal wound represents Nero, who initiated the persecutions. He committed suicide, and in his death the Roman Empire received a mortal blow. Three rival generals fought for the throne; but though the Empire staggered, it did not go under. It survived. *The Mortal Wound was healed.* It may be that there is some reference to a popular belief that Nero was not dead, but would return again. This, too, we shall discuss later.

In tabulating our results, we note that the same principles of symbolism are to be observed as in the case of the Two Witnesses, the Word of God, and the Woman in Heaven; each symbol represents an activity at work in the world which takes definite form in a definite epoch, and is finally focussed in a person or persons—

Two Witnesses.	*Word of God.*	*Woman in Heaven.*
Human witness to the truth.	God's truth, revealing itself.	Elect souls, faithful to the highest.
Law and Prophets.	Prophecies of the Christ, etc.	The true Israel.
Moses and Elijah.	Christ.	Mary.
Christian Prophets and Martyrs.	Apostles and Evangelists.	The Primitive Church.

The symbol represents a whole process, and must not be tied down to the persons in whom it is incarnate.

The results in the case of the Beast are as follows:

1. The Beast represents the Serpent-principle of Evil as it becomes incarnate from time to time in the world-empire.
2. At present in the E visions the world-empire is Rome; but the same spirit is to be found elsewhere, even in the streets of Jerusalem, which is the meaning in the J visions.
3. The Ten Horns connect the Beast with the Beast of *Daniel*, which stands for Antiochus, his divine claims and ruthless persecution.

4. The Roman Empire is summed up in its divine Emperor; and the mortal wound of one Head represents the death of Nero and the blow it dealt to the whole Empire.

5. Although the one Head symbolises Nero, the system is not so precise that the whole Beast may not be also identified with him; for in the Emperor resides the whole imperial power. The Satanic messiah is the head of the body, the empire.

The Vision, therefore, as it stands, must date from after the death of Nero, and was probably written after 68, the year of his death, and before 70, the year of the destruction of Jerusalem. It belongs to the period of confusion. But I do not wish to shut out the possibility that in its original form it may have referred to the mad emperor Caligula, who had a marvellous recovery from sickness, and who endeavoured to force the Jews to put up his image in the temple; but if so, it has been practically re-written.

The rest of this section describes the worship addressed to the Emperor by *every tribe and people and language and nation*, and reflects the enthusiasm with which it was taken up, especially in the East. But a period is set to his ascendancy *Forty and Two Months*, the familiar period of Three and a Half Years, which indicates that there is an end to persecution.

The Beast from the Land. (Second Beast: False Prophet.)

Satan, the Primal Serpent, has his Messiah, who is himself incarnate; he must also have his Prophet. Pseudo-prophets were expected as well as Pseudo-christs.

The Second Beast rises from the Land. He had *Two Horns like a Lamb, and spake like a Dragon.* Dr. Charles is distressed about this statement, because he says dragons do not speak; I am too ignorant about the natural history of dragons to contradict him here; but as St. John is not talking about flesh-and-blood dragons, the point need not detain us. The Second Beast is later on called the False Prophet; his exterior is Christian; his inspiration is not the Word of God, but the spirit of evil.

Now it is clear in the first place that this symbol denotes some power auxiliary to the divine emperor, and particularly to his worship. *He exercises all the authority of the First Beast before him, and makes all the earth (or land) . . . to worship the First Beast ;* he *makes fire descend from heaven ;* he gives *spirit to the Image of the Beast so that the Image speaks ;* he does other miraculous *Signs,* by which he *deceives those who dwell on the earth (or land).*

The theory of the Second Beast which holds the field is that of Ramsay, who says that it is a priesthood, or civil authority which enforces emperor-worship in Asia Minor; and if so this section is a later addition to the Vision, which is quite possible. As for the miracles, as Dr. Charles says, few oriental religions were without ingenious illusions of this kind; talking images and fire from heaven were common enough, and they were expected by the Jews at the coming of Antichrist.

The identification is supported by the wide powers of the Second Beast. Those who do not worship are to be killed. Those who worship receive *a Mark on their Right Hand and on their Forehead*, and without this Mark it is not possible to buy or sell.

But is it not possible that we are again on the track of the Ophites? We know from the letters to the seven churches that they were a more real danger to the Christians in time of persecution than the actual persecutors. They joined freely in heathen worship, and taught Christians to do the same; they had prophets, or at least prophetesses. They were Serpent-worshippers, and St. John is exhibiting the Emperor as a Serpent-Messiah; are not the Ophites the Serpent-Prophet?

It could much more truly be said of them that they looked like the Lamb and spoke with the voice of the Serpent; they persuaded orthodox Christians to lapse into heathen religious rites, and probably into Emperor-worship; they may have excited persecution against those who did not, just as the Jews excited persecution against St. Paul and St. Polycarp.

Further, they are identified with the false prophets foretold by our Lord, in the Pastoral Epistles of St. Paul, in

Jude, and in 2 *Peter*. The author of 2 *Peter* calls his heretics after the name of Balaam, just as St. John does; Jude says they walked in the way of Cain, and also mentions Balaam and Korah. This seems to identify them with St. John's heretics, and also with the Cainites, who are identical with the Ophites. It thus appears that Christians generally alluded to this sect as the false prophets.

1 *John*, which is a preface to the fourth gospel, identifies them with Antichrist (he is the only author in the New Testament to use the word) and with the false prophets; the spirit that inspires the false prophets is the Antichrist. He too mentions Cain; it is the only proper name besides that of Jesus that he does mention. He, too, strongly emphasises the hostility between Christ and the devil. His position is identical with what we find in *Revelation*.

It seems probable then that the Second Beast covers *every* influence which might seduce Christians into worshipping the power of evil in any of its incarnations.

The Mark of the Beast.

The Mark on the Forehead or Right Hand is not to be taken literally. It is identical with the worship; worship and Mark are one. It is a stain on the soul.

It is the Satanic counterpart of the Seal borne by the worshippers of the true God; this Seal corresponds to the " Chrism " of 1 *John*.

Its Old Testament origin is the Mark placed by the Lord upon Cain, a significant point.

It also bears some relation to the phylactery or amulet worn by pious Jews on their forehead and *left* hand; in the case of false Jews the positions are reversed. The Jewish amulet contained a verse out of *Deuteronomy* which proclaimed the Name of God: *Jehovah our God : Jehovah : One.* It is very probable that Cainites carried some such amulet; names and numbers appealed strongly to the Gnostic mind; but it could not carry the name of the creator they had rejected.

The Mark, says St. John, was *the Name of the Beast or the Number of his Name ;* it was also *the Number of a Man ;* that is to say, the name was expressed cryptically in the form of a Number. To interpret it required Wisdom and Mind,

> *Here is Wisdom,*
> *He who has Mind,*
> *Let him calculate the Number of the Beast.*

There is no veil at all here on the attack which is made on the Gnostic heresy. Wisdom (Sophia) is the errant æon, the Left-handed Wisdom who produced the creator; Mind (Nous) is the Serpent who inspired mankind to renounce their creator. The two words are not characteristic of St. John; they are never [1] used again throughout the book, except in one equally significant case (xvii. 9).

The Number, as everyone knows, is *Six Hundred, Sixty, and Six*. We have no right to expect to be able to unravel this mystery at this date, or to look for unanimity among commentators; but two ideas have won partial acceptance.

If Seven signifies divine perfection, then Six will signify that which falls short of divine perfection; and three sixes will signify the trinity of evil. This has in its favour that it agrees with St. John's use of numbers; it is the principle on which every other number in the book is to be explained. But this instance seems to require something more definite; it is the *Number of a Man*; it can be *calculated*.

In Greek and Hebrew and Latin there are no numerals; each letter of the alphabet has a numerical value, and therefore any name has a numerical value, which can be calculated by adding up the values of all the letters it contains. A surprising unanimity is found among commentators who have adopted this method; the name is NERON KAISAR (the Greek form of it) and the letters are given their Hebrew values:

Nun	=	50
Resh	=	200
Vav	=	6
Nun	=	50
Qoph	=	100
Samech	=	60
Resh	=	200
Total	=	666

[1] The word Wisdom is employed also in two purely lyrical passages (v. 12 and vii. 12) which belong to the latest strata in the book.

This also satisfies a reading found in some Latin authorities, 616; for the Latin way of spelling the name is NERO CAESAR; and the omission of the second Nun gives a total of 616. It should be remembered that Hebrew has no vowels.

It may be assumed, therefore, that the Number is meant to connect the Beast with Nero, in whose person the persecuting spirit of the world-empire became incarnate. The persecution of Nero is the appearance of Antichrist; and this identification enables us to date this vision shortly after A.D. 64. Thirty years later, when the visions were worked up into their present form, there was a second persecuting emperor, Domitian; the symbolism was brought up to date by using the current superstition of a return of the spirit of Nero; to St. John, Domitian is a second Nero (see pp. 282-6).

Now some of the imagery of this passage suits the time of Domitian better than the time of Nero, and must have been added then. *And it was given him . . . to make that any who do not worship the Image of the Beast should be put to death : and to make all . . ., to give them a Mark upon the Right Hand or upon their Forehead, and that no one can buy or sell except he who has the Mark.*

The curious grammar of this passage suggests that later insertions have been made; and it was certainly not till the reign of Domitian that the worship of the God-emperor was taken as seriously as this. Deissman has pointed out how a seal was placed upon meat and other articles sold in shops; and this no doubt explains the reference to buying and selling. The seal bore the titles of the " Beast," *Dominus Deus Domitianus.*

Though these references can hardly be doubted, it must be remembered that the root meaning of this symbolism is the inward and spiritual one, the stain on the soul, the brand of sin. The followers of the Serpent-Messiah must be marked with his Mark and bear his Name on their foreheads, just as the followers of the Lamb are sealed with the Seal of the Living God, and bear the Name of the Father on their foreheads, as the high priest in Jerusalem bore the sacred name Jehovah on his.

The Lamb and his Followers.

And I saw, and behold, the Lamb standing on the Mount Sion, and with him a Hundred and Forty-Four Thousand.

Over against the Beast and his Prophet and his world-wide army of worshippers, John now paints the Lamb, the Warrior-Messiah, with his faithful followers *who have his Name and the Name of his Father written upon their Foreheads*, just as the worshippers of the Beast have the Name of the Beast on their foreheads.

A New Song or triumphant psalm is heard from heaven; but no one can understand it except the Hundred and Forty-Four Thousand themselves, who represent all *the Redeemed from the earth,* Jew and Gentile. This chorus is probably a later addition, as it is sung before the Throne and the Living Creatures and the Elders.

There is some controversy over the identity of this army. Are they saints in heaven or saints on earth? The answer is that there are times when St. John does not trouble to draw the line. The Church or mystic bride of Christ includes beings visible and invisible, heavenly and earthly, as in *Ephesians.*

What, then, is Sion? Is it the earthly Jerusalem, or is it in heaven? Again we must remember that the earthly and heavenly Jerusalem are one. To quote the *Epistle to the Hebrews,* which has so much in common with *Revelation,* it is *Sion mountain and the City of the Living God, and myriads of Angels, and the whole assembly and congregation of the First-born whose names are written in Heaven; and God the Judge of all, and the spirits of the Righteous made perfect, and the Mediator of the New Covenant, Jesus, and a sprinkling in Blood which speaks better things than Abel (Heb.* xii. 22).

It is neither in Jerusalem nor above the clouds; it is the whole assembly of the saints, living and departed.

A curious literalism has spoiled this beautiful passage, as it has spoiled many others. Dr. Charles maintains that this Hundred and Forty-four Thousand represents all the faithful, and that all of them are martyred; this has to be noted, because it naturally vitiates his treatment of the second half of the book.

He also takes in a strangely material way the statement that *they were not defiled with women; for they are Virgins*, which he imagines to imply that all the redeemed are celibate. He then shows a very justifiable indignation with the monkish idiot who foisted it into the book; it is a pity that so much resentment should be wasted.

" Virgins " here is obviously a violent symbol for purity, just as " eunuchs " in *Matthew* is a violent symbol for celibacy; neither is meant to be taken literally. They are not men who have had no intercourse with women, but men *who have not defiled themselves with women*, which is quite a different idea, and is certainly not meant to describe marriage. It refers without doubt to the sexual rites connected with heathen temples like that of Ephesus, which gentile Christians found it hard to abjure, and the heretical sects encouraged them to adopt. It may even be more general than this; it may mean that they have been faithful to Christ and are not gone whoring after strange gods, and so are true members of his virgin bride, the church.

And then there is the odd criticism that under the terms of this description, none of the redeemed can be women!

Let us conclude this Book by gratefully acknowledging the magnificent work that Dr. Charles has done, and in particular the way he has brought out the sacrificial character of this passage. The word Aparche, translated " firstfruits," is really no more than " gift " or " sacrifice." The martyrs are here shown as offering themselves to the true God in union with the great sacrifice of the cross. *I beseech you, brethren*, says St. Paul, *by the mercies of God that ye present your bodies, a living sacrifice, holy, acceptable unto God, which is your reasonable service*, your " logical worship."

" Blameless," " without blemish," is also a technical term of the altar; but it is applicable to the priest as well as the gift. The candidate for priesthood, as I have pointed out before, had not merely to establish his genealogy, but also to show himself physically perfect, " without blemish "; only then was he given his White Robe of priesthood.

The phrase *These are they who have not defiled themselves with women* goes back to the same symbolic base. The priest

Ophite or Gnostic Universe

THE UPPER WORLD. "*PLEROMA*"

Bythos (Abyss).   Aion (Age).

The First Man Adam or Adamas.
The Unnameable Father.

The first existence from whom proceed:

Word (Logos).   Spirit (feminine).
Man (Anthropos).   Life (Zoe = Eve).
Son of Man.   Church (Ecclesia).
Second Man.   First Woman.
The Heavenly Adam.   The Heavenly Eve.

From the union of these two proceed:

Christ and   Sophia, Wisdom.
                  Second Woman who should have been the consort of the Christ, but fell from the Pleroma into the Void. She becomes the Harlot.

THE LOWER WORLD. "*KENOMA*"

The Void, *i.e.* The Nothing, the Emptiness, containing the Four Elements, Water, Darkness, Abyss, Chaos.

Sophia, The Harlot, takes a body from the "Waters" and by intercourse with Chaos produces:

The Seven Creator Spirits, Ialdabaoth, etc. or Jehovah.

From these proceed the world.

The Ophite or Gnostic Universe. This chart shows some of the main elements in the Gnostic cosmos; but it is already complicated compared with the primitive conception out of which it was framed. See Appendix II.

OPHITE OR GNOSTIC UNIVERSE

The first thing to note is the division between Upper and Lower (Right-handed or Dextral, Left-handed or Sinistral). The Upper is the part which has existence or reality, for it is all God, and everything in it is divine and exists in him; later on it came to be called the Pleroma or Fullness of God. Outside of God there is, strictly speaking, nothing; but the nothing (owing to the perpetual mental fallacy which visualises nothing as empty space) is thought of as Water, Darkness, Abyss and Chaos. Out of this inferior, evil, and strictly speaking non-existent stuff our world was made.

A creator is provided in the following way. The Unnameable Father or First Man, perhaps with the assistance of a consort (Silence), produces out of his own nature a divine pair, male and female, which in their turn produce another; in later gnostic systems this goes on almost indefinitely, producing the "endless genealogies" referred to in 1 *Timothy*. All are God; all are in the Pleroma; but each pair is further removed from the Father, and has less of his perfection.

The youngest, Sophia or Wisdom, aspires in her pride to know the Unnameable Father; she falls into the outer nothing or chaos, and is known as the Harlot. In some systems there is a heavenly Wisdom which remains in the Pleroma, the divine counterpart of the fallen Wisdom: so we may regard the highest female æon as Wisdom also.

From the union of the Harlot Wisdom with the Chaos is born Jehovah, the Creator, who imagines that there is no God above him; he is also thought of as the chief of the seven creator angels, who all proceed from the Harlot Wisdom. This is the origin of the world.

All Old Testament values are thus reversed. Jehovah is evil. He wished to keep the fruit of the tree of Knowledge to himself, out of mere selfishness. The higher æons in the Pleroma sent the divine Spirit or Mind in the form of a Serpent to help Man by making him eat of this fruit. This leads to the repudiation of Jehovah and the worship of the Serpent; his worshippers are "Ophites" (Serpentarians) or "Gnostics" (Men of Knowledge). My suggestion is that these heretics are the "Synagogue of Satan" mentioned by St. John, and that parts of the Revelation are directed against them.

St. John takes the Old Testament symbols which they distort into a heathen and anti-moral system, and uses them: (*a*) in the right sense, and (*b*) in the right manner. The Serpent and the Abyss symbolise evil and its origin, and are contrary to God; he provides the Serpent with a male incarnation or Messiah (the Beast) and a female one (the Harlot); but they symbolise actual historical movements, not mythological figures. God also has two ways of working in history; one is male or messianic (the Lamb), recurring as the Word of God, Michael, and Messiah; the other is female (the Bride), and recurs as the divine community or its energising Spirit. (See p. 278.)

had to be ritually pure before taking part in the sacrifice, and this purity was destroyed by any intercourse with women, even with his wife. From the point of view of the priest offering the sacrifice, such intercourse was "defilement." The ritual purity demanded of the Levitical priesthood was thus taken over as a symbol of the moral and spiritual purity demand of the Christian who had been made a member of the martyr church.

It is obvious that we are back again in the atmosphere of the early document J, with its Jewish liturgical background; we return to Jerusalem and the doom which is hanging over it. This passage, however, links itself beautifully with the vision we have just read of the great god-emperor, who demands the worship of the whole world. It is no longer merely the little church in Jerusalem which is marked with the character of the martyr and the witness; the battle against evil is to become world-wide.

The Lamb stands on Mount Sion, and with him the whole number of his true followers, all of them witnesses and martyrs in spirit, if not in fact. Now the battle may begin; now the sacrifice is ready to be offered. Now the liturgical and ceremonial movement of the book, after prophecy and interlude, is lifted up to its highest point. The victory and sufferings of the cross are to be repeated and multiplied throughout the whole world.

BOOK VI

THE AGE TO COME

PART I. THE DOOM OF BABYLON

The Three Messages.
The Son of Man.

The Seven Last Plagues:
> *The First Four.*
> 5. *The Throne of the Beast struck.*
> 6. *Preparations for Armageddon.*
> 7. *Babylon remembered before God.*

The Harlot and the Scarlet Beast.
Lamentations over Babylon.
The Bride of the Lamb.

HOW IS THE FAITHFUL CITY
BECOME AN HARLOT!
IT WAS FULL OF JUDGEMENT;
RIGHTEOUSNESS WAS IN IT;
BUT NOW MURDERERS.
Isaiah i. 21.

PROPHECIES AND OMENS IN JOSEPHUS, JEWISH WARS (vi. 5).

" A FALSE prophet was the occasion of these people's destruction, who had made a public proclamation in the city that very day, that God commanded them to get up upon the Temple, and that they should receive miraculous Signs of their deliverance. Now there was then a great number of false prophets suborned by the tyrants to impose upon the people. . . .

" 3. Thus were the miserable people persuaded by these deceivers . . . while they did not attend nor give credit to the Signs that were so evident, and did so plainly foretell their future desolation; but like men infatuated, without either eyes to see or minds to consider, did not regard the denunciations that God made to them.

" Thus there was a Star resembling a Sword which stood over the City, and a Comet that continued a whole year.

" Thus also before the Jews' rebellion, and before those commotions which preceded the war, when the people were come in great crowds to the Feast of Unleavened Bread, on the eighth day of the month Xanthicus, and at the ninth hour of the night, so Great a Light shone round the Altar and the Holy House that it appeared to be bright day-time, which Light lasted for half an hour. This Light seemed to be a good Sign to the unskilful, but was so interpreted by the sacred scribes as to portend those events that followed immediately upon it. At the same Festival a heifer, as she was led by the High Priest to be sacrificed, brought forth a Lamb in the midst of the Temple. Moreover the Eastern Gate of the Inner Court, which was of brass, and vastly heavy, and had been with difficulty shut by twenty men, and rested upon a basis armed with iron, and had bolts fastened very deep into the firm floor, which was there made of one entire stone, was seen to open of its own accord about the sixth hour of the night. Now those that kept watch in the Temple came running to the Captain of the Temple, and told him of it; who then came up thither, and not without difficulty was able to shut the gate again. This also appeared to the vulgar to be a very happy prodigy, as if God did thereby open them the gate of happiness. But the men of learning understood it, that the security of their Holy House was dissolved of its own accord, and that the Gate was opened for the advantage of their enemies. So these publicly declared, that this Signal foreshowed the desolation that was coming upon them.

"Besides these, a few days after that Feast, on the one and twentieth day of the month Artemisius, a certain prodigious and incredible phenomenon appeared; I suppose the account of it would seem a fable, were it not related by those who saw it, and were not the events that followed it of so considerable a nature as to deserve such Signals; for, before the sun-setting, Chariots and Troops of Soldiers in their Armour were seen running about among the Clouds, and surrounding of Cities.

"Moreover at that feast which we call Pentecost, as the Priests were going by night into the Inner Temple, as the custom was, to perform their sacred ministrations, they said that, in the first place, they felt a Quaking, and heard a Great Noise, and after that they heard a Sound as of a Great Multitude, saying, *Let us remove hence*.

"But what is still more terrible, there was one Jesus, the son of Ananus, a plebeian, and an husbandman, who, four years before the war began, and at a time when the City was in very great peace and prosperity, came to the Feast whereon it is our custom for every one to make Tabernacles to God in the Temple, began on a sudden to cry aloud, *A Voice from the East, a Voice from the Four Winds, a Voice against Jerusalem and the Holy House, a Voice against the Bridegrooms and the Brides, and a Voice against the whole People!*

" This was his cry, as he went about by day and night, in all the lanes of the City. However, certain of the most eminent among the populace had great indignation at this dire cry of his, and took up the man, and gave him a great number of severe stripes; yet did he not either say anything for himself, or anything peculiar to those that chastised him, but still he went on with the same words which he cried before. Hereupon our rulers, supposing, as the case proved to be, that this was a sort of divine fury in the man, brought him to the Roman procurator—where he was whipped till his bones were laid bare; yet did he not make any supplication for himself, nor shed any tears, but turning his voice to the most lamentable tone possible, at every stroke of the whip his answer was, *Woe, Woe to Jerusalem*. And when Albinus (for he was then our procurator) asked him, Who he was? and whence he came? and why he uttered such words? he made no answer or reply to what he said, but still did not leave off his melancholy ditty, till Albinus took him to be a madman, and dismissed him.

" Now, during all the time that passed before the war began, this man did not go near any of the citizens, nor was seen of them while he said so; but he every day uttered these lamentable words, as if it were his premeditated vow, *Woe, Woe to Jerusalem,* Nor did he give ill words to those that beat him every day, nor good words to those that gave him food; but this was his reply to all men, and indeed no other than a melancholy presage of what was to come.

" This cry of his was the loudest at the Festivals; and he continued this ditty for seven years and five months, without growing hoarse, or being tired therewith, until the very time that he saw his presage in earnest fulfilled in our siege, when it ceased; for as he was going round about the wall, he cried out with his utmost force, *Woe, Woe to the City again, and to the People, and to the Holy House!* And just as he added at the last—*Woe, Woe to myself also!* there came a stone out of one of the engines, and smote him, and killed him immediately: and as he was uttering the very same presages, he gave up the ghost.

"4. Now if any one consider these things, he will find that God takes care of mankind, and by all ways possible foreshows to our race what is for their preservation; but that men perish by those miseries which they madly and voluntarily bring upon themselves; for the Jews, by demolishing the tower of Antonia, had made their Temple Four-square, while at the same time they had it written in their sacred oracles—*That then should their City be taken, as well as their Holy House, when once their Temple should become Four-square.*

"But now, what did most elevate them in undertaking this war was an ambiguous oracle that was also found in their sacred writings, how, *about that Time, one from their country should become Governor of the habitable earth.* The Jews took this prediction to belong to themselves in particular; and many of the wise men were thereby deceived in their determination. Now this oracle certainly denoted the government of Vespasian, who was appointed Emperor in Judea.

"However, it is not possible for men to avoid fate, although they see it beforehand. But these men interpreted some of these Signals according to their own pleasure; and some of them they utterly despised, until their madness was demonstrated, both by the taking of their City and their own destruction."

(Translation of William Whiston.)

NOTE

The first half of section 3 is obviously to be taken as a short apocalypse which Josephus has worked into his narrative; it should be noted that, like *Revelation*, it is dependent on *Ezekiel* (x. 4, 18, 19 and xi. 23). It is interpolated with the story of the birth of the Lamb, just as in *Revelation* it is interpolated with the story of the birth of the male Child. (See also *Rev.* viii. 1, *Half an Hour*, and viii. 5: also xi. 13, 15, 19.)

The story of Jesus son of Ananus has many affinities with *Revelation*: the East (xvi. 12) and the Four Winds (vii. 1) as destroying agencies, and the woe against Bridegrooms and Brides (xviii. 23). This Jesus began his prophecies in A.D. 62, the year of the martyrdom of James the brother of the Lord.

Both stories are marked by poetic parallelism:

> *A Star like a Sword . . . stood over the City:*
> *And a Comet that continued a whole year.*

The Star and Comet are obviously one.

> *Nor did he give ill words to them that beat him . . .*
> *Nor good words to them that gave him food.*

The stories are further linked by the festival system; the Temple prodigies belong to the first two great Feasts, Passover and Pentecost, and the prophet begins his prophecy on the third, Tabernacles. It is possible, therefore, that one connected document lies behind the whole of section 3.

BOOK VI

THE AGE TO COME

Part I. The Doom of Babylon

Argument

We now return to the Judgment which is to fall on the Great City, mystically called Sodom or Egypt or Babylon. This is exhibited as a Coming of the Son of Man in the style of Mark xiii.: it corresponds in history to the overrunning of Palestine and approach on Jerusalem of the armies of Vespasian.

The Seven Last Plagues are now poured out, and symbolise the terrible events in Palestine, and the confusion which occurred in the Empire after the death of the Emperor Nero.

The avenging forces gather round "Babylon" (Jerusalem), which is completely destroyed by the "Beast" (Rome). The blood of the prophets and saints is avenged, and Jerusalem is lost to sight in a chorus of lamentation.

It has already been pointed out that the first half of *Revelation* comes to a natural end with chapter xi., and had we lost all that intervenes, we should have gone on at this point (xiv. 14) without suspecting our loss, except for an occasional reference to the Mark of the Beast.

It is necessary for the reader to refresh his memory, and forget for a moment the contents of the Great Interlude, which nevertheless are essential to the book. We left off at chapter xi., with the last of the Seven Trumpets of prophecy, and a heavenly chorus announcing that the kingdoms of this world were to become the kingdoms of God and his Messiah. Jerusalem had been depicted as the persecutor and murderer of the prophets of God, and we were led to expect a judgment upon her. We now find a

Coming of the Messiah in judgment, the Seven Last Plagues, and the Doom of Babylon, by which Jerusalem is meant. It is all beautifully in order.

But the literary task of the prophet now becomes extremely complicated. He has his original Jerusalem visions (J) marked by the thought of Jerusalem as persecutor and the Red Dragon as her ally; he has his intermediate visions (E) connected with emperor-worship and marked by the thought of Nero as Antichrist, and the Second Beast as his ally; and the two sequences of vision had to be delicately interlaced in this chapter of climax along with the reflections and explanations of the later period (P), the period of Domitian.

This work of interweaving begins in the threefold message which was necessary to form a bridge between the Great Interlude and the section we are now considering.

The Three Messages.

While the two armies led by Christ and Antichrist are facing one another, and waiting for battle, Three Angels with prophetic messages fly across the sky. Having entered the second half of the book, we are now definitely in Christian times, and these Three Angels represent the course of the Gospel and the work of the church prophets.

The First goes with *an Eternal Gospel to proclaim to all who dwell upon the earth;* it is the message that began in Galilee when Jesus said *Repent, for the Kingdom of God is at hand.* It proclaims *the Hour of his Judgment,* and bids men turn from vain idols to worship the Creator.

The Second proclaims as an accomplished fact the fall of the great city, which, we have already seen, is Jerusalem. *Fallen, Fallen, is Babylon the Great, who gave all the Nations (Gentiles) to drink of the Wine of her Fornication.* This, too, is part of the prophecy of Jesus.

The Third proclaims that whoever shares in the worship of the Beast, *he also will drink of the Wine of the Wrath of God, which is mixed strong in the Cup of his Wrath.* This implies that they will share the fate of Jerusalem. I have not the courage to translate it *mixed neat,* but that would be a very literal translation. It is a strong expression, as the ancients never did drink their wine neat. The following symbols are stronger yet: *they will be tortured in Fire and Sulphur before the Holy Angels and the Lamb ; and the Smoke of their Torture rises up into Ages of Ages.* Then, with a return to the spirit of parody, *They rest not day nor night, those who worship the Beast and his Image* . . . the restless unrest which is of the nature of evil is magnificently contrasted with the unresting rest of the blessed. The actual symbols which depict the " eternal " self-destructive nature of sin will be discussed later.

The Three Messages thus fall well into line; and they are worth remembering, for they are an outline of New Testament prophecy:

1. The Time has come. Repent.
2. Judgment upon Jerusalem.
3. Judgment on those who worship Antichrist.

These are the main lines of the prophecy of our Lord, as we can see by these comparisons:

1. *The Time is fulfilled :* . . . *Repent and believe the Gospel* (*Mk.* i. 15).
   First must this Gospel be preached unto all Nations (*Mk.* xiii. 10).
2. *Not one stone shall be left upon another* (*Mk.* xiii. 2).
   Thine enemies shall come upon thee and lay thee even with the ground (*Luke* xix. 43).
3. *False Messiahs and false Prophets shall arise and give Signs and Wonders, so as to lead into error, if possible, the Elect themselves. But as for you, beware* (*Mk.* xiii. 22).

All that is new, therefore, is the actual identification of the Antichrist.

The Three Messages are in the Present Time; they coincide with the very moment that St. John was penning them, the period A.D. 64 to 70; and even when he recast and re-wrote the prophecies about 96, he still adhered to this date. The whole apocalypse is written as from then.

This feeling for the *Present* (cf. *Now is the accepted time*, or *Now, if ye will hear his voice*) is characteristic of all good preaching. In the original Seventh-Day Adventist scheme, its existence here was strongly felt, and the passage was therefore applied to their own present time; it is perhaps worth recording as a typical misunderstanding of the *Revelation*. Their explanation of the threefold message was:

1. The calculations of William Miller that the Second Coming would take place 1843–1844. These calculations were based on *Daniel*.
2. The declaration that not only the Roman Church, but all organised churches, from that moment on were fallen and doomed. Not one member of any of them could be saved.
3. The Mark of the Beast was the observance of Sunday, which was held to be an invention of the Pope; all who kept Sunday would be destroyed along with the Beast.

The observance of Saturday (the Sabbath) was the *Seal* which marked the elect, and in the Day of Judgment precisely 144,000 Sabbath-keepers would be saved.

William Miller was an ignorant man who worked out the figures in *Daniel* with the aid of a slate and a concordance. His results worked up New England into a condition of frenzy; but when 1844 passed, he admitted he was wrong, and retired into silence. A group of his followers combined under the lead of a "prophetess" Ellen Gould White to form the present Seventh-Day Adventist Sect, which was only one among many. Her explanation of the failure of 1843 was that an invisible partial coming had taken place; Christ was "in the sanctuary," investigating the sins of his people; the outward visible coming could not be calculated, but would not be long. The third message about the Sabbath was one of her infallible revelations from heaven; "God has spoken, not an erring mortal." The sect is very strongly organised in every way, not excluding the financial.

The study of a modern Adventist sect is of great importance, for it illustrates the psychology and doctrinal ideas of the "montanist" type of heresy, to which St. John did *not* belong. Verbal inspiration, literal interpretation of symbols, God speaking through the prophets, puritan legalism, exact predictable dates, bodily visible angels, a bodily visible "Second Coming," a catastrophic "end of the world," a literal hell of fire and a sensuous heaven, are ideas which all hang together and mark the type of mind which is profoundly material at the very moment it prides itself on being spiritual. They depend on a hard, arbitrary, overwhelming view of God, in which human free will and the natural successions of events go for nothing; there must always be some depreciation of human nature, human knowledge, and the world in which we live. The Adventist commentator is a man of this type; the critical scholar of to-day often thinks that St. John and even Jesus were men of this type.

To return to the *Revelation*, we note that the Three Messages close with the glorious *Voice from Heaven* bidding the prophet *Write, Blessed are the Dead who die in the Lord from now on ; Yes, says the Spirit ; may they rest from their labours ; for their works do follow them.* It is the first Christian prayer for the dead, and possibly the model for later prayers: May they rest in peace.

A Coming of the Son of Man.

We now come to what followed the sounding of the Seventh Trumpet.

According to St. Mark, Jesus had promised, first to all his disciples, secondly to the chosen four, and thirdly to the priests and elders at his trial, that they would see him return *with the Clouds of Heaven*, and this return would be connected with the doom of Jerusalem. In this Vision St. John sees *a White Cloud, and one sitting on the Cloud like a Son of Man ;* nor is there any doubt that it refers to a visitation upon Palestine. It is similar to those conditional visitations promised in the letters to the Seven Churches. The Cloud, as in the transfiguration and ascension, symbolises the presence and power of God; and it originates in the story of the visible glory that filled the Tabernacle and Temple.

The Son of Man carries *in his hand a Sharp Sickle.* An Angel announces that the *Hour of Harvest is come, because the Harvest of the Land is ripe . . . and he who sat upon the Cloud cast his Sickle upon the Land and the Land was Harvested.* Note first the way in which the symbols reflect the majesty of God himself. The White Cloud is a reflection of the White Throne; *he who sat upon the Cloud* echoes the words *He who sat upon the Throne.* The word Kathemenos, as I have noted before, implies ruling and judging; it means president and sovereign. White is the colour of conquest and victory, as in the case of the White Horse.

I do not think that the Harvest of the Land is a symbol of judgment. In the gospels it symbolises the gathering of the elect. Now is the time to separate the tares from the wheat. The fields which are described in St. John's gospel as *white unto Harvest,* are now fully ripe, "dried up." The Sharp Sickle begins its work.

The gathering of the elect is symbolised by the Harvest of the Land; the judgment of the sinners is symbolised by the Vintage. There is a reflection here of the calendar of the Jewish Temple; Passover marks the beginning of Harvest, Tabernacles the conclusion of it, including the Vintage; and we have had reason to suppose that the J visions of the *Revelation* concluded with a passage based on the ritual of Tabernacles.

The Harvest was begun on the first day of the Passover week, the day following the actual eating of the Passover, that is to say the Saturday of Holy Week; *now that Sabbath was a High Day (Jn.* xix. 31). Christ rose from the dead, therefore, the very night on which the Firstfruit was cut and offered in the Temple; hence the symbolism in St. Paul, *the Firstfruits of them that slept* (1 *Cor.* xv. 20). There is an obvious connection between the Vision of which we are now reading and the gathering of the Firstfruits, which was itself the first act of the Harvest. (See Appendix I.) We see also a connection between the crucifixion of Jesus and the destruction of Jerusalem which becomes clearer as we proceed; the crucifixion is the beginning of that process of which the destruction of the city is the end. The crucifixion was the first act in the destruction; it was the beginning of the Coming of the Son of Man.

If Christ is the Firstfruits of the Harvest, we might have supposed that the Harvest of the Land here represented the resurrection of the just; but that is impossible as *Revelation* now stands. If, however, there was a time when St. John expected a bodily visible appearance of Christ at the destruction of Jerusalem, and if this Vision belongs to that period, then it is possible that in its original form the Harvest did mean the resurrection of the just, to join the Lord " *in the Air* " as in 1 *Thess.* iv. 17. The whole passage would then correspond exactly to *Mark* xiii. 26: *And then shall they see the Son of Man coming in the Clouds* . . . and *then shall he send his Angels and shall gather together his elect.* This gathering together would lead up to that celestial Feast of Tabernacles with which we have seen reason to suppose that J may originally have concluded. But all this, though a possible conjecture about a supposed original meaning, is not true of the passage as it now stands. There is another Coming of Christ in chapter xix.; and it is after that we find the resurrection of the martyrs to reign with him. The meaning here is shut up to what preceded the fall of Jerusalem.

In any case it is more satisfactory to connect this Vision with the Harvest symbolism of John the Baptist and our Lord. The thought there is the separation of the righteous from the wicked before vengeance falls on the wicked. He will *gather his Wheat into his garner ; but the Chaff he will burn with unquenchable Fire (Matt. iii. 12). In the time of Harvest I will say to the Reapers, Gather ye together first the Tares and bind them in bundles to burn them : but gather the Wheat into my barn* (*Matt.* xiii. 30). The simplest explanation is that the Harvest in *Revelation* means the escape of the Christian community from the horrors of the siege of Jerusalem. According to Eusebius, they fled to Pella immediately after the failure of Cestius Gallus to take the city; and this would fit chronologically into the other allusions to current events which I suggest are reflected in *Revelation*. The Harvest, we may conclude, is the salvation of the elect from the judgment which is to fall on the wicked.

(On the ritual of Firstfruits see Appendix I.)

We pass now from Passover and the Firstfruits to Tabernacles and Vintage. It is an Angel, not the Son of Man, who carries out the Vintage; and we should certainly prefer that the actual symbolism of destruction should be given to another. That destruction is, in any case, due to the natural course of events, and the laws of history. This Angel is bidden to carry out his task by an *Angel . . . out of the Altar who has charge of Fire.* Dr. Charles rightly connects this second Angel with the souls of the righteous dead, who are calling for vengeance; he comes in response to their prayer, and represents the burning of the City after the Blood-vengeance (the Vintage) has come upon it.

The Angel of vengeance *cut the Vine of the Land,* a very common symbol for Israel, *and cast it into the Great Winepress of the Wrath of God.* He does not cut the clusters; he cuts the Vine itself. The Winepress comes from *Second Isaiah* (lxiii.), where it relates to Edom.

And the Winepress was trodden Outside the City, and there came Blood out of the Winepress up to the Bridles of the Horses as far as One Thousand Six Hundred Furlongs. It is not stated here who trod the Winepress; but it is clear from later visions that it is the Christ himself. This is a necessity, as I shall show below, for the Blood-vengeance which came upon Jerusalem is regarded as a consequence of the Crucifixion, which is alluded to in this passage in the words *Outside the City.* It was then that Christ trod the Winepress; it was then that doom came upon the City.

One Thousand Six Hundred Furlongs represent roughly the length of Palestine from Tyre to El Arish; Dan to Beersheba is less. I do not feel very satisfied with this explanation; but it appears to be the best of those usually given.

The reference to the Bridles of the Horses is a picturesque piece of rhetorical exaggeration such as is frequently found in Oriental poetry; it has no reference to any particular horses who are going to swim in blood, as Sir Gilbert Murray supposes, in a moment of unpoetical literalism. It simply means a great deal of blood.

The Harvest symbolises the safe gathering together of the elect, those that love God; the Vintage symbolises the vengeance of blood that is to come upon the unfaithful nation. The political ambitions of the Jews came to a head in the mad and unscrupulous activities of the Zealots and Assassins. Feeling rose very high under the administration of two very bad Roman governors, Ventidius Cumanus and Florus Gessius; there was friction with the Greeks even in Cæsarea and Alexandria and other cities abroad. Mock messiahs and mock prophets arose and embarked on careers of brigandage.

When Florus massacred over three thousand people in Jerusalem and tortured men of high rank, the combined efforts of King Agrippa and the chief priests were unable to calm the mob. The taxes ceased to go to Rome, and the sacrifices for the Emperor ceased to be offered. The city was now divided by civil war; the priests and those who were in favour of peace held the Upper City; but the brigands, the Zealots, the assassins, and the rest who were in favour of war held the Lower City and the Temple. During this dissension Menahem, the son of Judas, the Galilean rebel mentioned in *Acts*, a family with royalist pretensions, came to Jerusalem and established himself as Messiah. After killing the High Priest, he was himself killed by Eleazar, a Zealot leader.

Cestius Gallus, the governor, now moved against Jerusalem in order to take it and come to the relief of the new High Priest Ananus and those who were in favour of peace with the Romans; the Zealots made a strong resistance, and Cestius unaccountably failed to take the city. His retreat gave the insurgent party time to garrison and fortify the towns of Galilee, as well as Judea and the surrounding country. The High Priest and his party in Jerusalem were practically in a state of siege; and, as Josephus remarks, " many of the most eminent Jews swam away from the City as from a ship when it was going to sink." Josephus himself was put in charge of Gamala, in Galilee.

In A.D. 66 Vespasian, who was not yet Emperor, together with his son Titus, came to take charge of the forces in Syria to which he added the fifth and tenth legions, and a considerable number of auxiliaries furnished by the surrounding kingdoms. He captured one by one all the cities which were held by the Zealots in Galilee, and then marched south to Cæsarea; after fortifying Jericho and other places round Jerusalem, he made preparations to attack it. Thus the whole of Palestine was overrun and deluged with blood with the exception of the city; and this may be the meaning of the Vintaging of the Land; I think it more likely, however, that it refers to the massacre of the priestly party by the Edomites, as I shall explain shortly. In any case, it was contemporary with the advance of Vespasian.

The Vine of the Land.

The conception of Israel as the Vine of Jehovah is a commonplace; and yet it may do no harm to illustrate it. The best passage is perhaps the fine *Psalm, Qui regis Israel* (lxxx.), in which, just as here, the invasion and devastation of the land by a hostile army are compared to the ravaging of the vineyard and the cutting down of the Vine.

> *Thou hast brought a Vine out of Egypt;*
> *Thou hast cast out the heathen and planted it.*
> *Why hast thou then broken down her hedges :*
> *So that all they which pass by the way pluck her?*
> *Return, we beseech thee, O God of hosts :*
> *Look down from heaven, behold and visit this Vine.*

The passage from *Isaiah* v. is well known:

> *For the Vineyard of the* LORD *of hosts is the house of Israel :*
> *And the men of Judah his pleasant plant.*

This is the passage used by Jesus as a basis for his parable of the Vineyard in *Mark* xii. The same thoughts are found in *Jeremiah*; and there is a whole oracle in *Ezekiel* (xv):

> *As the Vine among the trees of the forest which I have given for fuel, so will I give the inhabitants of Jerusalem.*

It does not seem possible to suppose that St. John could have intended to apply these words to any other country than Israel, or to any other city than Jerusalem. They echo the words of St. John the Baptist, with which the whole Christian prophetic movement began, *Even now is the axe laid to the root of the tree.* What is contingent in the Baptist is absolute in *Revelation.* Israel is rejected.

The Winepress.

The original Winepress prophecy in *Isaiah* lxiii. has to do with Edom. Jehovah is acting as the champion or blood-avenger of Israel, and in this capacity brings destruction upon Bozrah, which is a city of that country. That is to say, Bozrah has suffered disaster, and Jehovah is regarded as its author, since in the eyes of the prophets all such events occurred under the overruling providence of their God.

> *Who is this that cometh from Edom :*
> *With dyed Garments of Bozrah ?*
> *" I have trodden the Winepress alone :*
> *And of the People there was none with me.*
> *Their Blood shall be sprinkled upon my Garments :*
> *And I shall stain all my Raiment."*

Let us get the theology of this passage clear. It is human agency that has destroyed Bozrah, a Nebuchadrezzar or a Sennacherib; but there is Justice in it, for Bozrah has in times past shed the innocent blood; therefore the prophet sees the will of Jehovah in what has occurred. It is a way of saying that the calamity was just.

In the same way, Jerusalem had shed the blood of witnesses and prophets; and now her blood is being shed. It is therefore the action of God; or at any rate it is in accordance with the will of God. It is Justice.

Note carefully that it is not introduced as an interference of God in the natural order of events. It happens in the natural order of events. Any interference of God is only in the direction of delaying the vengeance; the Four destroying Angels are restrained for a period; and the Four represent the natural order of events. Those who take the sword perish by it. When the Seven Angels out of the Naos go forth to pour out the Last Plagues on the city, it is the Voice of God that gives the word; but the Plagues are actually delivered to the Angels by the Four. The natural order is allowed to proceed.

The events symbolised by this passage are not the final scenes of the siege and destruction; for they occur in consequence of the pouring out of the Seven Plagues; and the fifth of these Plagues represents the suicide of Nero in A.D. 68. I have suggested that they represent the original invasion of Palestine by Vespasian and the other calamities of 66 and 67.

I have, however, a precise identification to suggest.

Just before Vespasian heard of the revolutionary movements in Gaul and Spain, which led to the death of Nero, the Zealot leaders, Eleazar the son of Simon and John of Gischala, who had seized the Temple, sent to the Edomites for assistance against Ananus the High Priest, who was the rightful head of the nation, and was still endeavouring to bring about peace with Rome. The Edomites sent a force of about twenty thousand, which was admitted into the city by the Zealots, and massacred Ananus and eight thousand five hundred of his party. "From that day," as Josephus says, "dated the overthrow of the wall and the destruction of the fortunes of the Jews, that day in which they saw their High Priest, and captain of their own salvation, slain as a sacrifice." (The word is that which St. John uses in the phrase, the Lamb as it had been slain.) I have already quoted the passage in which he describes the cascades of blood in the Temple Courts, and his opinion that God had doomed the city to destruction, and determined to purge it with fire. (See p. 194.)

As a matter of sober history, Josephus thought that had Ananus remained in power he might have concluded some sort of agreement with the Romans, and avoided further warfare. But destiny decided otherwise. With the death of Ananus, Judaism was extinct. The three bandit chieftains, Eleazar the son of Simon, John of Gischala, and Simon of Giora, with their mock priests and mock prophets, dominated the city.

The parallel with the *Revelation*, so obvious in general tone, extends to many details.

1. It is the decisive moment; the Vine of Israel is cut down.
2. There is appalling bloodshed.
3. There is the reference to Edom.
4. There is the sense of divine purpose overruling the issue.

It is interesting to note that in the narrative of Josephus this event is at once followed by the account of the murder of Zacharias the son of Baruch, which has influenced the text of *Matthew* xxiii. 35. (See p. 132.)

Christ the Redeemer.

We have not yet exhausted the riches of this symbolism. We have established the underlying principle; *Whosoever sheddeth man's blood, by man shall his blood be shed*, as Moses said, *or They who take the sword shall perish by the sword*, as Christ expressed it. We have seen that this is regarded as happening in the natural course of events, under the operation of the "Four Living Things" which represent the laws of nature and history; laws for which man was not made, but which he comes under by taking up the sword at all; laws which grind out a kind of justice, though they grind exceeding slow.

Jerusalem had embarked upon a policy of imperialism and commercialism and political ambition; she aspired to the domination of the Mediterranean world; she had taken up the sword. Her history since the Maccabean period had been marked by intrigue and bloodshed; but she differed from any other city in being the shrine of the true religion. She had a conscience; and that conscience was incarnate in a continual witness of prophets and wise men. This conscience she had killed. She had killed the saints and prophets; and her wickedness had reached its height in the murder of Christ. That act was as symbolic as the murder of Ananus by the Edomites; it was the deliberate rejection of her last chance.

The Messiah had come to them with the true royalty and the true priestliness, with the gospel of the kingdom of God. They had killed him. That date, A.D. 30, is the first focal point in the theology of the symbolism of the blood-avenger. He had shown Jerusalem *the things that belonged to her peace ;* she had preferred the policy of violence and political ambition. *Not this man, but Barabbas.* She had chosen the way that led to ruin. With his clear prophetic insight into the motives of men and the secrets of history, he had told what would happen. The Jews had rejected and crucified their king; the kingdom would be taken from them.

The passage we are considering goes back to that scene *Outside the City;* for that is why St. John introduces this phrase. The shedding of all the innocent blood in Jerusalem is summed up in that terrible act. It was there he trod the Winepress alone; it is there that his Garments were dipped in Blood.

The words *Outside the City* have a connection with the sacrificial system. They belong to the mysterious rite of the burning of the Red Heifer, which was to be burned *Outside the Camp;* and, what is still more important, to the Sin Offering when offered for a High Priest or for the whole congregation. (The Camp, of course, is a word belonging to the wilderness period of Israel's history; in Jerusalem it was taken to mean the City.) The same sacrificial symbolism was used in the *Epistle to the Hebrews* (xiii. 11); *For the bodies of those beasts whose Blood is brought into the Naos by the High Priest for sin, are burned without the Camp; wherefore Jesus also, that he might sanctify the People with his Blood, suffered without the gate.* The same symbolism has influenced the Lucan and Matthæan texts of the parable of the Vineyard, where St. Mark's original *Killed him and threw him out of the Vineyard,* is altered to *Threw him out of the Vineyard and killed him;* an obvious alteration to suit this symbolism and the facts of the crucifixion.

Such is the first focal point in the meaning of the symbolism of the Blood-redeemer; the shedding of the Blood of the Messiah when he comes with his word of truth and peace. From that moment they go down the slippery slopes of bloodshed to ruin and destruction.

The second focal point is A.D. 70, when the Roman army is besieging the City, and it is open to anyone to see exactly where her policy has led her. The bloodshed of those years is nemesis, is retribution, is fate; whatever you like to call it. It is the facts of the case which St. John is describing under his symbolism. The policy which preferred imperial ambitions to the gospel of Christ went, in the nature of events, to destruction.

We shrink to-day from the insight which made St. John regard Christ himself as the avenger of blood; but in point of fact it was so. He brought the message of peace and goodwill; he preached repentance and faith in God; by rejecting him, they rejected that. They came to a point of critical decision, and they chose evil. His very message from heaven forced it upon them; his presence and word were a judgment; the faith of his followers kept the witness alive among them. He offered them peace, and when they rejected it, he foretold, with tears, what would come upon them. *If thou hadst known, even thou, in this thy day, the things that belong to thy peace . . . but the days shall come upon thee, that thine enemies shall put a fence about thee and encircle thee . . . and shall not leave in thee one stone upon another* (Luke xix. 42).

Christ, the messenger of peace, is made the messenger of rejection and destruction, by the choice of the Jews and the stern logic of events. It is in any case facts with which St. John has to do; and as he looks on the figure of the High Priest Ananus struck down as if for sacrifice, and the Temple courts flowing with priestly blood, he cannot help seeing the connection with the fatal day of forty years before when the High Priest and Nation rejected the gospel that was offered them, and crucified Jesus *Outside the City*.

These two points in time are correlative. In A.D. 70 the Vine of Israel is cut down and trampled in the Winepress; but this destruction is the culmination of a process which has lasted over forty years; it began Outside the City, when one whom they despised and rejected trod the Winepress alone, and of the People there was none with him. It was in that moment that Jerusalem fell.

The Seven Bowls.

Just as the Seven Trumpets were modelled upon a feature of the Temple ceremonial, so were the Golden Bowls. The first act in the daily sacrifice was to kill the Lamb and catch its blood in a Golden Bowl and dash it against the sides of the Altar; but we have seen that at this point St. John has in his mind the sin-offering made for the High Priest or for the whole nation. We have already had a reference to it in the phrase *Outside the City*, and as the same thought is found in the *Epistle to the Hebrews*, the thought of the death of Jesus as a sin-offering for the nation must have been well established.

The Day of Atonement was the grand example of such a sacrifice. It had three main points :

1. Blood was sprinkled seven times towards the veil of the Holy of Holies.
2. Blood was smeared on the four horns of the Altar.
3. The whole of what remained was poured at the foot of the Altar.

We can see that the pouring out of Seven Bowls is based upon this ritual, though the effect is both simplified and magnified.

It is also reversed; for this Blood, instead of bringing reconciliation, brings rejection and vengeance. Instead of being sprinkled seven times towards the veil, it is poured seven times on the Land. Instead of the appearance of the High Priest with the blood of reconciliation, we have Seven Angels with the Blood of Vengeance.

Here is the answer to the original cry of the Souls under the Altar (vi. 9) : *How long dost thou not Judge and Avenge our Blood on those who dwell on the Land ?* I have suggested already that the Altar means the Land on which the blood of martyrs and saints has been shed; the present vision seems to confirm that suggestion.

In Heaven the Sea of Glass appears mingled with Fire, on it stand the Martyrs having the Harps of God, and singing the Song of Moses and the Lamb; the Song of Moses because they have passed through the Red Sea and found deliverance : the Song of the Lamb because they have been redeemed in his Blood, the same Blood which is judgment to others. The Song tells of the Justice of God, and prophesies that the gentiles will come and worship him. It appears to be based on a song which was sung by the priests in the Temple in the interval between the preparation and the offering of the sacrifice. (See Appendix I.)

Then out of the Heavenly Naos came the Seven Angels

clothed in Clear Bright Stone, as the best text seems to read.
The reading is not impossible, for the Robe symbolises the
heavenly divine nature of the Angels; and in the Syriac
Gnostic *Hymn of the Soul*, the Robe which signifies the divine
element in the human soul is made of precious stones. On
the other hand, Dr. Charles points out that the Hebrew
word Shesh may be translated either White Stone or Fine
Linen. (See p. 312.)

Clothed in White Albs and Golden Girdles, they receive
from the Four Living Things the Golden Bowls full of the
wrath of God; for the Four represent those equal laws of
nature and history under which Jerusalem, like all false
civilisations and all false churches, is going to its doom.
The Smoke of the visible presence fills the Temple (it has
long deserted the earthly one), and no one can enter in until
the Seven Plagues are ended. The Voice of God himself
issues from the Shrine, commanding the Seven Angels to
pour out their Plagues.

We have here a reflection of the temple ritual in its detail.

The First Four Bowls.

The first Four Bowls are poured on the Land, the Sea,
the Rivers, and the Sun, corresponding exactly to the
incidence of the first Four Trumpets; and the Land is still
the Land of Palestine.

The First became *a grievous and evil Sore*, as in the plagues
of Egypt. The text adds that it falls upon those who *have
the Mark of the Beast and worship his Image*. This is hardly in
place in a purely Palestinian apocalypse, and was probably
added when the visions were pieced together. Dr. Charles
regards it as an interpolation.

In the Second and Third the waters become Blood, as in
the plagues of Egypt also. Under the Third (the Rivers
and Wells) the Angel of the Waters admits the justice of this
Plague; *they poured out the Blood of Saints and Prophets, and thou
hast given them Blood to drink ;* and the Altar, representing
the Martyrs, replies, *Yes, Lord God Almighty, true and just are
thy Judgments.*

The Fourth is a great drought; but all are symbolic of

the completeness and horror of the Roman invasion. None are to be taken literally.

In each sequence of Seven it is the last three that contain the most elaborate symbolism, and the Seven Bowls are no exception to this rule; they represent the confusion in the Roman Empire, the attack of Jerusalem itself, and the fall of that city.

The Last Three Bowls.

And the Fifth poured out his Bowl on the Throne of the Beast and his Kingdom was Darkened. This Egyptian plague of darkness symbolises the anarchy and civil war that befell the Empire after the suicide of Nero in A.D. 68. It meant a lull in the warfare in Palestine; for both Vespasian and Titus went to Alexandria. Vespasian went to Rome and became Emperor; Titus returned to Palestine also with the rank of Emperor.

No doubt the Zealot prophets in Jerusalem hailed the rise of the three pretenders, and the civil war to which Vespasian had to attend, as the end of the Roman Empire and an intervention of God. It was certainly very like the rebellion which had diverted Sennacherib from Jerusalem in the Old Testament.

The Sixth poured out his Bowl on the Great River Euphrates, and its water was dried up to prepare the way for the Kings from the East. This is usually taken to represent the march of Parthian kings who are going to destroy Rome; and if the words are taken literally, that interpretation is very just. But if the reader has followed me at all, he will see that this is quite untenable; and even if we take Babylon to be Rome, it comes awkwardly at this point.

Some writers suggest that they are Oriental auxiliaries who assisted at the siege of Jerusalem; but I must confess I do not like this. Where the Euphrates appeared before (ix. 14), we found that it was the position of the Four destroying Angels who were a recognised feature of the early chapters of the book. The Euphrates is the region from which both the Old Testament conquerors, Sennacherib and Nebuchadrezzar, came upon Jerusalem; it appears to mean no more than the quarter from which hostile attack may come. Surely the phrase "Kings from the East" means the Sennacherib and the Nebuchadrezzar that were now to come upon Jerusalem—that is to say, the Roman Emperors.

Who the kings and the army are we discover in the next verse: they are the Dragon, the Beast, and the False Prophet whose evil spirits have corrupted all the kings of the earth. It is the Roman Empire, with all its forces and allies, that is *gathering to the War of the Great Day of God ALMIGHTY . . . on the place called in Hebrew Armageddon.*

This surely represents nothing but the return of Titus to besiege Jerusalem with further reinforcements; and it is certainly odd that among them were three thousand men from the legions on the Euphrates frontier; it is possible that this irony of history suggested to the mind of St. John the parallel with Nebuchadrezzar.

The name Armageddon is significant because it is at Megiddo that the Jewish King Josiah was defeated and killed by an Egyptian army under the Pharaoh; and Titus had just returned from Egypt. Armageddon means Mountain of Megiddo; but Megiddo is a valley. It is the Mountain of Sion which has become Mountain of Megiddo or Mountain of defeat. The name, anyhow, shows that the field of battle is in Palestine, just as the phrase War of the Great Day of God Almighty is not compatible with a war between Romans and Parthians.

An extraordinarily interesting passage which St. John has inserted into this section shows that he still has the Temple in his mind. *Behold I am coming as a thief. Blessed is he who keeps watch and guards his Garments, that he may not walk naked, and men see his shame.* This passage was explained by John Lightfoot, the seventeenth-century Hebraist. He points out that there was an officer on duty at the Temple whose business was to walk round and see that those who were on watch kept awake; if he found them asleep he beat them; if he found them asleep a second time, he burnt their clothes. This is the only possible explanation of this passage. It means, Now is the time for those who are guarding the Temple to keep awake.

The whole symbolism of the Sixth Bowl, therefore, of which this is a part, has to do with an attack upon the Temple.

The Seventh poured out his Bowl on the Air, and there came a Great Voice out of the Naos saying : It is done ; and there came a Great Earthquake, such as has not been since men were upon the Land, such an Earthquake, so Great. And the Great City fell into Three Parts, and the cities of the gentiles fell.

I do not quite understand what is meant about the cities of the gentiles; but the phrase does suggest that the Great City is not a city of the gentiles.

Once before in *Revelation* an Earthquake befell the Great City, and we had no doubt that the Great City was Jerusalem, and the Earthquake some past judgment, from which it recovered. This time the judgment surpasses all past judgments. The City falls into Three parts.

This refers to the division into three factions, which became acute after the return of Titus. While Titus was besieging it from without, the three leaders of rival factions were fighting fiercely within: but for this the city might have staved off defeat for a long time, even perhaps indefinitely, for no great army could support itself for long in those days in the neighbourhood of Jerusalem; there was no water and no supplies. This fighting within the city delivered it quickly into the hands of Titus; " the days were shortened." So important is this point, and so exactly do the words of St. John fit the historical situation, that it will be worth while to quote Josephus again. After narrating the return of Titus to his headquarters at Cæsarea, he says, " While he was assisting his father at Alexandria . . . it so happened that the sedition at Jerusalem was revived and parted into three factions (the language is very similar to that of *Revelation*) and that one faction fought against another; which one might call in such a bad business the work of divine justice." The three leaders were the Simon, Eleazar, and John we have mentioned before.

I have pointed out already how the fall of Jerusalem and the crucifixion of Jesus are the two focal points in St. John's thought, one ending what the other began. The divine

Voice IT IS DONE of *Revelation* echoes the word from the cross IT IS FINISHED of the fourth gospel.

Note also the resemblance between the words *Unto the place which is called in the Hebrew tongue* ARMAGEDDON (*Rev.* xvi. 16) and *Unto the place which is called the Pavement, but in the Hebrew tongue Gabbatha* (*Jn.* xix. 13). Whatever may be our views about the authorship of the Johannine literature, it is certain that the resemblances in thought, plan, and diction between the *Revelation* and the Gospel are at times extraordinarily close, and those scholars who hold that they are from different authors and are inspired by different motives have some difficult points to explain. In the present case there is a contrast intended between Jesus, judged and going to his death at the hands of the Emperor's procurator, and Jerusalem, judged and going to her destruction at the hands of the Emperor.

The Detail of the Sixth Bowl.

The detail of the Sixth Bowl is found to be confused and perplexing by all commentators, and most of them regard it as interpolated. I am anxious not to resort to this expedient, as once it is adopted it becomes a fatal temptation to resort to it on every occasion; and in any case the question we must ask is, Why was it interpolated? My object is so far as possible to study the text as it stands; as a matter of fact, I feel certain that the author added two passages to his account of the events which took place under the Sixth Bowl; see how smoothly the passage runs if this is recognised.

And the Sixth poured out his Bowl on the Great River Euphrates and its Water was dried up in order that there might be prepared the way of the Kings from the East . . . (First Interpolation, 13 and 14a) *to gather them together to the War of the Great Day of God* ALMIGHTY . . . (Second Interpolation, 15 and 16a) *and he gathered them together to the place which is called in the Hebrew tongue* ARMAGEDDON. In *Revelation,* just as in Josephus, it is God who stands with the Roman army. It is possible that the drying up of Euphrates may have some connection with the drying up of the water supply of Jerusalem, which also helped to shorten the siege and to expedite the capture of the city.

I have already pointed out that the word Armageddon is difficult. Megiddo is not far from a hill (Har), but the famous battle-field was in the plain or valley; plain of Megiddo, valley of Megiddo, waters of Megiddo are the Old Testament terms. This has led to various suggestions for a new interpretation of the word; I should like to suggest Herem of Megiddo; the Herem was the ancient Hebrew "holy war" or "war of extermination," in which the enemy nation or city was "devoted" to complete destruction, all its people were killed, and its houses and goods completely burned.

As for the interpolations, I prefer to regard them as later insertions by our author himself, and if possible to interpret them in that way; and I have already dealt with the second. (*Behold, I come as a thief.*)

The first tells of the unclean spirits, *like Frogs coming out of the Mouth of the Dragon and out of the Mouth of the Beast and out of the mouth of the False Prophet . . . are the spirits of demons doing Signs, which go forth upon the Kings of the whole inhabited world.*

Now this prophecy fits its present position because it is based on the plagues of Egypt, like the rest of the symbolism of the Bowls. Frogs are mentioned four times in the Old Testament, every time in connection with the plagues of Egypt. In one case it is the magicians of Egypt who "bring up Frogs," so that St. John has Old Testament authority for connecting them with a prophecy which has not its origin in Jehovah.

False prophets were expected before the fall of Jerusalem, and St. John regards their activity as world-wide.

The Prophecies of Second Zechariah.

The only prophet who mentions Megiddo is *Second Zechariah* (xii. 11); it is natural, therefore, to connect this passage in *St. John* with him. I have so far not quoted *Second Zechariah*, because he is so confused and difficult; it is certain, however, that the primitive Jerusalem church studied him in detail; and it is easier perhaps to decide what they thought he meant, than it is to decide what he actually did mean. One point is clear; he expected hostile armies to besiege Jerusalem:

THE AGE TO COME   269

I will gather all nations against Jerusalem to battle, and the City shall be taken and the houses rifled (xiv. 2), so that we have now established two points of contact between *Second Zechariah* and the Sixth Bowl.

It will be worth while, perhaps, to go through a few of the more obvious passages in *Second Zechariah* which have influenced Christian thought.

1. ix. 9. *Rejoice greatly, O daughter of Zion . . . thy King cometh, etc.* This well-known passage is applied in *Jn.* xii. 15 and *Matt.* xxi. 5 to the first coming of Christ to Jerusalem, his coming in mercy. "St. Matthew's" additions to the gospel story, and his notes of prophecies fulfilled, have a high historical value in showing the beliefs of the Jerusalem Christians during this period; their close connection with St. John seems to demonstrate some dependence on him or on common sources.

2. x. 5. *I will strengthen the house of Judah and I will save the house of Joseph.* Does this explain the inclusion of Joseph in St. John's list of tribes (vii. 8)?

3. xi. In this chapter there are two " staves " (*i.e.* "instruments of shepherds," v. 15), called Beauty and Bands (*i.e.* unity). Beauty must have been identified with Jesus; for it is in connection with the " breaking " of Beauty that we read, *They weighed for my price thirty pieces of silver, and the Lord said unto me, Cast it unto the potter ; . . . and I took the thirty pieces of silver and cast them to the potter in the house of the Lord* (xi. 12, 13). This prophecy is applied to the betrayal of Jesus by " Matthew " (xxvii. 9).

4. There is evidence that the name Bands (Hoblim) was applied to James the brother of Jesus, who succeeded him as leader of Jewish Christianity; for Hegesippus tells us that he was called Oblias, which he explains as Bulwark of the People. The word for People is Am, so that this explanation itself demands a form like Hoblim or Hobliam.

5. The reason why James had this paramount position in Jerusalem is because he was of the house of Jesus, and that implied that he was of the house of David; this might mean that Jews generally would tend to rally round him in the time of false Messiahs. *Second Zechariah*, while he foretells the destruction of Jerusalem, mitigates the severity of his prophecy by saying that it will be rebuilt, and that the house of David will have a glorious future; he also has a distinction between the tents of Judah on the one hand, and the inhabitants of Jerusalem on the other; this is very like St. John's doctrine of the outer Jerusalem given over to destruction by the gentiles, and the inner Jerusalem that was to be established in glory.

xii. 6*b*. *And Jerusalem shall be inhabited again in her own place even in Jerusalem. The Lord also shall save the tents of Judah first, that the glory of the house of David and the glory of the inhabitants of Jerusalem do not magnify themselves against Judah.*

6. xii. 8*b*. *And the house of David shall be as God, as the angel of the Lord before them.* This interest in the house of David is found elsewhere in *Second Zechariah*. It was natural that the Jewish Christians should feel that in rallying round James and the other relations of Jesus they were rallying round the house of David.

Not, however, a military or an imperial David; that is the whole point of the prophecy. The King himself is *meek and lowly*; his followers are *the poor of the flock*. Jewish Christians at a later date called themselves *Ebionim*, or the poor.

7. *And they shall look upon me whom they have pierced and they shall mourn*

for him as one mourneth for his only son and shall be in bitterness for him as one that is in bitterness for his first born (xii. 10). This quotation has very great interest; the first line is quoted in *Rev.* i. 7, where it lies among miscellaneous texts without any direct application; our author has not worked it into its logical place in the book, though it obviously ought to belong to an appearance of the Son of Man at Jerusalem; perhaps it stood in such a place in the original J document.

The quotation in *Rev.* i. 7 is independent of the LXX, and appears to have been translated direct from the Hebrew; it is found in the same form in *John* xix. 37, another case of a mystical correspondence between the crucifixion and the fall of Jerusalem with which the coming of the Son of Man is connected. It almost looks as if it belongs to an early period, when a *visible* appearance of Christ was expected at the time of the siege; in that case its original place would have been after the appearance of the Son of Man on the White Cloud (xiv. 14).

The second part of the verse, in the form, *And all the Tribes of the Land shall wail because of him*, is found both in *Matt.* xxiv. 30 and *Rev.* i. 7; unfortunately it is mistranslated so as to mean all the kindreds (tribes, *Matt.*) of the earth. There is clearly some connection here.

8. xii. 11. The succeeding verse. *In that day shall there be a great mourning in Jerusalem as the mourning of Hadadrimmon in the valley of Megiddon.* This is the origin of Armageddon (Har Megiddon) in our text. The other O.T. writers spell it Megiddo.

9. xiii. 2*b*. *I will cause the prophets and the unclean spirits to pass out of the Land.* There seems to be some connection with the False Prophet and the Three Unclean Spirits of the Sixth Bowl; the second Beast is not called the False Prophet before the Armageddon passage.

10. xiii. 1. *A Fountain opened to the House of David.* A Fountain is found in St. John's New Jerusalem; but the dependence is on Ezekiel.

11. xiii. 5. *He shall say, I am no prophet, I am an husbandman; for man taught me to keep cattle from my youth; and one shall say unto him, What are these wounds in thine hands? Then shall he answer, Those with which I was wounded in the house of my friends.* I cannot resist narrating another of the Palestinian traditions of Hegesippus which is preserved in Eusebius. After the fall of Jerusalem the Jewish Christians continued to reverence the family of Jesus, and Symeon the son of Clopas was made bishop; the story of his martyrdom at the age of 120 may be based on fact, but its details are suspiciously like those of the death of Rabbi Akiba.

Eusebius states, however, that after the siege Vespasian did search out and persecute those who were of the family of David. Later, in the reign of Domitian, two grandsons of Jude were brought before him and charged with being of the family of David; in defence they showed him their hands, and, as a witness of the labour they had done, the hardness of their bodies, and the callouses which had developed on their hands through continual toil. The likeness is not very close, but it is a likeness. It is recorded that Domitian sent them back and that they ruled the church as "martyrs" and kinsmen of the Lord. The tradition shows a strong expectation of the coming of Christ, and it also states that his kingdom is not of this world or earthly, but heavenly and angelic (cf. *John* xviii. 36).

12. xiii. 9. *I will say, It is my people; and they shall say, The Lord is my God.* A similar form of words is found in many places in the Old Testament; *Rev.* xxi. 3 is probably derived from *Lev.* xxvi. 12.

13. xiv. 2 has been quoted above as a source for the Sixth Bowl.

14. xiv. 7. *It shall be one day, not day, nor night.* This is similar to *Rev.* xxii. 4, but that passage seems to be based on *Is.* lx. 19.

15. xiv. 8. *Living waters.* This is a well-known phrase found both in *Revelation* and in the fourth gospel.

16. xiv. 11. *And there shall be no more utter destruction.* This is quoted in *Rev.* xxii. 3, in a form which shows direct contact with the Hebrew, *There shall be no more Curse.* The word translated Curse or utter Destruction, is the word Herem, which I have suggested may be the first half of the word Armageddon. It means the curse or ban put on a city when it is " devoted " to utter destruction.

17. xv. 16. *And it shall come to pass that every one that is left of all the nations which came against Jerusalem shall even go up from year to year to worship the King, the Lord of hosts, and to keep the Feast of Tabernacles.* The vision of all the gentiles keeping the Feast of Tabernacles is the triumphant conclusion of the book; *Rev.* vii. 9 to 17 is a similar vision of the gentiles keeping a Feast of Tabernacles, and I have already suggested that it was designed as a conclusion to the book in one of its earlier forms.

These seventeen quotations suggest very strongly that the Jewish church made a complete and detailed study of *Second Zechariah*, and that this study has influenced *Revelation* and other New Testament literature. On the one hand they may do something to illuminate the history of Jewish Christianity, and perhaps assist us in tracing out the history of the hope of a Christian Davidic Jerusalem which was in time to develop into Chiliasm (see Book VIII, Part II); on the other hand they assist us in studying *Revelation.* From the Four Horsemen in chapter v. to the New Jerusalem in chapter xxii., traces of *Zechariah* appear; next to *Ezekiel* it has influenced St. John most. It is important to realise, therefore, that it speaks of the destruction of this Jerusalem and a vengeance upon its inhabitants; it looks forward to the glory of a New Jerusalem under the house of David, and the gentiles coming to worship there.

A study of *Zechariah* and its relation to our apocalypse would, however, be a study in itself; and we can establish the meaning of the book without it. It is sufficient for our purposes to note how strongly it has influenced the symbolism of the Sixth Seal, and the gathering to the battle of Armageddon; those armies are met to besiege the Great City, and that city is Jerusalem.

The Great City.

It is quite clear now that the Seven Bowl series deals with

the fall of Jerusalem and confines itself to Palestine; it follows the Seven Trumpets and the Two Martyrs section, and there is no need to suppose anything new introduced. Had we not been indoctrinated with the theory that it deals with Rome, it would never have occurred to us.

Only one City has been mentioned in the *Revelation*, and that City is certainly Jerusalem. In chapter xi. it is called the Great City, just as it is here, and there is no doubt that in that passage it means Jerusalem; it is *spiritually called Sodom and Gomorrha, where also their Lord was crucified*. It is the City that persecuted the martyrs and prophets, and God is going to exact vengeance. A part of it was destroyed in an Earthquake which symbolised partial judgments in the past; in the passage now before us *there came a Great Earthquake, such as has not been since men were on the earth, such an Earthquake, so great*. This is the judgment which is going to overwhelm it entirely. *And the City fell into three parts, and the Cities of the gentiles fell*.

It is connected with the previous vision by the title Great City and by the symbolism of the Earthquake, and of the Hail; there can be no mistake. The Three Parts represent the political parties into which it was so hopelessly divided at its fall; the phrase *Cities of the Gentiles* makes sure that the Great City itself is Jewish.

Those who deny that Jerusalem could be called the Great City underrate not only the importance of Jerusalem, but also the strength of national pride; they also forget that St. John called it the Great City in chapter xi., and that Josephus uses the same title. It seems to have been a local title, and may have been used like our phrase the Queen City, which I have heard applied to cities all over the Empire, including Auckland, Durban, Natal, and Sherbrooke, Quebec.

The second mention of it is the prediction of its overthrow in the Second Message of chapter xiv.: it is there given the mystical name Babylon, akin to the previous mystical names Sodom and Egypt. Nothing we have *previously* read in the *Revelation* gives us the least reason for supposing that this is a new city not mentioned before.

The third mention is in the Treading of the Winepress;

and here, as in the first case, there is general consent that Jerusalem is intended. If the *Revelation* ended at the point we have now reached, no one would have dreamt of suggesting that St. John had more than one city in mind; and I am sure that it will be agreed that this common-sense identification has given consistency and continuity to the whole book so far as we have got.

A further argument which will be developed later is the close parallelism which we have noted with *Ezekiel*. The structure of *Revelation* is based upon that book, and the central thing it prophesies is the fall of Jerusalem. Ezekiel, alone of all the Hebrew prophets, compares the destruction of Jerusalem to a great storm of hail; St. John does the same, *And Great Hail as of a Talent weight fell out of heaven upon men.*

The anonymous author of *The Parousia* makes a curious point about this Hail. A remarkable feature of the siege of Jerusalem was the artillery; a new kind of catapult was used which cast huge blocks of white limestone that did weigh a Talent. To this bombardment the fall of the City was largely due. The true text of Josephus tells us how the people of Jerusalem as they saw these great white masses of stone sailing through the air, said " The Son cometh."

Babylon the Great.

We have seen that there is no reason up to date to identify the city which is being destroyed as anything but Jerusalem. The arguments have been given as we have gone along; and their main lines can be summed up under these heads:

1. It is in line with the witness of the great prophets like Jeremiah, but especially with Ezekiel, whose book of prophecies was St. John's literary model.
2. It is the central point in the prophecies of our Lord, which St. John professes to reproduce and explain.
3. Jerusalem had persecuted the prophets and their Christian successors.
4. The identification gives consistency and continuity to the book, and shows that certain passages in it which had been thought to be discrepit are really essential and organic parts of the whole structure.

S

The identification which appears so obvious as we read through the book chapter by chapter, from the beginning, has been obscured by the introduction of a new factor not specifically mentioned in the prophecies of our Lord: the identification of Nero and Emperor-worship with the Antichrist of which he spoke in a vague and general manner. The " False Christ " and the " False Prophet " of which he spoke appear as the two Beasts, and their pictures have been elaborated because they are new. They have been elaborated to such an extent that they have obscured the original central theme of the doom of Jerusalem. Yet later on, in the very chapter which has led scholars to identify Babylon with Rome, it is the Beast that destroys Babylon; and if Babylon is Rome then it is very odd that Rome should destroy Rome. It leads, in fact, to the hopeless confusion in which our commentaries have wallowed. The Beast is certainly Rome; the city it destroys is Jerusalem.

On the other hand " Babylon " does mean Rome in the *Sibylline Oracles,* and perhaps in 1 *Peter.*

It is obvious that if the identification with Rome is given up, most of the confusion disappears. It must have come very early, as it is found in St. Irenæus about A.D. 175; but even St. Irenæus had lost the true tradition. We are at a loss to find an earlier reference to it. Had we any real light on the primitive stages of Montanism it might help us; but we know it best in its later and more respectable form. It was an Adventist heresy based on both books of St. John, the *Gospel* and the *Revelation,* and it accepted both as apostolic. It was prophetic in character, like early Adventism, and made much of the doctrine of the Spirit in the *Gospel,* and of the New Jerusalem in the *Revelation*; like Gnosticism, it must have linked them together in some way. The probability is that Montanists interpreted Babylon as the Catholic church which excommunicated them; and they appear to have charged the church with " killing the prophets," a charge which was indignantly repudiated. All " inner circles " of elect, especially if of a hard Puritan type, regard the official inclusive " catholic " church in this way. If this is the fact—and we only have a suggestion of evidence about it—then it was a natural development from the true meaning. In *Revelation* the Christian church is the inner prophetic circle and the Jewish ecclesiastical state is Babylon; in Montanism the heretics are the inner prophetic circle, and the orthodox church is Babylon.

In *Revelation* we have the viewpoint of the persecuted Christian minority in the " Holy City," which is drunk with the blood of prophets and martyrs and of their Lord himself. The Jewish circle for which it was originally written could not feel so keenly about Rome, which was far away. On the other hand, the gentile Christians, for whom the final form of *Revelation* was intended, were quite unable to enter into the feelings of the Hebrew Christians in Jerusalem. A great deal of the book they would find obscure; the key to it would soon be lost. In consequence of its difficulty and the use which heretics made of it, it was abandoned altogether in the East, though it was much valued in Rome; and it was in Rome, perhaps, that the new identification of Babylon was made.

The Latin identification with Rome held the field for many centuries, till the Abbot Joachim in the twelfth century attempted to give a fresh interpretation to its obscurities. One of his followers wrote *The Everlasting Gospel*, in which Babylon was first identified with the Papal Curia. This identification was rapidly adopted by the Imperial party and by the hundreds of anti-ecclesiastical sects which honeycombed the Middle Ages; it was adopted by Luther and Calvin and by all Protestants after them. It is to be found in Wordsworth and Alford.

Modern scholarship rejects the identification with the Papal Curia as impossible; but spiritually and essentially it is better than the identification with pagan Rome; for Babylon is the corruption of true religion, not the ignorance and brutality of the pagan. It is priestly not royal.

The Great Harlot.

The word " Great " links together the Great Harlot, Great Babylon and the Great City of the earlier visions; they are all one.

At the beginning of the difficult chapter xvii. one of the Angels who held the Seven Bowls takes John *into the Desert* to see *the Judgment of the Great Harlot*. The presence of St. John himself is brought to our notice, and we have, therefore, a Vision which he wishes to connect in a particular manner with himself. It is his own.

I have suggested already that *into the Desert* may be a synonym for *in the Spirit ;* but one object of the words here is to link this Vision with that of the Woman in Heaven, with which it forms so striking a contrast. We can see this at once when we set the particulars side by side.

The True Israel.	*The False Israel.*
The Bride.	The Harlot.
The Mother of the Messiah.	The Persecutor of the Messiah.
Persecuted by the Red Dragon.	Seated upon the Scarlet Beast.
Clothed in heavenly glory.	Clothed in worldly luxury.

This contrast has been noticed by commentators; but they do not see how impossible it makes the identification of Babylon with Rome. The first figure later on reappears as the New Jerusalem; this one must be the Old Jerusalem. This is the sixth great argument in favour of the identification.

In any case, Rome cannot fairly be described as a Harlot, though she may very fairly be symbolised as a Beast. It is true, as Dr. Charles points out, that Nahum calls Nineveh a Harlot, and Isaiah calls Tyre a Harlot; but this is done casually ; it is not the characteristic symbol of a heathen city. As against these two texts, we find that all through the prophets, beginning from *Hosea*, faithless Israel is called a Harlot or False Bride; it is to be found everywhere. In particular Ezekiel, who is St. John's literary model, develops the idea at great length in certain repulsive chapters (xvi. and xxiii.) which have profoundly influenced the *Revelation ;* it is precisely because they are so repulsive that they are unknown to the ordinary reader. But anyone who reads them through will have little doubt where St. John found his imagery; it is in *Ezekiel* that we find Jerusalem in all her finery playing the harlot with the heathen nations.

I am prepared to accept at its face value the translation of the Authorised Version, which says, *With whom the Kings of the Earth committed Fornication ;* for this is the exact picture of *Ezekiel.* It covers trade relations and treaties; and there were several millions of Jews scattered throughout the Empire, by whose trade with the *Kings of the Earth* Jerusalem had grown rich and luxurious and powerful. But we would be quite justified in translating it :

With whom the Rulers of the Land committed Fornication,
And the Inhabitants of the Land were intoxicated with the Wine of her Fornication.

It should be noted that the word King could be used very loosely; in Horace it is equivalent to millionaire, and our Lord tells his Palestine disciples that they will be brought before Kings.

The Fornication no longer implies that Jehovah is forsaken in favour of the unclean deities of Canaan; he is forsaken for trade with the Roman Empire. Jerusalem loves this world with an unlawful love, and has grown rich and prosperous and become a kingdom of the world, not a city of God. The commercial prosperity of Jerusalem will be found amply developed by Joseph Klausner, a modern Jew, in his great book, *Jesus of Nazareth ;* and there is plenty of evidence in Josephus of her worldliness and imperialism.

She is *seated upon a Scarlet Beast full of Names of Blasphemy ;* that is to say, her pride and prosperity are built upon her unnatural commercial alliance with Rome, and Rome will now turn and destroy her.

This unnatural alliance between two powers who ought to be enemies is also shown in a second way: she is *drunk with the Blood of the Saints and the Blood of the Martyrs of Jesus. The Cup of her Abominations and Harlotries* is certainly full, when she is found persecuting the Messiah and his followers in harmony with the god-emperor.

One point remains. She is *seated upon Many Waters.* Geographically this is more untrue of Jerusalem even than of Rome; but St. John found it in Isaiah's prophecy against the original Babylon, which was situated on a network of canals; later on he explains it: *the Waters are Peoples and*

SYMBOLISM OF THE DIVINE ACTIVITIES IN THE HUMAN WORLD

God the Almighty

works in the world of men in two ways, symbolised by two types of figures.

MALE.	FEMALE.
Word and Messiah (Christ). (Cf. Angel of Revelation in *Daniel* x.)	Spirit and Bride (Israel). (Cf. Wisdom of God in Apocrypha, *Wisdom* vii.)
In chapter x. of *Revelation*.	In chapter xii. of *Revelation*.
The Strong Angel = the Word aggressive. the process of prophecy. the progress of the gospel (Christ ?).	*The Woman in Heaven* = the Spirit among men. the holy souls. the elect in Israel (Mary ?).
The inspired leader. Prophet or martyr.	The inspired community. Mother of the inspired leader.

A break then occurs in the symbolism and in the structure of the book, and the Word becomes Incarnate.

The Christian Church.

(*Michael* : conqueror of evil.
The Lamb : saviour and leader of the elect.
The Son of Man : judging Jerusalem.)

In chapter xix. of *Revelation*.	In chapters xix.–xxi. of *Revelation*.
The King Messiah. The Bridegroom. The WORD OF GOD.	*The Bride.* The Beloved City. The New Jerusalem.

The Activities of Evil.

Over against his Trinity of Good, which is divine in origin, St. John places a trinity of evil arising out of the " Abyss."

THE SERPENT ABADDON,

the principle of evil, also working in the world in two ways.

MALE.	FEMALE.
The Beast. The kingdom of the world. Selfish Imperialism. The Satanic Messiah. The Roman god-emperor.	*The Harlot.* The corrupted kingdom of God. False religion. The earthly Jerusalem.

THE DIVINE ACTIVITIES

The first point to note is that St. John found the symbols of the Heavenly Man and the Heavenly Woman ready to his hand. They are derived from the writings of the Old Testament and Apocrypha, and were used by orthodox Jewish teachers as well as by the heretical Jewish sects, the forerunners of the Gnostics.

He does not regard them as mythological figures like Apollo or Diana, or as spiritual semi-substantial essences like the Gnostic aeons. They symbolise divine activities actually to be observed in the world of men; on the one hand the divine Word which animates the prophet, on the other the divine Spirit which animates the community without which the prophet would be an impossibility. The Strong Angel is the whole course of divine leadership in history, leading up to Christ; the Woman in Heaven is Spirit animating the faithful people of God, summed up perhaps in Mary.

Because God works in and through men, the symbols also include the inspired men and the holy community, as well as the Word and Spirit. This dual meaning is characteristic of the whole Revelation. The invisible spirit, in order to work in the world, must incarnate itself in human beings; the symbol blazons the whole process, and at one time may incline rather to the inspiring force, at another to the inspired persons. In the end they come to mean the Word incarnate in Christ, and the Spirit incarnate in the Church.

The spirit of evil also works in the world. It is incarnate in the "world," the society of mankind organised for its own selfish ambitions; for the moment it animates the Roman Empire and is summed up in the god-emperor with his blasphemous divine pretensions. But it can also animate what ought to be the Church of God; and the "holy" city of Jerusalem, with its commercial and materialistic ambitions and its record of persecutions, appears as the female incarnation of evil, the Harlot. Jerusalem and Rome are joined in an unnatural alliance to persecute the Messiah and the true Israel, his elect followers.

The Harlot (Jerusalem) is destroyed by the Beast (Rome), though this is also looked on as an act of God, or coming of the Son of Man. The Beast will later on be overcome by the Messiah and his martyr followers.

This system, which appears so complicated at first sight, owes its origin in part to the desire to refute the Jewish heretical sects who regarded the Serpent as a divine spirit coming from the high God. The trinity of evil is described partly in language which the gnostics applied to their divine æons, *e.g.* Mind and Wisdom.

The complicated system links together sections of the book which many critics have regarded as diverse in origin and contradictory in meaning. Once this system of trinities is grasped it becomes clear that the book as it stands is a luminous and crystal unity, the product of one mind, and that mind the mind of a great genius. The same result follows from a consideration of the intricate plan by which the whole book of *Ezekiel* has been reproduced. It is interesting that the two trinities are presented to us in the only non-Ezekielic portion of the book (chapters xii.–xiv.), but that they radiate out and link together the whole book.

Multitudes and Nations and Tongues, and symbolise, therefore, the " Diaspora," the vast number of Jews scattered throughout the known world, from all of whom Jerusalem drew her power and riches.

On *her forehead* is placarded *her Name,* as was the custom with Harlots; but it is prefaced by the word MYSTERY, which implies warning. " Stop to consider; the word Babylon does not mean what you think it does." Had it meant Rome, the identification would have been simple; it lies deeper. The Great City is not only called Sodom or Egypt, it is also called *Babylon the Great, the Mother of the Harlotries and Abominations of the Land.*

The Scarlet Beast.

In speaking of the Scarlet Beast I have spoken as if it were Rome and nothing more; but we must remember that it is a form or outward incarnation of the spirit of evil itself, evil outwardly organised and persecuting. I have suggested that two modes of symbolism have been blended; if I am correct it is in this chapter that they converge. In the J system there is a Woman and a Red Dragon (Scarlet Beast); in the E system there is a Serpent, a Beast, and a False Prophet (Second Beast). The presence of the Scarlet Beast with the Harlot here suggests that this Vision is part of a series which also contained the Vision of the Woman in Heaven and the Red Dragon. One point marks the combination of the two systems, J and E.

When the Beast was given his Name and Number we found the formula *Here is Mind : he who has Wisdom,* and I suggested that St. John was consciously using two Ophite catchwords. In this chapter, where the Harlot and the Scarlet Beast occur, we find them again exactly repeated. Nowhere else in the book are the words Mind and Wisdom [1] used. This new female figure appears to be an emanation of evil, just as the Emperor is a Messiah of evil. We have been given a complete and logical contrast between the powers of heaven and the powers of hell.

---

[1] For Wisdom only, see v. 12 and vii. 12. They are not found in the other Johannine books.

The Powers of Heaven.

GOD (in Heaven).

THE WORD.　　　　　　　THE CHURCH (Spirit).
Heavenly Man.　　　　　　Heavenly Wisdom.
True Messiah.　　　　　　True Israel.

The Powers of Evil.

THE SERPENT (from the Abyss).

THE BEAST (" Mind ").　　BABYLON (" Wisdom ").
False Messiah.　　　　　　False Israel.

The anti-ophite system is now complete. God is working in the world in two ways: his Word incarnate in Christ, his Spirit energising the Church. Evil also is working in two ways: the secular selfish world-state, and the corrupt faithless religion that should have been true to God: the false royal and the false priestly.

The completeness of this system is important for more serious reasons than the truth of any theories about anti-gnostic tendencies in the *Revelation*; it shows how intricate the unity of the book is, and how impossible it is to interpret without giving each part its true meaning and its true importance. Yet, intricate as it is, it is all very simple once the real clues are grasped and followed up. It completely rules out the theory of a diversity of authorship.

It is possible that the Many Waters on which the Woman was seated were originally equivalent to the Beast itself, and represent the primæval watery chaos, which in St. John means no more than the fundamental principle of evil. In the original Ophite cosmogony we learn that under the Woman lay the Four Elements, *Water, Darkness, Abyss, and Chaos; and the Spirit is feminine and is borne up upon the Four Elements.*

It must be grasped, however, that St. John is not creating a Christian cosmogony to refute the Ophite. He is taking the original Hebrew elements, which they had twisted into a heathen system, and using them in the way they should be used. It is not possible to make a system of mythology out of St. John at all; the Heavenly Woman, for instance, is both the Mother and the Bride of the Messiah.

The Angel Interprets.

The Angel now proceeds to give a clue to *the Mystery of the Woman and the Beast that carries her.* These clues were added in the latest period of all, to help bewildered gentiles, and they need very careful attention. Dr. Charles thinks that some of them may be marginal comments by a later hand; and this, of course, is quite possible.

He begins with the Beast, of which he says, *It was and is not and shall arise from the Abyss, and is going to Destruction. Those whose Names are not written in the Book of Life from the Foundation of the World gaze with wonder at the Beast because it was and is not and shall come.*

First we note again the clear intention to present the Beast as a blasphemous parody of the divine; it is not merely an Antichrist, it is an Antigod. We have a parody of the words *Who was and who is and who is to come.* It is the Roman Empire summed up in its god-emperor; and it is an incarnation of the evil one; it is doing the work of Satan.

Secondly, it is meant to recall the Emperor Nero, now dead; for the Mark of the Beast appears to be his name. In order to make this identification clearer, he makes use of a superstitious idea which we find in the *Sibylline Books* not very much later—that Nero was not dead, but would return and make himself Emperor again. As time went on, the belief in the return of a living Nero became impossible, and people began to believe that he would come back from the dead, or, as St. John says, *arise from the Abyss.*

St. John did not believe this myth, any more than he believed in the Ophite cosmogony; but he used it to express his own meaning. In fact, one of the most remarkable points about this great poet is his ability to assimilate new symbolic material from unexpected and even disreputable quarters, and weave it into his own starry vision. Ramsay has shown how the letters to the Seven Churches are marked by this feature.

The Beast, as we have seen, does not represent Nero solely, but the Empire as incarnate in Nero. Most of what he says can be applied to either. At the death of Nero the Empire *received a Mortal Wound, but the Wound was healed;* or, to put it in symbolic style, Nero died, but he is to come again. The Serpent Messiah must have his death and resurrection.

Here, remarks the Angel Guide (or possibly St. John; as in the gospel we cannot always see who is speaking), here is the need for intelligence; *Here is mind : he who has Wisdom . . . the Seven Heads are Seven Kings ; Five are fallen, One is, the Other is yet to come and when he comes he must remain a short time ; and the Beast who was and is not is also himself the Eighth and is of the Seven and goes to destruction.* St. John has exceeded his number of Heads, but has saved himself by regarding the Eighth as one of the Seven. It reminds us a little of the Ophite system of creators, which consists of the Harlot Wisdom and her seven angels; with them she makes Eight, and yet she is the Eight.

The numbers are, however, fairly clear; for they represent a succession of Emperors. Julius Cæsar does not count; he was not formally an Emperor, he did not receive divine worship in his lifetime, he did not assume the Name of Blasphemy, Augustus.

The First Five are:

1. Augustus, under whom our Lord was born (27 B.C.–A.D. 14).
2. Tiberius, under whom he was crucified (A.D. 14–37).
3. Caligula, who wished to force the Jews to worship his image (A.D. 37–41).
4. Claudius (A.D. 41–54).
5. Nero, the first persecutor (A.D. 54–68).

These *Five are fallen.* This is what gives us the chronological standpoint of the *Revelation ;* it is written as from the period that followed the death of Nero. During the confusion there were three pretenders, Galba, Otho, and Vitellius; but these do not count. They never received the worship of the whole Empire, " the world."

The Sixth is:

6. Vespasian, who began the siege of Jerusalem (A.D. 69–79).

It is in his reign that these visions are dated; we have already had other reasons for supposing this.

The Other is not yet come, and when he comes he must remain only a short time. This is

7. Titus, son of Vespasian, who completed the siege of Jerusalem, and afterwards succeeded his father. His reign was very short (A.D. 79–81).

The Eighth is the Beast himself again, Nero returned; his name is

8. Domitian, brother of Titus, who renewed the persecution of the Christians (A.D. 81–96).

St. John did not accept anything so crude as the superstitious idea of the return of a ghostly Nero from hell; but he found in it a valuable piece of symbolism. In Domitian, the spirit of Nero, the Beast incarnate, revived. Those who hold that St. John did believe in the return of Nero not only have no evidence for it, they are in great difficulties when they come to fit Domitian into their system. Domitian himself as a new Nero is the only solution of the mathematics of this passage. Thus, though the original visions date from the reign of Vespasian and earlier, and though the book as a whole is written as from that date, they have been worked over in the reign of Domitian.

So much, then, for St. John's system of seven evil world-rulers, which may have a reflection in it of the seven evil world-rulers of the Gnostics who were connected so closely with the Harlot Sophia.

Further Interpretations.

I have passed over the statement that the *Seven Heads are Seven Mountains on which the Woman sits.* This second interpretation of the Heads is a mystery. They have already been identified as the Seven Cæsars; and even in apocalyptic it is odd to conceive a Woman sitting on the Seven Heads of a Dragon. Apocalyptic symbols as used by St. John are sometimes absurd in the sense that they cannot be delineated; they are never absurd in the sense that they are comic. Dr. Charles wants to expunge the whole line as a foolish gloss by a later hand; and if we retain it, we are bound to suppose that it is corrupt and ran originally something like this, *The Seven Heads of the Beast on which the Woman sits are Seven Mountains.*

This text is, of course, the trump card of those who hold that the Woman is Rome; in fact, it is their one strong argument. It perishes when you remember that the Heads belong to the Beast, not to the Woman, and therefore identify him, not her.

The Ten Horns remain a mystery also. St. John received them from Daniel, and perhaps he was hard put to it to work them in. They are *Ten Kings who have not yet received a kingdom, but receive Authority with the Beast as Kings for One Hour. These have one Mind and give their Power and Authority to the Beast. These shall make war with the Lamb, and the Lamb shall conquer them because he is Lord of Lords and King of Kings, and those with him are Called, and Elect, and Faithful.*

No explanation has won general assent, and the points which are clear do not fit together. It is one of the last touches added to the book; the title Lord of Lords and King of Kings is quoted from a later Vision, and the words Called and Elect are borrowed from St. Paul, and appear nowhere else in the book.

There appear to be three possibilities. They may be:

1. Ten subsequent persecuting emperors; but this seems impossible, because they participate in the destruction of Jerusalem.
2. Ten governors of Roman provinces, holding authority from Rome for a limited period only (*One Hour*).
3. Ten auxiliaries or allies who assist in the destruction of Jerusalem (they have authority *with*, not from, the Beast).

But why, in any case, have they not yet, in the time of Vespasian, received a kingdom? On the other hand, they are his allies at Jerusalem. *They will hate the Harlot and make her desolate and naked, and devour her flesh, and burn her in fire.*

Probably there is no single and definite identification of the Ten. Ten itself may be merely a symbolic figure meaning persecution, as it does in the letter to Smyrna.

The Ten kings may be *any* allies or deputies associated with the Roman Empire in the war against the Jews and the persecution of the Christians. In this case we get a curious parallelism between our two strata of visions.

Nero Visions (E).		*Jerusalem Visions* (J).
The Serpent	corresponds to	The Red Dragon.
The Beast	corresponds to	The Seven Heads.
The Second Beast	corresponds to	The Ten Horns.

Only it is inexact, because the Beast in the first column himself has Seven Heads and Ten Horns: but I have pointed out that we must not expect to work out the interpretation of St. John too much in detail.

Dr. Charles takes the Eighth Beast to be the ghost of Nero returning from the Abyss and marching on Rome, with ten Parthian kings as his allies. But it is plain that the Beast does not mean simply and solely Nero; it means the Roman Empire summed up in him. So, in order to secure his interpretation, Dr. Charles has to find here a combination of two apocalypses, in one of which the Beast means the Roman Empire, and in the other Nero.

The incongruous conception of the ghost of Nero leading ten flesh-and-blood Parthian kings against Rome with the intention of destroying it is the kind of phantasy we find in the *Sibylline Oracles*; but it is not the kind of thing that appealed to St. John. It can be avoided, and the two-document theory along with it, by the natural and easy theory that the city destroyed is Jerusalem, the Beast is the Empire, the Seven Heads are the Seven Cæsars, and the Ten Horns whatever allies they found from time to time. If the parallel with *Ezekiel* is at all exact the Ten Horns should be powers with which Jerusalem had committed "Fornication"—that is, allied herself in unnatural intercourse.

The Destruction of the City.

The destruction of the City is never described. Three modes of symbolism come together at this point, and symbolism is left to do the work:

1. The Great City symbolism connected with the vision of the Two Witnesses; a Great Earthquake divides the City into three parts; a Great Hail falls upon it. These symbolise the divisions in the City and the bombardment by Titus. Stoning was the penalty for an adulteress.

2. The Blood Vengeance symbolism connected with the vision of the Souls under the Altar; this is a vengeance on the Land which has been defiled with the innocent Blood. It is also connected with the custom of pouring Blood at the foot of the Altar in the sin-offering.

3. The symbolism of Burning, which is connected with the Woman and Dragon visions. This is connected with the complete Burning of the daily offering, and the fact that Burning is the punishment for an adulteress, if a priest's daughter. The carcase of the sin-offering was also completely burned, when it was offered for the High Priest or for the whole nation.

A subordinate piece of symbolism is the Cup in the hand; I have already referred this to *Zechariah* xii. 2, and Jeremiah also uses it of Jerusalem. It is, of course, a common piece of symbolism. In my Appendix I suggest that it represents the last point in the daily sacrifice, the High Priest's drink-offering.

For the whole long passage is sacrificial, and Babylon is represented as priestly. The Gold with which she is "plated" (xvii. 4) recalls the Naos; the purple and scarlet recall the veil which hung in front of it; the very name Babylon reminds us that it was a "Babylonish web," like the "Babylonish garment" which Achan stole at Ai, and for which he was "devoted" to burning, he and his family. The long list of merchandise in xviii. 11–13 is surely a catalogue of materials for building the Temple, and stores for maintaining it.

The picture of the priestly City as a harlot committing fornication with the surrounding kings is drawn straight from the picture of *Ezekiel* xvi. and xxiii.; but when he tells us that her lovers will execute her punishment, St. John does so in priestly language, *They shall hate the Harlot, and make her desolate and naked, and eat her flesh, and burn her with*

Fire. The eating of the flesh is obviously connected with the sin-offering in which the flesh was eaten by the priests.

Josephus also sees in the burning of Jerusalem the execution of the will of God. "But as for that House, God had for certain long ago doomed it to the fire; and now the fated period of time was at hand." I need not quote from him to illustrate the completeness of the burning.

He also saw in the destruction of the City something in the nature of a blood vengeance, and records that he addressed his countrymen as follows, "Who does not know the words of the ancient prophets, and the oracle that is even now overhanging the miserable City? For they foretold that the capture of the City would come about when someone began the murder of his own countrymen. And is not the City and the whole Temple filled with your own dead bodies? It is God, therefore, it is God who is with the Romans, and is bringing upon it the fire of purification, and is rooting up the City which is full of such pollutions."

It is interesting to note the differences as well as the similarities between St. John the Christian prophet and Josephus the orthodox priest educated in the culture of the Greek. I have prefixed to this chapter other prophetic material out of Josephus, and I always wonder whether this curious inquirer after varieties of religion did not know more about the Christians than he thought it prudent to reveal. Where in the Old Testament is this "oracle" that the destruction of the City would date from the murder of their own countrymen?

He records an event in the final destruction which is harmonious with St. John's picture of the Blood Vengeance. "And round about the Altar lay a multitude of dead bodies in a heap, and down the steps of the Altar was flowing a stream of Blood, and the bodies of those who were being slain above, were falling down it."

Let us close this section with the epitaph, if I may so express it, which he writes over the whole scene. "And thus was the Temple burned, against the wishes of Cæsar. And much though a man might grieve over the fabric, since it was the most marvellous of all that we have seen or heard of, in respect to its structure and size and also to the preciousness of every part of it, and the Glory that was in it because of its Holiness: his greatest comfort would be in Fate which cannot be escaped whether by living creatures or by fabrics and places."

The Angel of Doom.

If the mention of Fate in the last extract from Josephus has a heathen sound, we should remember that the word literally means the thing spoken, and that Josephus was probably camouflaging under heathen terminology his own faith in the prophets of his race.

The same doom is now uttered by St. John. Another Angel repeats the words we have already heard, *Fallen, fallen is Babylon the Great, and become the dwelling-place of Demons and the haunt of every Unclean Spirit.*

It is taken from Isaiah's lament over the historical Babylon, just as in the next chapter St. John borrows from Ezekiel's lament over Tyre. He has reached the point at which he differs from Ezekiel. In *Ezekiel* Jerusalem is ultimately to be restored; in *Revelation* it is rejected for ever. The sentence passed of old upon Babylon and Tyre is to fall upon Jerusalem now; she is to join those ancient empires in the shades.

It is our first intimation that the sentence is irrevocable. Jerusalem is to become a ruin. It is to have no more history. And this, of course, is what actually occurred. The temple was burned; only ruins were left; and ultimately no Jew was allowed to set foot there. The Jerusalem of the following centuries was a little gentile village built in the ruins; and later, when it rose to more prominence, it was as a Christian gentile city.

The lyric parts of this chapter have a tragic power higher than anything else of their kind; there is exultation and triumph, it is true, but it is mingled with a poignant and terrible grief. For St. John was a Jew.

It may appear to us that too much is made of the greatness of Jerusalem; but this is only because it does not fire

T

our imaginations to-day. Jerusalem was perhaps more impressive than Rome. It had its marble temple roofed with gold; and no doubt the palaces of the priests were in the same style. It carried on commerce with the whole world. It was the oldest city in the world with a conscious and continuous history; and what a history! It had faced the archaic empires of Egypt and Babylon; it had come into real power and importance by defeating the successors of Alexander the Great; the leadership of Rome, the New York of its time, was a mere episode. Throughout that long period of time, the whole tract of man's history, as far as it really counts, she had been the elect of God; God had chosen her, and her alone, out of all the nations of the earth; the rest of the earth was in darkness. Now all that glory was to perish.[1]

It meant far more to a Jew than the fall of Rome; the Jews had seen many Romes pass by and decline into the shadows and oblivion of hell.

Come out of her, my people, thundered the Voice from Heaven, and, trembling, the Christians obeyed. With St. John among them, they fled into the desert, not to the mountains as their Lord had warned them, but to a little place called Pella, which was for a time to be the centre of the Hebrew Christian church. St. John, with some of the Elders, saw that the future of religion did not lie with this small band of legalist conservatives; he came to Ephesus, where he presided for a time over the destinies of Christianity.

Strange to relate, a small band of the nobler Pharisees also cast off the dust of the Great City; they came eventually to a place called Jamneh, where they organised the more spiritual Judaism of the future.

Jerusalem is now wholly Harlot, and her doom is approaching with terrible rapidity; yet she still feels secure, like Babylon of old, and has no fear for the future. *I sit as Queen and am not a Widow and shall not know mourning; wherefore in one hour shall her Plagues come upon her, Death and Mourning and Pestilence, and in Fire shall she be burned.*

---

[1] For a more detailed study of the priestly character of Babylon in this chapter, see Appendix I.

The Lamentation.

St. John does not see nor describe the actual destruction of Jerusalem, because he has escaped from it with the small company of the people of God; but he does see from afar the great column of *the Smoke of her Burning* standing up against the sky, and he does hear the lament of *the Kings of the Land* over her *terror and her torture*. They stand a long way off, and gaze at it with tears and lamentation, saying *Woe, woe, the Great City, Babylon the Strong City, because in one hour her judgment has come*.

He hears the lamentations of the merchants, and records the long list of luxurious wares that they traded with her. Many a merchant, many an investor, must have been ruined when the Holy City crashed. Palestine was mainly an agricultural country, but it appears to have produced every kind of farm produce in great plenty; no kind of country is richer or solider. There were great banking systems, great wholesale businesses, great shipping concerns; the salt fish of Galilee went to Rome, and the luxuries and delicacies of the whole world came to Jerusalem. The whole of this commercial system must have fallen into utter ruin; only the farmer would be left, much impoverished, and wringing his living from the soil. He alone remains, while emperors and millionaires perish.

Far off by the sea the sailors and masters of ships stand amazed at the great column of smoke; there is a lurid orange tinge in the sunlight, and men's shadows are a pale blue on the sand. Jerusalem is a pillar of cloud by day and a pillar of fire by night. They, too, are ruined. Joseph Klausner has shown the extent of the shipping of Jerusalem, and reminds us that after the siege Titus struck a medal bearing the words *Victoria Navalis*; no doubt in Roman eyes she was a second Carthage,[1] semitic, commercial, naval, *compassing sea and land*, as our Lord said. The sailors too lament over the great city which they have helped to enrich.

As we consider this chapter we find that it is more human, more poignant, than any other part of the book. It is

[1] The comparison is found in a speech attributed to Titus by Josephus.

personal. It moves us because it is real; St John is lamenting over what he actually saw, even though he *was standing afar off*, like some at the crucifixion; and it is his own city, that is being blotted off the face of the earth. Is there anywhere in literature such a lament over the death of a city by one who loved it? For it is clear from the tone of these lyrics that though he had denounced her as the Harlot, he had loved her as men love their own city.

In these three choruses we may perhaps trace the journey of St. John to the sea-shore, where he is going to take ship for Ephesus. He has not seen the horrors of the siege. It may be that he did hear the conversations in the shipping offices and warehouses; he was himself (or had been) partner in a Galilean fish-salting business; he would know where to get a ship. It may be that in this atmosphere there came into his mind the lament of Ezekiel, his master, over the sea-power of Tyre, and as he went about the streets the rimes began to sing themselves in his mind.

For the note of Ezekiel's Lamentation is its finality; the doom of Tyre is irrevocable. The ship of her commerce has gone down into the blue heart of the seas; she herself will henceforth be no more than a rocky ledge on which the fishermen spread their nets. The same note of suddenness and completeness marks St. John's lament over Jerusalem; *in One Hour . . . no more at all* are the chords on which his music is built,

> *And the fruit of the desire of life is gone from thee*
> *And all the bright and shining things are gone from thee*
> *And never shall they find them any more.*

The Heavenly Chorus.

Sorrow comes first in the mind of the poet; but it is crossed and slashed with notes of triumph and joy. There is nothing moderate in St. John, any more than in Blake or Shelley; there is nothing doubtful or indecisive or mixed; there is profound sorrow; but there is also high triumph and pure and radiant joy; for the downfall of Jerusalem is just.

If the reader thinks there is something unchristian in this triumph, let him try to consider the psychological state of those Hebrew Christians who had supported all their life the weight of persecution and fear, and witnessed the crucifixion of Jesus, the stoning of Stephen, the execution of James the son of Zebedee, and some seven years previously the brutal murder of James the brother of Jesus, a man respected by almost all Jerusalem. Let him read Josephus and see for himself the red and lawless anarchy that prevailed there, the deliberate policy of assassination, the atrocities and the party warfare. *Quem deus vult perdere prius dementat.* Jerusalem, mad-drunk, was staggering to her fall.

St. John calls upon the heavens to rejoice because there is such a thing as justice upon earth.

> *Rejoice upon her, you heaven,*
> *And you Saints and Apostles and Prophets,*
> *For God has brought your Judgment upon her.*

And a strong Angel raised up a Stone like a Huge Mill-Stone and hurled it into the Sea, saying Thus with a Rush shall Babylon the Great City be hurled down, and shall be found no more. The " No more " chorus is then taken up and repeated over and over again with an indescribable effect of sorrow, of triumph, and of finality, culminating with the last repetition of her crimes and of her sentence. *For thy merchants were the Great ones of the Land; for in thy Magic were all the Nations led astray,* and then, changing its tone, *And in her was found the Blood of the Prophets and Saints, and of all who were Slain in Sacrifice upon the Land.*

Here we lose sight of Babylon for ever in a last great blaze of worship out of Heaven, an *Alleluia* chorus of triumph and rejoicing in the *Righteous Judgments of God because he has judged the Great Harlot and avenged the Blood of his Servants at her Hand.*

The Hebrew word *Hallelu-Jah,* meaning *Praise ye the Lord,* is common in those last psalms of thanksgiving that close the psalter. St. John must have been familiar with them in the temple-worship; and here they are used to close the liturgical movement of the book. The whole Land had become an Altar on which the Blood of the Martyrs had been poured in Sacrifice; but there was another and more solemn sacrifice than the Blood sacrifice; this was the burnt-offering, an offering made twice a day, in which the whole victim was burnt and went up in smoke to God. The last such offering had now been made; Jerusalem herself had gone up to God as a whole burnt-offering;

Alleluia :
And her Smoke went up for ever and ever.

Nothing was left but the trail of smoke which marked the end of priesthood, law, and sacrifice for ever and ever.

Even the Temple in Heaven disappears; we are back where we began, with the Throne and the Four Living Things and the Four and Twenty Elders and the worship of all creation. Jerusalem is as if it had not been.

The Marriage of the Lamb.

Voices out of heaven now proclaim the coming of the better Israel, the New Jerusalem which is to take the place of the old. *Alleluia,* they sing, *for the Lord God* ALMIGHTY *has made himself King. Let us rejoice and exult and give him glory ; for the Wedding of the Lamb has come and his Wife has made herself ready.*

Now, without looking any further ahead, we know what this means; it is the divine woman, called in some books Spirit, and in some Wisdom, but in the prophets, both Hebrew and Christian, the true Israel, the home both of the Spirit and of Wisdom.

Two bodies might claim this title on earth. One was the group of Christian refugees at Pella with their fellow-believers throughout the world; the other was the group of Rabbis at Jamneh with their fellow-Jews throughout the world. It is naturally the thesis of the *Revelation* that the Christian churches form the true Israel.

The Harlot has disappeared, and the Bride is taking her place. It is impossible any longer to maintain that the Harlot means Rome; the antithesis must lie between the old Israel and the new, the false Israel and the true, the Israel that is to appear so soon as the New Jerusalem.

It was given her to be clothed in Fine Linen, Shining and Pure ; for the Fine Linen is the Righteous acts of the Saints, a deliberate contrast with the adornments of the Harlot.

Nothing remains but to wait for her Lord as he comes to the Wedding; *and he says to me, Write, Blessed are they who are Called to the Supper of the Wedding of the Lamb.* It is unnecessary to illustrate this from the gospels, for the parallels are so well known. But we ought to note that as our Lord's prophecy of the fall of Jerusalem was fulfilled, Christians must have looked with intense expectation for the event which was to follow it—that is to say, his Coming in Power and Glory. With this expectation we shall deal in the next Book.

But once more we have reached a stage which might almost form the end of a book; if it had stopped here we should have been disappointed, but we should not have expected any more. Still less should we have guessed that the best was yet to come.

The Angels of the Revelation.

There is appended here an account of St. John's attempt to worship the Angel who had been his guide and interpreter; it is the one authentic " doublet " of the *Revelation*, as it occurs again in the last chapter.

The Angel appears to be one of the Seven with Trumpets, and has attended the Prophet ever since. The episode may be a confession that in the past St. John has bestowed on Angels some of the worship and reverence that ought to have gone into the worship of God; and certainly they are more prominent in the earlier visions than in the later.

But it is more likely that it is inserted as a corrective for the honour given to Angels by the less reputable Jewish sects of the period. In the Apocalypses God was thought of as far distant, and the orders of Angels that came in between were classified and named and given great honour; in the pre-gnostic heresies they were grouped as emanations of God, or " æons." In both systems they were treated as mediators between man and an unapproachable God, and given great independence. St. Paul is distinctly anti-angelic, and we learn from him that angel-worship was common in the districts round Ephesus. It is this that really explains the inclusion of this section in the *Revelation*.

As it stands, the *Revelation* is remarkably restrained in its angelology; this is the only Angel who stands out as a personality, and even he has no name, or any personal characteristics except a desire not to be worshipped. The following classes of Angels appear in the *Revelation* :

1. The Seven Spirits of the Presence are not to be classified as Angels; they are identical with God, and symbolise the Holy Spirit.
2. The Seven Angels of the Churches are from one point of view identical with the above, and from another are personifications of the churches.
   They are a form of the Spirit-Church figure, covering the process of the Spirit energising the community.
3. The Angel of Revelation (the *First Angel*, with the voice like a trumpet in the Patmos vision) is either an activity of God or else the Angel Guide. He is mere background.
4. The Four Living Things are the agencies or "laws" at work in creation or history; they are separate from God.
5. The Strong Angel (identical with 3?) corresponds to the Ophite Heavenly Man; but he symbolises the progress of revelation, the Word of God.
6. The Angels of the Seven Trumpets;
   The Angels of the Seven Bowls;
   Various Angels proclaiming Messages;
   Various Angels performing Symbolic Acts.
   These Angels seem only to symbolise things that are being done or said. They have no character of their own. They are mere literary machinery. They are conceived liturgically as actors in a ceremony, not personally as actors in a drama.
7. The Angels of Water, Fire, etc., which are mere impersonations.

8. The Angel-Guide, who here, and here only, develops into a personality solely in order to disclaim divine honours.

Conclusion.

On the whole the Angels in the *Revelation* symbolise the activities or agencies of God, processes going on in history or creation, or even inanimate objects.

The Angel-Guide claims to be *of thy Brethren who have the Witness of Jesus ; for the Witness of Jesus is the Spirit of Prophecy.* With this important verse I shall deal later. (See p. 360.)

Michael, as has been shown, is not an Angel at all, but the victorious Messiah. He is not called an Angel.

OUTLINE OF HISTORICAL EVENTS REFLECTED IN REVELATION

A. *Possible background of earliest Visions.*

37. Accession of Caligula.
  Serious illness from which he re- xiii. 3 ?
  covered.
  Attempt to have his Image wor- xiii. 5, 6 ?
  shipped in the Temple.
41. Death of Caligula.
  Herod persecutes the church.
  Martyrdom of James brother of John.
  Herod's divine pretensions.
44. Death of Herod.

Break of Twenty Years.

B. *Events leading to the Fall of Jerusalem.*

62. Martyrdom of James brother of the Lord.
  (By Ananus the High-Priest.)
64. Persecution in Rome by Nero. xiii. The Beast.
  Martyrdom of St. Peter and St. Paul.
  Brigand-messiahs, false prophets, Assassins.
  Excesses of governors, Cumanus and Florus.
  Zealots seize Temple, declare the country independent of Rome.
  Cestius fails to take Jerusalem, and relieve priestly party who desire peace.
  Zealots fortify Galilee and Judea.
  Reign of Terror in Jerusalem.
66. Vespasian and Titus recover Galilee. xiv. Vintage of Land.
  High Priest killed and 8500 mas- Blood Vengeance.
  sacred in Temple by Edomites Vine of the Land
  admitted by Zealots. cut.
  Vespasian and Titus advance on xvi. *Seven Bowls* (First
  Jerusalem. four).
68. *Death of Nero:* civil war in Roman *Fifth Bowl.*
  Empire. Kingdom of Beast Darkened.
  War suspended: Vespasian and Titus go to Alexandria.
  Vespasian goes to Rome as Emperor.
70. *Titus returns* to besiege Jerusalem *Sixth Bowl.*
  with further forces. Armageddon.
  Three factions in City. *Seventh Bowl:* City in Three Factions.
  Bombardment of towers. Great Hail.
  Temple Burned. xvii., xviii.

BOOK VII
THE AGE TO COME

PART II. THE TRIUMPH OF CHRIST AND HIS CHURCH
    The King Messiah.
    The Wars of the Messiah.
    The Millennial Kingdom.
    Gog and Magog.
    The Judgment.
    The Lake of Fire.
    The New Creation.

II. THE PRINCE OF HEAVEN

Over the plains of the misty years,
  Over the hills of time,
I see the Son of the Mother go forth
  To trample the snake in the slime.
Babylon blackens the sky with towers ;
  The stars in the heaven are wrong ;
But the Man goes forth with his glittering sword
  And the terrible gift of song.

Eyes like a flame of fire, that are blind,
  And only behold the True,
And a wonderful Word like a whetted sword
  That pierces through and through.
I saw him taken and beaten and bound
  And whipped and stoned and dead ;
I saw him leap from the earth once more ;
  I saw him marching ahead.

The Truth himself with the eyes of flame
  And his sharp invincible sword,
You cannot bury or blind or lame ;
  He is master and king and lord.
I saw him once with his feet fast nailed ;
  I saw him laid in the grave ;
But he rose with a shout and a merry noise,
  Mighty and strong to save.

O who will follow, though earth do shudder,
  And sun and moon go black ?
Who will catch the wild horses of heaven,
  And mount and ride at my back ?
Who will smite at the gods and cæsars
  With weapons of fire and air ?
Who will fly on the clouds of heaven
  And die and suffer and dare ?

Over the years of hate and disaster,
  Corruption and blood and dearth,
Over the kings, and over the kingdoms
  I ride to the ends of the earth.
I shall bring you out into open spaces,
  And fair incredible skies,
And living waters, and golden meadows,
  Eden and Paradise.

BOOK VII

THE AGE TO COME

Part II. The Triumph of Christ and His Church

Argument

THE false religion having been destroyed, its place is taken by the true; the old Jerusalem goes and the new comes. The Bride takes the place of the Harlot; Israel is gone and the Christian Church flourishes.

Christ is seen triumphing among his Martyrs, and St. John foretells the end of the worship of the god-emperor, and the ascendancy of Christ and his Saints. This ascendancy, he says, will not be final; the principle of evil, though suppressed, is still in existence; after a long time (the Thousand Years or Millennium) there will be a final battle, and evil will disappear from the universe.

There will be a Judgment, and a new ordering of God's creation, in which all will be harmony; this new order is the Holy Jerusalem, which is being established on earth now, in and through the Catholic Church.

The destruction of Jerusalem was a stunning blow both to Christian and other Jews. The apocalypses of *Baruch* and *Esdras* were written at this time, and reflect the state of utter pessimism into which the Jews had fallen; the world now held nothing for them, and they could only look forward to the coming of their Messiah in vengeance, and its utter obliteration. Such at least is the tone of the apocalyptic writers; but we have no need to assume that their work represented the bulk of the nation; the Pharisee Rabbis at Jamneh had very different ideas, and laid the foundation of the new Judaism on other lines, a spiritual and ethical nationalism without prince, without altar, without sacrifice. It had in it much of St. John's own favourite virtue of Endurance, " the Patience of the Saints."

Christian thought was also very different. In Jewish myth Titus is the antichrist or arch-enemy of God, because he destroyed the temple; in Christian tradition Nero or Domitian is awarded this bad eminence. The destruction of Jerusalem had been part of their creed; Jesus the Messiah had foretold it; but many of them looked for no further world-history after it. He had also prophesied that at or immediately after the judgment of the city that rejected him, he would appear on the *Clouds of Heaven with his Holy Angels ;* and thousands must have taken these words in the literal and material sense.

It was natural, therefore, that after the fall of the great city the Christian church should be filled with an intense adventist expectation; the first prophecy had been fulfilled, and now men looked for the second. It was about this time that " St. Matthew's " gospel was compiled. Collections of the discourses of our Lord which had been made in Aramaic, probably by St. Matthew, were translated into Greek and combined with the outline of his life which St. Mark had made out of St. Peter's reminiscences. To this were added a number of traditions which must have been current in the Jerusalem church, and the whole was copiously illustrated with quotations from the prophets. This noble book, with its Palestinian and prophetic colour, rapidly became the most popular gospel, partly because it was the most complete and the most orderly; but it is no accident that in it the adventist expectation was considerably heightened.

Dr. Charles has pointed out that where the *Revelation* is echoing the prophecies of our Lord, its wording is closer to that of " St. Matthew " than the other gospels; this is best explained by supposing that " St. Matthew " has been influenced by the literary style of St. John's visions than *vice versa*. " St. Matthew " seems to be unknown to the author of the fourth gospel; and even if the fourth gospel and the *Revelation* come from different hands, they were written at the same place, at the same time, under the influence of the same man.

The church awaited her Messiah; but in point of fact he had only spoken in symbols, and then only in very general terms, about his ". Coming.". The *Clouds of Heaven* might be thought of as actual clouds conveying him here from some distant sphere, or they might be symbols of the might and majesty of God, as they are in the psalms and prophets. His Coming might be a visible journey in the sky, or it might be an invisible kingdom in the hearts of men. The Apostles had not been told which; they did not profess to know.

Simple believers of the literal or " montanist ". type took the whole thing materially, as they still do, and believed it. Academic scholars of the literal or " critical " type, like those at Athens, also took the whole thing materially, as they still do, and disbelieved it. Fleshly dreamers who think that in their dreams they have escaped from the flesh, fashioned out of it a materialistic dream-fantasy which they called the spiritual world; this is the " gnostic " or " theosophic " type. It takes a touch of poetry or prophecy to grasp the living spiritual truth that the symbols were meant to blazon out.

We have already seen that St. John has this last point of view. For him the imagery of Jesus is all symbolic of spiritual and invisible things, which are living actualities, at work in the world here and now; and his main object in writing the *Revelation* in its present form was to insist on the great fact that the Messiah had come, that he was present in the sufferings of his Martyrs and the witness of his Prophets, and that through them he was conquering the world.

It is possible that even he did not come to this conclusion till he came to live at Ephesus. He may at one time have thought that at the end of Jerusalem there would be no more earthly history to record; but after living in that circle of gentile churches, and seeing for himself the new and brilliant Christian life, he discovered that the church was only at the beginning of her work, and that the Spirit was inspiring her to new victories. In the faith of the Martyrs during persecution he saw the presence of the Messiah riding out to conquer the whole world; and this is the reason why he wrote his last visions, and arranged them in harmony with his earlier work to form the *Revelation*.

The last section of the book probably has a basis of older Palestinian work; but its two most glorious visions seem to me to show the influence of this later period. They are

1. The King-Messiah and his Wars.
2. The New Jerusalem for all the Nations.

At bottom they mean the same thing. Jesus and his Martyrs are at work conquering the world and reducing it to order; the New Jerusalem is the new order which is being brought out of chaos. *Behold I am creating all things anew.*

The Nuptial Christology.

There are two types of symbolism in the early church which did not pass into the main current of Christian thought. The first is the thought of Christ as an Angel, of which only a few traces remain; interpreted in the light of Hebrew prophetic tradition, it meant that he was identical with God, but this thought was too foreign to the European mind to be assimilated, and has been completely dropped. The conception of an Angel has since been so modified by Greek and Syrian art that it requires considerable historic and theological imagination to bridge the gulf. The other set of symbols still remains; it is the thought of the Coming of the Messiah as a Marriage.

The mystic of every type and every religion naturally thinks of his union with God as a nuptial union. In Christian phraseology, his soul is the Bride of Christ; but in Christian theology this individual union is incomplete and needs supplementing. It takes all the souls with whom Christ is mystically united to make up the true figure of the Bride: it requires, further, that they be united with one another. Nor is Christian theology satisfied with the thought of the soul only being united to Christ; the bodies of the true believers are to be brought into this mystical marriage. Their bodies, says St. Paul, make up the temple of the Spirit; their bodies form the body of Christ; for Christian thought will never accept that division of soul and body that comes so naturally to the "gnostic" or "theosophic" dreamer. The body is not an envelope out of which the soul can easily slip; there is a bond between the two which amounts to identity.

The definition of that union has always eluded the philosopher, and luckily it is not our business to define it; it is only our business to insist on it, even if we insist that it is a mystery. The union of spirit and body in man is a mystery; but it is there. Their radical unlikeness and their fundamental unity are both facts; it is only a too-refined sentimental spirituality which rebels against the grossness of the body, and sighs for an escape from it; a true strong spirituality accepts the body and masters it. It is a wedding; I know no better symbol for it; the two are two and yet become a unity.

Traditional Christianity is therefore very firmly founded on the actual constitution of man. It rejects a silly spirituality as strongly as it rejects a blind materialism. This is the key to all its characteristic doctrines; the inward deity and outward humanity of the Christ, the inward reality and outward sign in the sacrament, the inward possession of the Spirit and the outward order of the church.

Early Christians made no distinction at all between what has been called in modern times the visible church and the invisible church; they simply accepted the complex and mysterious unity. One figure—the figure of a Woman—symbolised both the Spirit in the church, and the church which formed a body for the Spirit; this was elaborately developed in Gnosticism as the Spiritus-Ecclesia figure; it appears to be older than Christianity. There was no distinction between the circle of true believers "known only to God" (to use the modern phraseology), whose souls are united to him in mystical union, and the visible official church which contained unworthy members; it was with this visible official church that the Christ united himself. Nor was there any distinction between the dead and the living; all were one in Christ. There is one whole tremendous process by which the Spirit is at work in the world, bringing men into union with God, and ordering the whole world afresh; this process has an outward and visible incarnation in the Christian church; but in the New Testament, and particularly in St. John, the word *Ecclesia* (Church) refers to the whole thing, where it does not refer to an actual local congregation.

Our last Book left off with the vision of the Bride arraying herself and awaiting her Bridegroom, the King-Messiah (or Lamb). Her figure can be traced through the whole of the *Revelation* as it gradually develops; the successive stages are:

1. The Woman clothed with the Sun, meaning Israel, and in particular the circle of true believers, the new Israel within the old.
2. The Mother of the Messiah.
3. The Christian church, but still conceived as an inner Israel within the old.

The external official Israel ceases to be the Bride and becomes the Harlot; the Harlot is destroyed, and we reach a new and important stage in the symbolism of the Bride. The believers in Jesus are no longer a sect of Jews within Judaism; they have been forced to become an independent body. We thus reach a fourth stage,

4. The Christian church, now an independent body, and claiming to be the true Israel.

The Marriage of the Lamb with his true Bride is therefore bound to follow the destruction of the Harlot; but this Marriage is only announced; it is not described. The reason for this is obvious. The symbolism, as symbolism, has broken down. To describe the Bride and insist on her identity with the Mother of the Messiah would be to introduce an immoral and disgusting element into the poem. Such immoral elements always are found in pagan mythology where it is based on this kind of symbolism; they disgraced the Gnostic systems; but St. John, with great literary skill, has used the symbols and avoided the pitfall into which they led others. Enough is said here to indicate that the rejection of the old Israel is followed by the union of Christ with the new Israel; a mere mention a paragraph or two later reminds us that we must not forget the existence of the "Beloved City"; it is not until the end of the book that it appears in all its glory; and when it does, the nuptial symbolism is forgotten, and the conception of the Bride is lost in that of the City of God.

Its position here is not an error in editing, as Dr. Charles thinks; it is a mark of supreme literary skill. St. John is saved from elaborating a symbolism which cannot be logically carried out, and his book ends with his vision of that redeemed and glorified community which is to him the end and object of creation:

> *One love, one law, one element,*
> *And one far-off divine event*
> *To which the whole creation moves.*

as Tennyson writes at the conclusion of his greatest poem.

Dr. Charles' reconstruction interposes a long description of the new Jerusalem which holds up the action of the poem.

It may be added that in the fourth gospel we find the same literary device used with great skill; important episodes are indicated without being described; the baptism of our Lord, for instance, in the first chapter is never actually narrated, though the average reader gets the impression that it is.

The Bridegroom.

The Hebrew reader for whom the visions of St. John were first intended had the advantage over us in understanding the background that was pre-supposed. This is particularly necessary in dealing with the nuptial passages in *St. John*; and it is worth indicating two Old Testament passages which would repay study.

The first is *The Song of Songs which is Solomon's*, more commonly called *Canticles*, which appears to be a collection of songs traditionally used at weddings. They are thick with Oriental mysticism and metaphor, and it is possible that when they were put together the compiler may have had some idea of referring them to Jehovah and Israel; Christians have always taken them as portraying the love of Christ and his church. The Pharisee Rabbis at Jamneh must have accepted a similar view, or they would not have included them in the Scripture, which they did only after some hesitation. We have noted that this book has already been quoted in the original description of the Bride in chapter xii., where she appears *clothed with the Sun, and the Moon under her Feet;* there is another trace in the letter to Laodicea, *Behold I stand at the Door and knock.*

In Jewish marriages the Bride and Bridegroom were given crowns and treated as king and queen for seven days; the Bridegroom was called King Solomon. We see, therefore, that the connection between King and Bridegroom was natural.

The second passage is *Psalm* xlv., which is also a marriage song, which has been converted into a messianic prophecy; but here the conversion has been more complete. The Bridegroom is both King and Conqueror, and after slaying his enemies, comes to claim his Bride. Although it is not quoted, it appears to be the basis of what follows in *St. John.*

This is the second " Coming " of the Messiah narrated by St. John; for he appeared upon a White Cloud before the Fall of Jerusalem, to reap the Harvest of the Land and to tread the Winepress. Nothing can make it more clear that the " Coming " is an invisible event. Two spectacular visible " Comings " would be absurd. St. John saw the fall of Jerusalem, and recognised in it the hand of God; it was not an accident, but a judgment of God; it was a visitation, a Coming of the Son of Man.

This Vision is linked with that by the word White and by the imagery of the Winepress. In the former Coming St. John has added the word White to the phrase used by Jesus; and the Rider on the White Cloud who brought judgment upon Jerusalem now appears as the Rider on the White Horse who is going to make war on Rome. The word White is also used of the Throne in the Last Judgment, and we may therefore regard this Coming also as a kind of Judgment. The link with the earlier Judgment is made even more secure by the Blood upon his Garments, and the words *he treadeth the Winepress of the Wrath of the Anger of God* ALMIGHTY. The two Comings are therefore planned quite deliberately, and do not represent any editorial confusion.

The Flaming Eyes and the *Sharp Sword which issues out of his Mouth* link the Vision with that seen in Patmos and described at the beginning of the book. The phrase *He will Shepherd the Nations with an Iron Staff* identifies him with the Male Child born of the Woman.

The whole picture is one of the grandest in the book. *The White Horse* blazons the idea of conquest; the Romans connected white horses with the thought of Triumph, and earlier in the book another Rider on a White Horse is used to symbolise Conquest. But what a difference between that picture and this! He wears *many Diadems*, the sign of kingly or imperial rule; but he has no armour; no sword or bow is given him; he has no weapon in his hands. *In Justice he Judges and Makes War ;* that is the real difference.

There is a Sword going out of his mouth; but this means the *Word of God*. Once again we have a cross-reference to the *Epistle to the Hebrews*, which has so many points of contact with these visions, though its own tone is so different. *For Living is the Word of God*, it says, *and operative, and sharper than any two-edged Sword, and pierces even to the dividing of soul and spirit ;* then follows a reference to the Flaming Eyes, *For all things are naked and revealed to his Eyes ;* while an earlier sentence summarises the whole Vision, *We see Jesus for the sufferings of death Crowned with glory and honour* (Heb. iv. 12, and ii. 9).

The Sword, therefore, is to be taken spiritually; and indeed one would not imagine that it could be taken in any other way. But contemporary Jewish apocalypses do represent the Messiah as destroying his enemies with sparks out of his mouth, and a few modern critics do think that St. John is using similar symbolism in a materialistic way; and so we must labour the point a little.

The matter is clinched by reference to *Psalm* xlv., to which the whole passage bears so strong a resemblance; in this psalm the following words are addressed to the Bridegroom-King; and in them the Sword and the Word balance one another:

> *Gird thee with thy Sword upon thy Thigh*
> *O thou most Mighty :*
> *According to thy worship and renown.*

Good luck have thou with thine honour.
Ride on because of the Word of Truth
Of Meekness and Righteousness,
And thy right hand shall teach thee terrible things.

Turning to St. John's vision, we naturally look to see the great Sword girded upon the Thigh; but we see instead that *he has upon his Garment and upon his Thigh a Name written, King of Kings and Lord of Lords.* He has no sword. His Name is his Sword: his Sword is his Word. Once it is seen, this symbolism is unmistakable.

He is a pacifist Messiah. He proposes to go out into the world armed only with the irresistible power of *the Word of Truth, of Meekness and of Righteousness.*

The Names of the Messiah.

He has three Names. The first *no one knoweth except himself;* the second is *The Word of God;* the third is the name written on the thigh and on the Garment.

The Word of God is a title which removes us very far from the notion of a heavenly Napoleon. It links the *Revelation* with the gospel, and though it is drawn from the Old Testament, it suggests the terminology of Greek philosophy, familiar, no doubt, to a church, like that of Ephesus, which was born in a philosopher's classroom. It is all part of that thrusting through of Jewish ideas into the world of Greek thought, which was taking place faster even in " gnostic " circles than in the Christian Ecclesia. Just as the vision of the Heavenly Woman, though built up of Jewish material, may have been so constructed as to appeal to gentiles who were looking for a world-redeemer and a new age; so this Jewish conception of the Word of God may have been deliberately chosen to appeal to Greeks who thought of the " Word " as the intellectual principle behind the universe. It was in Ephesus that Heracleitus had invented the term.

On the whole we confine the term " Word " in English to the expression of our thought as it comes from our lips; very rarely we use it of the thought as it exists in the mind before it is expressed. For example, we say, " You have taken the words out of my mouth," where they have been mentally formulated, but never expressed at all. In Greek and Hebrew it often refers to the thought formulated in the mind; it can mean either

1. The activity of the mind: thought-formulation,
2. The product or conception of this activity: the thought which is formulated,

and only finally

3. The thought as expressed in words.

The Word of God thus means either the mental activity of God (his only activity), or the thought resulting from that activity, or the expression of that thought, or it can sum up the whole process, as it does here. It is the highest and noblest of the energies which man (in his inadequacy) has thought of as proceeding from God; in fact it is God himself, God in his eternal self-activity. It is the creative activity by which he formed the universe: *By the Word of the Lord were the heavens made;* it is the creative energy that inspired the prophets: *The Word of the Lord came to me saying;* it was incarnate in the Messiah: *The Word was made flesh, and we beheld its glory.*

Such is the main conception of this passage, very far removed from the thought of the heavenly Napoleon going out to slaughter. It is possible that something is owed to the Jewish philosophical school in Alexandria; but that is not required. The conception of the *Word of God*, meaning the mental and creative activity of God, is common in the Rabbis, as Burney has shown in his study of the fourth gospel. The Alexandrian perhaps took a step towards making it a " person."

It will be seen now that the Sword issuing from the mouth is a characteristic weapon; the only weapon of the Word of God is *himself.*

The Garment Dipped in Blood.

The Garment Dipped in Blood is closely associated with the name "Word of God" and the name "King of Kings"; for it is on his Garment as well as on his Thigh that his name is written. It is obvious that the Blood is his own blood, though Dr. Charles will not have it. He says it is the blood of the Parthian kings, and that a passage has dropped out in which the slaughter of the ten Parthian kings and of their armies was described. The evidence seems precarious.

Apart from the general fitness of the situation, we must note that there is a correspondence between the Garments of Christ and those of his followers; theirs are *Washed White in the Blood of the Lamb*, and his is sprinkled with Blood too; whose but his own?

The Garment in question is a "Podērēs," which Dr. Charles himself describes as priestly; the Blood therefore is the Blood of Sacrifice. The Lamb is the sacrifice.

The Blood may also be associated with the Winepress; and we have already dealt with the treading of the Winepress which took place *outside the City* of Jerusalem. We noted then the back-reference to the crucifixion. The treading of the Winepress symbolises the crucifixion and is associated with the deaths of the Martyrs. The Land has been deluged with this sacrificial Blood; and it is on account of this "innocent blood" that Vengeance comes on the Great City.

The King-Messiah appears as High-Priest. His priestly robe is now dipped in blood; this blood must be sacrificial blood; the blood of the martyrs is sacrificial blood; the Blood of the Lamb is the supremely sacrificial Blood. The whole symbolism is consistent with itself and with the rest of the book; the Parthian kings cannot be proved to have any existence in the book at all, and their slaughter is admittedly not recorded.

It is through his sacrifice on the cross that the Messiah has gained his title *King of Kings* which is inscribed on the Garment along with the stains of Blood; it carries a distinct reference to the title on the cross. The priestly garment also recalls the seamless robe of the crucifixion, which is mentioned only in the fourth gospel.

The Heavenly Robe.

I must now make good some remarks which I made earlier on the subject of the heavenly Robe in general; but before doing so, I wish to deal with a verse I omitted to treat in the Letters to the Seven Churches.

ii. 17. *And I will give him a White Stone, and upon the Stone a New Name written which no one knoweth except he who receiveth it.* This passage has never been satisfactorily explained as it stands. Let me compare it with this: *Seven Angels . . . clothed in Stone, pure and white* (xv. 6).

Now in the latter case Dr. Charles has suggested an original Hebrew word Shesh, which means either fine linen or else alabaster or marble; he supposes, therefore, that Stone (or the whole phrase Pure and White Stone), which is probably textually correct, may be a mistranslation of Shesh. If this is so, it may also be the correct explanation of the first passage. I admit that the word translated Stone in the first passage is a different word (Psephos) and means a pebble or small tablet; but I submit that in the phrase *I will give him Shesh* the translator would necessarily visualise a small piece of stone only.

My own difficulty in accepting the theory is that it demands a translator who did not understand what he was translating; and the *Revelation* does not impress me as having gone through such a process.

If we accept ii. 17 as it stands, we are in the awkward position of having to illustrate it from pagan sources only, which is possible, but not likely. Dr. Charles does note the fact that according to *Yoma* 8, precious stones were said to have fallen with the Manna; and it is also true that a ticket of some kind was used in the organisation of the Temple ritual, those who drew stores or required animals for sacrifice receiving one from the official in charge.

In any case the main point is the Name, not the Stone, and it is interesting to note that it is linked with the passage we have just read by the expression *a Name which no one knoweth but he himself*.

Dr. Charles has rightly insisted that the Name written on the Stone is at the same time the Name of God and the character of the man. In symbolic thinking Name is nature. The Name of God is his essential being, what he is; the name of a man is what he is. But what is he?

As we go through life we clothe ourselves with a certain character (*he clotheth himself with cursing as with a garment,*

Ps. cix. 18), it develops with us and determines us; it is in our own power, and yet it depends upon our environment. In the case of the religious man it is felt to depend on God. The character he assumes as he goes through life is the gift of God (grace); and yet, for all that, it is an achievement. It is the Righteous Acts of the Saints; it is also the White Robe given by God. We are not surprised, therefore, to find *Revelation* insisting on what a man does—the keeping of the Commandments—as well as what a man receives—the White Robe of Royalty and Priesthood: *He hath made us a Kingdom of Priests.*

Scientific thought, which is the mode to-day, clings to the truth that the character is the man. " I acquire a character," we may say; but we do not think of the character as an external thing clothing the soul, as something which can be put off and on like a robe, leaving the self naked. Symbolic thinking can do this quite happily and, what is more, quite truly, so long as it remains symbolic thinking and is not converted into scientific thinking. That is why the psychology of St. Paul has been so badly misunderstood; his terms have been treated by theologians as if they were the terms of a scientific system, whereas in reality they are symbolic.

It is bad enough even where the symbolic nature of the thinking is grasped, and then an exposition is attempted in terms of scientific thinking, as everyone must feel in reading Sir J. G. Fraser's account of a rather similar psychological conception, which he calls the External Soul. Just as if an Internal Soul was a more satisfactory and scientific idea. In symbolism we have two things: the direct intuitive or imaginative grasp of the process to be described; the direct application to it of symbolism that does at once present it to the mind. Scientific thinking does not even come in; it can only affect a new presentation of the facts in its own way and its own terminology.

St. Paul, therefore, can readily look on death as the putting off not only of the body, but also of the self, the character that has grown and developed with it, changing from day to day; he can mix his metaphors on the subject, which is a sure sign that he is really contemplating the reality and desperately using whatever symbols come to hand to illuminate it. The " earthly house of this tabernacle " is to be dissolved; he is to be left naked; he groans, earnestly desiring to be clothed upon with the house not made with hands, eternal in the heavens; to be clothed upon, that mortality might be swallowed up in life. It is not merely the body to which he is referring; the word body itself has a wider meaning of a symbolic order. It is perhaps *contained* in the thought of the robe that he is to put off; but it is only a part of it. (See 2 *Cor.* v.)

The body of the self, the robe of the self, the house of the self; they are all symbols put out one by one to blazon that living tissue of thoughts and words and acts and habits and dispositions which the self has made for itself as it goes through life. And so in a sense the Robe is the body, as Dr. Charles says: but it is much more. Those who have *defiled their Robes* have stained much more than their physical bodies; and those who have *washed their Robes and made them White in the Blood of the Lamb* have purified much more than their physical bodies. It is their characters, their personalities, that which for good or evil they have let themselves become; their Name.

The plurality in the soul, demanded by symbolic thinking, corresponds to reality—that is to say, the actual facts of life; our nature is a thing we wrestle with, regret, judge, approve, or condemn. *Wretched man that I am,* says St. Paul, in a moment of depression, *Who will deliver me from the body of this death?* This is not theology at all (that is to say scientific terminology), it is poetry and symbolism.

The truth that we make it for ourselves is met and crossed by the contrary truth that it is given us by God. No one was more conscious than St. Paul that the life of the Christian was a thing of grace, a heavenly gift; *our life is hid with Christ in God.* It is something divine enfolding us and clothing us now (a foretaste of the Spirit), though we shall only possess it in security and perfection after death has stripped us naked, and we pass through that dreadful apocalypse into the life beyond. Yet we do in a real sense have it and hold it now. The life of the saint is a supernatural life; his virtues and victories are not his own; they are the power of God working in him:

> And every virtue we possess,
> And every conquest won,
> And every thought of holiness,
> Are his alone.

This gift of a heavenly nature, the "new creation," is what comes to us in baptism; and it is the symbolism of baptism which lies behind St. John's use of the Robe and of the Name. We are baptised *Into the Name ;* it occurs again and again. Christians are those *Who have been invoked with the Name of Jesus.* The Name was the earliest essential of Christian baptism, because it symbolised the very being of the divine person to whom we unite ourselves; his Name is put upon us.

Know ye not, says St. Paul (it is clearly a well-known piece of Christian teaching) *that as many of you as were baptized into Christ Clothed yourself with him? (Rom.* vi. 3). We have here the symbolism of the Robe which is also an essential part of baptism. Baptism by immersion must infallibly be followed by putting on clothes of some kind. St. Paul has seized upon this as symbolic of the new divine nature.

The Name and the Robe are both of them natural symbols of the new creation, the divine nature assumed by Christians. The Robe, the Name, the Washing, are the natural symbols in *Revelation* for the same thing: the new nature which is a gift of God, the new nature of which the glorious spiritual resurrection body is the perfect flower.

I have referred to the Syrian Gnostic *Hymn of the Soul* in the *Acts of Thomas.* In this composition the soul is conceived in Gnostic fashion as a stranger on earth who has forgotten his divine origin and nature. He has forgotten his Father (the King of Kings) and his Royal Mother (the Holy Spirit) and his Brother (Christ); it will be seen that this symbolic theology is very similar to that of *Revelation* xii.; but it is infinitely weaker, because it has got away from reality, and developed into a fantastic mythology. The divine nature forgotten by the soul is described as a Robe left behind before descending into this world; this thought of the soul as separable is the weakness of Syrian thought.

When the soul remembers its origin and returns to God it is described as a journey home and the resumption of the forgotten Robe; the Robe represents (*a*) the twin self, the forgotten part of the soul, and (*b*) the Christ, the twin brother. (The translation is that printed by M. R. James, *The Apocryphal N.T.*)

And suddenly I saw the Garment made like unto me as it had been a mirror,
And I beheld upon it all myself, and I knew and saw myself through it. . . .
And the lovely Garment which was variegated with bright colours,
And gold and precious stones and pearls of comely hue . . .
And the likeness of the King of Kings was all in all of it
Sapphire stones were fitly set in it above . . .
And it was ready to utter speech.
And I heard it speak,
" I am of him that is more valiant than all men, for whose sake I was reared up with the Father himself."

There is enough quoted to show that we have here the same conception, though it has been worked out into a poetic fantasia of some beauty. The divine Garment of the soul in this hymn is actually Christ himself, and the soul puts on Christ and is united with him. It contains the *likeness of the King of Kings*, and this sets us wondering whether its author had read the *Revelation*, in which the Garment of Christ is marked with the name King of Kings; if so it is interesting to ask how it reached the author, as *Revelation* had not been translated into Syriac. The phrase may have gone from the *Revelation* into Greek Gnosticism, and from Greek Gnosticism into Syriac.

Turning to Egyptian Gnosticism, we find a very interesting connection of Name and Garment. Names are all-important in Gnosticism. As the soul returns to God it has to pass each of the Seven Spheres; and at the gate of each of the spheres it is stopped by the spirit who guards it, and turned back, unless it knows the name of the spirit. There are, in fact, two ways of overcoming a spirit; one is to know its name; the other is to know a more powerful name.

When the great æon Christ came down from the Pleroma he dropped a Name at each gate so as to hide his identity; in symbolic language, it is said that he put off a Garment, and in the Garment was the Name. The conception probably is that he separated off part of his identity. After the resurrection he ascended from the Mount of Olives and passed through the spheres again, resuming a Garment at each gate. This progress upwards is described for us by Christ himself in *Pistis Sophia*, an Egyptian Gnostic production of the school of Valentinus, perhaps of Valentinus himself. My quotation is from the translation of G. Horner (S.P.C.K.), and as it is quite literal, it reads a little oddly. The first extract describes the return of the Garment; the second the passing through the spheres.

There came down a great Power of Light, my Vesture being in it, this which I left in the twenty-fourth Mystery, according as I have already said to you now ; and I found a Mystery in my Vesture written in the sort of, the writing of the things of the height, zama zama ozza rakhama ozai, namely its interpretation, The Mystery which is outside of the World, because of which the Universe became . . (It then appears there are two vestures.) *The first indeed being in it all the Glory of all Names of all the Mysteries with all the Emanations of the Arrays of the Spaces of the Ineffable ; and the second Clothing being in it all the Glory of all the Names of all the Mysteries of all the Emanations, these which become in the Arrays of the Two Spaces of the First Mystery, etc. etc.*

I put it on me in that hour, and I enlightened greatly greatly, and I flew into the Height, and I came at the gate of the firmament, enlightening greatly greatly, there being no measure unto the light which I was becoming. And were disturbed upon one another the gates of the firmament, all were opened at once, and all the Rulers with all the Authorities with all the Angels who were in it, they were all disturbed together because of the great Light which becometh from me. And they looked at the Vesture of Light which was on me, which enlighteneth, they saw the Mystery on which being their Name, they feared greatly greatly, and were loosened all their bonds . . . and they prostrated all before my presence, they worshipped saying, In what manner passed through us the Lord of the Universe, while we knew it not?

It will be seen from this that not only is the Name the same as the Garment, and that both signify the divine nature; but that it is in the power of the Name that the spirits of the firmament are overcome. We may add that there are signs of the influence of *Revelation* in *Pistis Sophia*; the female æon Sophia, for instance, is persecuted by a Dragon with Seven Heads.

These two extracts illustrate how the symbolism of the Name and Robe, meaning the divine nature, developed and proliferated in these amazing theosophic cults; they also show that the literal method of the Jewish apocalypses is not the only way of taking it. Even in these I often wonder whether we are doing them justice when we take them in a purely literal and prosaic way. In his additional note on the White Robe (Vol. 1, pp. 184–188) Dr. Charles has collected a great deal of extremely interesting illustrative material from his apocalypses; he has added to it a discussion of passages from St. Paul, and there are moments when he almost seems to be giving us the spiritual meaning which they undoubtedly had: in the end, however, he appears to sink back and repose on the eschatological and the material.

The conjunction of Name and Garment, then, in *Revelation*, symbolises the nature and character of the Christ. It is royal; it is priestly; it is human, for it is dipped in the Blood in which he suffered for us; it is divine, for it bears the Name King of Kings and Lord of Lords. These Names are the Names by which he will overcome the kings of the earth who stand up to oppose him; his Word and his own essential nature will win the day.

Let us now add a note about the Stone. The Garment of the Syriac Hymn appears to have been practically a tissue of precious stones; so that, after all, it may not be impossible to think of the angelic Robes as Stone, all the more because the alternative, the Fine Linen, seems to be reserved in *Revelation* for human beings.

The little White Stone with the Name is curiously like a passage in the Fourth Document of *Pistis Sophia*; it is describing the Eucharist.

Stood up Jesus in front of the Oblation : he put the disciples behind him, all being wrapped in Garment of Linen with the Ticket of the Name of the Father of the Treasury of the Light in their hands. This "ticket" seems to me to bear a distinct resemblance to the White Pebble; and that White Pebble, it will be remembered, stands in conjunction with the Eucharist, the "Hidden Manna." It suggests that the new nature which is received in baptism admits to the still more intimate union with the divine which is found in Communion.

The Wars of the Messiah.

Such is the divine figure which St. John saw going forth to conquer the world. It is the most important point in his book; it is a truth perhaps to which he came very gradually himself; Jesus is not a long way off, seated immobile and resting at the "right hand" of the King of Kings. (Has it ever been noticed, I wonder, that St. John avoids this very common expression?) He is in the world now, fighting with his prophets and martyrs and saints; the sharp sword of his truth flashes on through falsehood and error; his kingdom is even now extending itself; the evil systems are bound to fall before it. Those who idly await him from a distant star have missed his advent already; it is not a question of waiting; as in Galilee long ago, it is a question of following.

It may be that St. John once expected a literal and visible return before the fall of Jerusalem; if so, he did not expunge the passage from his prophecies. It was true; that was a visitation of Christ.

It may be that he then expected it shortly after. If so he has not expunged that passage either; he has transformed it into the present magnificent picture of the White Christ striding victoriously through the world. For that is what happened. In the preaching of the gospel, in the witness of the martyrs, Christ the King went forward. He went forward till the divine emperor himself saw the sign of the cross above the sun of Mithras, and assumed the White Robe of baptism. He went forward and tamed the barbarian races which the Romans themselves could not overcome; he added them to his kingdom. He goes on to-day, and the Indians and the Chinese are turning to him as Saviour. He goes on still; there is no limit to his victories. Even his enemies offer him honour; Lenin in Russia claimed to have completed the work of Christ.

The divine victorious Name of the perfect Man stands paramount in the world. There is no other Name given among men whereby they may be saved . . . the Name that is above every Name, that at the Name of Jesus every knee should bow.

The wars of the Messiah are the next step in the usual apocalyptic programme; and the advance of Christ and his gospel is now depicted as a great battlefield. The symbolism of war is carried so far that the birds who fly in midheaven are summoned to feed on the flesh of kings, and the flesh of colonels, and the flesh of horses and those that ride on them. It may seem to many that the symbolism has been carried too far, and that there is much unnecessary detail; but it is no more than symbolism. It is a strong piece of lyrical writing of the type of Kingsley's *Day of the Lord*. Yet there is this much literal truth in it; though the Christ is no Cæsar or Napoleon, though he strikes no blow and carries no weapon but the truth, nevertheless those who take the sword shall perish by the sword. The militarist empires shall go down in blood.

The words are taken from *Ezekiel*, but must be connected also with our Lord's saying *Wherever the carcase is, there shall the eagles be gathered together*. The original meaning of this saying is so obscure that it is not worth discussing here; but I think it means that wherever there are death and corruption there shall be a day of the Lord with the horrors of vengeance. All corrupt and cruel systems shall meet their Waterloo. This is clearly the general meaning of St. John; and though the Messiah does not himself slaughter kings and colonels, there were certainly to be battlefields with heaps of slain until the god-emperor came to an end before the rising glory of the Christ.

In the war between Christ and the emperor there is no sword in the hand of Christ, but only in his mouth; it is his Word that is going to run sharply and swiftly through the world and destroy all that is false. The last weapon of the faithful is not to kill, but to die. The great persecuting civilisation which radiates from the God-emperor is armed with swords in a million hands; its only weapon is to torture and to kill; before it goes down in final defeat it is to learn that those who take the sword shall perish by it.

The symbols from this point onward are very broad and general. St. John is now really looking into the future, and he only sketches in outline the sequence of events. He sees the contest begun, and he has no doubt that Antichrist and those who are with him will be overthrown. He does not say more. The *Beast and the False Prophet . . . were thrown, both of them, into the Lake of Fire that burns with Sulphur.*

The Lake of Fire has taken the place of the Gehenna of the Jewish apocalypses and of our Lord's own teaching. It was a valley by Jerusalem where rubbish was thrown to burn, a place where there were continual smouldering and continual corruption (*their fire is not quenched and their worm dieth not*). St. John has thrown over the local name, but retains something of the idea as a symbol of spiritual ruin and loss. But we must note that it is only *Systems*, (at this point) the god-emperor and his worship, that are cast into it; *the rest were killed by the Sword going out of the mouth of him that sat on the Horse, and all the birds of heaven were filled with their flesh.*

The symbolism is that of a battlefield; but it is only symbolism, dramatic as it is. The Word of God, the gospel running through the world, the witness of Jesus, the word of truth, does not kill in the literal sense, though it overcomes.

The result of the Messianic War, therefore, is not in doubt. St. John believed that in the end the Messiah and his saints must be victorious over the pagan system of the god-emperor and his worshippers. His faith was justified, though it was two centuries before it went into the Lake of Fire and men forgot the god-emperor for ever.

The Binding of Satan.

St. John may have thought that the "victory of the church," which he saw as a victory of the invisible Christ, would come sooner than it did; for it can be argued that it is included among the *things that were shortly to come to pass*. But he gives no indication of times.

He saw, however, that this victory would not be a final triumph for Justice. The Beast and the False Prophet would go for ever; but they were not the real enemy. *The Dragon, the Primal Serpent who is the Devil and Satan,* was not to be so quickly overcome. He is not killed; he is merely suppressed, and that only for a time, though for a very long time. For a whole age of human history, *a Thousand Years,* he is *Bound and thrown into the Abyss : after that he must be released for a little.*

The church will reign where once Cæsar was lord and god; Christ and his saints will be uppermost in political life and in the lives of men; but underneath *in the Abyss* which underlies the human mind he will still be powerful though bound.

The First Resurrection.

We come now to a thought which is always dominant in the mind of St. John—the question of the dead.

We have distinguished so far two classes of the dead: the Souls under the Altar who are merely represented as waiting, and the great witnesses or martyrs of the prophetic type who were assumed like Moses and Elijah, and ascended into heaven. We shall not go far wrong in supposing that these triumphant saints accompanied the Messiah in his war; *and the Armies in Heaven followed him upon White Horses, clothed in Fine Linen White and Pure.*

The Fine Linen (Bussinon), as we have been told only six verses above, symbolises the *Righteousness of the Saints;* Angels are clothed in Linen (Linoun) only. This Fine Linen is to be linked with the statement earlier, *they have washed their Robes White in the Blood of the Lamb,* which is not applicable to Angels. These are redeemed men who share the wars and victories of the Messiah.

The battle, therefore, is an invisible battle going on over our heads. St. Peter and St. Paul and St. James had not finished their warfare when they met their deaths as martyrs; they had only begun it. Because they died as they did, the armies of the Messiah were strengthened, and the glorious warfare could really begin.

It is surprising how little justification there is for taking this passage as the description of a bodily and visible resurrection of the saints, and the establishment of an earthly kingdom in Jerusalem. Dean Alford, it will be remembered, uttered some strong words about the dishonesty of anyone who doubted that this passage described a visible and literal reign on earth; and his words have been quoted from time to time by modern eschatologists whose own theology is at the opposite pole from that of Dean Alford. But the notion of the earthly kingdom is largely assumption, and Dr. Charles has to re-arrange *Revelation* pretty drastically before he can make much of it.

I deal with the rise of Chiliasm, as this belief is called, in Part II of my last Book; meanwhile it might be noted that there is nothing in this passage about a city, nothing about eating and drinking, nothing about earthly activities of any kind. All that is said of the Saints who took part in the First Resurrection is that they Lived, and they Judged, and they Reigned—a poor basis for the visions that have been spun out of this section. Furthermore, it is expressly said that it is the *souls* of the Martyrs who live, and judge, and reign; nothing is said about giving them a White Robe. Apart from the verse in which the merchandise of Babylon is described as the souls of men, there is only one other occurrence of the word soul in the whole poem, and that is the vision of the souls beneath the Altar, who are certainly the dead who have not yet been clothed in the resurrection body. The weight of the evidence is thus decidedly against a material interpretation of this passage.

It is worth noting, too, that there is nothing at all in *Revelation* to suggest that the New Jerusalem when it comes is to be built on the site of the old. Yet Dr. Charles and many others take this for granted. As a matter of fact it is seen in the air, in the act of descending.

The judging and reigning of this passage are merely a

continuation of the riding and fighting of the last; they are two ways of expressing the same thing, the supremacy in the human world of the invisible Christ and his saints.

Again, the inspiration of St. John was not at fault. During the period of persecution the Martyr was already receiving almost divine honours; but he was felt to be a comrade and a fellow-soldier in the good fight. After the victory of the church came the long catholic period of the Dark Ages and Middle Ages, in which Europe was being beaten on the anvil and re-forged into a new and more beautiful shape; in the new Europe the sacred was superior to the secular, and in the minds of all men Christ and his Saints held an unquestionable supremacy: not Christ only, but Christ and his Saints.

It is interesting to realise that the honour paid to the saints in the catholic liturgies is not merely a fulfilment of something which a keen prophetic vision was able to foresee; it is actually the outcome of what St. John said and saw. He saw the Martyrs suffering and the Messiah in their midst; he saw that this meant sweeping victory along a huge front; he expressed in his inspired poem the sentiment of the persecuted church, which associated the deaths of the Martyrs with the death of the Messiah, and elevated them to thrones of worship next to his. The cult continued throughout the long war till the age of persecution was over; but the impetus of it was so enormous that the very bodies of the Martyrs were carried into the churches and placed under the altars, and their names were repeated with wonder and veneration in the high places where the Beast and the False Prophet had once held sway. St. John is the leader of the movement whose culmination he foresees; it derives much from him.

This, he says, *is the First Resurrection; the rest of the Dead did not live till the Thousand Years were finished.* These are the saints expectant, or at rest.

The Loosing of Satan.

After the Thousand Years the symbols become even simpler and broader. They are in the far future now, and St. John deals only with gigantic general principles.

There will be reaction. The principle of evil has never

been destroyed but only suppressed. *Satan will be released from his prison and will go forth to deceive the nations in the Four Corners of the Earth, Gog and Magog, to bring them to war.* This looks as if it meant nations beyond the bounds of the old Roman Empire (now dominated by Christ and his Saints), the area which ancient writers called the world. I do not think this goes deep enough; it is only the symbolism, not the meaning.

A last battle against unidentified tribes is a common idea in the apocalypses, and appears to be based on passages in the prophets which had never been fulfilled. Jeremiah began his ministry by a prophecy that Palestine would be overrun by a barbarous nation from the north, probably the Scythians (*Jer.* i.); and this prophecy, which was never fulfilled, was taken up by Ezekiel, and brought out in a new form in which he christened the nations Gog and Magog (*Ex.* xxxviii), mere barbaric sounds that correspond to no known tribal names. St. John is following him in placing them in the Four Corners of the Earth.

Owing to Jeremiah's prophecy, the North became a mere symbol for the origin of destroying nations; in the *Revelation* this vague origin is symbolised by the East, by the Great River Euphrates, and by the Four Corners of the Earth, as in *Ezekiel*. But the Four Corners are associated with the Four Living Things, and imply that even these last barbarous enemies only come in accordance with the mysterious invisible laws of God's universe, and must eventually do his will.

They came up upon the Breadth of the Earth, and encircled the Camp of the Saints and the Beloved City. The City is not described until later, for reasons I have already given. Does St. John suggest that Christianity too may grow corrupt and need those destroying nations which are the scourge of God? He is far too wise to say anything so definite; all he tells us is that the end of Evil will not be rapid, and the victory over the god-emperor will not be the last battle.

On the other hand, he does say that Evil will eventually perish utterly from creation. The hostile armies will be destroyed by *Fire from Heaven . . . and the Devil be thrown into the Lake of Fire and Sulphur* along with the Beast and the False Prophet.

His general meaning is clear; and a general meaning is all he intends to convey. At the end of a long age there will be a reaction against the ascendancy of Christianity; it will be assailed by many enemies; but the issue is in the hands of God. The Beloved City, the true Israel, will be saved, and Evil will perish in its own flames.

The Judgment.

The Judging which is spoken of in the Millennial Kingdom is more of a ruling than a judging; it can only be called a Judgment in our sense because in the case of the great saints judgment is anticipated and they are given their blessedness now. The final universal judgment comes; but there is no indication how long it will be.

And I saw a Great White Throne ; the word White recalls the White Cloud and the White Horse on which the Messiah came to execute his Judgment; *And him who sat upon it, from whose Face Earth and Heaven fled, and no place was found for them.* Dr. Charles takes this quite literally and geographically, and is therefore much puzzled by the next verse, in which *the Sea gave up her Dead.* There ought not to be any sea. So he puts this down to an interpolator, with whose stupidity he is very angry. It would be just as easy to turn the argument round, and argue from the mention of the sea that the first verse was interpolated, or that it was meant to be taken symbolically, which is the truth.

It can only be a dramatic symbol. Men and women might flee like Adam and Eve in the garden if they were aware of the Presence of God; not so inanimate matter, which is as much in the presence of God as it ever will be. The whole verse is a dramatic symbol of the majesty of his Presence.

Then came the Dead, great and small; the Sea gives up its Dead, and so do Death and Hades, after which *Death and Hades are cast into the Lake of Fire.* They are the Last Enemy. They too perish from the Universe.

This picture of the Great Assize, as it has been called, is

symbolic of the universal nature of judgment; none will escape.

Books were opened . . . and the Dead were Judged according to their Works. Here too we have symbols of the great principles. All men are to be judged; and none of their deeds is omitted from the card-indexes of heaven. All that has been done has been done; nothing can alter the past.

> *The moving finger writes, and having writ*
> *Moves on ; nor all thy piety or wit*
> *Can lure it back to cancel half a line,*
> *Or all thy tears wash out a word of it.*

It is a grim thought—this Judgment according to Works, and a commonplace in orthodox Jewish writings of the day.

Justice, however, is crossed by another and opposite principle. *Another Book was opened*, the Book alluded to earlier as *the Lamb's Book of Life.* The dead are judged according to their works, but they are saved according as their *Names are written in the Lamb's Book of Life.* How explain this new symbol which seems to leave room for mercy and salvation? How reconcile it with the strict record of men's Works and the Righteousness of the Judge? There is no answer. St. John is content to outline the great principles.

The Lake of Fire.

A little has already been said about the Lake of Fire. It is an enlargement of another symbol, Hinnom or Gehenna, the valley outside Jerusalem where rubbish was burned, the place of perpetual smouldering and perpetual corruption. In the Jewish apocalypses the Messiah and his Saints who are enjoying their victory in the rebuilt Jerusalem watch the torture of their enemies in this valley. The idea is based on the last two verses of *Isaiah*.

There is more than a trace of this in the *Revelation*. The Second of the Three Messages in chapter xiv. declares that all who have the Mark of the Beast shall be *tortured in Fire and Sulphur before the Holy Angels and before the Lamb, and the Smoke of their Burning goeth up into Ages of Ages, and they have no rest day and night.* This is the most unpleasant passage in the book;

but it derives most of its unpleasantness from our habit of taking symbols as if they were descriptions of literal material fact.

Readers must decide whether the *Revelation* is good poetry, or bad history and geography.

In the first place, the Fire and Sulphur are not chemical, but spiritual phenomena. They symbolise the condition of utter loss and misery in which the deliberate sinner places himself; the man, that is, who, knowing God and knowing the right, deliberately turns his back on it and sets himself to hate what is good and follow what is evil. It is the sin against the Holy Ghost, spoken of by our Lord, the " eternal sin " that " has no forgiveness "; it cannot possibly have, because it does not ask it or want it. It has set itself against forgiveness too.

Fire and Sulphur, Gehenna, the Lake of Fire, and Eternal Fire, are all symbols for the condition in which such a man finds himself, utterly cut off from God, utterly given over to Evil. The Fire is not an added torment because he has chosen Evil; the Fire is the Evil which he has chosen. He has chosen the element which is self-destructive, and destructive of all that it touches; he has chosen it, embraced it, and is united with it. He possesses it and it possesses him.

We are recalled to the Gospel of Jesus, in which there only are two ways, each with its own destiny; but the way is itself the destiny and the destiny is the way; one is life eternal and the other is destruction, Abaddon. "Judgment " is no more than pronunciation of judgment, sanction of destiny; in this final fixation of destiny is seen the justice of God; good is good and evil is evil. As St. John says later, *He that is righteous let him be righteous still, and he that is unrighteous let him be unrighteous still.* That is the most terrible of all spoken dooms.

The Worshippers of the Beast are a case in point. St. John is probably only contemplating Jewish or Christian renegades who have gone over body and soul to the god-emperor and his system. He has particularly in mind, I suppose, the Synagogue of Satan who are nominally Jews, but in actual fact worship the author of evil, and practise immoral heathen rites. Such men are the opposite of the Martyr; they have sold their souls to the devil, and deserted the right they know, for what they perceive and know to be evil.

He is not considering, I think, the man who in a moment of weakness fails once at the trial; he is certainly not considering the honest heathen who is true to what light he has; the *Revelation* is not addressed to such. He is considering the man whose life is *marked* by it, the man with the *Mark of the Beast*. The severer view did, however, exist in some churches for a century or two; the man who failed in the hour of trial was never received back. There was no hope for him.

St. John's catalogue of sinners who are shut out from the heavenly Jerusalem suggests the deliberate renunciation of good of which I have spoken. *Cowards and unfaithful and dabblers in heathenism and murderers and harlots and witches and idolaters and all the hypocrites, their portion is in the Lake that burns with Fire and Sulphur.* The words are difficult to translate, but they include those who turn their back on Christ in persecution, those who play with heathen customs in defiance of the Apostolic Council, and all the sects that work with or worship the powers of evil. They are summed up in the expression *all the hypocrites* or *all liars* as the Authorised Version translates it. But the word Pseudos is one used in the fourth gospel instead of the *hypocrite* to which we are accustomed in the other three, and means a man whose life is grounded on a lie, fundamentally false, wrong through and through.

For Ever and Ever.

It remains to consider the words *for Ever and Ever*, or, as I have translated them, *Into the Ages of Ages;* this is the literal translation, and is not the same at all as our " Eternal " or " Everlasting." The same note should be made on the word *Eternal* found in the gospels; it means " belonging to the Age " or " characteristic of the Age " or " lasting for an Age." In the original Hebrew or Aramaic the construction consisted merely of two nouns side by side: Fire (belonging to or characteristic of) the Age. The phrase Eternal Life must be similarly construed: Life belonging to or characteristic of the Age.

Our conception of eternity was not present to the mind of the Jew; it is only in the case of God, who was and who is and who is to come, that he tries to conceive something free from the time-process. The Age is not free from the time-process; it rather emphatically is the time-process, and the space-process too, both rolled into one. The most he could realise was a succession of such processes, the Ages of Ages. In this expression he comes very close to our conception of everlasting.

In the gospels we have a contrast between This Age and the Age to Come; and the Age to Come means the Glorious Age, the Age of the Messiah, the Kingdom of God, the divine order of things which is rolling in upon and dominating the order of this world. Life of the Age (Eternal Life) appears to mean Life characteristic of this Age, participation in the Kingdom of the Messiah; in fact, the Kingdom of God and Eternal Life are convertible terms. I am not denying that such Life is eternal in our sense of the word; but such a sense is not necessarily conveyed in the Hebrew expression Life of the Age.

"Eternal" life means life in the times of the Messiah; an "eternal sin" ought to mean a sin whose effects endure into the times of the Messiah; "eternal fire" ought to mean "fire that burns even into the times of the Messiah"; and it has been pointed out that the times of the Messiah are usually conceived as temporary and limited.

I am not trying to prove that the expression "Eternal Fire" in the gospels cannot mean eternal fire in our sense; I am trying to show that it need not; that there is not, in fact, any doctrine of eternity (in our sense of the word) to be found in it, and that the real meaning of an eternal sin is a sin which bars the sinner from entrance into the Messianic Age; *it shall not be forgiven, neither in This Age, nor in that which is to Come (Matt.* xii. 32). It sees no further than the dawn of the New Age; it does not profess to see to the end of it.

Yet if the author had wanted to say "for ever" or "eternal," I admit that this is how he would have said it. Dr. Charles takes it in the literal sense of everlasting, even in the case of the quite earthly matter of the burning of Babylon *Her Smoke went up for ever and ever.* Now it seems quite impossible to accept the literalist meaning here; it must be a case of hyperbole; the smoke went up for a very long time, or even perhaps a very long way; St. John surely did not mean that the ruins of an earthly city would quite literally never stop burning.

There is a case in the fourth gospel where this expression means no more than "permanently." Talking about the status of a slave, it says, *He does not abide in the house eternally (into the Age)* (*Jn.* viii. 35), simply meaning he has no permanent status there. Here the meaning of the expression is very weak indeed.

It is worth noting that it is never said that the desperate sinners are cast into the Lake for Ever and Ever, or that the Lake burns for Ever and Ever; but only in one lyrical passage that the Smoke of their Burning goes up for Ever and Ever, exactly in the same way as the Smoke of Babylon is described as going up for Ever and Ever. That one passage is the only place where the thought of eternity even seems to be connected with the Lake of Fire. I submit that the *Revelation* gives actually less support to the doctrine of eternal punishment than the gospels do; and that if the one lyrical passage is pressed to support this doctrine, then we must give the same meaning to the other passage which describes the burning of Babylon in precisely identical words.

Whatever the Lake of Fire may be, it is not a literal mass of flame, and was never intended to mean that. A system of emperor-worship cannot be cast into a literal fire; neither can the principle of evil; nor can death and Hades. It symbolises the absolute obliteration in which these things are swallowed up, the *Second Death* that destroys death. Of men St. John says that the desperately wicked pass into it, have *their share* in it; but he sees no further. Looking into the future as far as human thought can reach, he sees the faithful and the penitent gathered into the City of God; but the cowards and unbelievers he sees outside, still restless day and night, still tormented by the destructive element they have chosen for themselves, still hugging the evil they have loved.

He can see no further. The solution of the problem lies

in eternity, and is not accessible to human thought. Their fate, as far as we can see it, is summed up in the word, Exclusion.

The New Jerusalem.

And I saw a New Heaven and a New Earth; for the First Heaven and the First Earth had gone, and there was no more Sea. This continues the symbolism of the appearance of God in Judgment. We need not take it to mean the physical constitution of the Universe; but the old principle on which human, social and political life was built. " The old order changeth, yielding place to new." The Sea appears to stand for all that separates and hinders; we remember that it has often symbolised the ancient enemy of God.

And the Holy City, New Jerusalem, I saw descending out of Heaven from God arrayed as a Bride adorned for her Husband. Dr. Charles, who expects our *Revelation* to conform to the pattern of the other apocalypses, points out that the descent of the Holy City should have come earlier; it belongs, he thinks, to the temporary millennial kingdom, and is out of place after the Last Judgment. This criticism is only valid if we think that St. John is outlining a programme of external events and expects a solid city of gold and diamonds to be let down from heaven by celestial engineers. If we think that the vision of the Holy City is a symbol of something spiritual and invisible, it will not worry us so much.

This apparently solid city of costly metals and precious stones symbolises a process which is actually going on—the process by which the Holy Spirit is redeeming and purifying men and women and fitting them into a new and more harmonious order. This process has an aim or objective which governs it and conditions it; in this it is like man himself, with his Way which eventually becomes his Destiny; it is like every other spiritual process. The symbol of the City blazons both the process, and the end which the process is to attain; for the end is only the process in its perfection.

This new ordering of the world has also been symbolised already by the Wars of the Messiah; but while the Wars of the Messiah more usefully represent the process, it can hardly be denied that the Holy City more usefully represents the end. Small wonder, then, if our present section opens with the Wars of the Messiah and concludes with the Holy City; opens with the coming of the Bridegroom and concludes with the coming of the Bride.

From an artistic point of view it is in every way the best arrangement, enabling the poet to repose at the last on his splendid vision of a redeemed creation, a universal order made perfect by the incorporation of a redeemed humanity.

He prefers, therefore, to describe the Holy City as it will be when all the counsels of God have worked themselves out to perfection; but he does not allow us to forget that it works itself out first as a process. It appears first as the Bride adorning herself for her husband. She is not yet ready; she must put on those White Garments which symbolise faithfulness and purity. It appears a second time as the Beloved City, to remind us that the City is there all the time. The word Beloved suggests the Bridal symbolism; the word Agape (Love) is rare in the *Revelation*, and refers to the close mystical union between Christ and his elect. It appears a third time now adorned, dressed, perfect.

Had he described the Bride earlier, it would have thrown out of gear the whole artistic harmony of the book; it would also have compelled him to describe the Bride as a Bride rather than as a City. Passing lightly over the nuptial Christology, and leaving his suggestion of it as far behind as possible, he gives us what he really wants to give us; and I have pointed out already that to dwell on the Bridal symbolism would only have drawn attention to the fact that the same figure had appeared earlier as the Mother of the Messiah.

We come therefore to the City after passing through the Wars of the Messiah and the Judgments of God,[1] because it is the divine order to which all those Wars and Judgments move.

Yet we must be careful to remember that while it takes the place of the heaven and earth which have passed away, it is also the means by which this far-off consummation is to be obtained; it is the earthly Catholic Church growing in love and holiness, as well as the Church made perfect, regnant in the heavens. It is not now one and now the other, but both at once; for the one is the other. The earthly imperfect Church *is* the heavenly ideal church; that is our only excuse for bearing with it.

The mystics have understood this identity between the earthly church and the heavenly Jerusalem very well; it has never been any difficulty to them. It has been particularly fruitful in Christian poetry. There are hymns which praise the church as the New Jerusalem establishing itself on earth; and there are hymns which sigh for it as the glorious heaven that follows the pains and toils of life; and there is a yet more mystic type which is nearer still to the heart of St. John, and looks on the New Jerusalem as an ideal city existing in the eternal above the changes and chances of this world, and yet incarnate somehow in the earthly brotherhood of believers. This is caught in one of the greatest of all Jerusalem hymns,

Jerusalem du hochgebaute stadt.

But its value is lost unless it is realised that the heavenly vision *is* the earthly church, with all its faults, just as the sprouting acorn *is* the oak it will become.

Now this is all contained in the statement that St. John saw the Holy City *descending out of heaven from God ;* not here, not there, but descending. There is, of course, a formal contradiction, because, as we know, the Bride has existed on earth all along; and yet she is now revealed as descending from heaven. There is no real contradiction. She has existed and developed on earth; but her origin and life are of heaven. She has existed on earth as a matter of mere outward human history; but her inward life, the power by which she grows and increases, is from heaven. Her maker and builder is God, and the process must go on until she has received and harmonised within herself every human activity.

The Tabernacle of God.

In order to put meaning into this Vision of the Holy City it is necessary to use even plainer and more glorious language, and to drop at last the figurative language of Hebrew poetry in which everything so far has been expressed.

I heard a Great Voice out of the Throne saying, Behold the Dwelling-Place of God is with men, and he shall Dwell with them and they shall be His People, and God himself shall be with them, their God.

The words are based on Jewish scripture and are found in the exclusive priestly book, *Leviticus*; but the narrow national limits of Judaism are transcended and forgotten. There are no mysteries now, and God dwells with men, and they know him. It does not depend on a local temple or hereditary priesthood.

The word Dwelling is untranslatable. It originally meant "pitching a tent," and so suggests the Tabernacle which the Israelites carried through the desert, and the Visible Presence of Jehovah in the Fire and in the Cloud. The word is used here in the same way as in the prologue to the fourth gospel of a Presence now among us and open to all,

> *The Word was made Flesh*
> *And set his Visible Presence among us*
> *And we gazed at his Glory.*

There, however, it refers to the incarnation, here to the presence in the church, the new Temple not made with hands.

The Visible immediate Presence of God was the greatest inspiration of Jeremiah, the greatest of the prophets. He looked forward to a day when men would not need to be taught about God by a priest, or the Law to be written on tables of stone; every man would know God for himself, and the Law be written in their hearts. *I will make a New Covenant with my People in those days, saith the Lord . . . and they shall be my People and I shall be their God.* The fulfilment of this noble prophecy is the principal mark of St. John's Holy City; its essential character is that God is in the midst of it and that he is directly knowable by all who enter it, small and great, Jew and gentile.

The same thought is conveyed in Isaiah's name for the Messiah, Immanuel (God with us). We have seen that St.

John has used this vision of Isaiah before, and it seems the best explanation of a superfluous God-with-us that has crept into the text here.

And they shall be his People,
And he (God with them) shall be their God.

The Temple in Heaven.

I have already given reason for supposing that St. John once intended to finish his poem, and in an earlier draft perhaps did finish it, with the picture of a Temple in heaven, the Temple spoken of by our Lord, not made with hands. I think that we have here the remains of that original ending. There are two reasons for this: (*a*) xxi. 1–8 are an undeniable ending; they are followed by a fresh start and another ending. (*b*) This little section began by promising us the New Jerusalem, but gave us instead the Tabernacle which is a movable Temple, not tied to any locality.

The fact that St. John has here described a new universal Temple for all mankind is not obvious on the face of it; but it becomes clearer when we realise that the central words of this vision are taken almost word for word from Leviticus, the book of priestly ceremonial.

And I will set my Tabernacle among you, and my soul shall not abhor you; and I will walk among you, and will be your God, and ye shall be my People (*Lev.* xxvi. 11).

I have known many good Christians who told me they were weary of the harps and robes of *Revelation*, and hoped that heaven may not be like that; it may help them if they realise that St. John grew weary of them too, and quietly suppressed them. He has given us a Tabernacle without any ritual at all, and then, in a quite superfluous Epilogue, has given us a City without even a Temple; superfluous, I mean, from the point of view of logic and theology; for he had finished his book, and needed to write no more.

The conclusion of the book is the passage we come to now. From *Leviticus* he goes back to *Genesis*; he sees the rising of another first day in which the whole world shall be new; not a destruction of the world in fire and brimstone, but a new process of creation: creation beginning all over again. The first week of the world's history is over; the new week begins, and God puts out his hands to the work. All eternity lies before him.

Behold, I am making all things new.

The New Creation.
And he shall wipe away every tear from their eyes, and death shall be no more ; and mourning and crying and toil shall be no more. The former things have passed away.

These, then, are the heaven and earth which have vanished. And though the words are spoken of the Jerusalem that shall be, it is true enough of the Jerusalem that is. The process of abolishing these things has begun in the Christian church. Nothing distinguished the early Christians so much as their contempt for death. They ignored it; for them it did not exist. They had no fear of death, and no sorrow over it; triumph rather, and alleluias. As St. Paul said, *The Last Enemy, Death, is being destroyed.*

With these thoughts St. John comes to the conclusion of his book.

And he that sat on the Throne said, Behold I am creating everything afresh.

And he said, Write because these words are Faithful and True.

And he said IT IS DONE.

And he said to me, I am the A and the Z, the Beginning and the End. I will give to him that thirsteth of the Well of the Water of Life Freely.

He who conquers shall inherit all things and I shall be his God and he shall be my Son.

I have again and again, quite casually, without looking for them, noted points of contact with the fourth gospel. The Well of the Water of Life is another; but more remarkable still is the fact that after his book has come to a perfect end, he adds an epilogue which is among the loveliest things he has written.

BOOK VIII
IN CONCLUSION

PART I. ST. JOHN'S EPILOGUE
   The Measurements of the City.
   Paradise Regained.
   Attestations and Conclusion.

PART II. RECEPTION AND INFLUENCE OF THE BOOK
   The Church in Ephesus.
   Gnostic heresy.
   Montanist heresy and the Prophets.
   Chiliasm.
   The Prophets in the Roman Church.
   Later history of Revelation.

CHORUS FROM "HELLAS"

The world's great age begins anew,
   The golden year's return,
The earth doth like a snake renew
   Her winter weeds outworn;
Heaven smiles, and faiths and empires gleam
Like wrecks of a dissolving dream.

A brighter Hellas rears its mountains
   From waves serener far;
A new Peneus rolls its fountains
   Against the morning star,
Where fairer Tempes bloom; there sleep
Young Cyclads on a sunnier deep. . . .

Oh, write no more, the tale of Troy,
   If earth Death's scroll must be!
Nor mix with Laian rage the joy
   Which dawns upon the free;
Although a subtler Sphynx renew
Riddles of death Thebes never knew.

Another Athens shall arise
   And to remoter time
Bequeath like sunset to the skies,
   The splendour of its prime;
And leave, if nought so bright may live,
All earth can take or Heaven give. . . .

                        P. B. SHELLEY.

BOOK VIII

IN CONCLUSION

Part I. St. John's Epilogue

THE construction of the last section of the *Revelation* forced St. John to depict the New Jerusalem as it will be when it is perfect. As a matter of fact, he does not depict it; he only enforces the two great principles which he thinks will be characteristic of redeemed society. The first is that God is among his People, open and accessible to all; the second is that through his People he is renewing his creation. He has so far made no use of the City symbolism. In the Epilogue he exhausts his imaginative powers in elaborating the symbolism of the City, treating it rather as it is than as it will be.

It is worth repeating that it is only on a literalist interpretation that the order of this last section much matters; for the spiritual processes with which it is concerned are going on all the time. There are, however, certain " events " which must be set down in the right order; they are:

1. The overthrow of the god-emperor: no suggestion of a date.
2. The ascendancy of Christ and his saints: lasting a very long time (a Thousand Years).
3. The overthrow of evil: no date.

The " Binding of Satan " is only another way of symbolising the ascendancy of Christ and his saints. This succession of events cannot be altered, and forms the skeleton of the section.

The spiritual processes are going on all the time, but have to be woven into the succession of events; the spiritual processes are also three:

1. The Coming and Wars of the Messiah: that is, the invisible process by which Christ is making himself master of the world.
2. The Preparing of the Bride or the Descent of the City: that is the process by which the invisible kingdom of God is extended throughout the world, in and through the church.
3. The Judgment of God, or separation of the just and unjust, by which some become members of the City and are mystically united with Christ, while others are left outside: it is easy to see that even this may be an invisible process going on all the time, though it seems more natural to us to dwell on its culmination in a "Last Day" of Judgment. St. John says nothing of a Last Day.

It is difficult to see how the symbolism of these inward and spiritual processes could be interwoven with the symbolism of the three "events" in any other way than St. John has done it; and coming in the place it does, his New Jerusalem must represent in the main the final order of things. That is why he is content to lay down only the broad spiritual principles of the new creation, and reserve a full study of the New Jerusalem for his Epilogue.

Ezekiel, his master, concluded his book with a long description of Jerusalem rebuilt and restored; but though it abounds with symbolic detail, it is on the whole a plan for the rebuilding of an earthly Jerusalem and a temple made with hands. St. John borrows little from Ezekiel, except perhaps the living waters, and the four-square shape, and some of the imagery of the gates; on the other hand, the example of Ezekiel may have led him to conclude his work with the vision of the New Jerusalem. But while the Jerusalem of Ezekiel is only a rebuilding, the Jerusalem of St. John is a New Creation.

Second Isaiah had pictured Jerusalem rebuilt after the exile in precious stones, and the author of *Tobit* (included in the Apocrypha) had carried the fancy even further; it is from these authors that St. John derives the imagery of this vision, though he prunes it of mere rhetoric and fancy, and stamps it with the mark of his own genius.

The conception of an "Upper Jerusalem" was quite common in Jewish thought; there is nothing new in that; but the characteristic Christian doctrine was the view that we are all even now members of it. St. Paul speaks of *Jerusalem which is above, which is free, which is the Mother of us all* (*Gal.* iv. 26); and in another place he says, *Our Citizenship belongs in Heaven* (*Phil.* iii. 20). It is true that a very similar view is to be found in Plato, who says that the just man lives on earth the life of the ideal city, the pattern of which is laid up in heaven; but Plato would have been very surprised at the notion of his heavenly pattern breaking in on our mundane existence. It is possible, however, that St. Paul and even St. John may have been stating their faith in a style that brought it a little nearer to the Greek ways of thought; it is possible even that St. John's vision may owe something to the heathen idea of the city of the gods; but the central notion is first Jewish and then Christian.

In Plato heaven is above this world and transcends it, and the sage abstracts himself from this world so as to be a member of it; in the gospels heaven is also "above" and transcendent, and yet it is very close; it is "within us." In the days of its preaching in Galilee it was beginning to break in on earth; in the days of St. John's last visions it was established on earth in the Christian church.

It is convenient here to tabulate the views of the different schools of ancient writers on this subject; as is natural, their view of the destiny of the world illuminates their whole system of thought.

1. *The Hebrew Prophets* looked forward to an earthly kingdom of righteousness here and now; they generally thought of it as coming within a genera-

tion; it would only differ from the present state of affairs in its justice, peace, riches, fruitfulness, prosperity, etc.

This bears a strong resemblance to the Utopia of the modern reformer; but its basis was theism not humanism.

2. *The Apocalyptic Writers* looked forward to a supernatural kingdom of God after this earth had been destroyed; this would be eternal, and its possessors would be the souls of the righteous clothed in new bodies. This earth and these bodies are inferior things.

The former conception could be combined with this by allowing for a temporary earthly kingdom before the end of the world.

3. *The Rabbis* believed in an Upper Jerusalem existing now in the heavens; this could be harmonised with the older views by thinking of it as " descending " at the Last Day.

4. *Our Lord* spoke of an invisible kingdom of God close at hand, breaking in upon earth, and establishing itself here in and through his own work, particularly his death on the cross; its continued presence was linked up with the community he left on earth, the twelve he chose, the practice of his " law," and the sacraments he instituted.

5. *The Gnostic heretics*, regarding creation as evil, could have no conception of a kingdom of God established on earth; certain human souls had in them a spark of divine essence, and the work of Christ was to rescue this divine spark and restore it to the heavenly places where it belonged.

Their view, therefore, is an escape from this world and from the body. They are also determinists; all such souls must eventually be restored to God and absorbed into him.

6. *The Apostolic Writers* develop the views of our Lord and deny the crude pessimism of the Apocalyptics and Gnostics. Christ in and through his Martyrs,

the Spirit in and through the Church, are even now reducing the world into harmony with the invisible kingdom of God.

The goal is the establishment of God's kingdom *on earth*; every day they prayed *Thy kingdom come, Thy will be done on earth as it is in Heaven.*

The Vision of the New Jerusalem.

This Vision is linked with the vision of the Old Jerusalem by the imagery with which it begins. *And there came one of the Seven Angels which had the Seven Bowls full of the Seven Last Plagues, and spoke with me, saying, Come here, I will show thee the Bride, the Wife of the Lamb; and he took me away in Spirit to a great and high Mountain, and showed me the Holy City, Jerusalem, descending out of Heaven from God, having the Glory of God.*

This follows the introduction of the vision of the Great Harlot almost word for word, except that the prophet goes to a Mountain, not to the Desert; the Bride is the antithesis of the Harlot; the New Jerusalem takes the place of the Old. The whole literary framework of the book becomes clear and simple once the Harlot Babylon is identified with Jerusalem.

I pointed out before that the phrase *into the Desert* seems to have become a symbol for prophetic union with God, and I referred to our Lord's temptation in the desert as one reason for this piece of symbolism. Here it is very plain that the symbolism is based on the third (or second: the gospels vary) temptation, in which he was taken up into an exceeding high mountain and shown all the kingdoms of the world and their glory; the temptation was to master these kingdoms by serving Satan and adopting his methods. The Messiah rejected this temptation and defeated Satan by his only method and weapon, to witness, to suffer, and to die. On this high Mountain St. John sees the great kingdom which the Messiah won by that victory: not the kingdoms of the world and their glory, but the City of God and his Glory, the kingdom which is eventually to dominate all the kingdoms of the world. *The kings of the earth bring their Glory into it.*

The Glory of God is the Visible Presence of the Old Testament, the open universal Presence of the new.

The word Descending, as I pointed out before, indicates that its coming is gradual; that it must conquer and extend till the kingdoms of this world become the kingdom of God and of his Christ.

The Measurements of the City.

The City is Four-square, like the temple of Ezekiel; its length and breadth and height are all equal; it is a perfect cube. This is very awkard for the literalist, as a city of this shape is difficult to visualise; one ingenious commentator of a very low order actually suggested that it must be pyramidal, and that the throne of God and of the Lamb at the top would give it a very neat finish. But as a rule even the most literal of theologians are impressed by the poetry of this magnificent chapter, and admit that it must be taken spiritually. The Four-square measurements symbolise God's New Creation, restored, redeemed, perfect. The cubic shape is probably based on the Holy of Holies in the temple. It will be remembered that Four is the number of creation, and this is the new creation.

The length of the wall is Twelve Thousand Stadia, about 1500 miles, an immense measurement, if taken literally. American Adventists claim that only in their continent could room enough for such a city be found, and therefore expect it to descend there; they also publish plans of it showing the gates, the streets, and the river, with illustrations of Adventist saints walking about in it. Acknowledged theologians have often treated the *Revelation* no better.

The figure Twelve symbolises the number of the redeemed; the figure Thousand has been used before as a clan or family of the Twelve Tribes; it has also been used to signify merely a large number. Its use here recalls the earlier visions of the multitude of the saints, those who had washed their robes in the blood of the lamb; and that is all the number means, for it is they who compose the walls of the Holy City. The City is composed of all who are elect and faithful, and Twelve Thousand simply means the full number of all of them.

There are Twelve Gates, and on them the names of the Twelve Tribes; there are Twelve Foundations, and on them the names of the Twelve Apostles. This merely continues the same symbolism. The old Israel was divided into Twelve, and the Twelve signified the fullness of Israel; the new Israel is founded upon the Twelve apostles. The whole vision symbolises the union of all holy and elect souls with Christ and with one another. The material of which the City is made is the bodies and souls of the faithful.

The Precious Stones.

The City is of Pure Gold like Pure Glass. . . . The Street (Open Square) is Pure Gold like Clear Glass. . . . The Foundations of the Wall of the City are adorned with every precious Stone, the First Foundation a Jasper, and so on. . . . The Lustre of the City is like a Stone most precious, like Jasper Stone sparkling. . . . The Twelve Gates are Twelve Pearls. . . .

The first and most obvious point about the symbolism of jewels is that they are precious. The Holy City is built of the most precious and beautiful materials; the lives of heroic men and women flashing and scintillating with all the virtues. But we must not forget that this City is no mere aggregate of human virtues; its maker and builder is God, and the light that shines in it is divine. What we call virtues in the lives of men and women is the glory of God reflected through their pure souls into our world.

The Pearls recall that parable of our Lord in which a man sold all that he had in order to possess the one precious stone that symbolised the kingdom of God. The Jasper is meant to recall the first vision of God as the Primal Light in which he is compared to a Jasper or a Sardius. *The Glory of the City is from God; her Lustre like a Stone most precious, as sparkling Jasper Stone.* It is the divine pure light of God that fills her and shines reflected from every facet.

God is the Primal pure light; but his saints shine like lights in the world in their several generations. In them the light is differentiated; it has different qualities and different values; it produces colours. In God it is invisible; in them it is made visible in a thousand ways: Twelve Thousand ways, St. John would say.

That is why Twelve precious Stones go to make the Foundation of the Wall. The saints are not all alike; they are not standardised, cut to a pattern; there is room for infinite diversity in the City of God. *The Foundations of the Wall of the City are adorned with EVERY precious Stone.*

There is a great dreariness in certain conceptions of the destiny of the soul; I mean those pseudo-oriental religions or philosophies of the gnostic type which insist that we shall lose everything that makes us personal or individual and that we shall be re-absorbed into the All. In Christianity the personality is valued because it *is* personal, because it is individual and different; and these individualities and differences are traced to the working of the Spirit of God (*Differences of gifts*, says St. Paul, *but the same Spirit*). There is no kind of precious Stone which cannot be built into the Wall of the City.

The Catholicity of the City.

I saw no Temple in it; that is to say, the Presence was no longer tied down to one spot of ground in one earthly city; *for the Lord God ALMIGHTY is its temple, and the Lamb.* The Presence does not depend on a sacred place any longer, but is found in any Ecclesia of the faithful; for any Ecclesia represents the whole Ecclesia or mystic church of God.

The City has no need of the Sun or of the Moon to shine upon it; for the Glory of God illuminated it, and the Candle of it is the Lamb. We are dealing with things spiritual and not things earthly. Darkness fell on the old sanctuary, but never on this one; it is perpetually filled with the Glory of God, and Christ himself takes the place of the old sanctuary lamp. He takes the place of King and Priest in the old vision of Zechariah in which Joshua and Zerubbabel were the two lamps of the sanctuary.

And the gentiles shall walk in the Light of it, and the kings of the earth shall bring their glory into it; and its Gates shall not be shut by day (for there is no night there) and they shall bring the honour and glory of the gentiles into it. Here we clearly have the universal visible Church on earth, with its gates open for ever to receive all the nations of the world into communion with itself, and to enlighten them with the knowledge and glory of God.

And there shall never enter into it anything unclean, nor he who makes an Abomination or a Lie—that is to say, a filthy or a false object of worship. It is equally clear that St. John is here thinking more of the " ideal " heavenly church, the invisible kingdom of God of which the baptised are inheritors.

But once more we must give the warning that he does not distinguish between the two. The outward visible church is the body, the earthly brotherhood through which we enter into the invisible Jerusalem, the communion of saints; but the invisible Jerusalem is itself the visible church as much as I am my body. What is the aim or object of the visible church is the accomplished fact of the ideal.

Paradise Regained.

Entry into the New Jerusalem means restoration into that condition of happiness for which mankind was made; it is restoration to Eden with its fourfold River and its Tree of Life—the New Creation.

And he showed me a River of the Water of Life bright as crystal, flowing out of the Throne of God and of the Lamb in the midst of its Street. The phrase Water of Life links this with the fourth gospel, where the mystic's communion with God is called by this name. It also has a reference to baptism.

And on either side of the River the Tree (or Wood) of Life, producing Twelve Fruits, and giving its Fruit every Month; and the Leaves of the Tree are for the Healing of the Nations. The mystic number Twelve, symbolic of the redeemed, is twice repeated here; for it lies concealed in the phrase Every Month. The Tree is the mystic food of the faithful, and there is a reference to the Eucharist. As for the Leaves of the Tree, I have no special identification to make; but it is worth pointing out, what is frequently forgotten, that medicines are distilled from plants, and that the symbol is a natural one. In Australia, where the forests are eucalyptus, it is literally true.

In the Holy City, therefore, there is not only Light, but also Refreshment, Cleansing, Food, and Healing.

It is worth noting that there is no reference at all to Palms, Crowns, Harps, or choral singing, which all seem to have passed out of the prophet's mind after the fall of Jerusalem; in the main they were a reflection of the temple worship. He now wishes to forget all that; and the condition of the blessed is described in terms of natural life: Light, Gold, Precious Stones, Rivers, Trees, Leaves. His Holy City is not entirely urban or ecclesiastical, as our modern hymnology suggests; it is simple and natural and of the open air. The older liturgies of Christendom did not omit this symbolism as we do.

All these blessings are summed up in what mediæval Christians called the Beatific Vision; *and the Throne of God and of the Lamb shall be in it; and his Servants shall worship him, and shall see his Face (Presence), and his Name shall be upon their Foreheads. And there shall be no night there; and they have no need of the light of a Lamp and the light of the Sun, for the Lord God shall shine upon them; and they shall reign for ever and ever.*

Such is the end of St. John's epilogue; and the force it has lies partly in the fact that he has allowed himself to forget the whole paraphernalia of Palms and Crowns and Songs, and the whole towering army of Elders and Living Things and Angels. We are left with the simple sunshine of blessing which God sheds upon his faithful servants, and the quiet paradisal landscape of rivers and trees and open spaces in the midst of the Beloved City; and that is the inconsistency of a great artist.

Nor is there anything in it we cannot understand; for

everything in it begins here. What we begin here imperfectly and timidly by faith is made perfect there in security; Light, Refreshment, Cleansing, Feeding, Healing, Worship are all freely given to us here and now. The very Presence of God is not hid from us; we have seen it in many a simple Ecclesia of Christian believers. But now we see in a glass darkly; then face to face.

The Attestations.

Even after the Epilogue, St. John cannot leave his book alone; exactly as in the case of the gospel, it has to be sealed by attestations and messages.

There is first the Attestation of the Angel: *These words are faithful and true; and the Lord God of the spirits of the prophets sent his Angel to show his servants what must quickly come to pass.* This is followed by the second attempt of St. John to worship the Angel.

He is then ordered to publish his prophecy, unlike Daniel, who was ordered to seal it up; *for the Time is near*; and this is followed by a number of disjointed fragments:

> *Let the unrighteous be unrighteous still*
> *And the filthy be defiled still:*
> *And the righteous do righteousness still*
> *And the holy be sanctified still.*

It is an inscription for the gates of heaven and hell:

> *Behold I am coming quickly,*
> *And my reward with me,*
> *To give to every man*
> *According as his work is.*
>
> *I am the Alpha and the Omega,*
> *the First and the Last,*
> *the Beginning and the End.*
>
> *Blessed are they who Wash their Robes,*
> *That they may have a right over the Tree of Life,*
> *And enter by the Gates into the City.*
>
> *Without are Dogs:*
> *And Witches and Harlots and Murderers*
> *And all who love and make Falsehood.*

The last contains an extra piece of symbolism about the City; for Oriental cities were full of dirty, mangy curs of the jackal type who fed on garbage. There will naturally be none of these in the Holy City; and they symbolise the men and women who nourish their souls on what is filthy and false.

Then follows the Attestation of Christ: *I Jesus sent my Angel to witness these things upon the Churches,*

> *I am the Root and Race of David,*
> *The Bright and Morning Star.*

Then comes the Attestation of the Spirit, *And the Spirit and the Bride say Come; and he who heareth, let him say Come; and he who thirsteth, let him come. He who wishes let him take the Water of Life freely.* This is remarkable for its plain identification of the Spirit with a female figure, the Bride; and for its plain statement that anyone who wishes may come into the Holy City and drink of the Water of Life now.

Then follows a warning to copyists not to add to or subtract from the words of the book; *if anyone adds to them, God will add to him the Plagues that are written in this book; and if anyone takes away . . . God will take away his share in the Tree of Life and in the Holy City, which are written of in this book.* It has been suggested that this warning is itself an addition by another hand; but though this is quite possible, there is nothing to prove it.

The whole book ends with a kind of versicle and response, *He who witnesseth these things* (Jesus) *says, Yes: I am coming quickly.* The response is, *Amen: Come, Lord Jesus.* " Come Lord " is a translation of the Aramaic phrase Maranatha (our lord comes), which was used in Greek churches as we use Amen and Alleluia, for liturgical purposes. It is a Eucharistic prayer in the *Teaching of the Twelve Apostles,* which is not much later than the *Revelation.*

> *The Grace of the Lord Jesus be with the saints.*
> *Amen.*

Having finished the exposition of the book, it now remains only to give a brief account of its reception and influence; for this will help us to understand how it was understood at the time, and why the key to it was lost.

Part II. Reception and Influence of the Book

The sub-apostolic period of the primitive church is very dark; but it is not so completely a matter of guess-work as some writers infer. There is, after all, a certain amount of evidence, which gives us a certain amount of solid fact.

Of Ephesus in the period when the *Revelation* was being written we can assert at least three solid facts. The first is that there lived and worked there a teacher of great eminence who had come from Palestine with certain others who are called Elders; his name was John. The theory of two Johns is based on a badly expressed paragraph in a writer of small intelligence named Papias; it is not sufficient to overthrow the quite solid evidence in favour of one John. It still seems rational to a good many to identify this John with the Apostle;[1] but I have not based any of my arguments on this identification.

The second point is that in his time and under his inspiration there was written a group of books which the church accepted as apostolic; they are all strongly Jewish in tone, though the gospel is linguistically Aramaic in tone while the *Revelation* is Hebrew. Towards the end of his life the epistles of St. Paul must also have been collected into a single volume; shortly after we find the four gospels have become a standard authority for the life of Christ, and the *First Epistle of St. Peter* is also accepted. Under his presidency, then, we find that an authoritative collection of apostolic literature was at least begun.

The third point is that in his life-time the government of the church was organised on an episcopal basis. Clement of Alexandria about A.D. 180 credits him with this work; but we do not need this testimony to show that it is contemporary with him. It is practically universal, at least in the East, in the writers who immediately succeed him; and we are told that St. Polycarp, bishop of Smyrna, one of the most prominent men of the time, was appointed "by apostles." Lightfoot's celebrated essay on the

---

[1] *E.g. According to Saint John*, by Lord Charnwood.

Christian ministry, although written fifty years ago, collects and arranges the evidence on this point in a manner which has made it a standard work on the subject.

The age of St. John, therefore, witnessed the solidification of the Christian institutions; it is probable that the first baptismal creeds were made about this time.

This institutional development was quite natural, because from the very beginning the apostolic order and the great sacraments had been essentials of the church life; there had always been a strong, visible, outward organisation. It became doubly necessary now because of the insidious attacks of heresy which accepted much of the new faith, but explained it away and blended it with false and fantastic systems. The view that Christianity at this period was indifferent to questions of organisation, that there were no set officials or "constitution," and that everything was settled haphazard at meetings of the Ecclesia under the direction of men who felt themselves inspired and could prove it by the gift of oratory, is not only contrary to the evidence, but contrary also to the experience of anyone who has ever organised a church. The church could not have come through its conflict with persecution and heresy without a very strong and uniform organisation; it had to have tests of faith, terms of communion, definite organisers, and powers of excluding the unworthy from communion. There is plenty of evidence that it did have all these things, and that in the time of St. John they were crystallised into constitutional form.

The inward invisible kingdom of God was strengthening its hold on the material world by forming for itself an outward and visible body, the catholic church, with its creeds, its ministry, and its canon of the scripture. The falsely spiritual, the "gnostic," defined religion as an escape of spirit from a world of matter; the genuinely spiritual, the orthodox Christian, defined it as the domination of the material by the spirit.

Gnostic Heresy.

The "theosophic" or "gnostic" teacher claims to be more "spiritual" than the ordinary humdrum church;

but his root error lies in supposing that what is spiritual is good and what is material is bad, that spirit must tend upwards and matter must tend downwards. The body is gross or evil, and religion is the escape from it; this is achieved sometimes by asceticism; in other cases dreams, visions, and other phantasies are welcomed as a temporary escape of the soul into another world.

Those who have had occult experiences of this kind believe that they have passed from this material world of shadow and error into the realm of pure and absolute truth; in comparison they depreciate historical fact or human reasoning. They look down on the " organised churches " and the ordinary believer; but though superior, they are tolerant. The churchman has his chance of salvation; but they are the " enlightened ". They are above the outward forms and historic facts of religion; they pick, they choose, they blend; they have the truth that lies at the basis of all religions.

As a rule the moral basis of their life is weak. They are above commandments and have no notion of a judgment. Their fundamental heresy is in thinking of God as a kind of essence or substance rather than a person or will. He is spirit; and spirit is a radiant and heavenly matter, over against the gross and visible matter of which the world is made. Morality does not consist in training the will to dominate the body; but in filling the soul with spirit and ignoring or trampling on the body.

The answer of the church was to assert the historic fact and insist on the need for ordinary morality and the doctrine of a universal judgment. We have seen already how the fourth gospel was written to insist on the historic fact, *That which was from the beginning, which we have heard, which we have seen, which we have gazed at, and our hands have handled, concerning the Word of Life,* as St. John says in the Epistle which he designed as an introduction to it. We have also seen how the *Revelation* insists on a strict morality on *keeping the Commandments of Jesus,* and on the judgment which Christ would bring on those that broke them.

Here is St. John's function as Witness; but he was also a Prophet. In both capacities the power of his work lay in his Palestinian origin, in his knowledge of Jesus, and his intimacy with the thoughts of the primitive Jerusalem church. He not only had the true Witness; he had also the true Prophecy. He was able to meet the dreams and visions of the falsely spiritual with the genuine revelations and visions of the true spiritual. As leader of the true prophets of the true church, he was able to confute the false prophets of the false church.

It must remain doubtful how far the *Revelation* succeeded in doing this. On the one hand it strengthened the church enormously and gave courage to the martyrs and prophets whose faith was liable to be sapped by the tactics of heresy; on the other hand they probably found a great deal of the book incomprehensible. St. John and his circle were Hebrews, and felt at home in the highly-coloured symbolism which they drew from the Hebrew scriptures; the members of the Asian churches were mainly Greeks, whose knowledge of the Old Testament was filtered through a translation. They could not, and apparently did not, understand the whole of the *Revelation*. Thirty years later they told St. Justin Martyr, who was converted in Ephesus, that it had been written quite lately in their midst by John, an apostle of the Lord; St. Irenæus, who must have left Ephesus rather later, and had grown up there among men who had known St. John well, was equally convinced of his authorship of it, and prized it highly; but he shows plainly how little he understood it. A generation later it was being abandoned in the country of its publication.

As Gnosticism developed it treated St. John much as it had treated St. Paul. Neglecting his plain statements of historic fact and his downright emphasis on common morality and divine justice, the heretics proceeded to "spiritualise" his characteristic conceptions and to weave his language into their theological systems. This may have occurred even in the undeveloped Ophite Gnosticism which preceded Valentinus; but Valentinus, who flourished in Alexandria about the same time that St. Irenæus was receiving his Christian education in Ephesus, boldly used the characteristic terminology of St. John; and one of his followers actually composed a further book, *The Acts of John*, which taught their views under his name. In this forgery there is no doubt that St. John is taken to be one of the Apostles.

Not long after, another and quite opposite heresy arose in Asia Minor, based almost exclusively on the works of St. John. It was owing to this heresy that the use of the *Revelation* was abandoned. Its name is Montanism.

The Prophetic type of Heresy.

The character of Montanism is clearly outlined for us; it was prophetic. Its date is very uncertain; but it is before 160. It arose in the inland parts of Asia Minor among a people accustomed to a religion of frenzy and excitement.

The " adventist " or " montanist " type of heresy is the opposite of the " gnostic "; but it makes the same claim to be " spiritual "; it is led by inspired prophets who claim to be the mouthpiece of God Almighty. The prophet is shaken by a great frenzy or emotion, and pours out torrents of words which are regarded as the voice of God speaking through him; sometimes he has visions which he reports; occasionally the spirit which possesses him takes control of his hand, and writes through him. Quakerism was exactly like this on its first appearance, as can be seen by reading Fox's *Journal*; Mormonism and Seventh-Day Adventism both began with inspired prophets whose words were divine and infallible. Mohammedanism is its supreme example. If this type of religion is to last it must settle down into something more worldly and commonplace; and that is what has happened in the case of the religions I have mentioned.

To the Montanist, morality is all in all, and morality is the training of the will, not the trampling of the body. Morality is very narrowly conceived as a matter of obeying written commandments which are very literally interpreted; God is pure arbitrary will, and has written down his orders for us on paper. The scriptures, like the words of their prophetic leaders, are submitted to in their literal and material sense. The flames of hell and the golden walls of heaven are both taken in their plain material meaning. Neither scriptures not prophets may be tested or questioned; that would be blasphemy.

The Montanists are known in English history as the Puritans; and Calvin is the great exponent of their theology. They are always hostile to the organised churches, which they consider corrupt, because they do not consist entirely of converted and severely moral men and women. They are in favour of a rigid exclusion of all but the perfect or pure. They first attempt to secure this reformation in the organised church, and on failing to do so, split off and form a church of the pure; this in turn is liable to further division. They always regard their separated church as a return to " primitive " " pure " religion; they are therefore the true church, and everything outside them is false.

These are the outlines of the heresy wherever it is found; but we should like to know more of the form of it held by Montanus, for it would shed a great deal of light on the way the *Revelation* was understood in his time. His characteristic teaching was the three ages of the world: the age of the Father was the period of the Jewish religion; the age of the Son was the period of the gospel; the age of the Spirit was the new age. It will be noted that this does fit the *Revelation* very well, the age of the Son being the intermediate or overlapping period between the old world and the new—the Great Interlude, as I have called it.

The third Age was to be marked by the coming of the Holy Spirit and the descent of the New Jerusalem at Pepuza, the place where Montanus preached. The promise of the Spirit is taken from the gospel, and the New Jerusalem from the *Revelation*; but the connection between the two shows that the Spiritus-Ecclesia figure had not yet been forgotten. It also shows that Montanus regarded his own prophetic community as the true Israel. As he reproached the organised church with persecution of the prophets it seems pretty clear that he regarded it as the false Israel or Babylon.

Now this dervish perversion of Christianity did not break out without preparation; it is a mark of the ecstatic prophet that while his utterances or visions are genuine in the sense that he does not fake them, they are never original. The *Book of Mormon*, for instance, is based on a religious novel to which Joseph Smith had access, and in part on the Methodist Book of Discipline; there was not one single new thing in the medley of prophecies with which Ellen White started Seventh-Day Adventism on its way.

An earlier stage of the prophetic heresy is to be found in a book called *The Teaching of the Twelve Apostles*; parts of this book may belong to the first century, and even as a whole most scholars date it within ten or twenty years of the *Revelation*. This book describes Christian institutions as they exist in some out-of-the-world country village, and the Prophet is very important. The church is governed by Bishops (a word which is here identical with Elder) and visits are paid from time to time by an Apostle or a Prophet. Directions are given for testing the Prophets when they arrive, as some of them are in the habit of using their gifts to obtain free board and lodging for themselves; but these directions are practically neutralised by a statement that their words are infallible revelations, not to be questioned.

This book has been accepted widely as depicting a primitive Jewish Ecclesia; it is, in point of fact, neither Jewish nor primitive. It is degenerate. In the first place there is no sign of the persecution or martyrdom which called the first prophets into existence; they gain a quiet and comfortable living by going the round of the churches. Secondly, they have become a professional class, living on their gifts, and often imposing on simple congregations. Thirdly, they are of the Greek,[1] not of the Hebrew type; their inspired remarks are not to be questioned or discussed, as in *Corinthians*; they are to be received with unquestioning submission. A God is speaking through them.

There is an appearance of Jewish Christianity about

[1] The word Greek is used very widely: the type may be Syrian, Phrygian or Asian.

this book; its authors no doubt thought that they were describing a Jewish type of Christianity; but it is the Greek prophet who is really described. We have reached the stage at which Greek converts are trying to carry on Jewish institutions. The prophetic revival of the persecution of Domitian has gone to seed in the years of peace; it has become professional and self-seeking, and even lends itself to fraud. It has also become ambitious. It seeks to exalt itself over the regular ministry by claiming to be the actual mouthpiece of God; it lays claim in so many words to the high-priesthood of the Christian church. *They are your high priests.* Here is the intermediate stage between St. John and Montanism.

It is possible that our version of the *Teaching of the Twelve Apostles* has been worked over in the interests of this ambitious class, who found that their claim to domineer over the church was being thwarted by the constitutional ministry. All prophets are autocrats.

Now the great dignity granted to the prophets can be traced back to the *Revelation,* where we are told that the *Witness (Marturia) of Jesus is the Spirit of Prophecy* (xix. 10). This verse places the Prophet on a level with the Martyr; the spirit in which the Martyr stands up for what he believes is the same spirit as that in which the Prophet proclaims his truth to a hostile world. They are two forms of the same kind of witness. We are reminded of the words of Jesus when James and John asked if they might sit one on his right hand and one on his left in the kingdom: *ye shall indeed drink of the Cup that I drink of . . . but to sit one on my right hand and one on my left is not mine to give (Mark* x. 40). James attained to actual Martyrdom; his brother John lived to a great old age, exercising courageously the witness of Prophecy; both drank of the Cup, *for the Witness of Jesus is the Spirit of Prophecy.*

But St. John does not confer upon the Prophet the function of ruling; there is no suggestion that he had any official position in the church, or any right to interfere in its discipline. For aught we know to the contrary, Prophet and Bishop were firm allies; St. Ignatius claimed both gifts. The Bishop and his Presbyters were the rightful constitutional rulers of the church; the Prophet was a private person with literary and oratorical gifts.

It has been suggested by some commentators that St. John exalts the inspired ministry of the prophet at the expense of the constitutional ministry. There is no trace of this in fact. The first vision of the book blazons the worship of heaven; and the symbolism he employs is the constitutional ministry of the Church. There is a circle of Twenty-four Elders seated on Thrones, with God himself as President or Bishop, just exactly as we find it described in St. Ignatius. The *Revelation* cannot be successfully employed to exalt the ministry of private gifts over the ministry of the community.

The modern attempt to depreciate the constitutional ministry of the church in order to exalt the ministry of personal gifts is without basis in the New Testament. The system advocated in the *Teaching of the Twelve Apostles* has to be read back into the New Testament to do it. The constitutional ministry was the safeguard of the liberties of the church and the faith of the gospels. Without it the church would have been at the mercy of any eloquent impostor; for Gnosticism as well as Montanism was spread this way. Prophets were not characteristic of a Palestinian type of Christianity; they were found throughout the whole church and in all heretical sects; and the exaltation of prophets is not a sign of anything " primitive " or " Jewish," but only of the ambitions of the prophets.

The true prophet served the church well in times of persecution; the false prophet domineered over it in times of peace; the exaltation of the false prophet led to Montanism. The " order " did not cease because a proud episcopate would not suffer it; it ran to seed, as it always does. Its claims could not be upheld.

Chiliasm.

Another perversion of views which we find in the *Revelation* is the Chiliasm which dominated even orthodox thought from about A.D. 130 onwards. " Chiliasm " comes from the Greek word Chilios, a Thousand, and refers to the Thousand Years' Reign of Christ and his saints described in *Rev.* xx. 4. This " Millennial " kingdom was thought of as a physical and literal event; a new Jerusalem would be built on the site of the old; Christ would descend bodily from heaven and reign there; he would be emperor of the world, and the earth would be incredibly fruitful.

This is simply a materialistic Jewish messianism masquerading as Christianity; but it would also appeal to the Greek, with his hope of the return of a Golden Age of peace and plenty. It is first found fully and explicitly in St. Justin Martyr's *Dialogue with Trypho*, which was probably written about 159 or a little later, but narrates a conversation said to have taken place just after the Jewish War of 132 to 135. He quotes St. John's *Revelation* as his authority for this belief, and calls him an apostle; on the other hand, he admits that there are orthodox Christians who do not hold it.

Needless to say, *Rev.* xx. 4 ought not to be interpreted in this material way. The Reign is spiritual; it is distinctly said that it is the *souls* of the mighty dead who lived and reigned. Nor is there a suggestion that the reign is in Jerusalem; the descent of the heavenly Jerusalem is described later. Nor is there any suggestion when it does descend that it descends on the site of the old Jerusalem. As we read St. Justin it is clear that the definite Chiliasm which he holds is an outcome of the second destruction of the city by Hadrian in 134; this time it was swept clear of Jews; no Jew was allowed to live there.

Nevertheless scholars permit themselves to write sometimes as if the Chiliasm of St. Justin and his successors was the same as the doctrine of *Revelation*, and had all along been a normal part of Christian belief. I am surprised as I survey the evidence how scanty it is. There was room for much development in the sixty years between St. John and St. Justin; and much development had taken place.

Immediately after the time of St. John we have three great Christian writers who have a right to speak for the church. St. Ignatius, "Bishop of Syria" (A.D. 110–117), shows no sign of it; St. Polycarp, Bishop of Smyrna in Syria, a man of great eminence, writing about the same time, shows no sign of it; St. Clement, writing in the name of the Church of Rome as early as 96, shows no sign of it; and it would be difficult for them to avoid any allusion to it at all if it was an important part of their faith. The *Teaching of the Twelve Apostles*, which also goes back to this period, has no sign of it, though it has a highly-coloured eschatological passage at the end with a Christ and an Antichrist whose coming appears to be conceived literally.

The prophet Hermas at Rome, who began his work in the episcopate of Clement, might be expected to show traces of this belief, but beyond a tendency to take the Christian eschatology rather simply and literally, we find none; his view seems to be that the church would be purified and perfected until it was ready for Christ to appear in the midst of it and rejoice.

Our only document previous to St. Justin which can be called Chiliastic is the so-called *Epistle of Barnabas*, a very queer production. It has been absurdly dated about A.D. 70; but its whole treatment of the gospel story forbids so early a date. This date is based on his explanations of the words of Daniel "There shall ten kings reign in the earth; and there shall rise last of all another little one, and he shall humble three kings." The deduction is that the tenth king is meant to be Vespasian and the eleventh Titus; but if we exclude the pretenders, Otho, Galba, and Vitellius, as we did in calculating out the seven Cæsars in *Rev.* xvii, then Vespasian is the sixth, Titus the seventh, Domitian the eighth, Nerva the ninth, Trajan the tenth, and Hadrian the eleventh. Trajan died in A.D. 117, and the *Epistle of Barnabas* may be placed in the early years of his successor, Hadrian. This date is confirmed by its explanation of the words of Isaiah, " Behold they that destroy this Temple, even they shall build it up," to which he adds, "And so it came to pass; for through their wars it is now destroyed by their enemies, and the servants of their enemies are building it up." Now Hadrian did attempt the rebuilding of Jerusalem about A.D. 120.

In *Barnabas* we find a simple and unreflective belief in the coming of Christ and in the day of judgment, but beyond that nothing which can be called Chiliast, beyond the one passage in which a Thousand Years chances to be mentioned. The meaning of the Sabbath, he says, is this, " that in six thousand years the Lord shall bring all things to an end; for the day with him signifieth a Thousand Years; and this he himself beareth witness saying, *Behold the day of the Lord is as a thousand years.* Therefore, children, in six days—that is, in six thousand years—everything shall come to an end. *And he rested on the seventh day.* This he means; when his Son shall come and shall abolish the time of the lawless one, and shall judge the ungodly, and shall change the sun and moon and the stars, then shall he truly rest on the seventh day . . . then shall we truly rest and hallow it (the sabbath) when we shall ourselves be able to do so after being justified . . . and all things have been made new by the Lord." It will be seen that in this passage there is one coincidence with *Revelation*, the Thousand-Year period, and one quotation *Behold I make all things new.* But in *Revelation* the Thousand-Year Reign is before this remark, not after it, so that the dependence is slight. What we have here is a fancy of the period, the interpretation of history as a " week " of seven periods of a thousand years each; this bears no relation at all to *Revelation*, though it may have its influence on St. Justin and later writers. But of the developed theory of Chiliasm there is practically no trace.

The study of this literature shows us just what we should expect; there were plenty of Christians (probably a majority) who set their hopes on the coming of Christ, and awaited that event with a simple literal faith. Such believers were bound to think of his advent as a bodily process, and his kingdom as a kingdom of eating and drinking. Such was the common Jewish expectation of the time, and many Christians were bound to share it. Such were the views of Cerinthus, the great Jewish-Gnostic opponent of St. John, as St. Irenæus tells us. Jewish Christianity generally must have held this view; in fact some Jewish Christians must always have held it; St. Paul had to tell them that the kingdom of God did not consist in eating and drinking, and that flesh and blood could not inherit the kingdom of God. But, as it happens, there is no sign of this sensual conception of Christ's kingdom in *Barnabas*; his tendency is to spiritualise.

The chief authority usually quoted for Chiliasm before St. Justin is Papias, who flourished about 130; of him St. Eusebius remarks that he was a man of small intelligence. Like the rising prophetic party, he tended to despise modern developments and to return to a more primitive form of Christianity; and the special form this affectation took was to depreciate the written gospels and to prefer his own memories of what he had heard from the Apostles (including St. John?) or their immediate hearers, the Elders. St. Irenæus preserves two of the traditions which he had received from the Elders. The first deals with the miraculous fruitfulness of the world in the days to come, " The days will come in which vines shall grow each having ten thousand shoots, and on each shoot ten thousand branches," etc., etc.; and when any of the saints shall have taken hold of one of their clusters, another shall cry, " I am a better cluster; take me." Now I must say I find it difficult to believe that Papias meant this literally, though it might be a hyperbolical account of a natural luxuriance.

The other saying preserved by St. Irenæus is certainly not sensuous or material; it divides the abode of the blessed into heaven, the paradise, and the city, and says that " in every place the Saviour shall be seen according as they shall be worthy to see him." This is certainly not a bodily, limited local presence.

There is nothing here that needs the *Revelation* to explain it; there is nothing about a thousand years' kingdom; there is nothing about Jerusalem; we cannot be sure that there is anything material; it is certainly not Chiliasm.

Chiliasm is, therefore, a development, not a true tradition about the meaning of *Revelation*. All we can say of the period between St. John and St. Justin is that simple believers everywhere would naturally expect a literal and visible return of Christ, and a day of judgment; beyond that we cannot go. Some may have been expecting a literal kingdom of the Jewish messianic type with eating and drinking, but there is next to no trace of it. It must, however, have been common among Jewish Christians. Chiliasm proper is a development from all this, assisted by two other influences: (*a*) the misunderstanding of *Revelation* and (*b*) the events in Palestine.

We must thank *Barnabas* for putting us upon the track of that. The tide of messianic expectation among the Jews was rising; this could not but influence the Christians who were still so closely connected with them. When Hadrian attempted to rebuild Jerusalem in 120, Christians of the type of Barnabas were interested, just as British Israelites are interested in our present policy of Zionism. It seemed to them to be a fulfilment of prophecy.

> *The world is very evil,*
> *The times are waxing late.*
> *Be sober and keep vigil,*
> *The judge is at the gate.*

That was the feeling of " Barnabas "; but that was all; it went no further; and that is not Chiliasm.

The messianic feeling among the Jews grew yet more intense; at last a Messiah was found, Bar-Kokhba, Son of a Star, and his claims were endorsed by Akiba, the leading Rabbi of the period. Bar-Kokhba raised an army and occupied Palestine; the Jews rallied to him in thousands. Christian Jews were in a terrible position; we know that they suffered, and it is possible that it is this war that really reduced the Jewish church to the level of a miserable sect. We can dimly see them reverencing the humble descendants of the family of Jesus, the bishops of the Poor, who had in their veins the blood of David; we can imagine them passionately affirming their belief in their Messiah of the poor, and their confidence that he would shortly come. The gulf that divides Jew and Christian dates from those days.

The Son of a Star came to a miserable end; the saintly and learned Akiba was put to death with horrible tortures, which he bore with incredible composure; Jerusalem was razed to the ground. This time it was not permitted to persist. On its site rose the gentile village of Ælia Capitolina. It was really gone.

It is not till now that Chiliasm takes shape. The Christians had their own interpretation of these events. Jerusalem was wiped away that the Lord might build his city there; justification for this view was found in *Revelation*. Is it possible that the correct belief still lingered that " Babylon " was Jerusalem, and that after " Babylon " was destroyed the true Jerusalem would come from heaven ?

We are now right into the period of literal interpretation, the period when literal-minded Greek Christians took the gospel prophecies at the valuation of literal-minded Jews. St. Justin was followed by Melito, Hippolytus, Tertullian, and Lactantius; not till Origen (fl. A.D. 200–254) did the spiritual view re-assert itself.

It should be noted that Montanism is not Chiliastic; it has developed in a different way. The New Jerusalem that is to descend in Pepuza is the kingdom of the Spirit, not of Christ; the reign of Christ would then be terminated. Behind that lies a very different way of regarding *Revelation*; it assumes that the reign of Christ was at that very time a fact. Apparently the coming of Christ lay in the past. Once more we wonder whether they were in touch with the true interpretation of *Revelation*.

The Roman Church and the Revelation.

After the death of St. John the leadership of the church rapidly passed westwards to Rome, and we are lucky in having some light shed on conditions there by the *Epistle of Clement*, which is almost contemporary with the *Revelation*, and the *Shepherd of Hermas*, the first part of which was written only a little later. In this early pre-montanist period we are able to see the prophet working hand in hand with the constitutional ministry, which is episcopal in form, though the terminology was different from that employed in the East.

Nevertheless the prophet is already beginning to make claims for himself. In his vision Hermas sees the Church as a goddess seated on a throne; there is a seat on each side of her, and when he is ordered to sit down, he suggests that the Elders have the first claim; but the Church tells him that the Martyrs are to sit on the right and the Prophets on the left. This goes further than St. John in the dignity given to the Prophet and the Martyr; it actually prefers them to the Elders in constitutional rank. It recalls more clearly than St. John the symbolism of James and John, one on the right, and one on the left.

Hermas also insists strongly on his right to read his vision himself in the Ecclesia.

The influence of the *Revelation* on Hermas is very strong, though we do not find many actual quotations. We have the White Throne and Four young men who carry it; the Woman sitting on it has a Book which represents the call of Hermas to prophecy; visions are seen in the Desert; the Woman is also a Tower (the city) and the Tower is Four-square; there is a Beast out of whose mouth goes a Locust cloud; and in the last vision the Woman appears as a Bride adorned in White for her husband. There is none of the glitter and colour of St. John; it has a pleasant rustic simplicity which sometimes descends as low as the ridiculous.

While we are certain that Hermas knew and used the *Revelation*, there is further material which shows that he was influenced by other authorities, heathen, Jewish, and Gnostic. He never got rid of the heathen beliefs of his pre-Christian days; God is not prominent in his *Visions*, and Christ is scarcely mentioned at all; his revelations are given by the divine Woman, who is identified with the Church. At first, however, he thought her the Cumæan Sybil; and her threefold appearance, first as old, then as middle-aged, and then as young, is clearly borrowed from the Italian Queen Mab, *Diana Triformis*. His adventures with the seven nymphs in Arcadia is also hardly of Jewish or Christian origin. Yet, in spite of this, and in spite of the pagan conception of prophecy itself, there are many scholars who look on Hermas as representative of a supposed primitive Jewish Christianity. In reality he shows how an Italian Gnosticism might have developed.

There is a good deal of symbolic material which is related to Gnostic speculation of the Jewish type; but it is innocent of system, and too vague to be called definitely Gnostic. It is part of the general atmosphere of the period. One point in which Hermas differs from the *Revelation* is that the Abyss (Bythus) or Water has a good meaning, and is connected both with baptism and martyrdom. For this reason the Tower which represents the church is built on the Water; and the Stones which represent the Martyrs are brought from the Abyss, not the land. Here is a distinct connection with the Ophite Divine Woman, who is closely related with the Waters. This connection is made clearer by the symbolism of the throne on which the Ecclesia of Hermas is seated; it has Four Feet because the world is held together by Four Elements. This is exactly like the Ophite Divine Woman who is borne up by the Four elements of water, darkness, abyss, and chaos. This agreement of Hermas and the Ophites confirms the contention that the Four Living Things in St. John must be connected with creation.

In the *Visions of Hermas* this Divine Woman practically takes the place of God, and in a later book she is referred to as " the Holy Spirit which spoke with thee in the form of the Church "; her connection with the Waters is therefore explained by the verse in *Genesis* which speaks of the Spirit moving upon the face of the deep. Hermas connects her closely with creation; " for her sake the world was made." It is possible that the word Life, which he constantly uses, also refers to her.

The Spirit is the female æon proceeding from God, and appears to be senior to the male æon or Christ, of which Hermas has much less to say; in a very confused parable in a later book he makes them the elder and younger sons of God. In his earliest book, the *Visions*, which we have been considering, a nuptial christology is about to be introduced; but it breaks off very suddenly, and this climax has most likely been deliberately omitted. In his last book, *The Commandments*, there is another version of the Vision of the Tower, which preserves some older features; in this vision there are six angels, the first-created; and the seventh,

A A

who is their chief, is Michael or Christ. This identification is extremely important for the study of the *Revelation*.

Despite his fondness for the nuptial christology, and his reverence for the Divine Woman Spiritus-Ecclesia, Hermas is not a Gnostic; and despite his endorsement of the ambitions of the prophets, and his strict legalistic morality, he is not a Montanist. He is a simple Christian with a muddled mind and a rather schoolmasterish morality; he has absorbed a large number of Jewish and Christian notions, and they float up to the top of his mind mingled with fragments of his original paganism. His charm lies, as he knew himself, in his sincerity and simplicity, and a quaint idealism which pervades his unsystematised amalgam of current religious notions; his value to us is that he reflects as in a very blurred mirror the various ideas that were current at Rome in his time.

Though the mention of Clement proves that his first visions date not much after the *Revelation*, the *Muratorian Canon*, a fragmentary document which gives a list of apostolic books authorised for public reading in the Roman church towards the end of the second century, has led some scholars to date them in the episcopate of his brother Pius, about A.D. 140. But the *Muratorian* does not say he wrote them then (scripsit) but that he compiled them (conscripsit); and it is better to suppose that it refers to the labour of selecting and editing previous prophecies so as to form a definitive edition.

The witness of Hermas therefore extends over a generation, and concludes with a triumph for the prophetic party; his brother Pius becomes bishop, and his prophecies are given authoritative position in the Roman church along with the apostolic writings. On the high prophetic view they are a new revelation from God. We must note again that there is no essential antagonism between the prophetic and the constitutional ministry; the prophetic party has actually been strong enough to capture the constitutional ministry, and if, as radical critics think, Clement was not a bishop, then the evolution of the episcopal system in Rome was actually conducted under prophetic influences.

IN CONCLUSION

The decline of the prophetic party in Rome must have been due partly to its extravagant and puritanical claims, and partly to the rise of Montanism. Tertullian tells us that when Rome first heard of Montanism it was favourable to it; and this would naturally be so if the episcopate was strongly prophetic; but the extravagances of the Montanists, and perhaps of the Roman prophets themselves, soon made it plain that it was not practical to permit ecstatic prophets to deliver new revelations which were bound to become more important than the original preaching of the apostles. The test of apostolicity was applied to the books which were read in churches, and *Hermas* was rejected, though it was still permitted to read it in private.

This stage has been reached in the *Muratorian Fragment*, which may be dated about 175 or 180; it speaks of the episcopate of Pius as recent. We gather from it that the prophetic party still exists, and still urges the reception of *Hermas* alongside of the apostolic books. Two apocalypses remain, *The Revelation of St. John* and *The Revelation of St. Peter*; the latter may be either a pseudonymous book influenced by Orphic ideas, fragments of which remain, or perhaps our *Second Epistle of St. Peter*, which is strongly apocalyptic. We do not hear much more of the prophets; but the severe puritan tradition remained, and appeared again in the schism of St. Hippolytus early in the third century. Some trace of this school may perhaps be found in the view that a man who had braved martyrdom was *ipso facto* to be regarded as an Elder.

We see now how it was that Rome clung to the *Revelation* although it was rejected in the East. But it probably never had understood it fully, and the prophetic party had probably expounded it in the same literal and material way as Papias in the East. The key to the situation is that the prophetic movement throughout Christendom early in the second century was not a relic of primitive Palestinian Christianity, but a wave of ecstatic pagan prophetism, using Jewish material.

It is fashionable to regard the " catholicising " movement of the sub-apostolic age, with its stress on apostolicity, as the Greek spirit capturing the church; the word " Greek " is, of course, used in a very wide sense to include the non-Christian and non-Jewish ideas of an age of syncretism. It is far more true to regard the prophetic movement as an uprush of such ideas; the pagan converts who led the movement had a non-christian view of inspiration, and did not understand the apostolic use of symbolism. They agreed with the less spiritual Jews in taking the symbolism of the Coming of the Messiah, the Messianic kingdom, the Last Judgment, and the flames of hell literally; and they influenced the whole church very strongly. The church of the second century was puritan and pessimistic; it expected the return of Christ and an earthly kingdom of prosperity and plenty; it believed in a literal hell. The thought of the earthly kingdom was elaborated from Jewish sources; the thought of the literal hell was elaborated from Greek sources.

This prophetic movement was needed in order to rescue the church from the much more dangerous fate of being swamped in the rising sea of Gnosticism, with its easy attitude towards morality and pagan religion; a church consisting now almost entirely of gentile converts, without any Hebrew background of theism and morality, needed more than anything else to be indoctrinated with the " Montanist " conception of the just God and the inevitable judgment. The function of the prophet was to give that desperate courage and that desperate faith without which they could not have faced the heathen persecutor and the semi-heathen heretic. It was a real question for a time whether the faith in the Saviour was to be grafted on to a Greek philosophy of an evil that was inherent in the world and even in the human body, or upon a Jewish faith in a good creator and absolute morals.

Further history of the Book.

The literalism of the second century was broken in Alexandria where East and West met. The *Revelation* was valued there, and Origen, the first great thinker of the Christian church after apostolic times, realised that it was meant to be taken spiritually. One of his successors, Dionysius, first noted how different it was in style from the fourth gospel, and how different it appeared to be in meaning. He first suggested the theory which appeals to many modern scholars that there were two Johns at Ephesus. From that time Alexandrians and Latins interpreted the book partly at least along spiritual lines; and later on when the Eastern churches received it again, their commentators took it in the same way. It is natural, however, that they did not really understand it.

In the West the authoritative work was that of St. Augustine whose thought was strongly influenced by it. In his *City of God* written shortly after Rome had been entered by some Gothic auxiliary troops under Alaric and partly burned and plundered, he developed the theory that the Fall of Babylon meant the end of the old secular empire of Rome, and that the coming of the New Jerusalem meant the ascendancy of the Christian church. This so dominated the thought of the West that our view of the actual history has been coloured by it, and we still look on the sack of Rome by Alaric as a spectacular end of the whole Roman empire. As a matter of fact it was only an episode in a long succession of decline and revival; and in any case St. John did not mean Rome by Babylon.

On the other hand St. Augustine was brilliantly right and brilliantly prophetic in his interpretation of the New Jerusalem. That symbol does mean the Church; and the Church was to rule western Europe in the place of the Cæsars. What is more, St. Augustine worked out in its classic form the relation between the invisible and ideal rule of God and the outward catholic church in which it was incarnate, the church which is called holy, not from the holiness of its members, but from the holiness of God which pervades it and makes its members holy. This system of thought was accepted until the Reformation; but as the centuries went by the outward catholic church made stronger and stronger claims to be in itself, on its human side, the kingdom of God. Theologians and mystics, however, constantly witnessed to the other side of the truth.

On the Last Judgment and the punishment of the lost, St. Augustine took a more literal view, and the mediæval church followed him in its preaching of literal fire. This view was not, however, universal.

In the twelfth century when the temporal power of the papacy was reaching its height, society was honeycombed by anti-ecclesiastical and anti-social sects, in many of which the outlines of Gnosticism and Montanism may be discerned. There is certainly actual continuity in the case of the Gnostic and Manichean sects; and it may be that there were still traces of Montanism. I have already pointed out how Abbot Joachim and his followers revived the Montanist teaching of the Three Ages and identified Babylon with Papal Rome. This identification was taken up by the followers of the Empire and by the rebellious sects; and spiritually they were right; Rome as they saw it was in precisely the same condition as Jerusalem in the time of St. John. It was worldly, luxurious, politically ambitious, and drunk with the blood of the saints.

Luther and Calvin both identified Babylon with Papal Rome, and so the doctrine became an integral part of orthodox Protestantism. But Protestantism was "montanist" in theology; it held fast to verbal inspiration, and this generally carried with it literal interpretation of the symbolic; the symbols of *Revelation* were tied down to events in history, and the Last Judgment and the Lake of Fire were taken literally, just as in popular catholicism. The insight of the theologians, of mystics, and of poets had little effect. Popular preaching depended on bodily fear, and most of the theologians continued to back it up.

Quakerism, Moravianism, and Methodism succeeded the severe puritanism of the seventeenth century and insisted on the need of emotional experience; this emotional wave which swept the Protestant churches produced in its train hysterical prophets like Ann Lee and Joseph Smith and Ellen White, who founded the "adventist" religions of Shakerism and Mormonism and Seventh-Day Adventism; soon the "gnostic" systems of Theosophy and Christian Science were being organised. The "adventist" systems revel in a literal Judgment and a literal hell; the " gnostic " ones eliminate the ideas completely.

The orthodox preacher, as in the early Greek church, has not known what to do about the *Revelation*; it is read very little in church and few sermons are preached upon it. On the other hand, its symbolism still appeals very strongly to the average man, and the hymn-writers have used it with great success; the truth is that it is only as a poem that it can be understood.

Theology for a long time has been "critical"; and "critical" means analytical; and the analytical mind is powerless to understand a poem. Most critics have prosaic minds, and their comments on *Revelation* have revealed how low the prosaic mind can sink. Recent study has brought to light the Jewish apocalypses which were written in the same epoch as our *Revelation,* and because most of these were written by men with prosaic minds who expected a literal end of the world and a literal Messianic kingdom, it has been assumed that our *Revelation* must mean the same. It has even been assumed that our Lord meant the same. These scholars do not see how comic it is to suppose that our Lord was an Ann Lee, and St. John a Joseph Smith; they do not see the difference between poetry and prose; they are not merely deficient in spiritual insight, they have no literary taste.

Our Lord was great because he had in him something original and different from those around him; the *Revelation* stands out as a great poem because it is not like the dreary ruck of Jewish apocalypses. Every time our Lord used one of the standard phrases of his day he put into it a powerful and original new meaning; every time St. John took up some old and faded device of the apocalypses he gave it new vigour and made a new thing of it. His great work is not to be judged by taking it to pieces and bringing every piece down to the level of the low journalism that had so often employed it before. The clothes of it are nothing; the soul of it is everything.

A modern work on the *Revelation*, like Dr. Charles' great Commentary, is a mass of profound learning and often of acute judgment; but the judgment is only in detail. The grammar, the style, the text, are laboured over with titanic diligence, and really understood; every point of symbolism is illustrated by copious illustrations from contemporary works. But the poem is lost. As Dr. Charles tracks his dreary Parthian kings or his monomaniac editor between the lines of this great book, one can only ask in vain how it is that such futile hunting can draw his attention away from the glorious landscape of the world's greatest poem. I suppose it is a legacy of the piecemeal classical scholarship of the last century, which looked on Vergil and Homer merely as fields for quarrying grammatical forms out of.

Even a more moderate commentary like those of Swete and Anderson Smith does not really do much better; they quote what other scholars have said, they elucidate many points; but they seem unconcerned with the question of the meaning of the poem as a whole.

The best attempt to get at St. John's meaning was made by the prophetic mind of F. D. Maurice, who refused to be satisfied with "identifications" and "meanings." The literary form of the book was first displayed by Archbishop Benson in his celebrated edition, in which he printed it as a drama. Its poetic grandeur is best appreciated through Christina Rossetti (*The Face of the Deep*). A sound and sane theological approach is that of Dr. Milligan. But in spite of everything I have said, we would not stand where we now do without the great learning of critics like Dr. Charles; his Commentary must be the constant handbook of anyone who wants to work seriously at the poem. We cannot do without his critical insight and his masses of illustrative material; but it is quite impossible for us to agree with him on the meaning of the book.

APPENDICES

I. THE LEVITICAL SYMBOLISM IN REVELATION.
II. PRIMITIVE HEBREW GNOSTICISM.

THE LITURGICAL STRUCTURE OF REVELATION

A. HEBREW SACRIFICE

Revelation.	*The Jerusalem Sacrifices.*
i.–iii. Introductory.	The High Priest.
iv. Christian Worship A. The Creator.	The Temple Ornaments.
v. Christian Worship B. The Lamb.	1. *The lamb killed at dawn.*
vi. (The Four Horsemen).	
Souls under Altar.	Blood splashed on altar.
(Sixth Seal.)	
vii. Christian Worship C. The Martyrs.	(Feast of Tabernacles.)
viii. *The Trumpets.*	Three Trumpets.

      Offering of Incense. This does not occur at this point in the daily ritual; but it does on the Day of Atonement. See below. In the Temple ritual the Silence *follows* the burning of the Incense.

  ix. (The Trumpets, originally *three*, symbolise the prophetic message.)
  xi. (The Call of St. John, and his witness against Jerusalem.)

Opening of Sanctuary in Heaven.	Gates of Temple and Sanctuary opened.
xii. and xiii. (The Great Interlude.)	
xiv. *The Lamb and his Followers on Mount Sion.*	2. *Preparation of Sacrifice.* Lamb skinned, cut up, washed, laid by altar.
First fruits. Without blemish.	
The Harvest (Passover).	The meal offering. Bread.
The Vintage (Ingathering).	The drink offering. Wine.
xv. *Song of Moses and the Lamb.*	Pause for prayer and praise.
The Sanctuary Opens.	3. *Offering of Incense.*
The Smoke of the Glory.	Silence.
No one may enter the Sanctuary.	Intercession.

      St. John has placed the Incense symbolism earlier, though the smoke recalls it here. On the Day of Atonement no one might enter the sanctuary till the High Priest had finished his work there.

xvi. *Pouring of the Blood.*	
The Seven Bowls. In the daily ritual this is done at the beginning; but on the Day of Atonement the High Priest smeared the mercy seat and altar with blood at this point.	
xvii., xviii. *Babylon Burned.*	4. *The Burning of the Victim.*
Her Cup.	The Cup poured out.
xvii. 16 refers to the ritual of the sin-offering;	
xvii. 2, 3 is reminiscent of the scapegoat.	
xix. *Alleluia Chorus.*	5. *The Psalms.*
	Song and Instruments.
The Marriage Supper of the Lamb.	
The High Priest out of Heaven (cf. Ecclus. l.).	
The Great Supper of God.	6. *The Feast on the Sacrifice.*
xx. (Wars of the Messiah and Judgments.)	
xxi., xxii. *The Tabernacle of God with Men* (cf. Lev. xxvi. 11–12).	
Christian Worship D. The Universal Worship of Mankind.	

NOTE.—This chart shows how the structure of the older part of *Revelation* follows the events of the daily sacrifice, with variations suggested by the ritual of the Day of Atonement. It confirms our impression of the unity of the book, and its division into earlier and later strata. The liturgical symbolism is dealt with more fully in Appendix I.

THE LITURGICAL STRUCTURE OF REVELATION

B. CHRISTIAN WORSHIP

1. SCHEME FOR CHRISTIAN SACRIFICIAL WORSHIP

A. *The Worship of the Creator.*
iv. 1. " Come up."
      In spirit, in heaven.
   4-6. Throne, Elders, Lamps, and Living Creatures.
   8. HOLY, HOLY, HOLY.
  10. Elders join in : Worthy art thou, etc.

Lift up your hearts.

The " Preface " : With angels and archangels.
The Sanctus.
Conception of communion with heaven.
It is meet and right.

B. *The Worship of the Lamb.*
v. 6. The Lamb Sacrificed.
  8. Adoration of Lamb.
 14. Amen.

Recital of redeeming life and death.

Amen.

2. THE WORSHIP OF THE TRIUMPHANT SAINTS

This is a literary anticipation of the vision with which St. John closes his poem; it symbolises his faith that the martyrs are triumphant and do anticipate the bliss prepared for all.

C. *The Martyrs in their Worship.*
Note that they are not included under A and B.
vii. 9. Robes and Palms.
  10. Hosanna.
  15. Worship him day and night in his Sanctuary.
     God shall " Tabernacle upon them."

Hosanna.
Borrowed from ritual of the Feast of Tabernacles.

3. THE IDEAL UNIVERSAL WORSHIP

St. John here sketches a worship free from the limitations of time and space or of a national religion and a hereditary priesthood. The symbolism of Jewish liturgical worship is deliberately excluded.

D. *The Universal Worship of Mankind.*
xxi. 3. The Tabernacling with Men.
  10. The Glory of God.
 22. No Sanctuary in it.
 23. Its Candlestick the Lamb.
 24. The kings of the earth.

 25. No night.
xxii. 4. Worship him : see his face.
     Name on their forehead.

Not a temple made with hands.
His " visible " presence.
Not local.
Seven-branch candlestick.
Royal sacrifices by gentile kings at Jerusalem.
Free of times and seasons.
Open universal presence.
High priest's petalon : all are priests.

NOTE.—These four sections are all late additions to the book, and confirm the division into earlier and later strata made on other grounds. They make a framework for the main composition, which is placed between C and D, though a little of it is to be found after B. In A and B St. John is consciously constructing a pattern for Christian worship, a pattern which was followed in every Eucharistic liturgy of the Catholic Church. It is based on Hebrew ritual, and no doubt reflects the custom of St. John's own day.

APPENDIX I

THE LEVITICAL SYMBOLISM IN REVELATION

THE liturgical character of sections in *Revelation* has often been pointed out; but I have seen no attempt to study and elucidate the liturgical scaffolding into which the visions are built. Archbishop Benson came very near to it when he treated the book as a drama, and printed it so as to display the choric structure. But *Revelation* is not a drama; it is a liturgy. A drama deals with the unfolding of personality, and the actors in it must use their own personalities to interpret it. In liturgy the hierophants must submerge their personalities and identities in the movement of the whole composition. It is a real literary triumph that a sustained poem like *Revelation* should grip the attention as it does without the assistance of human interest in character; and that triumph is liturgical in character.

The author of the *Revelation* frequented the temple and loved its liturgy; when he shut his eyes in Ephesus, he could see the priests going about their appointed tasks at the great altar of burnt-offering. That vision forms the background of the whole poem.

I am astonished to find so few discussions on the temple ritual, not only in connection with the *Revelation*, but also in connection with the Palestinian background of the New Testament generally. The recent advance in this study has concerned itself with the eschatological literature, and the oral teaching of the Rabbis; it has neglected the temple, its priesthood, and worship. But in the New Testament period the temple system was central; after its destruction the Rabbis organised a new Judaism on enlightened Pharisee lines. But it was a new religion, not the old. The old religion died in the year A.D. 70, and gave birth to two children; the elder was modern Judaism without temple or priest or sacrifice; the younger was Christianity, which was proud of possessing all three.

What links *Hebrews* with *Revelation* is its insistence on this fact. Christianity is the true heir of the old faith. To it have been transferred the priesthood and the sacrifice.

The New Universal Worship.

When St. John came to the work of publishing his visions twenty years after Jerusalem had fallen, one of his main tasks was to provide a scheme or pattern for Christian worship. There can be no doubt that he set himself to do this consciously and deliberately; what is more, he was successful. The "Anaphora," as the consecration prayer of the eucharist is called in the East, follows the pattern he laid down. The

"Canon" of the Roman Mass and the Consecration Prayer of the English Prayer Book do so, though less faithfully.

It seems reasonable to suppose that his liturgical work was not done at random or in a spirit of theory. It must have borne some sort of relation to the way Christian worship was actually conducted at the time; analogy suggests that if the older part of the book reflected the worship of the old religion that had passed away, the newer part would reflect that of the new religion which had taken its place. Now the opening chapters iv. and v., though they belong to the later period of St. John's inspiration, do seem to be built upon a foundation of older work, in which the following changes appear to have been made: (1) a Throne takes the place of an Altar, and (2) Twenty-four Elders on Thrones are added. (See Charles, *ad. loc.*) But these changes correspond to the picture of the Christian congregation of the period suggested in the writings of St. Ignatius (see Rawlinson in *Foundations*, on "The Origins of the Christian Ministry"). The Throne of God represents the chair of the bishop, and round him are grouped the Elders. The number is chosen because of the Twenty-four courses into which the Hebrew priesthood (and even the Levites and people) had been divided; we may compare the picture of the High Priest Simon in *Ecclesiasticus* l. with his " garland " of priests.

We may therefore feel some confidence that we have before us the actual arrangements for the Christian liturgy, which was in its turn dependent on Hebrew origins.

I have dealt in the text with the parallelisms between the Four Zoa, the Seven Lamps, the Glassy Sea, etc., and the Cherubim, Candlestick, and Laver of the Temple. In *St. John* they are variously applied to the universal worship of all creation. This universal worship finds expression in the Sanctus (Holy, Holy, Holy), which is also used in the morning prayers of the synagogue, where it is associated with the thought of creation; in the *Revelation* the praise of God for his creation is uttered by the Elders, who prostrate themselves at the sound of the Sanctus.

This is the "first movement" of the Anaphora, of the Christian Eucharist, in which men "join with angels and archangels and all the company of heaven." Most of the Greek liturgies show traces of the "Axios" or "Axion" (worthy) of *Revelation*; at rather a long remove it is reflected in " It is meet and right (*justum et dignum*) so to do."

The *Revelation of St. John* then proceeds to show us the Lamb as it had been slain for Sacrifice; and the Christian liturgies follow him by narrating the life and death of Christ, and so leading up to the consecration and offering. The word Standing, which is applied to the Lamb, is a translation of Tamid, the technical name for the lamb which was offered every morning in the temple as a whole burnt-offering. It was the " standing offering."

This is followed by the offering of Incense, which stands for intercessory prayer; and then comes a New Song. The New Song was also mentioned in a hymn used in the temple after the killing of the lamb, and before the Incense. I shall refer to it later.

The liturgy ends with praise to God and the Lamb, and the singing of the Amen, which was characteristic of the eucharist at this point. All the liturgies follow this outline, and it is from this point onwards that they vary. The first two parts of the Te Deum follow the same lines of construction.

We now turn to chapter vii., verses 9 to 17, a short passage which is also the work of the latest period, anticipating the end of the book. It represents the worship of the Martyrs in heaven.

The thought of martyrdom as sacrifice is as early as the Maccabean period, and has behind it *Isaiah* liii. The man who gives his life for God or country is both priest and victim; he offers, but what he offers is himself. In *Revelation* his priesthood is dependent upon that of Christ.

In chapter i. Christ has been shown as priest and King. He is wearing the long white robe and the girdle at the breasts; he stands "in the midst of" the seven lamps; that is to say, he is in the sanctuary where the seven-branched candlestick is, and robed like a priest. This plain linen was worn by the high priest on the Day of Atonement. At the end of *Revelation* the same figure comes out of the sanctuary with the same robe splashed with blood.

The martyrs also wear white robes, which are connected with that of Christ by the statement that they are washed in the blood of the lamb; the same mixed character of priest and victim belongs both to the martyrs and their lord; but their deaths are lifted to the level of sacrifice by association with his.

The martyrs offered their bodies, and more than their bodies: their lives, their courage, their *patient endurance;* this is the *living sacrifice* of *Romans* xii., *holy, acceptable, your logical worship.* Giving the word body this wide sense, we may well agree that the white robes mean all that the martyrs offered to God, purified now in the blood of the perfect sacrifice. (See treatment of Robe in text, p. 311.)

Later on the white robes are called *fine linen*, which is priestly material.

In the text of the book I have compared the palms and the hosanna (Salvation) to the triumphal entry of Christ into Jerusalem, his going up to be sacrificed. This is only part of a wider comparison. Both are connected with the ritual of the Feast of Tabernacles, which occurred at the time of Ingathering, when the vintage and all the other harvests were in. In this festival priests encircled the altar waving palms and singing Hosanna; here the martyr-priests are in the sanctuary waving palms and singing hosanna round the throne which has taken the place of the altar.

The thought of Tabernacles is carried further in the statement that God *will Tabernacle upon them;* they are themselves to be his Tabernacle or dwelling-place.

We turn to the end of the book for the fourth and last section dealing with Christian worship. In xxi. 3 the last statement is taken up again. It is, strange to say, a quotation from *Leviticus*, where it implies that the holy God will dwell among a holy people. Here it is widened to mean that men generally make up the sanctuary of God; his Tabernacling is with them. The noun and verb "Tabernacle" are connected with the Hebrew Shekinah, the visible glory of God which is said to have filled the tabernacle in the desert and the temple when Solomon consecrated it. St. John is announcing, therefore, that the old local sanctuary is gone, and henceforth the Presence is with men in general, and God is making himself visible in and through them.

The thought is developed in the Epilogue which begins with verse 9. It is first repeated in the language of symbolism. The holy city has the Glory of God; its lustre is like the Jasper Stone; in chapter iv. God was said to be like the Jasper Stone, so that all this only repeats the previous statement about the Tabernacling. God's "visible" Presence is in this city. It replaces the old temple. The whole city is filled with the

Presence, not merely a sacred part of it. Even its foundation is Jasper—that is to say, divine.

The precious stones built into its walls mean the elect souls in which God dwells; the twelve foundations being the apostles of the lamb. The clear bright gold of its streets means that God's tabernacle is built out of the pure in heart; this symbolism corresponds to that of the white robes.

There was no sanctuary in it; that is to say, the Presence is not localised. There is no alternation of light and dark upon it; no need to calculate suns and moons; it lives in the perpetual light of the presence. No seven-branched lamp needs to be kindled to burn through the night; the Lamb is the lamp.

Through the lives of the elect souls in which God dwells the light shall shine into the world. The community of the elect is wide open; its gates are never shut. It has no national distinctions. The kings of the earth bring their glory into it; a reference to the sacrifices offered by Roman emperors and others at Jerusalem. The honour they gave to that sanctuary shall come to this. Free to all shall be the waters and fruits of the spiritual paradise.

No hereditary and monopolist priesthood shall have sole possession of this sanctuary and mediate between God and his people. All his servants shall stand in his presence, and every one of them shall be like the high priest, and have his name on their foreheads. Open universal vision: open universal priesthood.

This epilogue builds up a picture of the Catholic church in which it is contrasted at every point with the old Jewish temple, and shown to be more glorious because every part of it is filled with the illumination of the Presence which had been confined to the Holy of Holies. St. John deliberately avoids all the ornaments of temple worship—white robes, golden girdles, harps, incense, altar; they are all gone. Note also its square shape, its gates, and its living waters, which are all taken from Ezekiel's temple.

The Temple Sacrifice.

We have gone through the later additions to St. John's poem and seen how illuminating it is to test them from the liturgical point of view; we now turn to the older visions which are preserved within this scaffolding.

Chapters i. to v. are new material which forms an introduction to this older system; and no doubt older elements are to be found in them. I have pointed out already how the High Priest is to be seen in the vision of Christ in chapter i., the sanctuary and its ornaments in chapter iv., and the slain lamb in chapter v.

Let me now outline the course of the daily burnt-offering at the temple; it may be divided as follows:

1. The killing of the lamb.
2. The preparation of the offerings.
3. *Interval* for prayer.
4. Offering of Incense.
5. The burning of the offering.
6. Psalms, etc. The " shout."
7. Feasting on the sacrifice: if a sin-offering.

APPENDIX I

1. *The Killing of the Lamb.*—Four events took place simultaneously: the trumpet was blown three times, and the gates of the temple and the gates of the sanctuary were opened; at the same moment the lamb was killed and its blood dashed against the altar.

Of necessity St. John must begin with the lamb killed, as he wishes to work it into the Christian scheme of worship which he has prefixed to his older series of visions; v. 6 is therefore the culmination of one and the opening of the other. *I saw a lamb standing as sacrificed.* I have already pointed out that the word " standing " is a literal translation of Tamid, the technical name for the morning burnt-offering. The verse should therefore be translated, " I saw the lamb of the Tamid as slain." The expression recurs in xiv. 1.

(A " New Song " is sung by the Twenty-four Elders, who now have harps and incense as priests; but this has to do with the Christian scheme, which overlaps at this point. The " New Song " in the temple came a little later; and St. John has deferred it till xiv. 3.)

Passing over the non-liturgical episode of the Four Horsemen, we come to the souls under the altar (vi. 9). Immediately after the lamb was killed its blood was splashed on to the altar; there is a strong connection in Hebrew thought between blood and soul, and the souls here are described as the souls of the sacrificed. They pray also for vengeance on their blood. The blood is thought of as poured on the ground; the blood-soul is thought of as going up to Jehovah. The same thought ultimately underlies the blood sacrifice and blood vengeance. We see that already the deaths of the innocent dead are associated with the death of the Lamb; perhaps they are thought of as cleansed by his blood, for they are given a white robe (see above).

Passing over the sixth seal and the later Christian liturgical passage which has been linked to it, we come to the trumpets and the incense offering (viii. 1). The incense offering appears to be out of its place, and we will neglect it for the moment, noting, however, the feeling of St. John for correct and beautiful ceremonial. One of the beauties of ceremonial is simultaneous action designed to prevent delay while preparations are being made.

1. Seven angels are given seven trumpets.
2. The Incense is offered.
3. The trumpets are sounded.

The same particularity is shown in the case of the seven bowls. (See xv. 1.)

Let us return to the killing of the lamb. The signal for the killing of the lamb was three blasts on the trumpet; these three blasts were also a signal for the gates of the temple and sanctuary to be opened. This is what we find in *St. John* :

Seven Trumpets (viii. 1 to xi. 18).
Opening of the Sanctuary of God in Heaven (xi. 19).

We are justified in concluding, therefore, that he is following, though in a rough manner, the temple ceremonial. The likeness becomes more exact when we recollect that Dr. Charles has given very good reason to suppose that in *Revelation* also the number of trumpets was originally three. The argument from ceremonial converts Dr. Charles' hypothesis into a certainty. The series of seven seals and seven trumpets,

B B

as I have observed in the text of my book, is *not* a key to the construction of *Revelation ;* it obscures it; it was introduced to bind together visions that did not cohere.

In dealing with the Naos or Sanctuary in Heaven, we are on very delicate ground. Two things seem clear. One is that the "visible" Presence or Glory is departed from Jerusalem so that the Naos there is a Naos no longer; the other is that the Naos in heaven is the number of elect believers in which the Presence is henceforth to Tabernacle. It is universal, in the "heavens," open to all. I believe that the older series of visions was to have ended, or perhaps did end, with the descent of this *Temple not made with hands.* Two traces of it, I think, are to be found: the promise in iii. 12, *I will make him a pillar in the Naos of my God,* and the statement about the triumphant martyrs, vii. 15, *They serve him day and night in his Naos.* (See note to Book IV.)

This thought of the new Naos from heaven was superseded by something better, the vision of the New City which has no Naos, and no day or night either.

Now we see why the death of the lamb had to come first. It was the death of Christ that opened the way. *When thou hadst overcome the sharpness of death, thou didst open the Kingdom of heaven to all believers.* Comparing St. John with the temple ritual, we now get:

Temple. Simultaneous.	St. John.
Three trumpets.	Lamb killed.
Lamb killed.	Blood on altar.
Blood splashed on altar.	Three trumpets.
Gates opened.	Gates opened.

The Incense Offering (Rev. viii. 3–5).

Why, then, is the incense offering put in its wrong place?

There are one or two suggestions which can be made on this point. The first is a literary point of some importance. St. John is following out several complicated systems in this book, and the logical order of one sometimes has to give way to another. I have shown how faithfully the order of *Revelation* follows the book of *Ezekiel*; now this passage is based on a vision of Ezekiel's which comes at this point. If he remains true to *Ezekiel* it must immediately succeed the vision of the sealing.

Further, there was one day of the year when the offering of incense did come earlier; and this day was the Day of Atonement, the only day when the high priest was bound to officiate in person. We shall find other reasons for supposing that St. John has the Day of Atonement in mind. We have had one already. The high priest (Christ) has been shown to us in chapter i. wearing a white vestment, and the only day the high priest wore white was the Day of Atonement.

If this suggestion is true, St. John has not confined himself to the ceremonial of one type of sacrifice only. His ceremonial is conflate. We may note that he could not have used the Day of Atonement ceremonial only, as he would then have had to have symbolised Christ by a goat.

The ceremony described by St. John seems to be based on the daily ritual, as it is done by an angel, not by Christ the high priest; but possibly this need not be pressed, as the angel symbolises the whole process of intercession. The half-hour's silence which preceded the incense offering corresponds to the silence and prostration which followed it in the temple system. We may note that in the daily ritual the Naos was entered at this point, and the incense altar cleansed; the heavenly Naos would not need this. On the other hand, when we come to the point where the incense offering took place in the daily ritual, we find that St. John has a very significant passage corresponding to it.

To sum up. St. John desired at this spot to symbolise the prayers of the innocent dead coming before God and being answered. He therefore moves the incense offering to this point, as on the Day of Atonement. He thus preserves his parallelism with *Ezekiel*.

A long non-liturgical passage follows. The three trumpets are made to symbolise the voice of prophecy in its denunciation of sin. Lengthened to seven, they recall the fall of the city of Jericho (viii. 6 to ix. 21).

Then comes the completion and fulfilment of the prophetic ministry in the Christian evangel, in connection with which he relates his own call, and his peculiar and distinctive work which is to prophesy against Jerusalem. Jerusalem is to be destroyed; the Naos only is to be preserved; and by the Naos we have seen that he means the community of elect souls in which the Presence of God is Tabernacling. The real Israel is now the Christian church (x. 1 to xi. 13).

All this is concluded by the last trumpet and the opening of the heavenly Naos (xi. 14–19).

The Great Interlude is also non-liturgical. It narrates the appearance of the Deliverer, his victory over Satan, the persecution of his followers in Jerusalem, and the appearance of the Beast (the Roman god-emperor system) which persecutes his followers abroad (xii. and xiii.).

2. *The Preparation of the Sacrifice.*—After the lamb had been killed and its blood splashed on the altar there was still much to be done. It had to be skinned and cut into pieces; its entrails and legs were washed in the laver; and it was laid out on the slope that led up to the altar. The priests then went to the Hall of Polished Stones for Prayers.

Chapter xiv. opens with the *lamb standing on the Mount Sion*, or rather *the lamb of the Tamid on Mount Sion*. As Mount Sion is the site of the temple, I need not labour the sacrificial aspect of this verse.

With him are the hundred and forty and four thousand who were "sealed"; they have *the name of his father written on their foreheads*. These are the martyrs, who, together with the lamb, form the sacrifice. They are also priests. The high priest carried on his forehead a golden plate, the petalon, bearing the sacred name of Jehovah, *Holiness unto the Lord*. In verse 4 they are described as "firstfruits," a definitely sacrificial term; and in verse 5 they are said to be "without blemish"; perfect material for sacrifice.

I have dealt in the text with the statement in verse 4 that they were not defiled with women. The priests at the sacrifice had to observe certain ceremonial taboos which kept them technically "holy"; among these was abstinence from intercourse with women.

Then follows the New Song, sung not in the Hall of Polished Stone, but before the Throne; but I shall deal with this later.

After the three woes which are non-liturgical, we find the coming of one like a son of man upon a white cloud, followed by the harvest and vintage of the land. These are strongly liturgical in tone. Let us set it out liturgically.

And I looked and lo a White Cloud, and upon the Cloud one Seated like a Son of Man, having upon his head a Golden Crown and in his hand a sharp Sickle.

And another Angel came out of the Naos, crying in a loud voice to the one Seated on the Cloud,

Send thy Sickle and reap : for the hour is come to reap ; for the Harvest of the land is dried up.
And the one Seated on the Cloud put his Sickle to the Land and the Land was reaped.
And another Angel came out of the Naos in Heaven also having a sharp Sickle.
And another Angel came out of the Altar who had charge of the Fire and said with a loud voice to the one that had the Sickle, saying
Send thy sharp Sickle and cut the clusters of the Vine of the Land ; for its Grapes are full-ripe.
And the Angel put his Sickle into the Land, and cut the Vine of the Land, and put it into the Great Winepress of the wrath of God.
And the Winepress was trodden outside the City, and there came out Blood from the Winepress.

The liturgical form and tone of this section are obvious, and invite closer study than we were able to give it in the text of the book. It is a very complicated passage.

1. Its primary reference is to *Mark* xiii. 26, which speaks : (*a*) of the Son of Man coming on the Clouds, (*b*) of his sending his Angels to gather the elect into his kingdom, and (*c*) of the sun darkened, etc., by which is meant the fall of Jerusalem.

2. The meaning of a resurrection of the just is impossible as the passage stands, though it may have meant that in an early recension of the poem. As it stands it means the separation of the elect, and their escape from the doom of Jerusalem.

3. There is a reference to the Jewish Calendar and the system of feasts observed at the Temple : (*a*) Passover at the beginning of the year, marking the beginning of harvest, and (*b*) Tabernacles or Ingathering at the end of the year, marked by the vintage. This allusion relates the vision to our previous supposition that the early recension J ended with symbolism based on Tabernacles. xiv. 1 ff. would have followed this vision.

4. The liturgical form suggests that it may be based on the ritual of gathering in the harvest. Now the cutting of the first sheaf was itself a ritual, known as the Omer of Firstfruit. It occurred on Nisan 15, the " high day " of *John* xix. 31, and as it was done at night it was contemporaneous with the resurrection.

Nisan 14. Lamb killed.	Crucifixion.
Passover eaten.	Burial.
15. High day.	
Firstfruit cut.	Resurrection.

In the year of the crucifixion it chanced that Nisan 15 was also a sabbath; but this was, of course, a coincidence. I have dated the crucifixion, etc., as in the fourth gospel, which I take to be correct; but in any case the references in *Revelation* are to the crucifixion story as related in that gospel.

5. Lightfoot in his account of the Temple and its services gives an outline of the ritual for the Omer.

" Those that the Sanhedrin sent about it went out at the evening of the Holy Day (the first day of the Passover Week); they took baskets and sickles, etc.

" They went out on the Holy Day when it began to be dark, and a great company went out with them; when it was now dark, one said to them,

" On this Sabbath, On this Sabbath, On this Sabbath.

" In this Basket, In this Basket, In this Basket."

APPENDIX I

"Rabbi Eliezer the son of Zadok saith, With this Sickle, With this Sickle, With this Sickle, every particular three times over,

"And they answer him, Well, Well, Well; and he bids them reap."

This is not perhaps on first sight as close a parallel as one might have desired to the passage we are discussing; but there are points of likeness:
(a) There was a dialogue which took place at the beginning of harvest.
(b) It explicitly mentions the time: This Sabbath = The Hour is come.
(c) It explicitly mentions the Sickle. (d) The reaper is then commanded to do his work; but the words of this command are not given. The two dialogues are of the same character, have the same purpose, involve similar speakers, and have points of resemblance; we could not expect much more.

(The word Sabbath demands a note. I think I am right in saying that Nisan 15, though not necessarily a Sabbath, might be called a Sabbath, because it was in every respect equal to a Sabbath and observed in the same way. The breach of the Sabbath involved in cutting the first sheaf was excused.)

6. A further very interesting parallel is afforded by the stage we have now reached in the Tamid, or daily offering. To the pieces of the lamb were added (a) the meal offering of fine flour, and (b) the daily offering of the high priest, which consisted of bread and wine. The Son of Man is, of course, the Christian high priest; the wheat harvest and the vintage afford some parallel to the bread and wine. The connection, which seems rather fanciful, will amount to a certainty if we accept the relation proposed in the text of the book between the cutting of the Vine of the Land and the murder of the high priest Ananus; for this provides a second point of contact with the thought of the high priest.

To a poet of St. John's type, the thought of the high priest's offering of bread and wine would prove a basis for rich and complex symbolism. (a) Considering the crucifixion, there is the thought of the high priest Jesus offering himself on Calvary, and antithetically the thought that his offering was the work of the official high priest Caiaphas; and linked with this the institution of the sacrament of bread and wine the night before the crucifixion. (b) Taking the murder of Ananus as the starting point of the ruin of Jerusalem, there is the thought of the official high priest lying dead, sacrificed, as Josephus describes it, in the courts of the temple itself; a vengeance of blood.

7. The Winepress imagery makes clear the blood-vengeance symbolism, and suggests at once the Edomites who murdered Ananus.

The words "outside the City" are the link with the crucifixion, and provide a connection with the sin-offering when it was offered for the high priest or for the whole nation, as in the special case of the Day of Atonement; for it was then that the body of the victim was taken outside the city to be burned. (*Note*: the Day of Atonement follows the festival of Ingathering.)

The parallelisms in the second section may therefore be summarised as follows:

Temple.	*St. John.*
Preparation of Lamb.	
Pieces laid on slope of altar.	Lamb of the Tamid on Mount Sion.
Meal offering.	
Offering of high priest.	Appearance of son of man.
Bread.	Harvest.
Wine.	Vintage.

Those with the Lamb in *St. John* may perhaps be compared to the numerous free-will offerings which accompanied the Tamid.

3. *Interval for Prayers, etc.*—At this point in the temple ritual, when all was ready for the sacrifice, the priests retired to the Hall of Polished Stone for prayers, which included the Ten Commandments and Shema. Amongst them was a " G'ullah," which includes the following verses in the form still used among the Jews:

> *True and firm it is that thou art Jehovah : our God and the God of our fathers.*
> *Thy Name is from everlasting : and there is no God beside thee.*
> *A new song did they that were delivered : sing to thy Name by the sea shore.*
> *Together did all praise and own thee as king : and say Jehovah shall reign who hath redeemed Israel.*

We are not surprised, therefore, to find St. John introducing at this point *the song of Moses the servant of God and of the Lamb*. It is sung by the martyrs standing by the glassy sea in heaven, which now appears as if mingled with fire, a clear reference to the Red Sea of the Mosaic deliverance. St. John's song is very like the temple ceremonial:

> *Great and wonderful are thy works ; Jehovah God of hosts.*
> *Just and true are thy ways ; O king of the world.*
> *Who shall not fear thee O Jehovah ; and glorify thy Name ? for thou only art holy.*
> *For all the nations shall come and worship before thee : for thy righteous acts have been shown forth.*

The " New Song " mentioned in the temple ritual is alluded to earlier in xiv. 3 by those who stand with the Lamb on Mount Sion; but this song is only known to those who sing it. The song at this point, however, serves to identify them as priests as well as victims.

A " New Song " has also been given to the twenty-four priestly elders who lead the Christian worship in chapter v. This also follows the revelation of *the Lamb of the Tamid as slain for sacrifice* (v. 9). " *Worthy art thou to take the book . . . for thou wast slain for sacrifice and redeemed to God in thy blood, out of every tribe and tongue and people and nation, and hast made them a royal priesthood to God and they reign upon the earth.*"

It is impossible to say how much of this psalmody is based on the temple ritual, or how much it has influenced Christian liturgiology. May not the " True and firm " have suggested the " Meet and right? "

A form of the True and Firm is still used in the Synagogue morning prayers.

4. *The Incense Offering.*—The next section of the daily ritual of the temple was the offering of the incense at the golden altar inside the Naos. We have noted that St. John has placed this piece of ceremonial earlier; but that has enabled him to place something far more significant here.

Let us note first that he has arranged the ritual of the seven bowls exactly as he arranged the ritual of the seven trumpets. A comparison will suffice to show this:

The Trumpets.	The Bowls.
The Trumpets given.	The Bowls ready.
Incense offered.	The Song of Moses and the Lamb.
The Trumpets sounded.	The Angels with Bowls appear.
	The Smoke of the Glory.
	The Bowls poured out.

It will be noted that in the case of the bowls, to which we are now coming, the ritual is more elaborate, as the greater importance of the event warrants. They are, of course, the real answer to the prayers offered with the incense; the trumpets were warnings.

The point we have now reached was the most solemn in the daily ritual. The priest with the incense went in with four assistants, who placed everything in readiness and then withdrew; the priest in charge of the incense, who was now alone in the Naos, threw the incense on the coals, and the Naos was filled with smoke. Then came the solemn silence for intercession, the people and priests outside prostrating themselves. This was the moment for prayer and answer to prayer. St. Luke gives an account of it in the first chapter of his gospel.

In *St. John* we read that the Naos was filled with smoke from the Glory of God and his Power. As in the story of Solomon's dedication, the " visible " Presence of God appears in the temple, the outward signs which corresponded to the pillar of smoke by day and the pillar of fire by night in the temple. The Glory and the Power are both words which mean nothing else in Rabbinic Hebrew but God himself in his glory and power. After the Incense and the trumpets in chapter viii. we read that the Naos appeared in heaven with the ark which was the outward sign of God's covenant; now the Naos is filled with the Shekinah.

Just as in the former case we saw some parallelism with the ceremonial of the Day of Atonement, so the same is to be found here, *No one could enter into the Naos till the seven plagues of the seven angels were completed.* On the Day of Atonement, once the high priest had entered the Naos, no one could enter it till he had finished his work.

But in St. John's ceremonies there is still no sign of the high priest. All is entrusted to angels; and the splendour of his coming is delayed.

The Pouring of the Blood.

We now come to another point in which St. John deserts the order of the Tamid, which has no pouring of blood at this point; it has been done at the beginning.

There are several reasons for this.

St. John is bound to have two pourings of blood, because he is using the symbolism of blood avenging; blood has been shed, and more blood must avenge it.

It was at this point on the Day of Atonement that the High Priest came out, after cleansing the Naos and Holy of Holies, in order to smear blood upon the horns of the altar and cleanse that, following the custom in all sin-offerings.

The offering on the Day of Atonement was a special version of the sin-offering, a sin-offering for the High Priest and for the whole nation; in such cases it was directed that the carcase should be taken and burnt " outside the Camp "—that is to say, in historic times, " outside the City." I have pointed out how our author and the author of the *Epistle to the Hebrews* have brought out the likeness between this custom and the crucifixion of our Lord " outside the city."

In the sin-offering the whole of the remainder of the Blood was poured out at the foot of the altar; and this ceremony has provided the basis for what follows in *Revelation*. On the Day of Atonement the High Priest entered the Holy Place and sprinkled Blood Seven times towards the veil; he then came out with reconciliation and atonement for the people. Nothing of the sort occurs in *Revelation*, because there is no reconciliation. No High Priest appears. Only a " great voice " from within the Naos directs the seven angels to pour out their bowls, and the seven angels in " white stone " and golden girdles come out with a sevenfold libation to pour upon the land. It is to be presumed that in St. John's thought the land that has been soaked in the blood of Jesus and his martyrs is one great altar of burnt- and blood-offerings.

It is a reversal of all values and expectations. There is no atonement, no reconciliation; what is to follow is rejection, retribution, and destruction.

The blood-avenging symbolism recurs throughout the seven bowls. Under the second the sea becomes like the blood of a corpse. Under the third the rivers become blood, and a versicle and response follow:

And I heard the voice of the Angel of the Waters saying,
Righteous art thou, who art and who wast, the Holy; for thou hast judged these things.
For the blood of saints and prophets they poured out; and blood thou hast given them to drink.
They are worthy.
And I heard the Altar saying,
Yea, Jehovah God of hosts: true and just are thy judgments.

I pointed out in the text of the book that the altar here signifies the martyrs, or their blood spilt on the land.

When the seventh is poured out on the air, a Great Voice came out of the Naos from the Throne, saying, IT IS DONE . . . and Babylon the great was remembered before God to give her the cup of the wine of the anger of his wrath. Here too the liturgical tone cannot be missed. " Remembered before God " is a devotional phrase; and we shall recur to the cup.

5. *The Offerings Burnt.*—The next stage in the daily ritual was the burning of all the offerings except the drink-offering, which was poured out at the foot of the altar.

Babylon is priest as well as victim. Her fine linen is priestly. Her purple and gold and scarlet and blue are priestly. The fine linen recalls the stones of the temple gleaming white like snow. She is " gilded with gold," like the temple. There was in front of the door of the Naos a " Babylonian tapestry in which blue, purple, scarlet and linen were mingled with such skill that one could not look on it without admiration," as Josephus tells us.

The merchandise of xviii. 11, which critics say could never have come to a small town like Jerusalem, would all have been used in building and furnishing the temple; the merchandise of these things must have employed many ships. And note the irony at the end, *horses and chariots and slaves, yes and the souls of men.*

The conjunction of the desert and the scarlet in xvii. 3 suggests the scapegoat.

Her former lovers are *to make her desolate and naked and eat her flesh, and burn her with fire,* and the only excuse for this horrible symbolism is that it is drawn from the sin-offering.

A verse of masterly irony is found in xviii. 5, *Her sin-offerings have mounted up to heaven, and God has remembered her unrighteousness.* Hattah in Hebrew means both sin and sin-offering; not till the last word of the line, when we read unrighteousness, is the meaning of the first apparent: it means sins.

Babylon, falsely priestly, is herself the burnt-offering. It is another reversal of expectations. *In fire shall she be burnt, When they see the Smoke of her burning ;* and finally when the shout of triumph goes up, *Alleluia : for her Smoke goeth up forever and ever.* She is turned into a continual burnt-offering. (Compare *Lev.* vi. 13.)

Nor is that the end. One ceremony remains. The high priest's cup of wine, the drink-offering, must be poured out. This too is not forgotten, but it is turned into a communion. *To give her the cup of the wine of the anger of his wrath* for she is *drunk with the blood of the saints and with the blood of the martyrs of Jesus. Repay to her as she repaid ; and double and redouble according to her works.* So ends the blood avenging. *In her was found the blood of prophets and saints and all who were slain for sacrifice upon the land* (xviii. and xix.).

6. *The Psalms.*—After the drink-offering was poured out, came the psalms; there was a "shout"; there were trumpets; there were prostration and silence; there was for the first time instrumental music. All this is reflected in the Alleluia chorus which goes up after the fall of Babylon. The detail of it need not detain us here, except that the Alleluias recall the last psalms of the book; and that each chorus begins with Alleluia, though in one case it has been translated into " Praise our God " (xix. 1–10).

7. *The Feast on the Sacrifice.*—Sin-offerings were followed by the eating of part of the sacrifice by the priest. Two feasts follow the psalmody here, one for God's friends, and one for his enemies. The first is the marriage feast of the lamb, with its obvious reference to the eucharist (xix. 9). The other is the invitation to the birds of heaven to feed on the flesh of those who fall in the wars of the messiah (xix. 17).

The Hebrew part of the book has two further liturgical points in it before it closes:

(i) *The Coming Out of the Great High Priest* (xix. 11) in which the liturgical symbolism is already gone; he comes out of heaven, not out of the Naos. The Naos in heaven seems to vanish with the earthly temple. I have dealt with the symbolism of this passage; but it is worth noting again the fine linen, and the priestly garment splashed with blood. One fine point is the name written on the thigh; I have given an explanation in the text, which I think is the central one. But it is worth noting that priestly sacredness attached to the thigh; it was a part of the sin-offering that went to the priest. I have seen mediæval Jewish drawings with a letter engraved on the thigh. But I do not know the explanation.

(ii) *The New Naos* (xxi. 3). Here too the liturgical symbolism is gone, though the description of the new order which replaces the old Jerusalem is taken from *Leviticus : Behold the Tabernacle of God is with men, and he shall Tabernacle with them, and they shall be his peoples, and he (God with them) shall be their God.*"

The word Tabernacle is used, but there is only a ghost of the old priestly symbolism. The new sanctuary is universal, human, catholic, not national or local. He goes on to describe it more fully in chapter xxii.; but that belongs to the later part of the book, that deals with Christian worship.

I have dealt fairly fully in this appendix with the liturgical background of the book, because it seems to have been neglected and yet to be all-important. It sheds a great deal of light on the tone and motives of the book. It reinforces the view that Babylon is priestly Jerusalem. It may shed some light on the development of Christian worship, and even on the worship in the temple.

I cannot pretend to have done more than blaze a trail through a dense forest of obscurities; and what I have revealed, I do not profess to understand. Until we know what a Jew felt when he saw the blood being splashed on the altar, or the fire consuming the lamb of the Tamid, we can hardly expect to enter into the complexities of the liturgical poetry of St. John.

APPENDIX II

PRIMITIVE HEBREW GNOSTICISM

As I have made frequent reference in the text of the book to second-century gnosticism and its Hebrew forerunners, I have thought it wise to add an appendix giving an outline of the ideas which I believe to have been current when St. John wrote his book, and some notion of the evidence on which that outline is based.

It will be remembered, in the first place, that the first two chapters of *Revelation* itself speak of a strongly organised sect of pseudo-Jews, and give us some positive information about them. They claim to be Jews, but are not; they claim to have apostles, but have not; they have false prophets, or at least a prophetess, " the woman Jezebel "; they can be described as a synagogue of Satan; they join freely in pagan worship; their morality is open to attack.

In the second place, it is admitted on all hands that the other Johannine literature (the gospel and epistles) which were written in the same circle of Christians, and at the same time, had in view a Gnostic sect which the author or authors wished to refute.

Thirdly, we know of a Jewish Gnostic, Cerinthus, who is said to have lived in Asia at this time; and we are told on the excellent authority of Irenæus that John of Ephesus regarded him with horror. Irenæus was an intimate friend of those who had been intimate friends of St. John. The same Irenæus is our principal authority on the Gnostic sects in general; he came originally from Ephesus, but wrote in Gaul about the decade 170 to 180; the authority of next importance is his disciple Hippolytus, bishop in Rome, whose writings may be dated about 220 to 230. They are both of them more concerned with the developed philosophical Gnosticism of their own times, but they have something to tell us about the earlier and less philosophical stages.

Fourthly, they tell us that the original sects who first assumed the name of Gnostics were Ophites or serpent-worshippers. We may date them in the first quarter of the second century (100 to 125), the generation succeeding that of John. They were Christian sects, of course—that is, they accepted Christ as redeemer, and worked his name into their system. Now in *Revelation* Satan is called the old serpent, and the pseudo-Jews are said to be worshippers of Satan, so that it is quite reasonable to try out the hypothesis that the pseudo-Jews are Ophite in character, fore-runners of the more developed sects treated of in Irenæus.

Fifthly, the second-century Gnostics claimed that they had a secret tradition of the truth handed down to them on apostolic authority, and there is no special reason to suppose that they did not believe what they said. If we credit their statement, a tradition came their way which was Hebrew in character and apostolic in authority. Looked at from

395

the Christian point of view, it would claim to be Jewish and apostolic, without being either. This also fits in with the description of the sect given by St. John.

The Gnostic traditions are obscure, unintelligible, and inconsistent; the different sects contradict one another; they are liberally adulterated with Greek philosophy, Greek religious ideas, and mythical fancies from all quarters; yet there must have been an original deposit of Hebrew speculation and pseudo-Christian tradition. It is not impossible to get some notion of what this was, by comparing the different systems together.

There are three tests which must be applied. We must look first for what is early in date, unphilosophical, and unsystematised; secondly, for what is common to various systems, even contradictory systems; thirdly, for what is best explained from Hebrew sources. On the other hand, we must not forget that there had been fusion between Hebrew and Greek ideas even before St. John wrote, and that it was in this syncretist atmosphere that Gnosticism originated.

It does seem possible to get a glimpse of ideas which were based upon a reading of *Genesis* in Hebrew, and may be illustrated from Rabbinic sources; something which in its origins may come from Palestine itself. This Hebrew heretical speculation seems to have developed out of orthodox Hebrew speculation, or parallel with it; the twist that made it worship the serpent instead of detest it will probably come from very old magical or atavistic cults, comparable to the witchcraft cults of the mediæval and reformation periods. The worship of the serpent is too old to need illustration from the first century.

A. THE SYSTEM OF IDEAS

1. *Of God and of Chaos.*—All Gnostic sects agree in denying that the universe was created by God, and in asserting a sharp and fundamental opposition between the two. This thorough-going dualism is fundamentally non-Jewish, and may be illustrated from many heathen systems of religion and philosophy; yet it is stated in early Gnosticism with a wealth of symbolic terminology drawn from the book of *Genesis*.

Gnostic systems have a spiritual world " above " or on the " right hand," where the high God and his æons dwell; this is the Pleroma or fullness, where alone is reality. They have also a material world " below " or on the " left hand " subject to the creator (Jehovah, Ialdabaoth) and his angels; this is the Kenoma (void), or even the Hysterema (minus quantity), where there is evil, illusion, or unreality.

Nothing so definite as this underlay those primitive Hebrew Gnostic speculations; but they depend on the idea that the world is evil.

2. *Of the Seven World Rulers.*—There are seven creating and world-ruling angels in whom or through whom or by whom the universe was made. Their importance varies in different systems.

3. *Of the Male and of the Female.*—Though the Gnostics regarded the relations of the sexes as evil (as, indeed, all material things were evil), they saw it as a principle deeply implanted in the nature of things, and even in the nature of God. It was essential both to the upper world and the lower.

The male is intellectual, powerful, creative, initiative; the female is emotional, erratic, fertile, productive. It is on this point that contact is established with a hundred myths, and Gnosticism breaks into a prolific and bewildering complication of symbolism.

It is enough to say that in God himself there must be a division between male and female; that from him proceed male and female; and that male and female in the cosmos reflect his nature. For the lower, left-handed, world is a copy of the higher, right-handed world. Between the two worlds there are an abhorrence and a division which is absolute; God and creation are at extreme ends of the scale of existence; yet the filthy gross world of creation reflects in its clumsy way the nature of the intellectual world which is the only reality. Through the relation of the sexes matter achieves in its way what God achieves in his way through pure intellect—that is, conception, creation, reproduction.

4. *Of the Threefold Nature.*—Pure dualism, however, cannot stand. You cannot divide the universe into two halves without any relation at all. Such thought calls loudly for relationship, or mediation. How did the world come into being? How did creative activity become implanted in matter, which is only void and nothing? In the same way how does our intellect, which belongs to the world of light, come to exist in our body, which belongs to the world of darkness?

Contrary to the system, then, a mediator, a something in between, must be allowed, in order to link the two together and permit relations. We find, therefore, that the Gnostics also assert a threefold nature for man and for the world.

First, between the intellect (spirit) of man, which belongs to the upper world, and the body, which belongs to the lower, they place the living soul; this living soul (in Greek, psyche) is the living principle of all animate flesh; we share it with birds and beasts. It is the emotional part of us which Greek philosophy thought so inferior. It is the female part.

Illogical though it is, the Gnostics frequently regard the intellectual spirit in us as the male principle, and the emotional animating soul as the female principle; illogical because it makes it difficult for them to make up their minds whether the latter is divine or earthly in origin. It turns out, in point of fact, to be the something in between, which their system does not allow, sometimes one, and sometimes the other.

The system is as follows:

1. Mind. Spirit. The part that is made for Knowledge of God. (In Greek, pneuma or nous.)
2. Soul. Animating life. Our emotional and instinctive nature. (In Greek, psyche.)
3. Body. Evil, dark, gross matter. (In Greek, soma.)

So much for the psychology. The cosmology follows suit. The universe is likewise three-fold: it has mind; it has animating soul; it has body.

1. Intellectual. God, the Pleroma, the æons.
2. Intermediate. The errant element. The unknown feminine quantity: inordinate ambition: source of emotion and animal life: origin of creation.
3. Material. Creation, matter, void.

This correspondence between psychology and cosmology is of great importance.

5. *Of Creation.*—It is plain that though the Gnostics will not allow God to be the creator, the cause of creation must come from within the

Pleroma—that is, the abode of God and the æons or beings which proceed from him. It must come from the Pleroma and pass over into the Kenoma, or nothing, out of which creation is made. Hence the necessity for the intermediate element, the force, the impulse, sufficiently remote from God himself as to make this lawless and unnatural move. Such a move is best attributed to a "female" æon remote in order from the fountain of the godhead; and this æon is generally named Sophia or Wisdom.

In any case, creation is achieved by some existence of a divine nature whose origin is in the pleroma; and almost in every case there lies behind the imagery the thought of the relation of the sexes. Something unnatural and unbecoming took place even in those high abodes of light before the mystical power of creativeness found its way into the dark waters of chaos, and the visible universe arose.

Sometimes the female is imprisoned in creation like the spirit in the flesh, and aspires upwards to the male who has deserted her, as in the case of Israel and Elohim in the system of Justinus.

Sometimes the male is abandoned by the female after she has inspired him to create; he then plays at being God, innocently thinking that there is none above him. This is the case of Sophia and Ialdabaoth.

Sometimes the female is divided. An earthly Sophia, as in the Valentinian system, is imprisoned in the material, and aspires upwards to her mother, the true wisdom in the pleroma.

Sometimes, as in the Marcionite system, there is no system; you are presented with two gods, the high God and the creator, and no questions are asked; or, as in the system of Satornilus, God may simply depute the work of creation to the seven angels. This simple crude assertion is much more likely to be the characteristic of primitive Hebrew Gnosticism than any subtle theory like that of Valentinus.

6. *Of the Redemption of Man.*—The Redemption of man is essentially a redemption from his body, from this world, and from the power of the creator.

The characteristic of the Ophite system is that the serpent is the first messenger of redemption; he persuades the man and the woman to eat of the tree of knowledge (Gnosis) which the jealous creator is guarding from them. Hence the term Gnostic; Knowledge is the redemptive power. The serpent is a messenger from the high God; he is Mind or Spirit.

Throughout the history of the Jews he continues to inspire rebellious and reforming spirits in spite of the efforts of Jehovah through the law to keep the race in subjection. Here is a clue to the nature of the sect. They were antinomians, rebelling against the law, and seeing through St. Paul that Jesus had broken the power of the law and redeemed the nation from it. This explains how it was that they could take into their system the figure of Jesus as redeemer; he was the heavenly æon come down with the true Knowledge of the Unnameable Father.

7. *Of the Three Types of Men.*—Salvation was not open to all men, according to the Gnostic system. There were three classes of men corresponding to the three constituents of their personality, the spiritual, the psychic, and the earthly; this classification was deduced from the three sons of Adam, Cain, Abel, and Seth.

According to the system that later on came to be accepted, Seth represented the spiritual, the true Gnostics, who were sure of salvation; Abel represented the psychic, or ordinary Christians, the "righteous" who had not arrived at the true Knowledge, but were capable of being saved by faith and keeping the commandments; Cain represented the material and the earthly, who could not be saved at all. "For, according to them," says Hippolytus, "there are three kinds of all existing things, the angelic, the pyschic, and the earthly; and there are three churches, angelic, psychic, and earthly; and their names are the elect, the called, and the captive." The angelic church is clearly the æon Ecclesia in the pleroma, the new Jerusalem of St. John, to which all elect souls are joined; the psychic church is the actual church on earth all of whose members are called to redemption; the earthy is probably the Jewish nation and the earthly Jerusalem (who is "in bondage," Gal. iv. 25).

This view, however, which was adopted by Valentinus, and therefore became general, is that of the Sethian Gnostics, as they are called. The earlier branch is known as Cainites, and to them Cain was the type of the true Gnostic, while Abel, one supposes, the "righteous," with his sacrifices of blood, was the type of the Jew. The Cainites were thoroughgoing revolutionaries and enemies of law; they held to Cain and Korah, and the rebels of the Old Testament.

We have outlined the general principles of Gnosticism; but it must not be supposed that any one system is described. Some Gnostics adopt only parts of our outline; in others it is blended with so much myth and philosophy that it is almost lost; others develop its logicalities and illogicalities interminably. Even in its early and unsystematised stages it varied so freely that St. Irenæus compares it to the Hydra or waterserpent with a hundred heads, that grew another as fast as one was cut off; he saw, however, that the early confused contradictory teaching provided the material for all that followed. We shall therefore confine ourselves to the early sects, only using Valentinus and the later systematisers when they appear to preserve some earlier piece of material; for our knowledge of the earlier sects is scanty.

It is worth while now to give the reader some idea of these sects and teachers:

1. *First Century.* Individual teachers.
    Simon Magus in Samaria.
    Cerinthus in Ephesus.
    Saturninus in Antioch (early second century), founded a sect, but still unsystematic.
2. *Early Second Century.*
    Gnostic sects develop. Ophite.
    Cainites.
    Sethians.
    Peratæ.
    Note also the heretic Justinus and the Book of Elchasai.
3. *Philosophical Gnosticism.*
    Valentinus works Gnosticism into a "Platonic" system.
    Basilides reduces the Hebrew element to a minimum.
    Carpocrates.
  Note also at the same period.
    Marcus, a charlatan, who nevertheless preserves interesting formulæ in his ritual.
    Marcion, not strictly a Gnostic, but adopting Gnostic elements in his teaching.
4. *Gnostic Literature* A.D. 150 and after.
    Pistis Sophia, Epistle to Flora, heretical Gospels and Acts.
    See also traces preserved in Origen.

B. The Earliest Hebrew Elements

1. *Of God and Chaos.*—The simplest account of the Ophite view of God is to be found in *Irenæus* i. 28. "But the Sethians, whom some call Ophians or Ophites, call the God of all things Man, naming him also as Light, and calling him Blessed and Incorruptible, and affirming that he has his dwelling in Bythus (the deep); and his Thought (mental conception) they call Son of Man or Second Man; and after him they say exists the Holy Spirit; and below these are four elements, Water, Darkness, Abyss, Chaos; and they call the Spirit feminine, and say she is borne upon the four elements." In the previous chapter, which forms an introduction to the study of the Ophites (though he here calls them Naassenes, and does not realise that this word comes from the Hebrew Nahash, a serpent, and has the same meaning), we read, "They suppose a certain Indestructible Æon, dwelling in a Virgin Spirit, which they name Barbeloth." The word Barbeloth is very interesting, because it appears to be a corruption of Barbelo, which means in Hebrew "God in Four." (She is the Virgin of Light in *Pistis Sophia*.)

The common names of God are Unnameable Father, and Incorruptible Æon (or Age); Adam (or Adamas) and First Man are doubtless older; he is sometimes called Bythus (the deep), sometimes said to dwell in it; he is given a shadowy sort of feminine counterpart, his Thought (Ennoia) or Silence; the Virginal Spirit (feminine in Hebrew) of my second quotation seems to be a confusion between consort and daughter. Simon Magus (or his followers) definitely made Ennoia into a feminine existence which God separated off from himself; in the Ophite system it appears to be co-eternal or older. Marcus certainly seems to think so; he speaks of Sige (Silence) as the womb and receptacle of the Kolarbasus;[1] another word of Hebrew origin, appearing to mean "all the Four," and appears to claim that she revealed herself to him; but then Marcus was a feminist and had prophetesses in his church, and needed a strongly developed female side to his system.

A word I do not find much employed for God in these passages is Arche (beginning), though it must have been in use. Valentinus, basing his terminology on that of previous Gnostics, calls God Forefather, and Fore-beginning, and Fore-unnameable, and Bythus. This seems to suggest that he had found Arche (beginning) in use among Gnostics, as he had found Father and Unnameable.

The account of the Sethians in Hippolytus is simplified and yet more philosophical; they had, no doubt, much modified their teaching by his time. We read of a God who is called Light, and of the dark waters of chaos; between these is generated the Spirit like a wind or fragrance. The anthropomorphism is gone; the ancient cosmology and the sexual element remain.

We note that there is no sign of a dogma of abhorrence between God and matter; we note also that matter is co-eternal with God.

Let us now examine the Hebrew basis of this symbolism. *In the Beginning God created the Heavens and the Earth : and the Earth was Wasteness and Emptiness and Darkness upon the surface of the Gulf, and the Spirit of God brooded upon the surface of the Waters.*

[1] Kolarbasus is not the founder of a sect. Another derivation is Voice of the Four.

APPENDIX II

Here, at any rate, is the origin of the four elements. The Gulf (Tehom) seems to mean a great mass of waters, and the phrase surface of the Waters only goes back to this. The four are, therefore:

1. Wasteness, desert. Tohu.   or   1. Chaos. Tohu-bohu.
2. Void, Emptiness. Bohu.   2. Darkness. Hoshek.
3. Darkness. Hoshek.   3. Abyss, gulf. Tehom.
4. Waters, gulf. Tehom.   4. Waters. Mayim.

Over these waters, according to Genesis, goes a breath, a wind (Ruah) from God; the word Ruah is feminine, and this is the feminine spirit spoken of by the Gnostics. The Hebrew word for God (Elohim) is plural, and this may be some excuse for the Gnostic reduplication of God into Man and Second Man.

Genesis i. 3. *And God said, Let Light be, and Light was.* We have already seen that Light is used by the Gnostics as a title of God; they would therefore interpret this verse as an emanation of God from God (Light out of Light, as the Nicene Creed says).

So also of the speaking or Word. In *Irenæus* i. 8 there is a quotation from Marcus which he claims was revealed to him by " All the Four " appearing in feminine form; he says, " When first the Father travailed in birth, he who is inconceivable and without being, he who is neither male nor female, he desired to bring to birth that in him which was unuttered and to give form to that which was invisible; he opened his mouth and put forth a Word (Logos) like unto himself, who, standing alongside of him, showed him what he was, he himself shining forth as the image of the invisible. And the uttering of the name came to pass in such a way as this; he spake the first Word (Logos) of his name, which was Beginning (Arche) and was a composition of four letters." This passage is late, of course, and occurs in a section which is typically Marcosian; it may also be influenced by *St. John's Gospel* (and by St. Paul?); but it serves to show how the Logos was thought of " way-y'omer elohim " . . . " God spoke " . . . and the very verb Amar is given substantial existence.

It is not surprising, therefore, to find the same substantial existence conceded to the word Beginning, the first word of *Genesis*, or, as Marcus puts it, " The first Word of his name." It is true that he uses the Greek word Arche, which was made up of four letters, and thus forms a basis for his cabalistic calculations; but the Hebrew word Reshith can be written in four letters (Resh, Aleph, Shin, Tau or Resh, Shin, Yodh, Tau, as in *Deut*. xi. 12). It is possible, therefore, that he may be adapting some prior Hebrew speculation for Greek readers.

Let us look a little closer. Marcus says that when God spoke there came forth a word of four letters, which was the " first word of his name"; turning to *Genesis*, we read, *God said, Let there be Light*, so that the first recorded word is Yehiy, Let there be. Now this word is practically identical with the name Y-hu-h, the sacred name of four letters which we pronounce Jehovah, so that according to the text God does begin by enunciating his name, and that too a name of four letters, the sacred four. This name, however, is not accepted by Gnostics as a name of God; Jehovah is the evil or bungling creator of the cosmos, not the originator of all being. The Gnostic therefore moves back to an earlier verse, and chooses the first word of the whole bible, Reshith, the Beginning, which may also be regarded as a word of four letters. This is

God's first utterance and the name of the nameless. It is before speech: it comes forth out of silence.

My guess is (it can be no more) that there are three stages: an orthodox Hebrew stage in which it is pointed out that God began creation by uttering his own name, the mystic tetragrammaton, Jehovah; a heretical Hebrew stage in which God is said to begin the production of the æons by uttering his own name, a four-lettered name, Reshith or Beginning; a Greek Gnostic stage in which this is adapted to the Greek language.

In any case, we must note the primitive elements of Hebrew Gnostic heresy all closely connected with *Genesis*:

1. God is unnameable. Of the names in *Genesis*, the one most rightly his own is Reshith or beginning. He cannot have a particular or personal name like Jehovah.
2. He dwells alone in the deep (Bythus).
3. His Ruah, a feminine influence proceeding from him, broods over (fertilises?) the surface of the Waters.
4. The Ruah is intermediate between him and the four elements, Waste, Void, Darkness, Waters.
5. There comes from him also a Word: way-y'omer, he spoke; this word is himself, his name. It is the active instrument in the divine creation.
6. *Genesis* next speaks of a division made by God between light and darkness, and a firmament dividing waters above from waters below; this certainly harmonises with the Gnostic dualism.

The close connection of all this with contemporary orthodox thought is also clear. *The Book of Jubilees* records the creation on the first day of heaven, earth, waters, spirits, abysses, darkness and light (*Jub.* 2) and the *Pirke de R. Eliezer* (3) has a similar list. The Gnostic differs in making Waste, Void, Darkness, and Waters coeternal with God and contrary to him; the Gnostic exegesis is nearer to the literal meaning of *Genesis*.

The first verses of *St. John's Gospel* belong to a similar school of thought: *In the Beginning (Reshith) was the Word, and the Word was with God, and the Word was God; this was in the Beginning with God*, etc. But St. John agrees with the orthodox Hebrew in asserting that everything came into existence through him.

As for the *Revelation*, God is not only Beginning, but Beginning and End. The elements of Gnostic thought are there, but are woven into a harmony. The Waters are spread, calm and subdued before the Throne; between God and the Waters is the Spirit symbolised as sevenfold Light; there is no sign of Chaos or Void or Darkness. More important, the Throne is supported by the four living things; these take the places of the four insubordinate Gnostic elements, and symbolise the order of God's creation. So far from being contrary to him, the four form his throne.

Of the Gnostic " God in Four " we shall write later.

2. *Of the Seven World Rulers.*—In one early form of Gnosticism the work of creation was simply deputed to seven angels. In chapter xviii. Irenæus tells us that Satornilus of Antioch early in the second century taught that the unknown Father "made angels and archangels and powers; and from a certain seven angels the cosmos received its origin, and all things in it, and that man was a creation of angels after a bright image which

APPENDIX II

shone out from above . . ." Even though man was made after this bright image, he was incapable of standing erect, but sprawled on the ground like a worm until the high God imparted to him a flash of divine light.

A similar view of man's creation is found in the Rabbis; but it need not detain us, as we are dealing with the seven creating powers.

In Irenæus' account of the Sethian Ophites they are said to have been generated by the feminine divine being Sophia out of the waters of chaos; each of them created one of the seven heavens. Their names are given in the Latin translation, and they are Ialdabaoth, Iao, Sabaoth, Adoneus, Eloeus, Oreus, and Astaphaeus; and later on he allots each one of them a day of the week. In Valentinus they *are* the seven heavens.

Only the first and the last names cause any difficulty; the rest are interpreted as follows:

2. Iao = Jehovah.
3. Sabaoth = of Hosts.
4. Adoneus = Adonai, Lord.
5. Eloeus = Elohim, God.
6. Oreus = Or, Light.

It will be noted that with the exception of the last they are all titles of Jehovah; the last (Light) occurs in i. 3 as produced from Elohim; Elohim said, Let there be Light. This connection shows that we are not far from someone who read *Genesis* in Hebrew. 1 and 7 (Ialdabaoth and Astaphaeus) are uncertain; Ialdabaoth may be Yah El Da-abahoth, as Harvey suggests in his note *ad loc*. This is Aramaic for Jehovah, God of the fathers—that is, of Abraham, Isaac, and Jacob. A recent suggestion is Yalda Bahoth, Child of Chaos.

There can be little doubt that the seven angels are the seven hostile guardians of the spheres associated in gentile thought with the seven planets; Irenæus says that the Sethians "wish the holy seven to be the seven stars which they call planets"; they rule the cosmos and are jealous of man.

At some point in the first century these seven hostile world-rulers were identified with Jehovah, the "jealous" God of the Jews; the work was done by a man who read Hebrew, but was heretical in his faith, holding that the creator was not the high God. At least he knew enough to understand that the word for God, though always taking a singular verb, was plural in form. The cosmos was created by Elohim; and Elohim means gods, mighty ones, angels; it is even used of kings and judges. He found the work of creation divided into seven days, and it was simple to allot one of the Elohim to each day, and distribute the titles of Jehovah among them.

It is possible that he translated the first three words of *Genesis* as follows: Bereshith bara Elohim; The Beginning (Reshith) created the Elohim? It would be a very bad, an impossible translation, but once Reshith is considered a name for God it might not be impossible to the kind of exegetes we are considering. Besides, the name Bereshith (Be = In and Reshith = beginning) may have been accepted holus bolus; see below on Barbelo.

It is worth noting that his sixth angel, Eloeus, has his name correctly turned into the singular, Eloah.

If the translation suggested above is unacceptable, we must suppose that he translated (quite correctly) " In or through Reshith (the supreme God) Elohim (angels) made the heavens and the earth," or " B'reshith created the Elohim, even the Heavens . . ."

In *Jubilees* and Rabbi Eliezer angels are created on the first day, and in Jewish orthodox thought generally they are introduced and made prominent at the important moments of the sacred history. St. Stephen in *Acts* speaks of the law on Mount Sinai as being given by angels. There was a strong tendency in Jewish thought (*a*) to think of God as having in him an infinite multiplicity of spiritual powers, and (*b*) to surround him with a host of angels of various ranks and grades. The former conception is a half-way house not only to Gnosticism, but also to the Christian doctrine of the Trinity. The two views tend to coalesce.

It will be noted that neither among the Gnostics nor in the New Testament is the " apocalyptic " series of seven great angels beginning with Michael adopted. In both, the figure seven is connected with the divine. St. John's seven lamps which symbolise the Holy Spirit are not so grotesque as Dr. Charles thinks; the multiple energies of the divine spirit are symbolised by the number seven, just as among the Gnostics the semi-divine work of creation is allotted to a semi-divine creator who is broken up into seven in order to identify him with the seven astrological world-rulers. We can hardly help seeing in St. John a deliberate correction, and an authentic reason for the use of the number.

So much for his positive use of the number seven. His negative use is yet more interesting.

The divine Word of God, the Lamb, is given seven horns and seven eyes, signifying that he is by nature endowed with the plenitude of the divine power. His antithesis, the Beast, is given seven heads; and these seven heads are not taken from Daniel or any other Hebrew prophet. It has always been supposed that the dragon was a current mythological conception familiar to his readers, and that in some familiar myth (unknown to us) the dragon had seven horns.

Now Swete points out that in *Pistis Sophia*, the only Gnostic work which has survived (it is of the Valentinian school), there is a serpent with seven heads; the evidence is late, but it is all we have. Now in the cosmic myths which were adopted and worked over by the Gnostics the dragon or serpent stood for the waters of chaos, the old enemy of God, the matter out of which the world was made; in Hebrew thought and in the writings of St. John matter and creation are not hostile to God; but we have seen how the dragon and the waters stand for whatever is hostile to him. These forces of evil (moral evil) are incarnate in the beast with seven heads which stands for the Roman imperial power.

Now the whole Gnostic system appears to be reflected and reversed in the picture of the harlot Babylon and the beast. The harlot represents the errant feminine æon (actually called Prunicos or Harlot by the Ophites), from whose union with the waters of chaos sprang Ialdabaoth and the other of the seven creators and world rulers. St. John's harlot is seated on the waters, just as the Gnostic feminine æon was " borne up by the four elements, water, etc."; she is also represented as seated on the beast with seven heads, and in one verse (impossibly) as seated on the heads. The heads in St. John also signify world-rulers, the seven Cæsars.

One need not note how the titles Jehovah, Sabaoth, etc., are all applied to the supreme God who is worshipped as the only creator.

3. *Of the Male and of the Female.*—When we come to the division of all existence into male and female, we find ourselves embarrassed with a confusion of material which makes quotation difficult. The subject can be divided into two sections, one dealing with the heavenly, and the other with the earthly; for though the Gnostics loathed the relation of the sexes, they were bound to hold that Ialdabaoth assisted by Sophia only worked out in a gross and material fashion a poor copy of the patterns in heaven. Even Satornilus, whose system appears not to be sexual so far as our short account of it goes, exhibits the creators as making man in the likeness of a shining image from the world above.

Ialdabaoth and Sophia are doing over again in the world of matter what Bythus or Arche the Unnameable Father did in the world of thought with his consort Ennoia (Thought) or Sige (Silence).

The supreme God, Marcus asserts, is neither male nor female; but his assertion would appear to belong to a later period. Others say that he is hermaphrodite—that is, both male and female; and for practical purposes the two statements come to the same thing. That is why the relation to Ennoia is so hard to fix; while Sige might be thought of as co-eval or even prior, Ennoia is more naturally thought of as subsequent. Sige is the womb of All the Four, says Marcus; but then he was a feminist and emphasises the female. Sige and Ennoia are shadowy and vague, because they are only abstract concepts, the result of speculation. They have no biblical basis; they play no part in the scheme.

We have already seen how the Word, a masculine power, springs from the Unnameable Father, or from his union with Ennoia, who is no more than part of himself; we have also seen the importance of Spirit, Ruah, the feminine influence which proceeds from him and broods upon the waters. We have here a small system in itself, perhaps originally independent. Its character is that of cosmic myth; out of Bythus, the incorruptible Age (æon), the Father of all, comes the feminine influence, wind or Ruah, which moves upon and fertilises the waters of chaos. Here also is the threefold division of being; for the Ruah or Spirit is the intermediate or psychic element between the contrary principles of mind and matter.

But there is another system which needs investigation. In the 28th chapter of *Irenæus* I we learn that the (Sethian) Ophites "call the God of all things Man . . . affirming also that he has his dwelling in Bythus; and his Thought (Ennoia) they call Son of Man and Second Man; and after these exists the Holy Spirit." Two systems here exist side by side.

A.	B.
Bythus Ennoia.	Man.
	Son of Man. Holy Spirit.
	Second Man. (First Woman).

The word Holy applied to Spirit must certainly be a piece of Irenæus' own phraseology; she is often called First Woman in the later part of the exposition of the Ophite system, and the word implies that she is the first of two; the second is the errant Sophia who fell into the world of matter. There seems to be implied a simple system of this kind:

First Man (= the God of all things)
Second Man. First Woman (Spirit).
Second Woman:

but Second Woman has fallen from the world above into chaos.

The identification of Spirit (the daughter) with Ennoia (the consort) of the God of all serves to show the confusion of the whole system, and the difficulty of reconciling different systems. It seemed natural, of course, that the First Woman should be the consort of the First Man. In any case such confusion exists in the identification of the female æons that there is no point in attempting to recover an original consistent system or systems; the division of the female æon into two seems to follow upon the division of the waters by the firmament in *Genesis* i. 6; for, as we have seen, Spirit is closely associated with the waters. The feminine existence which is cut off and submerged in the lower waters is the Second or Latter Woman, sometimes called Hystera (latter), to whom creation is due. She remembers, however, her mother, the First Woman in the heavens, and through this recollection is able to impress on creation the image of what is heavenly.

Now Hystera, the lower feminine spirit, stands to Ialdabaoth, the creator, much as the First Woman stands to the supreme God, so that the lower creation reproduces the higher; the deduction is almost irresistible that the First Woman must have been thought of as equivalent to Ennoia, consort as well as daughter of the supreme God.

Let us now turn our system into Hebrew:

Adam Rishon (compare Reshith, beginning)
Adam Ahēr   Isshah Rishonah.

(Ruah: spirit. Hauuah: Eve, Life.)

Let us note in passing that the word Rosh, from which are derived Reshith and Rishon, has the meaning of Head, Supremacy, Beginning, and First. Note also the use of Adam as a name for God and the division of God into Man and Woman; we have here primitive elements with Hebrew affinities which were very soon lost as Gnosticism progressed and denied that God could be named or that he was male or female. But the assertion that there are male and female in God can be proved from *Genesis* and seems to be implied there.

Genesis i. 27: *And Elohim created Adam in his image: in the image of Elohim he created him: male and female he created them.* And again in *Genesis* v. 1: *This is the book of the begettings of Adam, in the day of Elohim creating Adam: in the likeness of Elohim he made him: male and female he created them.* The image in God, therefore, after which Adam was made, may reasonably have been considered male and female.

The thought of the image of Adam existing in God was not new. Ezekiel (i. 27) speaks of *the likeness as it were the appearance of Adam* seated on the throne of God. The same thought may explain *one as a Son of Man with the clouds of heaven* in *Daniel* vii. 13; for the clouds of heaven are the throne and power of God; Son of Man (*bar enosh*) is Aramaic for man (Adam); for *Daniel* at this point is written in Aramaic. It is unquestionable in *Enoch*. In the Rabbis we frequently meet the heavenly man, Adam Qadmon (ancient or original man, pre-man), after whose likeness the earthly Adam was fashioned.

Once this deduction of a heavenly Adam has been made, the further deduction of a heavenly Eve seems almost necessary.

Now so simple, so anthropomorphic a system was not likely to stand long; and we must be grateful to Irenæus for preserving for us the evidence that in the earliest forms of the heresy it did exist. We need not consider any further the Son of Man or Second Man; the figure of the First Woman needs further elucidation.

APPENDIX II

In the first place, we note that in *Genesis* itself, rightly or wrongly, the name Eve is explained as meaning Life; she is the mother of all living. The name Mother of All Living is frequently applied to the heavenly woman of the Gnostics; we are right, therefore, in regarding her as a celestial Eve. The name Eve does not occur; we find instead Zoe, the Greek word for Life; but this is the natural translation; the Septuagint (*Genesis* iii. 20) says, *Adam called the name of his wife Zoe.*

Secondly, she is identified with Eden or Paradise, which was regarded as part of the upper (or intermediate) creation. In Justinus, a later Gnostic of independent views, the heavenly couple are Elohim and Israel or Eden; in Valentinus (*Irenæus* i. 1. 10) the lower female æon is called Earth and Jerusalem, and as she reflects the nature of her heavenly mother, it is reasonable to suppose that in some sense she too was Earth and Jerusalem, heavenly Earth and heavenly Jerusalem. We thus have two independent witnesses to this fact, besides hints in other places. In Justinus, however, there is no division into upper and lower; the lower female existence is Babel or Venus or Omphale.

It has been pointed out that in *Genesis* i. the Gnostics thought they had a description of the upper creation, the sevenfold realms of heaven. Now in the first verse Elohim is said to have created Heavens and Earth, and we have already seen how in one system the Elohim were interpreted as angels or æons; still more was this possible with the Heavens, a name frequently given to the spirits that controlled them. The Heavens then were masculine, the Earth was feminine; the Heavens and the Elohim were practically one and the same; the Earth was the Eden or Paradise from which Man and Woman were expelled.

Here also we are in a state of extreme confusion owing to the supersession of a dualistic scheme by a division into three:

1. The angelic. Heaven.
2. The psychic. Eden.
3. The material. Earth.

Nothing much, however, hangs on the name Eden; we may pass on to the quite certain identity with the holy community.

Thirdly, the heavenly woman is the true church. We have seen how Justinus calls her Israel, while Valentinus calls her earthly counterpart Jerusalem; but we are fortunate in finding the following words in Irenæus' description of the Ophites, "They say that the first man and the Second were enamoured of the beauty of Spirit (the heavenly woman), and brought to birth Light, whom they call Messiah, and that the Feminine element, not being able to bear the excess of light, boiled over, and the Messiah with his Mother was caught up to the Incorruptible Æon; and they call her also the true Church."

We may note in passing the very close connection with *Rev.* xii. 5, the production of a new male æon, Messiah, and along with him the fall of a portion of the female element into chaos; but our main point just now is the title Ecclesia, given to the heavenly woman. We have seen that she is called Spirit; she also stands for Israel, the Church or holy community in which the Spirit moves, the body or outward visibility of the Spirit.

Now throughout the Gnostic systems we find one group of four æons high up in the scale who do not change their positions one to another; they are:

Male.		Female.
Logos (Word)	and	Zoe (Life).
Anthropos (Man)	and	Ecclesia (Church).

There can be no doubt that this is the original Tetrad or Four, produced in God out of his Ennoia or Thought; it is true that in Marcus, in Valentinus, and in the books ascribed to Simon Magus (produced, no doubt, within his sect) there are prior existences, and even a prior Tetrad or Four. But the names fluctuate and the concepts themselves are vague and shadowy. The higher Four in Marcus are Bythus, Sige, Father, and Truth; in Valentinus they are Bythus, Sige, Mind, and Truth; they are an attempt to systematise what before was shadowy and vague. The Tetrad, Logos, Zoe, Anthropos, and Ecclesia, is not only constant, but primitive, and is made by combining together the two couples which can be deduced from *Genesis*:

A.	B.
Bythus.	Man.
Word. Spirit.	Second Man. Eve (Life).

This is the original Tetrad referred to when Sige is called Voice of the Four or All the Four (Kolarbasus = Kol-ha-arba) and God in Four (B'arba-eloh = Barbelo). The ritual formulae used by Marcus refer to these names.

In the original system, then, there was an upper Four and a lower Four:

Above.

God (masculine)
  on the Four.
  Word, Life, Man, Church.

Below.

Spirit (feminine)
  borne on the Four elements,
  Water, Darkness, Abyss, Chaos.

As time went on the system of seven world-creators was added to the lower part of the system, and the Spirit now called Sophia combined with them to make the Ogdoad or Eight. It was necessary then to make an Ogdoad or Eight out of the upper world, and the addition of a higher Four such as Bythus, Thought, Mind, and Truth not only made the correspondence exact, but gave a much more philosophical appearance to a still rather anthropomorphic system.

Turning to the *Revelation*, we note that in chapter iv. God is introduced not only as creator of all things, but as sole creator. We find that there is no fourfold complex of divine being issuing from him; he is not, if I may so venture to express it, a four-cylinder deity; nor is there a fourfold system symbolic of matter, contrary to him. Yet he is Barbelo, God enthroned upon Four, the four living things which express the harmony and worship of his own creation.

In chapter v. we find proceeding from him neither Logos nor Adam, but the Lamb; the Lamb is introduced, I think, in the place held by the Serpent in the Gnostic scheme. (See below.)

The title Son of Man is avoided except in the one place (xiv. 14) where it must be employed to be true to the prophecies of Jesus (*Mark* xiii. 26). It is avoided in the same way by all New Testament writers. No doubt this is due to the Gnostic use of the terms, which is refuted in 1 *Corinthians* xv. 44. *If there is a body psychic there is also a body pneumatic. Thus also it is*

APPENDIX II

written Adam the first man became a psyche, living ; the last Adam became a pneuma, life-giving. But the pneumatic does not come first : but first the psychic, then the pneumatic. The First Man is of the Earth, material ; the Second Man is from heaven . . . and as we have carried the Image of the material, so let us also bear the Image of the heavenly. We cannot stay to elucidate this passage ; we must only note the rejection of Gnostic doctrine and the employment of Gnostic terms.

On the other hand, as I have pointed out in the text of the book, the mighty angel of *Revelation*, x., descending from heaven with the book and the symbols of divinity, symbolises the progress of the Word of God on earth, and that progress is consummated in chapter xix., and summed up in the triumph of the Messiah who rides out armed and named with the Word of God. Here St. John is using in a sound and true way the Old Testament symbolism out of which the Gnostics have built their heretical system of æons—Man, Word, Messiah.

The heavenly woman appears in chapter xii. as the spiritual community that gives birth to the Messiah, and is painted as a second Eve ; the details of the divine birth and her subsequent history are closely parallel to those of the birth of the Gnostic Christ from his mother the First Woman, and the further fortunes of that overflow from the substance of the First Woman which boiled over into chaos. (See text *ad loc.*, Book V.) The female figure in *St. John* now symbolises the Christian church, and she ultimately appears as the bride of Christ, the new Jerusalem from heaven ; like the male Word of God figure, she is divine throughout, and suffers no fall or defilement ; in the last chapter she is the Spirit and the Bride. (In the Gnostic system Christ descends through the seven heavens, is nuptially united with Sophia, and returns with her to heaven.)

The Term Sophia.—The term Sophia is applied in Gnosticism to the fallen æon, the portion of the heavenly feminine spirit which fell into chaos ; she is also called Harlot or Hystera (Latter Woman). St. John's Harlot Babylon is partly modelled upon her.

In the Valentinian system Wisdom is divided. There is a heavenly Wisdom, Sophia, and there is her daughter Achamoth, the lower Wisdom, formless at first, who was thrust out into the void. Achamoth is the Hebrew word for Wisdom, Hokhmah.

If a mere guess may be permitted, we may suggest that the elaboration of this figure was the work of heretics in Alexandria, where the orthodox Wisdom theology was also worked out. In the orthodox theology the wisdom of the creator was personified after a poetical fashion ; for instance, the *Wisdom of Solomon* says (chapter vii.) :—

22. There is in her a Spirit of Understanding : Holy, Only-begotten, subtle.
25. For she is a Mist from the Power of God : and a simple flowing forth of the Glory of the Almighty (= Jehovah Sabaoth) . . .
26. For she is a Radiance from the light invisible ; and a spotless mirror of Energy of God : and an Image of his goodness . . .
27. And through the generations she passes on into holy souls : and equips them as friends of God and prophets . . .
29. For she is more glorious than the sun : and above every constellation of stars : being compared with Light she is found before it.

It would be tempting to compare this term by term with the Gnostic theology : spirit flowing from God : light flowing from spirit : the inspiration of the prophets: the queen of the seven heavens and their stars: it is interesting also to compare verse 29 with *Revelation* xii. 1; but our business here is to point out that this sort of teaching has been worked over by a heretic who held a low view of creation. Something of the heavenly radiance still clings to the fallen spirit Sophia, who inspires the creator Ialdabaoth in his blind and clumsy labours.

Except v. 12 and vii. 12, which are purely lyrical and belong to the latest strata of his book, the author of *Revelation* only employs the word Wisdom allusively in referring to his two evil mysteries, the name of the Beast and the name of Babylon (xiii. 18 and xvii. 9).

It is worth noting that St. James knows the contrast between the two wisdoms: *This is not the Wisdom which cometh down from above, but is earthly, psychic, daimonic . . . the Wisdom from above is first of all sacred, then peaceful . . .* (*Jas.* iii. 13–18).

4. *Of the Threefold Nature.*—It is a commonplace of Johannine criticism that he tolerates no middle terms; he knows only of good and evil, God and the devil. Such simplicity is impossible to those who suppose that the opposing terms are spirit and matter; an intermediate has to be found, the element which the Gnostics call psychic. This classification (conscious, sub-conscious, and bodily) is useful in psychology if it is not carried out into a relentless subdivision of the man; St. Paul used it in an admirably loose and descriptive way; the Gnostics applied it with relentless logic not only to psychology, but also to cosmology.

In *St. John* there are no middle terms. There are opposites: God and the Devil; the Lamb and the Beast; the Bride and the Harlot. This is characteristic of primitive Christianity, which knows Two Ways only, a Way of Life and a Way of Death (*Teaching of the Twelve Apostles*, i. 1.). It is often remarked that in the *Revelation* we do not find the common antithesis of the fourth gospel, Light and Darkness. This omission is so pointed that it is worth while looking for a reason. It may be found in the possibility that had Darkness been included in a book of symbols, it would have been considered to have a substantial existence. The fallacy of the Gnostics which we most easily detect is their treatment of nothing as a substantial existence; Sophia falls into the void outside of real existence; but the whole point of the void outside real existence is that it is not there. Had Void and Darkness appeared in the *Revelation*, they would infallibly have been thought of as substantial. Even the Abyss which he does employ to symbolise the depths of moral evil is only too readily thought of as an existence in time and space.

The omission gives this divine poem its peculiar clarity; it is like God: for God is Light, and in him is no Darkness at all.

For the rest, St. John excels in depicting processes which are double. The progress of the Word of God is, for instance, a divine progress; it is also a human progress; but it is not mixed. The growth of the Church is a divine progress, the advance of the Spirit in the world of men; it is also a human progress; but it is not mixed. There are no half-way existences in *St. John*.

The Serpent.—Under this head we may now consider the Serpent in primitive Gnosticism. This is very hard to do, because such references as remain are contradictory. It is easy to see that the Serpent was benevolent, leading men to the tree of Knowledge (Gnosis) which the jealous creator was keeping from man; but his place in the system is hard to define. The twenty-eighth chapter of *Irenæus* 1, which has been our guide so far, is Sethian in character, not Cainite, and regards the

Serpent as the son of Ialdabaoth and matter; even here the Latin text gives us a hint in its allusion to "Mind (Nous) coiled in the shape of a Serpent." It goes on to tell us how the heavenly mother uses the Serpent (who is regarded as evil) to tempt mankind to eat of the tree of Knowledge; this is plainly not the teaching of the original Ophite Gnostics, who worshipped the Serpent as good. The Serpent, being cast out of Paradise along with Adam and Eve, begets six more spirits in imitation of his father Ialdabaoth, and the seven become the spirits of the world. (Compare our Lord's parable of the devil cast out, taking seven spirits worse than himself.) He is thus the creator of the earth, as Ialdabaoth is creator of the heavens.

It is unfortunate that at this point we have only the Latin translation (and expansion?) of the Greek of Irenæus, which we have followed so far; and even Irenæus may not have fully understood the sect he was describing. Still there are certain points even in the Latin.

The first is the name Nous or Mind given to the Serpent, together with the word "coiled"; this agrees with the description in Hippolytus which compares the Serpent to the convolutions of the brain. The second is that the serpent is said to have two names, Michael and Sammael. Now these must surely be the names given in opposing sects, and it is in the original "black" Ophites that the Serpent would have been called Michael; and as the "white" or Sethian Ophites make him the chief of seven earthly and evil spirits, it is likely that the black Ophites made him the chief of seven celestial spirits. The third point is a note added in the Latin to the account of the Sethians; but as it is worked into the later Greek writer Theodoret, who makes copious use of Irenæus, we may feel fairly sure that it stood in the original. "There are some who say that Sophia herself became the Serpent; and that is why he opposed the creator of Adam, and instilled Knowledge into man, and therefore it is said that the Serpent is wiser than all." There follows a comparison of the Serpent with the intestines, "showing the hidden generative substance of the shape of the Serpent in us."

What does become clear is the connection between Sophia and the Serpent; all the more so when we note the evidence for a double nature in her. In describing the Valentinian system Irenæus says, "Her they call Mother and Ogdoad and Wisdom and Earth and Jerusalem and Holy Spirit and in the masculine sense, Lord"; she is therefore bisexual, a very significant point. Add to this that in Justinus the female being who co-operates in creation is half woman and half serpent. Note too that in the Valentinian system we find next to the supreme God and above the Tetrad (Logos, Zoe, Anthropos, Ecclesia) the figure of Nous or Mind, the title of the Serpent; he is also called Monogenes or Only-begotten, and he alone understands the Father and can declare him to the other æons. There is no accident in the conjunction of terms which we find in *Revelation* xiii. 18 and xvii. 9.

<blockquote>
Here is MIND (= Serpent?)
He who has WISDOM (= Sophia).
</blockquote>

We have discovered, perhaps, still another form of the male and female couple which proceeds from the supreme God; perhaps not a couple in this case, but a bi-sexual existence like that of the supreme God himself.

For our purpose, however, it is unnecessary to conjecture precisely what place the Serpent may have held in Cainite Ophism. It is enough to note that even in the Sethian and later systems, where the Serpent became less and less prominent, and less and less beneficent, it is easy to find traces of the mediating position which it once held. In Hippolytus, who deals with later and more philosophised stages of the same sects, we find in the case of the Peratæ that the Serpent is the Mind, the Word, the Son of God, and that in the case of the Sethians the Serpent is the " wind " (*i.e.* spirit) that moved between God and the waters of Chaos; it is also called the wise Logos of Eve: and the Aramaic word Hiuuiah (Serpent) closely resembles the Hebrew Hauuah (Eve).

The recovery of any definite Serpent theology is the more hopeless because Serpent worship existed in so many forms in the heathen systems which surrounded the Jew, and Serpent symbolism is as manifold and changeful and Protean as the Hydra itself. Actual Serpent worship is bound to have existed on Palestinian soil and though a form of Judaism was forced upon the population, such a cult would not die out; I have already compared the survival of such a cult to the heathen survivals which were called witchcraft in the Mediæval and Reformation periods.

The undoubted cardinal points of primitive Hebrew Gnosticism are as follows:

1. Rejection of Jehovah, the creator, who is looked on as a jealous or an evil God.
2. Consequent rejection of his law, and of those who act as mediators of his revelation.
3. Worship of the Serpent who is sent by a higher power to bring men to Knowledge.

The Serpent is the Nous or Mind of the high God; his only-begotten; the eldest of all the æons which proceed from him. He is also connected with the highest of the female æons, the heavenly Eve, the mother of all living; he is the " wise Logos of Eve "; in some systems he actually is the female power, " the wind that blows between the worlds." He mediates between God and matter in creation; he mediates between God and man in inspiration; he is that intermediate divine power which makes such commerce possible. Just as the constellation Draco (or Serpent) was seen to revolve round the Pole Star in the northern sky, so the mystic Serpent was placed next to the unmoved original deity; just as the convolutions of the brain are the medium of our thought and control our bodies in accordance with our thought, so the Serpent is the mind or brain of the highest God, controlling all things in accordance with his will.

That is why the author of the *Revelation*, though he bases his vision of the creator in chapters iv. and v. on the vision of Ezekiel, nevertheless fails to introduce the image of Adam or the figure of the Son of Man in the midst of the throne of God; for this language was also employed by the Gnostics; he places there instead the Lamb as slain for sacrifice with his seven eyes and seven horns, as a contrast and contradiction to the Gnostic Serpent with seven heads. And all through the book this contrast is developed.

5. *Of Creation.*—We need not (fortunately) linger over that " fall " among the divine æons to which the Gnostics attributed the misfortune of creation; it is doubtful, in any case, whether it can be reduced to anything like system; its fundamental dogma is one which must inevitably lead to confusion, and always does so. It is as old as mankind, and may be roughly summed up as follows:

1. There are two opposed principles in the universe, spirit and matter; they are found in man as spirit and body.
2. The spirit is the source of good, and the body (or matter) is the source of evil.

It is impossible on these grounds to explain the facts of creation without assuming two further points which are contradictory to the first principles already laid down; these are:
3. A kind of fall, or tendency to evil, in spirit which produced creation.
4. An imprisonment of spirit in matter.

After creation there is no fall, but only an ascent or aspiring upwards on the part of the spirit which is thus imprisoned.

We need not delay again to point out how abundantly St. John emphasises the fact that the whole material creation is good, and that its origin is to be found in the will and pleasure of God.

How, then, about evil?

Evil is the true contrary of God. " Sin," says the *First Epistle of St. John*, " is lawlessness ": Anomia, rejection of law; Gnosticism also is Anomia or rejection of law. Rejection of law can only take place in a mind possessed of reason and free-will; the only contrary to God, therefore, is a contrary mind or personality.

In the *Revelation*, the origin of that which is contrary to God is not matter or chaos or darkness or waters; nor is it eternal. It had a beginning. A Star fell (viii. 10 and ix. 1). The symbolic language of St. John makes it unnecessary to decide whether the " fall " was that of an angel or of a man. But I have pointed out in the text of the book that the fall is a contrary to law; anti-Moses and anti-Sinai. As Moses sweetened the bitter waters at Elim, so the fall embittered the waters that were sweet; the " waters " are not naturally contrary to God. They become so. We are told in xvii. 15 that they symbolise " peoples and crowds and nations and languages."

After this we find the Abyss (ix. 11); it has not existed before; it is only opened by the fall. Out of this Abyss proceeds all that is contrary to God; it symbolises the origin of moral evil. It was not part of creation, and it will ultimately disappear.

When I use the word " origin " I do not mean historical origin in time, of which nothing is known. It is the *nature* of sin in which St. John is interested, not its history; I use " origin " to mean cause, birth, breeding-place.

The word Abyss was a term from Hebrew theology (*Genesis* i.) used by the Gnostics in a sense contrary to Hebrew faith; St. John takes it and uses it in a sense compatible with Hebrew faith. Both use it as the origin of what is contrary to God, the Gnostics of original eternal matter, St. John of the depths of moral evil in human nature.

As we pass on in *Revelation* we find that it turns into the Serpent who tempted Eve, the enticing spirit of evil itself; as we go further it embodies itself more clearly in a male incarnation, the Beast with Seven Heads, a Serpent Messiah contrary to the Lamb with Seven Horns who is the Messiah of God. The older Hebrew prophets had also delineated the world-power as a beast or even as the old dragon of the waters; in *Revelation* too he rises out of the sea, the watery element. But nothing cosmical or Gnostic clings to him in *Revelation*; he is the false claimant to world-empire and world-worship. The seven word-rulers are seven actual world-rulers; the only " mystery of lawlessness " working in the world is that which originates in the human heart and incarnates itself in human bodies or human communities.

We pass further and find the use which St. John has made of the Gnostic female figure, the lower Wisdom called the Harlot; the Babylon of chapter xvii. which is associated with the Beast. Her likeness to the errant Gnostic æon (or to the primitive female spirit in creation) may be seen in her being enthroned on the Beast and upon the Waters; but here also St. John is carrying on the traditional orthodox doctrine of the Hebrew prophets. As in the heretic Justinus, she is the bride of God who has gone a-whoring after strange deities; the Israel or Jerusalem that should have been the Bride of God, but is, in fact, the Harlot. (In Justinus, Babel = Aphrodite, the Omphale of Heracles.)

Babylon is therefore the second or female incarnation of the Serpent principle of evil; but nothing cosmical or Gnostic clings about her; she is the unholy community of the old Judaism from which the presence and glory of God have long removed.

I have dealt with the detail of this in the text of the book, and it need not be repeated here. Enough to say that in the *Revelation* the Serpent and the Harlot represent not the Mind and Wisdom of the high God (however fallen or far removed), but the Mind and Wisdom of the spirit of evil which has its origin in the heart of man. (" It is the Number of a Man.")

6. *Of the Redemption.*—The Gnostic doctrine of redemption can be summed up under two heads sufficiently well for our purpose:

1. It is a liberation of the soul from matter and the body.
2. In this process the Serpent plays a part.

In *St. John* the redemption is the work of the Messiah, who is represented as redeeming mankind *in his Blood*. He is regarded as offering a sacrifice in which he is both the high priest and also the lamb of the sacrifice. But more interesting for our purpose is the passage in chapter xii. where this act of redemption is represented as a war with the Serpent. In this passage the name Michael is taken from the Serpent and given to Christ, and the Serpent is conquered and cast down.

It is this passage which is most thick with references to Gnostic mythology, as I have pointed out in the text of my book.

As for the body, it is probable that Dr. Charles is right in seeing some reference to the body in those white robes which are given to the redeemed; but it would also seem proved that these are not totally new bodies by the statement, *they have washed their robes white in the blood of the Lamb.* Their actual bodies are redeemed and made new.

The reference to the blood of Christ also makes it clear that the Messiah himself had a true body in which he suffered.

7. *Of the Three Types of Men.*—The Valentinians, following the Sethians, divided mankind into three types corresponding to the three sons of Adam and Eve:

1. Seth: the spiritual.
2. Abel: the righteous.
3. Cain: the fleshly.

This subdivision is a necessary consequence of their principles, but it is unlikely that it was found in the original Cainites, who regarded Cain as the superior type. What they taught was probably a contrast between

APPENDIX II

Cain and Abel only. When the Sethians produced their white Gnosticism, and made the system more respectable, they probably introduced the threefold classification.

I have pointed out that Serpent-worshipping sects must actually have existed in Palestine; the Old Testament tells us also of a nomadic tribe called the Cainites (usually spelt Kenites), related by blood to the Israelites; and there is no reason to suppose that groups may not have remained in Palestine who claimed to trace their descent from it. In some such non-Israelite or semi-Israelite community, forced into outward conformity with Judaism, Gnosticism may have had its beginning.

In this tribe must have been told a form of the legend favourable to Cain; Cain must have been the tribal hero, forefather, and perhaps god. The word Cain (fabricator) may even mean creator.

Among orthodox Jews Abel became the type of the innocent dead, and this use of his name is common in the New Testament; he is righteous in the sense of law-keeping; his sacrifice pleased Jehovah. His name is not mentioned in *Revelation*, but the thought of the blood of Abel crying to God for vengeance lies behind the symbolism of vi. 9, a passage which depends upon some words of Jesus in which Abel is actually mentioned; there are traces of the Cain and Abel story in xii. 16 and 17; and the mark of the beast has a close connection with it.

More important is the continual stress on " keeping the commandments " and on the salvation of the " righteous," the law-abiding. This emphasis is different from what we find in the writings of St. Paul, where the stress is laid on faith; but the emphasis on " works " and " commandments " which we find in *St. James* as well as *St. John* is not due to some " primitive " anti-Pauline Jewish Christianity; it is anti-Gnostic. The faith of St. Paul was a faith which issued in good works; when it was suggested that he was destroying law, he said " God forbid." The " works " of St. James and St. John issue from faith. The common enemy of both is the enemy of " law," the Gnostic (whether Cainite or Sethian) who describes himself as " spiritual," and considers himself above law. Released from any such bonds or duties, he aspires to a salvation which is open to him through Knowledge. Such " spiritual " claims appear to be alluded to in 1 *Corinthians*.

The attitude of St. Paul to the law was very difficult, and the Gnostics appear to have claimed him as their ally; an enemy of the law, that is, and a champion of liberty. St. Paul himself denies it; *the law is holy, and the commandment holy and righteous and just* (*Rom.* vii. 12). For him love is the fulfilling of the law, not something antagonistic to it. On the other side, St. James, when he praises the law is careful to qualify and spiritualise it, " the perfect law," " the royal law," " the law of liberty." The apostolic writers, though they supersede the letter of the law with the spirit of the gospel, are nevertheless on the side of Abel the righteous.

St. Paul, St. James, and St. John agree together in upholding a kind of " righteousness" and rejecting the Cainite " Anomia " or lawlessness. The whole contrast is very clearly set out in 1 *John* iii. 1–12, where the Devil is said to be the origin of sin, and Cain the child of the Devil.

The Christian church was therefore in a very difficult position. It absolved its gentile members from a literal obedience to the law, and preached the glorious liberty of the gospel of Christ. On the one hand it was attacked by the Jews because it gave up the law; on the other hand it was eagerly welcomed by antinomians who regarded the law as evil. Christianity regarded the law as good, and yet only a stepping-stone to something better; it could also speak of its own " free " morality as a kind of law. It is natural that as the opposition of the Jews became less important, and the danger from Gnosticism became more urgent, they should lay more and more stress on "works," "righteousness," and " commandments." This is precisely what we find, not only in St. John, but also in other writings of the period, in the *Teaching of the Twelve Apostles* and the *Shepherd of Hermas*. But it is not, as most critics say, a survival of primitive Palestinian Christianity; it is a development to meet antinomian Gnosticism.

To the Gnostic, therefore, the Christian church would seem a halfway house, a church of compromise; and so they fitted it into their scheme:

1. Seth: the spiritual or angelic church: Gnosticism.
2. Abel: the psychic or intermediate: Christianity.
3. Cain: the bodily: Judaism?

This is, of course, the Sethian scheme. The original Cainite scheme must have run like this:

1. Cain: the spiritual or Gnostic: of the Serpent.
2. Abel: the righteous or legal: Judaism: of Jehovah.

How they worked in Christianity, when it arose, is hard to say.

With these we may compare the rather similar contrast of St. Paul:

1. Ishmael: the slave: child of the flesh: Judaism.
2. Isaac: the free: child of the promise: Christianity.

Or the other contrast of Jerusalem above, which is free, and Jerusalem which is on earth, which is in bondage. This contrast is not, however, a contrast between body and spirit, as in Gnosticism, or of good and evil, as in St. John; it is a contrast between two possible relations with God—the legal and the spiritual, that of the slave and that of the Son.

St. John uses the old Hebrew idea of the Jerusalem above to illuminate his contrast of the good and the evil:

1. *Jerusalem.*	2. *Babylon.*
Church of the Redeemed.	Church of the Disowned.
True to her King.	False to her King.
Suffers with him.	Crucified him.
Bride of the Messiah.	Harlot of the Beast.
Adorned in heavenly glory, etc.	Adorned in earthly luxury, etc.
The Christian Church.	The official Jerusalem.

to which may be added a third classification, perhaps,

3. *The Beast*, and his worshippers, those who, not knowing God, cannot be called faithful or faithless, but whose god is nevertheless self, ambition, conquest, wealth, force, fraud.

Despite this distinction, however, St. John's ultimate division is into two classes: the holy and righteous on one hand, the filthy and unrighteous on the other (xxii. 11).

Note.—The Greek word Demiurge applied by later Gnostics to the creator has exactly the same meaning as the Hebrew word Cain (workman, smith).

INDEXES

PASSAGES FROM THE REVELATION
OTHER BIBLICAL PASSAGES
SUPPLEMENTARY SUBJECT INDEX

PASSAGES FROM THE REVELATION

Revelation.
1. 1–3   Title, 71
    4–8   Greetings, 74
    9–20   Vision of Risen Christ, 76, 383
2 and 3. Letters to Seven Churches, 91
2. 17   White Stone, 313
4. 1–2   Door in Heaven, 109, 179
    3   Throne, 110, 327, 402
    4   Elders, 112, 361, 382
    5   Seven Lamps, 89, 404
    6   Sea of Glass, 114
    6–7   Four Living Things, 115, 369
    8   Sanctus, 115 ff., 122, 382
5. 1–4   Sealed Book, 117
    5–7   Lamb, 119, 382, 385
    8–14   Worship of Lamb, 122, 382, 404, 412
    9   New Song, 123, 382, 390
6. 1–8   Four Horsemen, 124
    9–11   Souls under Altar, 130, 262, 385
    12–17   Earthquakes, etc., 135
7. 1   Four Winds, 139
    2–8   Sealing of Elect, 140
    9–17   Great Multitude, 141, 144 ff., 311, 383
    10   Hosanna (Tabernacles), 142, 271, 383
8. 1   Silence, 153, 386
    2   Trumpets, 154, 385
    3–5   Incense, 153, 385
    6–12   Trumpets (Wormwood), 154
    13   Eagle, 157
9. 1–2   Fallen Star, 158
    3–11   Locusts (Abaddon), 161, 413
    12–21   Demon Horsemen, 165
10. 1–3   Angel of Revelation, 168, 173, 409
    4   Seven Thunders, 169
    5–7   Voice of Angel, 174 (79)
    8–11   Call of Prophet, 175
11. 1–2   Measuring Temple, 176
    3–13   Two Witnesses, 187
    8   Great City, 191 (61)
    15–18   Seventh Trumpet, 192
    19   Temple in Heaven, 193 (181), 385
12. 1–2   Woman in Heaven, 202, 210, 409, 416
    3–4   Red Dragon, 208
    5   Birth of Child, 218
    6   Flight of Woman, 224
    7–12   Michael, 218, 370, 414
    13–17   Persecution of Woman, 224
13. 1–10   Beast from Sea, 226, 413
    11–15   Beast from Land, 231
    16   Mark of Beast, 233
13. 17–18   Number of Beast, 234
14. 1–5   Lamb and Followers, 236, 387
    3   New Song, 236, 390
    6–13   Three Messages, 248
    14–16   Son of Man (Harvest), 251, 387
    17–19   Vine of Land, 256
    20   Wine-press, 257
15. 1   Seven Vials, 261
    2–4   Song of Moses and Lamb, 262, 390
    5–8   Shekinah in Temple, 263, 383
16. 1–21   Last Plagues, 263, 391
    6   Blood-Vengeance, 263 (131), 251 ff.), 391
    10–11   Kingdom of Beast darkened, 264
    12   Euphrates dried up, 264, 267
    13–14   Frogs, 268
    15   " Keeping his Garments," 265
    16   Armageddon, 265, 268
    17–21   Babylon remembered, 266, 271
17. 1–7   Great Harlot, 275, 392, 414
    8–14   Scarlet Beast, 280
    15–18   Great City, 286 (191)
18. 1–8   Doom of Babylon, 289, 393, 416
    9–24   Lamentations, 291
19. 1–6   Alleluias, 292, 393
    7–9   Marriage of Lamb, 294, 393
    10   Angel Worship, 295, 360
    11–16   King-Messiah, 307, 393
    13   Garment dipped in Blood, 311, 383
    13   Word of God, 310
    17–21   Wars of Messiah, 320
    20   Lake of Fire, 322, 328
20. 1–2   Satan Bound, 323
    3   Thousand Years, 324, 362 ff.
    4–6   First Resurrection, 323
    7   Satan Loosed, 325
    8–10   Gog and Magog, 326
    11–13   Judgment, 327
    14–15   Lake of Fire, 328
21. 1–2   New Jerusalem, 333
    3–8   Tabernacle of God, 335, 383, 393 (144)
    9–11   Vision of Holy City, 345, 416
    12–17   Measurements of City, 346
    18–21   Precious Stones, 347
    22–27   Catholicity of City, 348, 383
22. 1–5   New Eden, 349
    6–21   Attestations, etc., 351
    8–9   Angel Worship, (295)

OTHER BIBLICAL PASSAGES

	PAGE
Genesis	166
1^{1-2}	105, 400
1^3	401
1^{26}	79
1^{27}	406
2 and 3	64, 158
2^9	166
3^{15}	210
4^{11}	131, 225
5^1	406
6^2	159
37^9	207
49^9	118
Exodus	64
3^6	73
15^{23}	156
19^4	225
Leviticus	
4^{12}	260
8^{17}	260
26^{11}	64, 145, 184, 270, 337, 383
Deuteronomy	
6^4	233
11^{12}	401
Joshua	
5^{15}	87, 222
6	64, 152
7^{19}	192
2 Samuel	
8^2	182
1 Kings	
6^{23}	115
Job	
15^{15}	45
Psalms	
2^{7-9}	218
45	64
45^3	309
74^{14}	114
80	256
82^3	138
93	114
98	123
109^{18}	314
113^5	38
114	136
118	143
Canticles	64, 307
5^{24}	308
6^{10}	207, 308
Isaiah	
1^{10}	208
1^{21}	242
6^{1-3}	64, 115
7^{10}	204

	PAGE
Isaiah	
7^{14}	336
9^6	223
10^{15}	35
11^2	90
11^{10}	118
13^{10}	56
13 and 14	64, 289
14^{12}	160
24 to 27	37
36^{17}	205
51^9	114
53	132, 383
54^{12}	343
60^{19}	271
63	254, 257, 383
65^{22}	136
66^{24}	328
Jeremiah	
1	64, 326
31^{33}	64, 336
Ezekiel	63
analysis of	64
1	125
1^{10}	115
1^{26}	79, 122, 173, 406
2^{10}	175
8	168, 173
$8^{1, 2}$	79
9	140, 193
10	193
10^2	154
11	193
13^{11}	273
14^{21}	126
15^6	256
16^{23}	276, 287
24^{6-8}	133
36^{27-8}	145
37^{10}	190
38	326
39^{17}	321
40–end	342
40^3	185
47	146
48^{16}	146
48^{30}	146
Daniel	33 ff.
3^{25}	122
7^{1-8}	33, 64
7^2	125, 228
7^7	285
7^{9-14}	36, 64
7^{13}	406
7^{18}	41
7^{15-28}	41, 64

	PAGE
Daniel	
7^{28}	41
8^{16}	64, 79
9^{20}	174
9^{21}	64
9^{27}	187
10	64, 168
10^{13-21}	64
10^{21}	220
12^1	64
12^7	64, 79, 174
Hosea	276
Joel	
1 and 2	64, 161
3	64
Amos	
2^9	136
Haggai	
2^7	136
Zechariah	37
1	64, 125
2^1	185
4	64, 188
9, etc.	37
9^9	269
10^5	269
$11^{12, 13, 15}$	269
$12^{6, 8, 10}$	270
12^{11}	268, 270
$13^{1, 2, 5, 9}$	270
14^2	269, 270
14^7	271
14^8	146, 271
14^{11}	271
15^{16}	271
Matthew	302
3^{10}	256
3^{12}	253
4^1	225
4^8	345
7^1	185
12^{32}	331
13^{30}	253
13^{39}	64
16^{18}	160
21^5	269
23^{34-39}	55, 64
23^{35}	132
24^{25-28}	55, 64, 157
24^{30}	270
24^{31}	152
24^{37}	190
27^9	269
Mark	
1^{15}	52, 174, 249
7^{21}	164

OTHER BIBLICAL PASSAGES

Mark	PAGE
9^1	251
10^{40}	360
12^1	256
13	64, 60, 62, 302
13^2	249
13^{3-8}	64
13^{10}	169, 249
13^{14}	58, 187
13^{22}	249
13^{24-26}	64
13^{26}	253
13^{30}	251
14^{58}	56, 64 f., 183
14^{62}	251
14^{63}	55

Luke	PAGE
1^{26}	222
10^3	120
11^{49-51}	55
17^{23-27}	55
17^{37}	157
18^7	154
19^{42}	261
19^{43}	249

Acts	PAGE
6^{14}	57
7^{56}	58
12^1	60
19^{14}	104

Acts	PAGE
21	180
Romans	
6^3	316
7^{12}	415
7^{24}	315
12^1	237, 383
14^{17}	365
1 Corinthians	
2^{10}	100
3^{16}	183
4^9	133
12^4	348
14^{29}	359
15^{20}	252
15^{26}	338
15^{44}	408
2 Corinthians	
5	315
5^4	134
6^{16}	183
12^2	170
Galatians	
2^9	183
3^{27}	316
4^{26}	343
Ephesians	
6^{12}	73
Philippians	
2^{10}	321

Philippians	PAGE
3^{20}	342
Colossians	100, 213
3^3	315
1 Thessalonians	58, 171
1^5	169
4^{16}	152, 222
4^{17}	253
Pastorals	100, 213
Hebrews	
4^{12}	309
12^{22}	236
13^{11}	260
James	
1^{13}	164
3^{13-18}	410
4^1	164
1 Peter	
1^{20}	120
2^5	75
5^{13}	274
2 Peter	
3^{15}	96
	98
1 John	
1^1	156
2^{27}	233
3^4	156
3^{1-12}	415
Jude	
9	221

SUPPLEMENTARY SUBJECT INDEX

Abaddon, 163
Abel, 131, 225
Abyss, 45, 105, 160, 204, 323, 413
Adam, 79, 158, 173, 214, 217, 406
Adventism, 72, 74, 81, 94, 250, 274, 346, 357, 359, 374
Æons, 212 f., 295, 369
Agabus, 58
Ages, 46, 48, 52, 67, 96, 196, 330, 358, 364
Alexander, 33, 35
Alexandria, 31, 35, 311, 372, 409
Alford, Dean, 275, 324
Alleluia, 293
Almighty, 76
Ananus, 258 f.
Angels, 44, 72, 80, 86 ff., 220 ff., 295 ff., 304
Antichrist, 48, 141, 227 ff., 233, 274, 282
Antinomians, 103, 156
Antioch, 35, 92
Antiochus, 35, 41, 47, 58, 60, 187, 230
Apocalypses (non-canonical), ix ff., 37 ff., 46 ff., 62, 66, 88, 93, 95, 109, 134, 137, 193, 220, 295, 309, 333, 344, 375
Archangels, 86, 220
Asia, churches of, 81, 91 ff., 97 ff., 174, 353
Atonement, Day of, 153, 262, 386, 391
Augustine, 47, 373

"Babylon," 62, 65, 67, 266, 272 ff., 287, 294, 345, 358, 367, 392, 404, 414
Baptism, 316
Bar-Kokhba, 366
Barnabas, Epistle of, 363 f.
Bishops, 113, 353, 359, 361, 370
Blood, symbolism of, 132 ff., 254, 257 ff., 288, 294, 311 ff., 392
Boanerges, 172
Bride (divine), 206, 276, 294, 304 ff., 334, 409

Cæsars, list of, 283
Cain, 103, 131, 210, 225, 233, 399, 414 ff.
Cainites, *see* Ophites
Caligula, 58, 170, 231, 283
Cerinthus, 364, 395, 399
Charles, Dr., ix, 37, 62, 74, 110, 132, 134, 165, 182, 263, 282, 302, 307, 312 ff.

Cherubim, 115
Chiliasm, 271, 324, 361 ff.
Chorus, *see* Worship
Chronology, 59, 61, 170 ff., 196, 227, 255, 259, 264, 283, 298
Church, 81, 88, 97, 113, 208, 213, 224, 236, 305 ff., 333, 349, 354, 368 ff., 373
Coming, *see* Parousia
Cross, 75, 121, 140
Cyrus, 33, 42, 126

Daniel, 33, 36 ff.
Darkness, 410
David, 32, 46, 174, 269 ff., 366
Dead, 48, 131 ff., 154, 190, 251, 305, 323
Desert, 224 ff., 276, 345
Docetism, 103
Domitian, 59, 61, 284, 302
Door in heaven, 110, 179
Dragon (*see* Serpent), 105, 114, 209, 319

East, 140, 245, 265, 326
Elchasai, 214
Elders, 113, 359 ff.
Energies of God, *see* God
Enoch, 38, 43 ff., 93, 121, 158
Ephesus, 92, 303, 310, 353 f.
Eschatology, ix, 47, 52, 135, 375
Euphrates, 129, 165, 264, 267, 326
Eve, 102, 158, 173, 210 ff.
Everlasting, 48, 330
Ezekiel, 63 ff. and *passim*

Fall, 44, 155, 158
Forty-two, 187, 224, 231
Four, 115, 125 ff., 139, 165 f., 213, 245, 257, 259, 263 f., 281, 326, 346, 407

Gabriel, 79, 86, 173, 215, 221 f.
Gallus (Cestius), 253, 255
Garment, 133 f., 143, 265, 312 ff.
Gehenna, 45, 48, 177, 322, 328, 374
Gnostic, 101, 211, 303, 305, 344, 348, 354 ff., 368, 372. *See also* Appendix II
God: energies of, 42, 73, 79, 87 ff., 111 ff., 119, 173, 212, 215
——multiplicity in, 42, 90, 111 ff., 119, 212, 348.
——and the world, 41 f., 53, 111 f.
Gospel, ix, 51, 169 ff., 174, 196, 248 ff., 329

SUPPLEMENTARY SUBJECT INDEX 423

HEAVEN, 32, 43, 52, 110, 157, 163, 168, 183, 193, 204, 343
Hell, see Gehenna and Punishment
Hermas, 215, 223 f., 363, 367 ff.
Herod, 58, 60, 170
Hippolytus, 101, 371, and Appendix II
Hosanna, 142, 146
Hymn of the Soul, 317

IGNATIUS, 361, 363
Inspiration, 93 ff. See also Prophets
Irenæus, 101, 274, Appendix II

JAMES, brother of Jesus, 61, 269, 245, 269
Jamneh, 290, 294, 301, 307
Jerusalem above, 44, 343
——Council of, 100, 330
——described, 176
——doom of, 55, 60, 176, 183, 189 ff., 259
Jesus, symbolism of, 50, 56, 136
——prophecies of, 54, 62, 65, 131, 183, 196, 249, 251, 256, 259
——see Gospel
Joachim, Abbot, 275, 374
John, Acts of, 357
John (of Ephesus), 92, 353, 356, 362, 373, 395
John, Gospel of, 103, 120, 142, 172, 206, 267, 312, 336, 338, 349, 388
John (author of Revelation), 77 ff., 82 ff., 118 ff., 176, 182, 195, 276, 289 f., 303, 331, 333, 362
——(son of Zebedee), 82, 171 f., 191, 213, 353, 362
Josephus, 60, 176, 188, 194, 242, 258, 266, 277, 288
Justin Martyr, 356, 362
Justinus the Gnostic, 129, 166 and Appendix II

KINGDOM (temporary), 45, 48, 333, 344, 362
Kingdom of God, 52 ff., 57, 59, 66, 88, 343 f.
Klausner, J., 277, 291

LAKE of Fire, 322, 328
Language of Revelation, 74, 120
Lightfoot, John, 265, 388
Literal interpretation, ix f., xv, 39, 56, 66, 93, 97, 135, 161, 250 f., 303, 324, 331, 341. 346, 356, 358, 364 ff., 372, 374. See also Adventism and Montanism
Liturgy, see Symbolism
Lyric, see Worship

MACCABEES, 35 f., 47, 121, 132
Marturia, 77, 118, 134, 188 ff., 325
Martyrs, cult of, 55, 132, 325
Mediums, 93
Messiah, 44, 48 ff., 95 ff., 121 f., 218 ff., 236, 251 f., 259, 278, 304, 307 ff.
Michael, 86 ff., 218 ff., 370
Milligan, Dr., 62, 67, 376

Monotheism, see God
Montanism, 94, 274, 303, 357, 371
Mormonism, 94, 357, 359, 374
Muratorian, 370 f.
Myth, ix, xiv, 39, 114, 158, 203, 368

NAMES, 112, 229, 233, 236, 310, 313, 318, 321
Naos, 144 ff., 153, 179 ff., 193, 262, 294, 337, 348 and Appendix I
Nebuchadrezzar, 33, 41, 139, 165, 264
Nero, 61, 227 ff., 258, 274, 282 ff., 302
New heaven and earth, 47, 333
North, 177, 326

OLAM, 48, 76
Old Testament, 32, 35, 62, 64 f., 159
Ophites, 101 ff., 160, 166, 210 ff., 225, 232 ff., 238, 281, 356 and Appendix II
Origen, 372
Orphism, 45

PAPIAS, 365
Parousia, 81 f., 95 ff., 251, 270, 302, 308 ff., 320, 367
Parousia, The, author of, 273
Parthians, 124, 161, 165, 167, 286, 312
Paul, 73, 97, 100, 154, 183, 185, 295, 314
Pella, 61, 253, 290, 294.
Peter, Revelation of, 45, 371
Philip, 57
Pistis Sophia, 134, 221, 318
Planets, 43, 110
Plato, 343
Pompey, 49
Priesthood (Christian), 116, 122, 133 f., 143, 237, 312, 383, 387
Prophecies of Jesus, see Jesus
Prophecy and Marturia, 55, 58, 98, 360, 368
Prophets in general, 54, 72, 93
——Christian, 57 ff., 94, 170 ff., 370
——"false," 94, 232, 250 ff., 255, 268, 357, 359 ff.
Protestant exegesis of Revelation, 275, 374
Psalms of Solomon, 49
Pseudonymity, 37, 71, 93
Ptolemy, 35.
Punishment, 45, 48, 132, 138. See also Gehenna
Puritan, see Montanism

RAMSAY, Sir W., 91, 232
Raphael, 86, 221
Robe, see Garment
Rome, 45, 48, 49, 132, 229, 274, 277, 282, 285, 321, 328, 367

SACRIFICE (Christian), 119, 130, 132, 179, 237, 260 ff., 312, 381 ff.
Sanctuary, see Naos
Satan, 35, 101, 209, 323
——Synagogue of, 99 f., 211

Sceva, 104
Seleucus, 35
Sennacherib, 33, 41, 126, 165, 264
Serpent, 101 ff., 158, 209, 229 ff., and Appendix II
Seven Angels, 72, 86, 90, 121, 221
Seven Churches, *see* Asia
Seven Spheres, *see* Planets
Seven Spirits, 74, 88 ff., 369
Sibylline Books, 274, 282, 286
Silas, 58, 171, 222
Simon Magus, 214, 399
Sin, 158 ff.
Sion, 236
Son of Man, 40, 44, 47, 53, 57, 59, 61, 79, 122, 173, 212, 223, 251, 270
Soul, 314
Sources, *see* Strata
Spirit: feminine, 212 ff., 305, 333, 358, and Appendix II
—— Holy, 74, 88, 169 f., 173, 212 ff., 294, 305
Stephen, 57 f.
Strata, 110, 129 f., 138, 141 ff., 152 ff., 165, 184, 203, 209, 228, 240, 248, 279 f., 286, 382
—— different, harmonised: 129, 152, 165, 247, 280, 286, 287, 306, 334
Structure, 58 f., 61, 63, 95, 120, 132, 152, 156, 165, 216, 278, 281, 333, 341, 382
Suffering, 119, 121
Symbolism of Jesus, *see* Jesus
—— in general, 38, 56, 82, 91, 116, 314, 321, 375
—— Liturgical, 113, 116, 119, 142, 144 ff., 152 f., 181 ff., 193, 252, 260 ff., 293, 337, 350, and Appendix I
—— Processes, 58 f., 61, 63, 91, 95, 127, 154, 169, 174, 189, 208, 230, 311, 333, 342

Symbolism, Double sense of, 88, 126, 130, 133, 154, 208, 215, 313, 333 ff., 349, 351, 389
—— Spiritual, *see* Literal interpretation
Syncretism, 31, 42 ff., 50, 203, 368

Tabernacles, 142 ff., 385 ff.
Tamid, 119, 385 ff.
Temple, *see* Naos
—— daily ritual, 119, 123, 133, 153 f., 193, 261 ff., 293
—— described, 178 ff.
Theosophist, *see* Gnostic
Titus, 255, 265 f., 284, 302
Twelve Apostles, Teaching of, 359

Uriel, 72, 86, 221

Valentinus, 101 f., 318, 356
Vespasian, 255, 258, 264, 283
Virgin-birth, 204 ff.
" Virgins," 237
Vision: psychology of 82 ff.

War, Jewish, 255, 258, 260, 264 ff., 266, 366
Waters, 32, 114, 225, 277, 281, 333, 369, 413
Ways, The Two, 51
Wisdom, 90, 215 ff., 225, 234, 280, 294, 409
Witness, *see* Marturia
Word of God (*see* God), 79, 89, 173 ff., 213, 215 ff., 310, and Appendix II
Worship, 75, 113, 116, 122 f., 142 ff., 192, 219, 236, 293, 336 ff., 348, 361, and Appendix I

Zealots, 172, 178, 181, 186, 255, 264, Zechariah, 63, 268 ff.

www.ingramcontent.com/pod-product-compliance
Lightning Source LLC
Chambersburg PA
CBHW070058020526
44112CB00034B/1434